Russian Research Center Studies, 64

Struve: Liberal on the Left, 1870–1905

P. B. Struve as a student, early 1890's

STRUVE

Liberal on the Left, 1870–1905

Richard Pipes

Harvard University Press
Cambridge, Massachusetts
1970

The Russian Research Center of Harvard University is supported by
a grant from the Ford Foundation. The Center carries out interdisciplinary
study of Russian institutions and behavior and related subjects.

Library of Congress Catalog Card Number 77–131463
SBN 071 81505 1
Printed in the United States of America

To Isaiah Berlin

ACKNOWLEDGMENTS

In preparing this book, I have been helped by many witnesses and scholars, some no longer living. A list of them will be provided in the second volume, covering Struve's life from 1905 to his death in 1944, to be subtitled "Liberal on the Right." Here I would like only to express particular gratitude to the sons of Peter Struve, Professor Gleb Struve and M. Alexis Struve, who have rendered me invaluable assistance in a great variety of ways. M. Maximilien Rubel has been kind enough to give me the benefit of his expertise in reviewing the sections dealing with Marx, Marxism, and Social Democracy. The Russian Research Center of Harvard University, the Guggenheim Foundation, and the Center for Advanced Study in the Behavioral Sciences in Stanford, California, have been most generous in assisting me to carry out my studies.

R.P.

Menlo Park, California
March 1970

CONTENTS

ILLUSTRATIONS

Frontispiece   P. B. Struve as a student, early 1890's
Courtesy of Mr. Alexis Struve

Following page 80

Struve's parents, Anna and Bernhard Struve
Courtesy of Mr. Alexis Struve

Struve as a child with two of his brothers, ca. 1872
Courtesy of Mr. Alexis Struve

A. M. Kalmykova, ca. 1916
From *Polveka dlia knigi, 1866–1916* (Moscow, 1916)

A. N. Potresov, 1925
From *A. N. Potresov: Posmertnyi sbornik proizvedenii* (Paris, 1937)

Following page 240

Editorial board of *Nachalo*
From *Al'bom po istorii VKP(b)* (Moscow, 1928)

Struve, ca. 1905
From A. Törngren, *Med Ryska Samhälls Bygare O. Statsmän* (Tampere, 1929)

ABBREVIATIONS

ARR   *Arkhiv russkoi revoliutsii*
ASEER   *American Slavic and East European Review*
ASGS   *Archiv für Soziale Gesetzgebung und Statistik*
ASS   *Archiv für Sozialwissenschaft und Sozialpolitik*
B&E   *Entsiklopedicheskii slovar' Ob-a Brokgauz i Efron*
Belokonsky   I. P. Belokonsky, *Zemskoe dvizhenie* (Moscow, 1914)
BK   *Bor'ba klassov*
BSE   *Bol'shaia sovetskaia entsiklopediia*
BV   *Birzhevye vedomosti*
Frank   S. Frank, *Biografiia P. B. Struve* (New York, 1956)
GM   *Golos minuvshego*
IsSSSR   *Istoriia SSSR*
KA   *Krasnyi arkhiv*
KL   *Krasnaia letopis'*
KrKh   P. B. Struve, *Krepostnoe Khoziaistvo* (St. Petersburg, 1913)
KS   *Katorga i ssylka*
Lenin   V. I. Lenin, *Sochineniia*, 3rd ed., 30 vols. (Moscow, 1926–1937)
Lenin PSS   V. I. Lenin, *Polnoe sobranie sochinenii*, 5th ed., 55 vols. (Moscow, 1958–1965)
LisOsv   *Listok Osvobozhdeniia*
LM   *Letopisi marksizma*
LN   *Literaturnoe nasledstvo*
LR   *Letopis' revoliutsii*
LS   *Leninskii sbornik*
MB   *Mir Bozhii*
MERR   *K. Marks, F. Engel's i revoliutsionnaia Rossiia* (Moscow, 1967)

MG   *Minuvshie gody*

MV   *Moskovskie vedomosti*

N   *Nachalo*

NO   *Nauchnoe obozrenie*

Nrt   P. B. Struve, *Na raznye temy (1893–1901 gg.) — Sbornik statei* (St. Petersburg, 1902)

NS   *Novoe slovo*

NV   *Novoe vremia*

NZ   *Die Neue Zeit*

NZh   *Novyi zhurnal*

Obzory or *Obzor*   *Obzory [Obzor] vazhneishikh doznanii o gosudarstvennykh prestupleniiakh proizvodivshikhsia v Imperii*

OD   L. Martov and others, *Obshchestvennoe dvizhenie v Rossii v nachale XX veka*, 4 vols. (St. Petersburg, 1909–1914)

Osv   *Osvobozhdenie*

PN   *Poslednie novosti*

Potresov   B. I. Nikolaevsky, Introduction to *A. N. Potresov: Posmertnyi sbornik proizvedenii* (Paris, 1937), 9–90

PR   *Proletarskaia revoliutsiia*

RB   *Russkoe bogatstvo*

RBS   *Russkii biograficheskii slovar'*

RiS   *Rossiia i Slavianstvo*

RM   *Russkaia mysl'*

RR   *Revoliutsionnaia Rossiia*

RS   *Russkaia starina*

RV   *Russkii vestnik*

RVed   *Russkie vedomosti*

SaV   *Samarskii vestnik*

SB   *Staryi Bol'shevik*

SC   *Socialpolitisches Centralblatt*

Shakhovskoi   D. Shakhovskoi, "Soiuz Osvobozhdeniia," *Zarnitsy*, Vyp. 2 (St. Petersburg, 1909), 81–171

SK   *Severnyi kur'er*

SoV   *Sotsialisticheskii vestnik*

SP   *Soziale Praxis*

SR   *Slavonic Review*

StPV   *Sankt-peterburgskie vedomosti*

SZ   *Sovremennye zapiski*

Trudy IVEO *Trudy Imperatorskogo Vol'nogo Ekonomicheskogo Obshchestva*

VE *Vestnik Evropy*

VFP *Voprosy filosofii i psikhologii*

VI *Voprosy Istorii*

VIKPSS *Voprosy istorii KPSS*

Voden A. M. Voden, "Na zare 'legal'nogo marksizma," *Letopisi marksizma*, No. 3 (1927), 67–82, and No. 4 (1927), 87–96

Voz *Vozrozhdenie*

Zh *Zhizn'*

References to Struve's writings before November 1905 are keyed to the bibliography given at the end of this volume. The first number refers to the title of the work, the second, to the pagination. Thus: #89/298 refers to "Osnovnaia antinomiia teorii trudovoi tsennosti," *Zhizn'*, IV, No. 2 (February 1900), p. 298. The numbering system for Struve's works corresponds to that used in the xerographic edition of Struve's *Collected Works* which the author is readying for publication.

Ask the young; they know it all.

Joseph Joubert

PART ONE

IMPLANTING SOCIAL DEMOCRACY

1. YOUTH AND FIRST THOUGHTS

Peter Struve came of a German family whose ancestral home was the partly German, partly Danish province of Schleswig-Holstein. In the sixteenth century — which is as far back as they can be traced — they engaged in farming. The first intellectual in what was to become a remarkable dynasty of scholars and scientists was Jacob Struve (1755–1841), a stone-cutter by trade who turned mathematician and held a variety of educational posts in and around Hamburg.[1] It was his son Wilhelm, born in 1793, who founded the Russian branch of the family. To escape being pressed into the Napoleonic army, he fled his native Altona for Dorpat and there enrolled at the University. Dorpat (now Tartu) had been annexed to the Russian Empire by Peter the Great and was nominally a Russian city; but as was the case in all the Baltic towns, power there continued to reside with German nobles and burghers, and the culture remained thoroughly German. After a brief try at philology, Wilhelm transferred to the Faculty of Mathematics and Astronomy. In these disciplines he displayed such unusual talents that in 1819, when barely twenty-six, he was promoted to a full professorship and entrusted with the direction of the university observatory. A few years after assuming this post, he acquired a reputation as one of Europe's foremost astronomers. His fame rested principally on the identification and measurement of "double stars," that is, stars placed in such close proximity as to appear undistinguishable, single bodies. In 1827 he published the first of two catalogues containing a list of over three thousand double stars, the majority of which he had been the first to identify.

The appearance of Struve's catalogue coincided with the decision of Nicholas I to give Russia its first national observatory, one

---

[1] I am indebted for most of my genealogical information to the late Miss Olga Tomaschek of Vienna, a member of the Struve family.

able to equal the best in England and on the continent. Together with several German scientists Struve played an active role in its design, and in 1839, when its construction was completed (it was located at Pulkovo, not far from St. Petersburg), he was appointed its first director. At this time he moved from Dorpat to St. Petersburg with his large family of thirteen children. He became a Russian citizen, received the rank of hereditary noble, and was elected to the Academy of Sciences. Under his management, Pulkovo not only equaled the best foreign observatories, but surpassed them all, becoming the leading center of astronomical studies in the world. It is largely to him that Russia owes its great school of astronomy. Showered with honors, he held his post until 1857, when illness forced him to retire. He died in 1864.[2]

Directly descended from Wilhelm (or Vasily, as he came to be known after acquiring Russian citizenship), were four successive generations of distinguished astronomers, some of whom continued his investigations of double stars. The last of this line, probably without equal in the history of science, died in 1963 in the United States.[3] Wilhelm's other descendants either became educators or joined the civil service. His connections gained them entry into Russia's best schools, and there they rapidly assimilated. By the middle of the nineteenth century, notwithstanding the recentness of their connection with Russia, the Struves were well ensconced in Russia, and felt more at home there than many educated Russians of native origin. By domestic upbringing and the Protestant culture that they had carried with them from Hamburg and Dorpat, they were attuned to the "system" of Nicholas I, which sought to inculcate in Russians the rather foreign ideals of selfless duty to the state and respect for scholarship. It was certainly easier for them to adjust to the imperial state service with its national-conservative ethos drawn directly from Restoration

[2] Wilhelm Struve's biography was written by his son, Otto (*Wilhelm Struve,* Karlsruhe, 1893). There is also an account of his life in RBS, XIX (1909), 549–557, and in the *Encyclopaedia Britannica,* 11th ed., XXV (1911), 1044–1045. Recently, A. A. Mikhailov (ed.) and Z. N. Novokshanova have published studies dealing with his life and scientific work.

[3] Otto Struve succeeded his father as director of the Pulkovo Observatory in 1862. His sons, Herman and Ludwig, headed the Berlin and Kharkov observatories, respectively. Both had sons who followed in their footsteps. Ludwig's son, Otto, directed until his death in 1963 several major North American observatories, including the National Radio Astronomical Observatory at Green Bank, West Virginia. The German branch of the family also produced its share of scientists and scholars.

Austria and Germany than it was for that sizable segment of the Russian gentry which had been raised on the ideals of the French Enlightenment or German Romantic Idealism. And so they prospered and became Russian patriots as only Russified Germans knew how.

Peter Struve's father, Bernhard, was the son of Wilhelm's first wife, a German woman of Huguenot descent. Born in Dorpat in 1827, he spent there the first twelve years of his life. After moving to St. Petersburg, he was enrolled at the Tsarskoe Selo Lyceum, the country's most prestigious school, whose pupils, drawn from the leading landowning and bureaucratic families, were trained for high government posts. He graduated in 1847 and for a while worked in a St. Petersburg chancery, but he did not remain there long, for something more exciting soon turned up. N. N. Muraviev had just been appointed by Nicholas governor general of Eastern Siberia and instructed to carry out sweeping reforms designed to stop flagrant fiscal abuses and oppression of the natives, and bring the enormous area under closer scrutiny of the central state organs. An outstanding representative of that type of enlightened state servant which imperial Russia produced in greater numbers than is generally realized, Muraviev attracted many idealistic youths to his side. Bernhard Struve spent five years in his service, in the course of which he explored the length and breadth of Siberia. Because reliable people were in short supply on the frontier, he was given greater responsibilities than would have been the case had he remained in St. Petersburg. He was only in his mid-twenties when Muraviev placed him in charge of the administration of the province of Irkutsk, whose territory exceeded that of any country of western Europe. These were the happiest years of his life, a nostalgic record of which he left in the recollections of Muraviev that he wrote forty years later, shortly before his death.[4]

Yet even then he revealed that uncanny knack for getting into trouble that was never to leave him. Bernhard Struve seems to have belonged to what Dostoevsky called "the strange category of 'unlucky' Germans" and described as forming a distinct class in imperial Russia. Many of these Germans, like the Struves, worked zealously for king and country; yet they always ran into a deep-

[4] B. V. Struve, "Vospominaniia o Sibiri," first published serially in *Russkii vestnik* (April–June, October, and November, 1888) and then as a book bearing the same title in St. Petersburg in 1889.

seated hostility which sooner or later brought them to grief. They
never ceased to be "foreigners," even if they knew no other country than Russia. (During the War of 1812, the Russian general
Prince Bagration — ironically, himself a Russified Georgian —
expressed the wish to be promoted to the status of a German,
thereby voicing not only his own resentment at having to serve
under a Baltic officer, Barclay de Tolly, but that of many other
Russian officers and officials.) Struve's colleagues vowed to "get
that German" and began to intrigue against him. His troubles multiplied after 1853, the year he married Anna Fedorovna Rosen,
who not only was of German Baltic stock but also was a rather
temperamental person with a disagreeably overbearing manner.
After this marriage his relations with Muraviev deteriorated to the
point where he thought it wise to feign illness and request a transfer. The request was granted, and in 1855 he returned with his
wife and their year-old baby, Vasily, to St. Petersburg.[5]

The only intimate glimpse of Struve's parents at our disposal
comes from the fragment of a novel, unmistakably autobiographical
in intent, published by Peter Struve in Paris in 1926–1928.[6] The
action of this novel takes place in Odessa during the Russo-Turkish
war of 1877. Struve's father is portrayed here in the guise of Alek-
sei Gavrilovich Desnitsky as a robust outdoor man, sound and
steady, a creature of regular habits, a lover of dogs and horses.
Such he appears also in the only extant photograph of himself and
his bride, which was probably taken shortly after their marriage:
every feature of his open face here conveys integrity and content-
ment. Struve's mother, Anna Fedorovna, appears very different,
her knitted brows and pouting lips giving her an expression of re-
proach suggestive of a discontented woman. In Struve's novel,
where she is named Antonina Fedorovna, she is depicted as obese,
flabby, and highly excitable. Attractive in her youth, she

---

[5] RV, November 1888, 207–216.

[6] The novel, called *Vremena* (Times) appeared serially over the signature
"Sergei Lunin" in two newspapers which Struve edited in Paris, *Vozrozhdenie*
and *Rossiia*: *Voz*, No. 264 (February 21, 1926); No. 275 (March 4, 1926); No.
513 (October 2, 1926); No. 537 (November 2, 1926); and *Rossiia*, No. 26
(February 18, 1928), and No. 27 (February 25, 1928). The facts bearing on
the Desnitskys so closely coincide with the biographies of Struve's parents that
the novel's autobiographical intent is unmistakable. Like Bernhard Struve, A. G.
Desnitsky graduated from the Tsarskoe Selo Lyceum and spent the Crimean
War in Siberia (Kamchatka). In *Vremena* Struve tried to combine the historical
narrative of Tolstoy with Dostoevsky's political pamphleteering. He gave up with
the sixth installment.

had gained much weight [and], by contrast, could not stand that sensibly regulated and active "working" life that so engrossed her healthy husband. She always ailed, always complained of something or other, and, indeed, began early to suffer from gout and asthma . . . Her puffy body seemed to contain no muscles whatsoever. She organically feared all exertion and shuddered at every physical danger . . . She neither knew how to work nor liked to work. With all these qualities, she was a fairly intelligent and interesting woman, endowed with that indescribably attractive (though not insistent) quality of femininity always compounded of helplessness, instinctively decorous coquettishness, and capriciousness — qualities often irresistible to fairly intelligent and physically strong men.[7]

Her husband was utterly devoted to her; but for Antonia (read: Anna) Fedorovna

the world of men was by no means limited to her husband, although she never betrayed him and probably was not capable of betraying. Still, she always found other men enchanting and formed strong attachments — insofar as she was capable of anything strong at all — to men other than her husband. She was nervous and emotional. Almost everything excited her.[8]

That Struve's mother had the reputation of a trouble-maker and man-chaser is confirmed in the few references to her in contemporary sources.[9] All of this suggests that she bore at least some responsibility for her husband's failure to fulfill his early promise in the civil service.

Having returned to St. Petersburg from Siberia, Struve was reassigned to the post of the deputy governor of Astrakhan province. Although much closer to central Russia than Irkutsk, Astrakhan was no less a frontier outpost, whose population consisted largely of Muslim tradesmen and fishermen. While Struve was in charge of the province, Alexander Dumas the Elder visited it on his tour of southern Russia. In his travel account he had very little good

[7] *Voz*, No. 264 (February 21, 1926).
[8] *Ibid.*
[9] See, e.g., the remarks of the exiled Decembrist Volkonsky, recorded in N. P. Chulkov, *Dekabristy* (Moscow, 1938), 102, and of the poet P. V. Shumakher in P. I. Shchukin, ed., *Shchukinskii sbornik*, VII (Moscow, 1907), 186.

to say about this Oriental village where all his requests, including one for an ordinary bed, caused undisguised amazement among his hosts. It was his good fortune that shortly after his arrival in Astrakhan Struve, now governor, invited Dumas to pay him a visit; and once the acquaintance had been struck, Struve catered to every wish of his famous guest, sparing him further dealings with the natives. Dumas was delighted to find that the governor of so remote and barbarous a province spoke French like a Frenchman (he had learned it at the Tsarskoe Selo Lyceum) and altogether kept a household that seemed a veritable oasis of Western culture. "A table chez M. Struve . . . nous étions à Paris," he wrote in his account, "au milieu des arts, de la civilisation, du monde enfin." To explain this strange phenomenon he informed his readers that Struve was "d'origine française." [10]

Struve did not long remain in Astrakhan. In 1861, for reasons which cannot be ascertained from available documents, he tendered his resignation and left. How and where he spent the next four years is also unknown. In 1865 he was assigned to the post of governor of Perm, another outlying province, on the western foothills of the Urals. He already had five children — all boys — when on January 26/February 7, 1870, his wife gave birth to the sixth and last, Peter.

Immediately after Peter's birth, tragedy struck. The government in St. Petersburg, apparently in receipt of disquieting reports from Perm, on March 5/17, 1870, appointed a commission headed by Senator P. N. Klushin to carry out there what in the bureaucratic language of the time was called a "revision." It did not take Klushin and his investigators long to corroborate the rumors. They unearthed a mass of evidence testifying to bureaucratic incompetence, corruption, and blackmail shocking even for the low ad-

---

[10] Alexander Dumas, "Voyage en Russie," *Oeuvres*, IV (Paris, 1866), 16ff. Little did Dumas suspect that Governor Struve's attentiveness was at least partly dictated by ulterior motives. The imperial police kept a close watch on Dumas during his journey, and concluded from his questioning of various people he met that his real purpose was to incite peasants to rebel. It therefore instructed Struve to keep an eye on the French visitor throughout his stay in Astrakhan. After Dumas had departed, the local chief of police reported to St. Petersburg: "In general, as during previous visits of foreigners to Astrakhan, the Governor of the province, State Councellor Struve, sought by his attentions to attract the foreigner to himself so as to facilitate the surveillance of his activities." "Aleksandr Diuma-otets i Rossiia," LN, XXXI–XXXII (1937), 544. See also Struve's remarks in *Rossiia*, No. 30 (March 17, 1928). How many visitors to Russia since have mistaken concealed police observation for genuine and disinterested hospitality!

ministrative standards of imperial Russia. Under Struve's lax government, local officials, especially the police, treated the population as they would inhabitants of a conquered territory. Extorting tribute took so much time that the police had none left for the performance of their proper duties, the result being that Perm had the highest crime rate recorded in any province of the Russian Empire. State revenues, on the other hand, were collected in an agreeably tolerant manner: tax evasion was brazen and in one district the local citizens banded in the Society of the Nonpayers of Taxes. The findings of the Klushin Commission received wide publicity, especially in the liberal press, always eager to expose bureaucratic malpractices. As soon as the evidence was in, Struve was retired from the service. His retired rank — Deistvitel'nyi Tainyi Sovetnik (Wirklicher Geheimer Rat) — was the second highest in the civil service, which indicates that he was not personally disgraced. However, he never received another government post.[11]

The movements of Bernhard Struve and his family after the Perm disaster cannot be reconstructed except in the most general terms. In his novel Struve suggests that his family lived in Odessa in 1877, but there is no hard evidence to this effect. What is certain is that in 1879 the family left Russia and settled in Stuttgart. Here the Struves spent three years, during which the children attended German schools. It is at this time that Peter acquired excellent command of German, which he subsequently spoke and wrote with nearly the same facility as his native Russian.[12]

In the summer of 1882 the family returned to St. Petersburg,[13] Peter was enrolled in the Third Gymnasium, the leading classical school in the city.[14] Bernhard Struve found employment as head

[11] The records of Klushin's committee, to which I had no access, are deposited at the Central State Historical Archive in Leningrad (TsGIAL, Fond 1390). Its findings are summarized in *Moskovskie vedomosti*, No. 12 (January 16, 1871), and in an article in *Vestnik Evropy* (October 1871, 629–659), called "Doreformennaia guberniia." Struve seems to have been charged with negligence rather than with complicity in corruption and extortion. B. I. Nikolaevsky believes that he was innocent of all wrongdoing and fell victim to bureaucratic intrigues but furnishes no evidence: NZh, X (1945), 311.

[12] At home, among themselves, the Struves always spoke Russian: BV (morning edition), December 17/30, 1914.

[13] The sole authority for dating the family's sojourn in Germany is a casual remark in Struve's reminiscences of Ivan Aksakov: "Aksakovy i Aksakov," RM, VI–VIII (1923), 350.

[14] The Third Gymnasium was located near the Struve residence at Gagarinskaia 5.

of a major publishing house, and in his free time worked on a
biography of Muraviev, a history of peasant emancipation, and his
memoirs.[15] Of Peter's mother during these and subsequent years
nothing is known save that her obesity assumed pathological dimensions. According to family gossip, "die grosse Tante Annette"
once became lodged in the compartment door of a train, delaying
its departure until she could be extricated. With the exception of
one brother who came to grief in some sort of a financial scandal,
Peter's brothers went on to make respectable if not brilliant careers
as educators and diplomats.[16]

It was this conventional household of a civil servant cashiered
for tolerating corruption that produced one of the most unconven-
tional minds and incorruptible spirits of modern Russia.

It must be stated at the outset that very little is known of
Struve's childhood and youth. He left no memoirs, and except
for occasional reminiscences which he scattered in obituaries of
friends and public figures kept his memories to himself. His earliest
available writings date from 1892, when he had already completed
two years at the university and was about to begin work on what

---

[15] NV, No. 4657 (February 14/26, 1889). His publications, in addition to the
memoirs listed above (note 4), include: "Graf Nikolai Nikolaevich Muraviev-
Amurskii: epizod iz ego zhizni," RS, December 1883, 505–512; "Neskol'ko slov
o Grafe Muravieve-Amurskom," RV, July 1884, 354–361; "K istorii raskola i
uprazdneniia krepostnogo prava v permskoi gubernii," RS, September 1884,
663–676; and, "K istorii uprazdneniia krepostnogo prava v permskoi gubernii,"
Rus', No. 13 (July 1, 1883), 50–58. There is a letter from him to the editor of
the daily newspaper Novoe vremia: "O vozmozhnosti udobnogo vnutrennogo
puti po Sibiri," NV, September 21, 1880. Struve told A. A. Kizevetter that his
father had a "religious adulation and admiration" for the Emancipation Edict
and became an expert on its history: GM, No. 2 (February 1915), 230–233.

[16] Bernhard Struve's eldest son, Vasily (1854–1912), for a time taught mathematics and foreign languages at the St. Petersburg Pedagogical Institute, and
at the time of his death was director of the Surveyor's Institute in Moscow. On
him, see Pamiati Vasiliia Berngardovicha Struve (Moscow, 1912), and obituaries
in RM, February 1912, Pt. 3, 67 (probably by Peter) and IV (March 1912),
1150. Of Fedor, the second eldest, nothing is known save his dates, 1858–1903.
The third son, Nicholas, after a stint as German language teacher, joined the
diplomatic service. He held posts as Russian Consul in Frankfurt am Main and
in Montreal, where he died. Michael (1865–1913), worked in the Ministry of
Agriculture and State Domains. Alexander (1866–?) came to a bad end. He
prepared for a scholarly career and worked in the Ministry of Finance, but in
1898 he was tried on charges of embezzlement and subsequently dropped out
of sight (Odesskie novosti, No. 4432, October 19, 1898). Peter broke all relations with him (letter to N. N. Ilin, dated September 27, 1917, Pushkin House,
Leningrad, Arkhiv Il'ina, Fond 385, No. 37).

became his first book.[17] There is little mention of his early years in memoirs of others: the little there is was written after a lapse of half a century by old men. Such dearth of information on a man's formative years would be a handicap to any biographer, but it is particularly frustrating in the case of Struve because he was an extraordinarily precocious youth who made himself a name in St. Petersburg intellectual circles while still a gymnasium student and became a national celebrity at twenty-four.

A personal description of him, written in 1944 by V. A. Obolensky, a fellow student from St. Petersburg, depicts him as a pallid and sickly young man of nineteen who resembled more his neurotic mother than his robust father: "He was a slender, tall youth, with a sunken chest. His hair was closely cropped, fair, with a reddish tint. Despite his rather regular features he seemed unattractive because of his unusually pale face, full of freckles, and his moist mouth and white lips." [18] Later on he grew a thick beard to conceal his unappealing mouth and let his hair reach to the shoulders to hide his equally unattractive thick and protruding ears. His whole appearance as a young man had something utterly helpless about it, and Vera Zasulich, on meeting him in 1896 in Geneva, at once dubbed him *telënok* — the calf; this name stuck as his Social Democratic code word.

But in this limp frame there burned a moral and intellectual fire of such constancy and such intensity that all who met him soon forgot his external appearance. Struve was an intellectual of a type that is nearly extinct today and that in another century will probably be as difficult to imagine as a medieval ascetic, a Renaissance humanist, or a Prussian Junker are today. From the moment of earliest awareness until his death his life centered on an inner dialogue. He was forever debating with himself. Everything that went on around him, even when it concerned his own person, was to him utterly insignificant unless it related in some way to that

[17] Sergei Vodov says that Struve published his first article in the newspaper *Russkie vedomosti* on January 31, 1890: "P. V. Struve," *Studencheskie gody* (Prague), No. 1/18 (1925), 34. There is indeed in this issue a brief item on German school reform signed with the initial "S," but neither in content nor in style does it bear any resemblance to Struve's authenticated writings. According to I. F. Masanov, *Slovar' psevdonimov*, III (Moscow, 1958), 47, the letter "S" was a cipher used by Struve's oldest brother, Vasily.

[18] V. A. Obolensky, untitled reminiscences of Struve written in 1944; manuscript in the B. I. Nikolaevsky Archive, Hoover Institution, Stanford, California.

which occupied his mind. He had no particular interest in other people except as they either taught him or were willing to learn from him. Although capable of forming warm friendships, he selected his friends from among those who shared his way of thinking and were in tune with his outlook. Obolensky aptly said that just as there are many "egocentrists of feeling" Struve was a "singular egocentric of thought." He never attended to his private interests unless they grew desperate; indeed, the very notion that he might exert himself to live better seemed to him somehow indecent. In 1938, when he was living in Belgrade in destitution, a friend suggested that he do something to improve his situation. Struve replied indignantly:

> It follows from my entire "nature" that I never impose myself on anyone and never seek anything for myself as a public figure and only in extreme need for myself as a private person, and never "arrange" anything. For that reason in my day I have done only that which I could not help doing, "inspired by some demon" (in the Greek sense of the word) . . . This is my "nature," and I could not act otherwise.

If his life needed "arranging," he added, that was for his friends to worry about, not for him.[19] These were not the idle boasts of a man struck by misfortune and attempting to justify himself, but a firm principle of conduct to which he adhered also when life was good to him and when it would have taken little effort on his part to feather a comfortable nest.

For Struve, to think meant to speculate not *in vacuo* but from a position of knowledge. From his earliest years he thirsted for it. So important was learning to him that in the snatches of recollections which he left behind he talks of nothing else; and where others measure the stages of their life by what had happened to them, he measures it by what he had learned. Even as a school boy he displayed an extraordinary range of intellectual interests and read widely on sociology, politics, literature, philology, economics, philosophy, and history. Before reaching his teens, he mastered the classics of Russian prose (Tolstoy, Turgenev, and Dostoevsky, for example),[20] as well as the standard sociological literature, in-

[19] Letter to N. A. Tsurikov, dated March 31, 1938; manuscript in possession of Professor Gleb Struve, Berkeley, California.

[20] RiS, No. 83 (June 29, 1930), and *Voz*, No. 362 (May 30, 1926).

cluding most of Darwin and all of Spencer.[21] He followed regularly the "fat" journals, and while still in grade school devoured political periodicals and pamphlets. Many years later he recalled the vivid impression made on him by Ivan Aksakov's protest against the Treaty of Berlin and Dostoevsky's Pushkin speech, events which occurred when he was eight and ten, respectively.[22] He was so impatient to learn that he plowed through his elder brother's university notes.[23] He attended disputes of doctoral dissertations on historical and philological subjects, and funerals of writers and scholars of note.[24]

All this happened before he had graduated from school. By the time he had done so, he had acquired an astonishing store of information on a wide variety of subjects. And what he learned he retained, for he had a photographic memory that never let go of any information imprinted on it:

His memory, which he retained to old age, astonished all who knew him. Everything he had read, seen, or heard he remembered for the rest of his life. He remembered even the most useless trivia, which were sealed in his memory as it were automatically, without any exertion on his part, even without an effort of attention and so contrary to his characteristic absentmindedness. He could repeat in detail a conversation which he had with you twenty years ago, tell you where it took place and under what circumstances. If his memory retained trivia that were utterly indifferent and uninteresting to him, it must be apparent how firmly it retained all that which he took in with interest . . . He was a remarkable bibliographer. He knew where, by whom, and when this or that book had been published. And as concerns great and even not so great men of all

[21] Pamiati V. A. Gerda," Voz, No 450 (August 26, 1926).

[22] "Aksakovy i Aksakov," 350, and RiS, No. 117 (February 21, 1931). "This discovery and disclosure of Pushkin by the prophetic utterances of Dostoevsky represents for me, who was then still a child, the first strong, purely spiritual, purely cultural experience, upheaval, and revelation": "Dukh i slovo Pushkina," in E. V. Anichkov, ed., Belgradskii Pushkinskii Sbornik (Belgrade, 1937), 270. Struve also recalled the powerful impression made on him when he was eleven (1881) by Vladimir Soloviev's funeral oration for Dostoevsky, although in this case he says that he was more moved than enlightened: "Iz vospominanii o Vladimire Solov'eve," RiS, No. 95 (September 20, 1930).

[23] "Iz vospominanii o S.-Peterburgskom universitete," RiS, No. 65 (February 22, 1930).

[24] "Russko-slavianskie pominki," RiS, No. 223 (August 1933); in June 1889, for example, he witnessed the obsequies of Orest Miller: Slovo, May 10/23, 1909.

nations and times, writers, scholars, musicians, artists, crowned heads and statesmen, he not only knew accurately their names, but he could often furnish the precise dates of their birth and death. Peter Berngardovich carried in his head, as it were, a whole library, which in the course of his long life filled with new volumes.[25]

These remarks, applied to the mature Struve, also hold for the very young man. A. Meiendorf, who entered school in Stuttgart shortly after the twelve-year-old Peter had departed with his parents for Russia, recalled being told wonders about the Struve boy who, perched on a table, recited poems by heart.[26]

In Struve's youth, passion for knowledge in general and for knowledge which had no social and political "relevance" in particular was not only out of fashion but decidedly frowned upon. Young Russians, raised in the spirit of anarchism which worshiped action, regarded pure learning as incompatible with service to the people. As they saw it, one had to choose between study and revolution. Active revolutionaries, by the very nature of their vocation, had little time to read and were poorly informed on any subject outside of radical polemics. But even their sympathizers who stayed in school and cheered the revolutionaries from the sidelines — that is, the vast majority — confined their reading to standard "progressive" monthlies, sociological treatises, and pamphlets. In belles lettres their tastes were confined to novels that portrayed "realistically" or "naturalistically" (in other words, unfavorably) Russia's condition. Even such literature, however, was regarded as inferior to literary criticism, which in the 1860's had developed in Russia into a powerful instrument of political propaganda. Poetry and the fine arts were altogether ignored unless, like Nekrasov's verse or the paintings of the "Ambulants," they dealt with social themes. Of academic subjects, the intelligentsia between 1860 and 1890 favored only the natural sciences, especially chemistry and biology, which were useful in fighting the idealism and religion of the older generation.

Struve was sufficiently a child of his time to share its passion for sociology and its respect for natural science. But he was constitu-

[25] V. A. Obolensky's unpublished memoirs of Struve.
[26] A. Meiendorf, "P. B. Struve," unpublished manuscript in the possession of Professor Gleb Struve, Berkeley, California.

tionally incapable of putting fences around his curiosity or of judging that which intellect or taste had created by the standard of "relevance." He regarded the ignorance and militant anti-intellectualism of the Russian intelligentsia of the 1880's with profound contempt as a symptom of cultural deficiency.

He was never, therefore, not even in his teens, a true Russian intelligent. His unstinted admiration for every great achievement of the human spirit, whatever its political orientation or utility, perplexed those who knew him, especially his friends among radical youth. N. K. Krupskaia, Lenin's plodding wife, recalled with amazement the sight of Struve, tired from work on some Marxist publication, withdrawing to relax with a volume of poetry by Fet.[27] Her Volodia, in this respect a far more representative Russian intelligent of the period, could never have done anything like that, for he had little use for any poetry, and certainly none for that written by a reactionary like Fet. The radicals, in the midst of whom Struve spent much of his life until the age of thirty, instinctively (and rightly) interpreted his insistence on separating knowledge and art from politics as symptomatic of an imperfect commitment to the "cause." For that reason they never fully trusted him, and he reciprocated by treating them with a certain measure of disdain. Struve's quarrel with the Russian intelligentsia, which was to break into the open after 1905 and form one of the stormiest chapters in his biography, may be said, therefore, to derive from a fundamental trait of his character, one of which he gave evidence from his earliest years.

Nationalism constitutes the lowest substratum of Struve's mind. Before he was anything else — a liberal, a Social Democrat, or what he himself called a liberal conservative — he was a monarchist, a Slavophile, and a Pan-Slavist. Nationalism is one of the several continua in his intellectual biography, a constant of which most of his other political and social views were merely variables. A great, vital, cultured Russian nation was for him, from the earliest moments of political awareness, the principal objective of public activity.

[27] N. K. Krupskaia, "Iz vospominanii," in Istpart, *O Lenine*, I (Leningrad, 1925), 19. Struve discovered Fet in 1888, when in the library of a friend he chanced on a volume of his poetry called *Vechernye ogni*. He read it with enormous excitement, even though aware of Fet's reactionary political opinions: "O Fete — 'prozevala'-li Rossiia Feta?" RiS, No. 214 (February 11, 1933).

He absorbed this nationalism at home. His parents were sub-scribers and avid readers of the leading Pan-Slav organs, Ivan Aksakov's *Rus'* and Dostoevsky's *Diary of a Writer,* as well as of the "semilegal, oppositional conservative" (as he calls them) pamphlets of A. I. Koshelev and R. A. Fadeev.[28] The intellectual idol of the Struve household was Ivan Aksakov, to whom the Struves wrote letters expressing gratitude and admiration for his courageous critique of the government's domestic and foreign policies. In the summer of 1882, when on their return from Stutt-gart to St. Petersburg they stopped in Moscow at the Slav Bazaar, the city's leading hotel, Aksakov came to thank them personally for these expressions of support.[29] Struve's mother also entered into a correspondence with Dostoevsky, from whom she sought spiritual guidance.[30] From these clues it is not difficult to recon-struct the political atmosphere of the home in which Struve grew up: loyalty to the crown, hatred for "nihilism" and terror, admira-tion for the Great Reforms, unbounded faith in Russia's future as a great nation, support of imperial expansion in the Balkans. It was the ideology of the upper echelons of the enlightened imperial bureaucracy to which Peter Struve's father had belonged. Until the age of fifteen, Struve tells us, he shared these ideas. "I had patriotic, nationalistic impulses, tinged with dynastic and at the same time Slavophile sympathies, verging on hatred of the revolu-tionary movement. Ivan Aksakov and Dostoevsky, as the author of *Diary of a Writer,* were my principal heroes in the realm of ideas." [31]

The nationalism to which these statements refer was a very spe-cial phenomenon connected with the reforms of Alexander II. The purpose of the Great Reforms was to bring Russian society into closer participation in the life of the country: to transform it from a body of passive subjects into one of active citizens. By in-troducing them in the 1860's the monarchy for the first time de-parted from the ancient tradition of bureaucratic authoritarianism and estate privilege and sought to bring to life a Russian nation. The mood of the country during these years resembled that of Prussia half a century earlier, in the age of the reforms of Stein and Hardenberg. Those who had been active during that decade

---

[28] "Vremena," *Voz,* No. 264 (February 21, 1926).
[29] "Aksakovy i Aksakov," 350–351.
[30] RiS, No. 117 (February 21, 1931); "Aksakovy i Aksakov," 350.
[31] "My Contacts and Conflicts with Lenin," SR, XII, No. 36 (April 1934), 575.

or had grown up in its shadow never quite rid themselves of that optimistic liberal nationalism characteristic of societies in transition from traditional to modern politics, from static bureaucratism to dynamic democratism. As the reign of Alexander II drew to a close, the monarchy, responding to revolutionary violence, gradually abandoned its earlier course and returned to a policy of reliance on bureaucracy and police. But the liberal nationalism which it had stimulated in the 1860's remained very much alive in society during the following decade, when the precocious Struve began to interest himself in politics. His mind was molded by the Great Reforms and he always held fast to the belief that national greatness was attainable only through popular involvement, which had inspired this experiment.

The thinker from whom Struve had absorbed this brand of nationalism and who of all the figures in Russian intellectual history exerted on him the profoundest influence was Ivan Aksakov. Struve's admiration for him was born early and never flagged. As a twelve-year-old, Struve recalled, "his first love in the realm of ideas were the Slavophiles in general and [Aksakov] in particular." [32] As a child, carried away by Aksakov's powerful editorials, he wrote, in secret from his family, an article for *Rus*.[33] Forty years later, on the occasion of Aksakov's centennial, Struve described him as the "foremost among Russia's publicists," ranking him higher than both Herzen and Katkov, who, as he put it, "had played themselves out performing for their own generation." [34] Aksakov indeed provides the key to the innermost recesses of Struve's political thought. His unique conservative-liberal-nationalist ideology explains a great deal that is otherwise puzzling in Struve.

Aksakov's politics cannot readily be fitted into the familiar categories of Western political thought. He was the leading spokesman of Slavophilism in its final phase, after it had abandoned the cultural idealism of its early years and turned into a political movement with strong xenophobic overtones. As he grew older, Aksakov became increasingly paranoid, inciting his readers against Poles, Germans, and Jews, whom he blamed for Russia's misfortunes, and whipping up public frenzy for imperialist ventures.

[32] SR, II, No. 6 (1924), 515.
[33] "Aksakovy i Aksakov," 350.
[34] *Ibid.*, 349.

Viewed from this side, he may be characterized as a reactionary nationalist and one of the ideological forerunners of twentieth-century fascism.

But Aksakov's nationalism had to it another side, a strong liberal strain not commonly associated with someone of his xenophobic disposition. Like all the Slavophiles, he drew a clear line separating the state (*vlast'*) from the land (*zemlia*), or people (*narod*). To the state he conceded full political authority, unrestrained by either constitution or parliament, with the customary Slavophile qualification that it respect the civil liberties of the people. In interpreting the state-land relationship, however, he went beyond the usual vague generalizations of his fellow Slavophiles. Unlike them, he did not idealize the common people of Russia. He did not think that the narod carried in its soul the secret of some higher truth lost to the educated; nor did he think that it was capable — as then constituted — of giving Russia a true national culture. Illiterate, and therefore of necessity culturally passive, the Russian people were to him only potentially a nation. To become one in reality, the narod had to raise itself to the higher level of *obshchestvo*, a term Aksakov understood in the sense of "society," and occasionally referred to by that English word.[35] "Society" was what the people created at a more advanced stage of its historic evolution. It was "that environment in which a given people carries out its conscious intellectual activity, an environment which is created by the entire spiritual might of the people engaged in working out its national consciousness." [36]

The achievement of this level of consciousness was not possible without civil liberty. A passive people could create an active "society" only when permitted to educate itself, to engage in open discussion, to gain experience in local self-government. True to his conviction, Aksakov fought relentlessly to improve and extend Russia's elementary and secondary schools, to safeguard the power of the zemstva and of the reformed courts, and to assure for the country freedom of speech. He detested the bureaucratic police regime of Nicholas I which he had known in his youth. In the 1880's, when reactionaries were urging Alexander III to liquidate what was left of the reforms of his father and revert to the

---

[35] Aksakov's remarkable essays on "society" from the early 1860's can be found in Volume II of his *Sochineniia* (Moscow, 1886).

[36] I. S. Aksakov, *Sochineniia*, II (Moscow, 1886), 33.

authoritarian regime of Nicholas I, Aksakov's was one of the loudest voices warning against the disastrous consequences of such a course. He thought it essential that the government draw its strength from the support of an enlightened citizenry and not from police repression. For his blunt critique of the government's foreign and domestic policies he was constantly harassed by the authorities, and he had more publications shot from under him than any contemporary liberal or radical publicist.

Aksakov's nationalism was as hostile to the radical intelligentsia as to the bureaucracy and police. To him, the intelligentsia was not an acceptable alternative to the Westernized elite that had run the country since Peter the Great, for it too had arrogated to itself the right to speak for the people. Its desire to reorganize the country in a preordained manner was as contrary to Russia's true interests as were the efforts of the bureaucrats to prevent Russia from developing at all. The people alone, speaking and acting freely, could work out its national destiny. No one had the right to prevent it from so doing, and no one could act on its behalf.

Struve early adopted Aksakov's national ideal, which envisaged the creation of a Russian nation through the exercise of freedom of speech, education, and local self-government. Like Aksakov, he never treated the nation as something already given, something that, in order to flourish, merely required insulation from foreign influences, as did the run-of-the-mill Russian nationalists. From his earliest years he regarded Russian nationhood as lying still in the future: to him it was a task, not a thing. That which Aksakov called by the English term "society" Struve described by the German word "culture": it is one of the basic terms in his vocabulary and means the conscious creation of an environment assuring the individual's and society's unrestrained search for identity. When in 1894 Struve spoke of the United States as enjoying the highest level of culture in the world,[37] he used the word in this Aksakovian sense; and so it appeared often in his subsequent writings.

Until the age of fifteen Struve adhered to this kind of nationalism, partly conservative, partly liberal. He expected the monarchy to continue along the lines charted by the Great Reforms, to raise the level of "culture" and help the country create a nation. He detested the revolutionaries for hindering this work. If the mon-

[37] #15/91–92.

archy had indeed remained faithful to the reformism of the 1860's, he probably would never have changed his political views, for in his heart he was very much a German with an instinctive respect for the state as a creative force. But the government, as is known, chose otherwise. In 1881, after brief hesitation, it decided to abandon further attempts at bringing society into partnership and to rely henceforth on repressive administration by the bureau-cratic-police apparatus. The story of Russian politics during the quarter of a century that followed the assassination of Alexander II was one of relentless constriction of that relatively limited sphere of public activity granted society by the Great Reforms.

Aksakov saw all that happening, but he was too old to change. He expected to the end of his life to work for Russian "society" within the framework of monarchical absolutism. He rejected constitution and parliament, convinced that they would serve only to divert the attention of the Russian people from more urgent cultural tasks and to perpetuate the domination of the country by the Westernized elite. He was therefore content to confine his demands to civil liberty.

As long as Aksakov was alive, Struve seems to have thought in a similar manner. Then, in the winter of 1885–86, came an intel-lectual crisis, the first of several to come: his faith in the monarchy was shaken. He now became aware of a fatal disparity that had developed between the government and the country. The autoc-racy which since Peter the Great had led a reluctant country toward culture had after 1881 lost its capacity to lead: worse than that, it had become a burden which prevented the country from developing further on its own. An ossified bureaucratic-police establishment could not direct a people whose leading spokesmen had created a world literature and art, and whose educated classes were engaged in an endless and impassioned discussion of fundamental religious, political, and social questions. The country had outgrown its government and could not survive any longer without political liberty. As Struve recalled half a century later, his love of political liberty was "born of the enormous wealth of Russian spiritual and cultural life, which obviously [had] ceased to fit the traditional legal and political framework of autoc-racy or absolutism, even if enlightened." [38]

This conviction must have come to him as a sudden illumina-

[38] "My Contacts and Conflicts with Lenin," 584.

tion, for he says his conversion to liberalism occurred "with something like an elemental force." [39] Under what circumstances this happened can only be surmised. But there are strong indications that the crisis was connected with the last brush which Aksakov had with censorship just before his death in January 1886.

In November 1885 Aksakov published in *Rus'* a particularly audacious attack on the government's policies in Bulgaria, in which he blamed Russian diplomats for the deterioration in Russia's position in the Balkans. For this editorial he was formally reprimanded by the Minister of the Interior, who sent him a note accusing him of interpreting events "in a tone incompatible with true patriotism." As required by law, Aksakov published the reprimand without comment in the next issue of *Rus'*; but in the one that followed he took it as the text for a scathing indictment of the whole bureaucratic conception of patriotism prevalent in the Russian government:

> We take the liberty of saying that the law itself does not empower the Main Publishing Administration to use such a formula of accusation, that it does not authorize the police, even its uppermost ranks, to cast doubts on anyone's "patriotism." We say "the police" because the Ministry of the Interior, in whose charge Russian literature has been since being removed, in 1863, from the competence of the Ministry of Education, is in the main a ministry of state police and can only administer literature from the police point of view . . .
>
> Indeed, what is "true" and "untrue" patriotism? What are reliable symptoms of one and the other? What are the criteria for evaluating or even distinguishing them? From our point of view, for example, for a publicist true patriotism means to tell the government the truth, courageously and to the best of his understanding, no matter how hard and unpalatable; and for the government it means to listen to the truth, even when it is hard and unpalatable. In the opinion of many from the so-called higher spheres, the most genuine patriotism consists in cowering silence . . .
>
> Is the government itself always acting in the spirit of faultless patriotism? . . . After all, the Russian enthusiasts of the Treaty of Berlin considered themselves also "true patriots,"

[39] *Ibid.*, 576.

while "untrue patriots," like the editor of *Rus'*, see in their actions only patriotic thoughtlessness and cowardice. And can one, for instance, call unpatriotic that sense of alarm which sent a shudder through all Russia when it learned the terms of this treaty, an alarm which the writer of these lines expressed in a public speech for which the government meted out to him the well-known punishment? . . . If this were so, then one would have sometimes to charge all of Russian society and the whole of the Russian people with lack of "true patriotism," and to bestow a monopoly of genuineness exclusively on official circles! . . .

The point is that in Russia the very word "patriotism" still has a very imprecise meaning. Translated, it means "love of attending the development of our public life since the time of fatherland." However, because of the special circumstances Peter the Great, there have emerged in Russia, especially among its higher social strata, not a few "patriots" who manage to separate the idea of the "fatherland" from that of Russian nationality, and who are ready to sacrifice their lives on the field of battle to protect the fatherland's frontiers and honor, while at the same time being estranged from their Russian nationality and from Russian history and its legacy, of which they want to know nothing and, of course, know nothing! In other words, loving the vessel they scorn its content! Loving the "fatherland" they ignore and even feel contempt for that which contains the inner meaning and cause of its spiritual, moral, and political place in the world, and which, consequently, defines its very destiny and mission. It is understandable that such empty or one-sided patriotism often enters into unconscious contradiction with Russian national life, with the true national interests of Russia, causing between the one and the other at times a vast unbridgeable chasm of tragic misunderstandings.[40]

This editorial made an overwhelming impression on Struve. "Men of our generation read and reread it literally with trembling and exultation," he wrote, "as a condemnation, unexampled in its courage, of bureaucratic stupidity, and an equally courageous

[40] *Rus'*, No. 23 (December 6, 1885), 1–2.

defense of free speech." [41] "In our family everybody read with enthusiasm Aksakov's passionate and forceful answer to the censorship department, and in my case it acted as the warm or even hot breeze in which my own love of freedom finally matured." [42]

For Struve, the essential point of Aksakov's reply lay in the final sentence quoted above: the implication that the imperial government and its ideologues had ceased to represent the "true national interests of Russia." Aksakov himself did not draw from his charge the obvious political conclusions. True to his Slavophile heritage, he treated the government as simply misguided. He was content to play the role of critic, on the assumption that by telling the government what the nation felt he would bring it to its senses. Struve, however, pushed Aksakov's premise further: if it was true that the autocratic government no longer served Russia's national interests, then it had lost its usefulness and had to go.

The impulse of Struve's liberalism thus came from nationalism and remained rooted in it. Struve never gave up the hope that the government would come to realize the country's absolute need for freedom, and would, of its own accord, for the sake of the future of Russia, transfer power to the people. Its stubborn refusal to do what he considered both right and unavoidable incensed him and drove him steadily leftward, from hatred of revolutionaries to admiration and even verbal support. But he was always willing to make peace with the monarchy, and would at all times have preferred to have it grant political liberty on its own accord than to have liberty wrested from it. To understand Struve's political evolution it is essential to keep this fact in mind. His opposition to absolutism was the fruit of the disappointment of a man who had grown up on the ideals of the Great Reforms, who throughout his youth saw them betrayed, and whose fondest hope it was to see them reactivated.

Between 1885 and 1888 Struve drew his liberal inspiration mainly from two sources. One was the monthly *Messenger of Europe* (*Vestnik Evropy*). Around 1885 he met and made friends with K. K. Arseniev, the leading writer for the *Messenger*. Struve greatly admired the column "Domestic Survey" ("Vnutrennee

[41] "Aksakovy i Aksakov," 352.
[42] "My Contacts and Conflicts with Lenin," 575.

obozrenie"), in which Arseniev month after month flayed the bureaucracy and championed the cause of law and freedom.[43] In his apartment on the Moika Arseniev held a literary salon to which he invited young men to lecture to his guests, luminaries of the St. Petersburg intelligentsia, among them many contributors to the *Messenger*. Struve began to frequent this salon while still a gymnasium student and continued to do so after enrolling at the university. There he became acquainted with the philosopher Vladimir Soloviev, the literary historian Alexander Pypin, the trial lawyer A. F. Koni, and many others.[44] There too he made his literary debut. At Arseniev's invitation he read two papers, one on Shakespeare's *Tempest*, the other on the poetry of Nadson. The Shakespearean lecture was so brilliant that it dazzled even Arseniev and his sophisticated audience.[45] Arseniev took Struve under his wing and by his patronage helped him to enter unusually early in life the circle of St. Petersburg literati.[46]

The other source of Struve's liberal inspiration was the novels of Saltykov-Shchedrin, his favorite reading in school.[47] The picture which Saltykov-Shchedrin painted of contemporary Russia,

[43] *Ibid.*, 575–576.

[44] Struve left scattered recollections of Arseniev's salon in the following newspaper articles: "Pamiati A. F. Koni," *Rossiia,* No. 12 (November 12, 1927); RiS, No. 38 (August 17, 1929); No. 39 (August 24, 1929); and No. 214 (February 11, 1933). Among those who frequented it he listed, in addition, the literary historians V. D. Spasovich and S. A. Andreevsky and his university friends B. V. Nikolsky, N. D. Vodovozov, and N. P. Pavlov-Silvansky.

[45] I. V. Gessen, *V dvukh vekakh* (Berlin, 1937), 252. On Struve's Nadson lecture see his own remarks in RiS, No. 214 (February 11, 1933).

[46] On November 15, 1907, on the occasion of Arseniev's literary jcbilee, Struve sent him the following letter: "In your person I would like to hail a remarkable Westerner-humanist, a man who firmly upheld the standard of true liberalism during the most difficult years in Russia's existence. I would like to tell you how much I owe to you in my political development both as an individual and as a representative of that Russian youth which in the 1880's and 1890's learned so much from the *Messenger of Europe*." (Manuscript, Pushkin House, Leningrad, Arkhiv Arsen'eva, Fond 359, Item No. 467). The same archival deposit has another letter from Struve to Arseniev, dated December 3, 1894, expressing admiration for the masterly survey of the reign of the recently deceased Alexander III which appeared in the *Messenger* (see VE, December 1894, 840–853). In one of those casual asides so exasperating to his biographer, Struve said that while a student he had contributed regular listings of current books to "a periodical"; *Mech* (Warsaw), No. 42/75 (October 27, 1935). This periodical was almost certainly the *Messenger of Europe*.

[47] "My Contacts and Conflicts with Lenin," 576. Saltykov died in the same apartment house in which Struve lived from the spring of 1889 onward as a permanent house guest of A. M. Kalmykova (on whom see below): RiS, No. 83 (June 29, 1930). Struve seems to have attended Saltykov's funeral: *Rossiia,* No. 26 (February 18, 1928).

like Gogol's somber to the point of grotesqueness, increased Struve's loathing for absolutist Russia and sharpened his resolve to see it radically changed.

As he entered the last year of gymnasium (1888–89) he was a nationalist and a liberal, but as yet he lacked a political program. He knew what he wanted but not how to get it. His politics were still less of an ideology than an attitude.

In February 1889 Struve's father suddenly died. The cause of death was not announced, but his death was unexpected and gave rise to rumors of pressing debts and suicide.[48] Peter had been for some time on bad terms with his neurotic mother.[49] As soon as his father had been buried, he left home, moving in with a classmate, the son of Senator A. D. Kalmykov. There is no evidence of his having subsequently maintained contact with his mother. Apart from the fictionalized account cited above, he did not mention her in his writings, and her death, in 1905, made no perceptible impression on him.[50]

Struve probably thought of his move to the Kalmykovs as a temporary arrangement to tide him over until he entered the university. But, as it turned out, it was the beginning of a protracted and crucial episode in his life. His friend's mother, Aleksandra Mikhailovna Kalmykova, at once took him in tow, offering the kind of firm adult guidance which, given his poor health and helplessness in practical matters, he required but had never received from his own mother. He was to spend seven long years in her apartment on Liteinyi 60, in the heart of the St. Petersburg literary district.

At the time of their encounter, Kalmykova was approaching forty. She was a native of Ekaterinoslav in southern Russia, where, as a young woman, she had taught secondary school and worked for various philanthropic and educational organizations. She be-

[48] Information supplied by Miss Olga Tomaschek. The obituary in *Novoe vremia* (No. 4657, February 14/26, 1889) confirms that death occurred suddenly.

[49] V. A. Posse, the brother-in-law of Vasily, Peter Struve's oldest brother, says that Peter had early entered "into opposition against his mother"; *Moi zhiznennyi put'* (Moscow and Leningrad, 1929), 123.

[50] She died on June 11, 1905, and was buried by her husband's side at the Smolensk Orthodox Cemetery in St. Petersburg: Velikii kniaz' Nikolai Mikhailovich, *Peterburgskii nekropol'*, IV (St. Petersburg, 1913), 186. There is no indication in Struve's biography of that Oedipal complex which according to some "psychohistorians" explains youthful radicalism. Nor, for that matter, can any trace of it be found in the biography of Lenin, the archetypal revolutionary.

longed to that first generation of emancipated Russian women who had managed to escape the tutelage of the family and then threw themselves with unbounded energy into civic work. At twenty, she fell in love with a judge fifteen years her senior. Impressed by his "democratic" background (his ancestors were serfs), she consented to marry him. The marriage proved a disaster. Kalmykov, notwithstanding his low origin (or perhaps because of it) had little else on his mind than his career, and found his bride's civic proclivities silly. The two soon became estranged, and led separate lives although continuing to maintain a joint household. Kalmykov doggedly climbed up the service ladder, while Kalmykova pursued her civic work and, in her free time, read a great deal.[51] In the early 1880's, when her husband was transferred to Kharkov, she became acquainted with a group of "progressive" writers who published the newspaper *Southern Land* (*Iuzhnyi krai*) and under their influence she became radicalized. She brought out several educational pamphlets for mass distribution, the sort of publications which afterward were to become her specialty and earn her a national reputation.[52]

In 1885, Kalmykov at last reached the top of the judiciary profession: he was promoted to the rank of senator and transferred to St. Petersburg. Here Kalmykova again immersed herself in civic affairs of all kinds. She became a leading spirit of the Literacy Committee of the Free Economic Society, whose goal was to spread mass education. She also worked as a volunteer teacher in Sunday and evening schools for workers founded by the enlightened St. Petersburg industrialist V. P. Vargunin. At these schools she made contact with radical youths, among them N. K. Krupskaia, the future wife of Lenin.[53]

She was intensely and constructively active, but nevertheless

[51] Biographical information on Kalmykova can be found in the following sources: a fragment of her memoirs, "Obryvki vospominanii," *Byloe*, No. 1/35 (1926), 64–80; "A. M. Kalmykova," KL, No. 4/19 (1926), 138–55; B&E, XIV (1895), 64; and a brief obituary in *Leningradskaia pravda*, No. 75 (April 2, 1926). 3he is depicted as a fictionalized Daria Mikhailovna Kolchugina in Struve's *Vremena*: Voz, No. 537 (November 2, 1926).

[52] V. M. Muratov, *Knizhnoe delo v Rossii v XIX i XX vv.* (Moscow and Leningrad, 1931), 122–123, gives a glimpse of her in Kharkov. Her booklets from that time include one on the Jewish question (*Evreiskii vopros v Rossii*, Kharkov, 1881), a bibliography of literature for the masses, and several pamphlets on sanitation.

[53] Kalmykova, "Obryvki," 64; Richard Kindersley, *The First Russian Revisionists* (Oxford, 1962), 44–45; and Richard Pipes, *Social Democracy and the St. Petersburg Labor Movement, 1885–1897* (Cambridge, Mass., 1963), 45.

lonely and frustrated. She had long ceased to have any contact with her husband. Her son brought her no consolation for a miserable marriage, for he seems to have resembled his father and resented a mother who was "different" from the others. One day he introduced to her a friend whom he had brought from school. "Here is a real son for you, mother," he said, introducing Peter Struve; "he always walks with his head downcast, he is forever lost in thought, and he knows more history than the teacher." [54] After graduating from school in the spring of 1889 in Struve's class, the young Kalmykov seems to have dropped out of her life entirely.[55] Her husband died later that year. Struve stayed on in her now deserted apartment, and before long was introduced everywhere as her adopted son. From then on they became inseparable.

[54] KL, No. 4/19 (1926), 141. Ariadna Tyrkova-Williams (Villiams) told me she believed Struve first met Kalmykova when he was sixteen.
[55] Kindersley, *Russian Revisionists,* 44.

2. THE 1880'S: INTELLECTUAL BACKGROUND

For one who has concluded — as Struve had done in 1885 — that his country had to have political freedom as a matter of national survival, the next natural step should have been to join that movement which in the nineteenth century had everywhere made the attainment of political freedom its main objective, namely liberalism. But in 1885 there was in Russia no liberal movement in any meaningful sense of the term. Why this was so will be discussed later (Chapter 12). Suffice it to say here that when Struve began his search for an antiautocratic ideology, those Russians who subscribed to liberal principles no longer wanted to fight the monarchy. Rather than struggle for constitution, parliament, and civil rights they preferred to devote themselves to the great task of improving the material and cultural condition of the Russian people. The value of this activity, known as "small deeds," must have been apparent to Struve even then, and he always spoke of it with the highest admiration. But clearly the founding in villages of cooperative societies and mutual insurance organizations, or drives against rural illiteracy and low sanitary standards, could not satisfy a youth of fifteen bent on toppling a tyranny. And in fact until 1900 Struve treated Russian liberals with a certain contempt for their ready acquiescence in a lawless government. In 1898, in the Manifesto of Russian Social Democracy, he explained their behavior by a famous formula according to which the further east in Europe one moved "the weaker, more cowardly, and baser in the political sense" the middle classes became.

What then? There was no alternative but to turn left, to the radicals. But here too the situation was far from satisfactory. The anarchist movement, so daring in the reign of Alexander II, collapsed after his assassination. In the 1880's, Russian radicalism was in disarray, uncertain what to do and where to aim. Every now and then attempts were made to revive the People's Will and the terror. But the dominant mood on the left, as in the liberal center, was one of accommodation. Some radicals converted to Tolstoyism and gave up politics altogether. Others — the majority — adopted the policy of "small deeds" and went to work in the countryside, usually as salaried employees of zemstva. The leading radical journalists continued to criticize lawlessness and injustice and hold out the prospect of a free and equal society; but they tended to treat freedom and equality as remote desiderata rather than as pressing needs. Their outlook — reformist and cultural — did not much differ from that of the liberals.

It was dissatisfaction with the spirit of the antiautocratic movement, liberal and radical alike, that drove Struve in 1888 to Marxism and Social Democracy. Before proceeding to this phase of his life, however, it is necessary to digress and to deal at some length with Russian socialism of the 1880's. Unless one has a clear conception of that which Struve found and rejected in the socialism of his youth it is not possible to understand what he came to advocate as an alternative; and failing that one cannot understand the origins of Social Democracy in Russia, for it was he who launched it.

The historical literature on the subject is uncritical and hopelessly entangled in controversies of the past. That Struve was a "Marxist" (usually qualified as of the "Legal" variety) and that in Russia "Marxism" superseded something called "Populism" are assertions made in every respectable history of Russia. In this historiographic scheme Populism is understood to be a theory originated by Herzen and Chernyshevsky according to which Russians, owing to their unique spiritual qualities, were predestined to solve the social problems plaguing the modern World. They were to fulfill this historic mission by constructing on Russian peasant institutions (the repartitional commune and artel') a socialist society, thus bypassing the purgatory of capitalism. The critical role in this whole process was to be played by the intelligentsia. This supposedly utopian scheme is said to have been exposed in the 1890's by the "Marxists," who won over the radical intelligentsia by advancing the allegedly realistic thesis that Russia's economic and social development would inexorably follow the path of development first beaten by the advanced countries of Western Europe, socialism arriving in Russia, as there, as an outgrowth of capitalism.

In fact, matters were much more complicated than the traditional picture allows. The pattern of doctrinal succession — "Populism," the partial truth, supplanted by "Marxism," the truth in full — derives from the Christian conception of the New Testament as a revelation that superseded the Old, and bears no more semblance to reality. There never was any "Populist" movement with a consistent theory and strategy, any more than in the West there was anything identifiable as "Utopian Socialism": both these terms were launched by Marx and his disciples in order to discredit rival socialist movements. The phenomenon usually labeled Populism was a broad and diversified anarchist current whose adherents constantly experimented with theories and strategies of revolution, seeking an effective means of overthrowing a regime resting on a non-Western economy and social structure — in other words, seeking a revolutionary technique suitable for what today would be called an underdeveloped country. They never regarded the theory of Marx and Engels as an alternative. Quite the contrary: they absorbed a great deal of the doctrine of Marx and Engels, believing to have found in it conclusive "scientific" proof that Russia need not follow the Western path. Marx and Engels encouraged the Russian radicals to make such a creative adaptation of their theories and furnished them with additional arguments.

My analysis of Russian socialism will stress those of its doctrinal elements which Struve and other Social Democrats subsequently singled out for critique as "utopian": the theory of historical progress connected with the so-called subjective method in sociology: the theory of economic development identified with the notion of a "separate path"; and the interpretation of the theories of Marx and Engels as they applied to Russia.

Radical thought in Russia during the second half of the nineteenth century rested on foundations supplied by Comtean positivism. Positivism had two features which particularly attracted Russian intellectuals. One was its denial of a qualitative difference between nature and society, with the corollary proposition that identical laws explained the operations of both. The other was the definition of human progress as progress of enlightenment, understood to mean the transition from "theological" and "metaphysical" ways of thinking to the scientific or "positive" one. Positivism put a premium on knowledge and extolled the intelligentsia as its carrier. It made the latter the prime mover of history, teaching that an intellectual, by the simple fact of converting his way of thinking to the "scientific" mode, made a decisive contribution to the advancement of the human race. It was an outlook admirably suited to a large and ambitious elite long on education but short on wealth and political influence. As such it won for itself an impressive following not only in Russia but also in other countries situated on the periphery of Europe (for example, Brazil) where the Westernization of education and thought outdistanced significantly the modernization of society and government.

Russian youths who saw themselves as the vanguard of mankind received their first rude shock from Darwin. Natural selection, especially as reinterpreted sociologically by Spencer, depicted progress in terms very different from Comte's. In its view what counted was not enlightenment but adaptability, and that as often as not meant cunning, rapacity, and brute physical force. The agent of progress was seen to be not the individual — a "negligible quantity," in Spencer's words — but the biological or social group. These ideas posed for Russian radical intellectuals a cruel dilemma. As positivists committed to the scientific outlook they had to grant that natural selection, like any other demonstrated law of nature, had universal validity, and therefore also explained the operations of society. But to accept natural selection as an explanation of human evolution was tantamount to denying themselves any meaningful role in history. The other alternative — denial of the universal applicability of scientific laws — produced the same effect because it meant the rejection of the basic premise of positivism — that is, the scientific way of thinking as the essence of progress — on which the intelligentsia based its claim to being the vanguard of the new era.

Initially, Russian intellectuals responded to the difficulty by repudiating Darwin's theory on scientific grounds. Such was the case with Chernyshevsky. Others did not reject natural selection out of hand but ascribed to it limited validity. Kropotkin, for example, held that both in animal and in human evolution, cooperation (mutual aid) contributed more to the survival of the species than did competition and conflict. In general, Darwinism had a poor reception in Russia. Although it did not encounter there the kind of religious hostility common in Protestant countries, it did run into firm resistance of an ideological kind from an intelligentsia whose position and self-conception it seriously threatened. N. K. Mikhailovsky voiced a widespread sentiment when he paired Darwin with Offenbach on the grounds that the former's pseudo-science, like the pseudo-operas of the latter, served the same purpose, namely to justify or conceal bourgeois exploitation.[1]

Of all the anti-Darwinian and anti-Spencerian theories, the "subjective method" formulated by Mikhailovsky and P. Lavrov around 1870 gained the greatest currency in Russia. Its proponents resolved the contradiction between positivism and Darwinism by diluting the former so as to accommodate an anti-Darwinian conception of progress. They claimed that man and society should really not be approached in a strictly objective manner, such as was proper in the study of natural phenomena, because man possessed subjective values and goals: hence there was no warrant for an automatic transfer of laws operative in nature to society. The intellectual inspiration of "subjective sociology" came from the late writings of Comte, especially his *Système de politique positive*, where the founder of positivism, after having been struck by love in old age, conceded that in human affairs there was indeed room for "subjective" factors absent from inanimate nature. On this slender authority, Russian sociologists erected an elaborate philosophy of history which dominated Russian radical thought from 1870 to 1890 and which in the opinion of some scholars represents Russia's principal contribution to the store of sociological ideas.[2]

Credit for the theory must be divided equally between Lavrov and Mikhailovsky. But Lavrov was in Siberian exile when he wrote his influential *Historical Letters,* and he subsequently fled to Western Europe, from where he could not directly communicate with Russian readers. Mikhailovsky, on the other hand, stayed out of trouble, and as principal writer for *Notes of the Fatherland* (*Otechestvennye Zapiski*) won for his ideas an immense following. Although not a systematic thinker, he managed to formulate

---

[1] N. K. Mikhailovsky, "Darvinizm i operetki Offenbakha" (1871), in his *Sochineniia,* I (St. Petersburg, 1896), 391–422.

[2] The contributions of the Russian sociological school are discussed in T. G. Masaryk's *Spirit of Russia,* II (London and New York, 1968), 115–190.

a fairly consistent theory of sociology and philosophy of history.[3] It was against his theories that Struve directed his first sociological writings and it was Mikhailovsky that he dethroned in the mid-1890's as the chief spokesman for the left.

Mikhailovsky proceeded from the premise that the main difference between natural and sociological phenomena consisted in the presence or absence of purpose. Nature is aimless. It functions from day to day in accord with prescribed rules but it has no goals beyond self-preservation. The law of natural selection which underlies progress in biology is not purposeful activity because of its negative character: it is a technique for preserving that which already exists, but it gives no indication of how the existing can improve itself.[4] In history things are different. Man possesses ideals and he struggles not only for self-preservation but also for self-perfection. He transforms his environment in accord with his ideals. "The history of life on earth strives to become the history of human ideals." Man's aspirations are an essential part of his nature and therefore of his evolution. This would be the case even if it could be shown that these aspirations are a delusion. Whether they can be realized or not, whether man has or lacks free will does not alter the fact that he possesses ideals and believes himself to possess free will. The purpose of "subjective sociology" was to provide a necessary corrective to strict empiricism by making allowance for these factors. Its essence, according to Mikhailovsky, lay in the ability of the observer to place himself in the situation of the object of his observation, to share his aspirations and sufferings, and thus to understand him and his behavior.

For the subjective method the primary object of observation was the individual. A thoroughgoing nominalist, Mikhailovsky refused to hypostatize nation, society, or class. He had nothing but contempt for Spencer's absurd analogy between society and the biological organism. In the organism, Mikhailovsky argued, it is the whole that experiences pain and pleasure; in the former,

[3] Mikhailovsky's ideas are summarized admiringly by E. E. Kolosov in *Ocherki mirovozzreniia N. K. Mikhailovskogo* (St. Petersburg, 1912), and critically by S. N. Ransky in *Sotsiologiia N. K. Mikhailovskogo* (St. Petersburg, 1901). See also Masaryk's study cited above, Arthur P. Mendel, *Dilemmas of Progress in Tsarist Russia* (Cambridge, Mass., 1961), and James H. Billington, *Mikhailovsky and Russian Populism* (Oxford, 1958).

[4] Mikhailovsky seems to have owed this as well as several other basic ideas to his friend N. D. Nozhin, a brilliant youth who died at the age of twenty-three.

the individual human being. The sociological counterpart of the biological organism, therefore, is individual man. From this it follows that a society can be said to be good only if its members are content: a happy society composed of miserable individuals is a contradiction in terms.

What makes for man's happiness? What is his main aspiration? Following Comte, Mikhailovsky believed that man strives for an integral personality, that is, one which allows both his mental and physical capacities to receive their fullest realization. Such a personality can be acquired only through meaningful work because man is by nature a doer, *homo faber*. To enable man to develop all his capacities, work has to be correspondingly diversified, engaging fully both mind and body. Monotonous, repetitive work that calls only for one particular skill stultifies man and turns him into a "toe on the foot" of society.

The great problem is that man's quest for an integral personality collides with a contrary tendency of society. As society matures it promotes division of labor. The initial step is the separation of mental work from physical; then, gradually, there occur ever greater refinements within each of these two categories and greater specializations of productive functions. The result is superior efficiency of production, but the cost is heavy, for it brings with it the steady restriction of opportunities for the individual to develop his latent capabilities. To Mikhailovsky, division of labor was the worst threat inhering in human evolution. Because of his fear of it he went to great lengths to refute Spencer's organic theory of society. By defining society as an organism, Spencer could equate the division of labor occurring in society with the specialization of organs in biological organisms occurring in the process of evolution, and designate it progressive. To Mikhailovsky it was a regressive phenomenon, because it degenerated the individual, the true "organism" of society. In his celebrated definition of progress he described it as consisting in the "gradual striving of indivisible personalities for completeness, for the fullest and most diversified possible division of labor among the organs of the human body, and the least possible division of labor among men."

One of the worst by-products of the division of labor was class war. Where everyone took turns doing everything, class war was not possible because there were no social distinctions (Mikhailovsky identified these with occupational distinctions). As soon as men took up specific vocations, however, society broke up into occupational groups, each with its ideas and interests; thus divided, men ceased to understand one another, lost the sense of common humanity, and clashed. Class war, like its cause, division of labor, was not a biological fact of human nature, but the consequence of a particular arrangement of production.[5]

The alternative was cooperation. Division of labor, of course, was also cooperative activity, but of a lower type, one which Mikhailovsky designated "complex." He preferred "simple" cooperation, under which every individual performed every productive function. He believed that the progress of history required the replacement of complex cooperation with simple. Unless that happened — and the question was an open one, for in his philosophy of history there was no room for inevitability — mankind would steadily dehumanize and ultimately perish.

Although not free of inconsistencies and in the main quite eclectic, Mikhailovsky's system of sociology had one great virtue: it reconciled in a persuasive manner the scientific commitment of the intelligentsia with its deep yearning for a role in history. As formulated by him and other theorists of the school, "subjective sociology" established a relationship between scientific inevitability and human volition with just the right degree of flexibility; and because of this quality, in the 1870's and 1880's it all but monopolized the sociological and historical outlook of Russian radicals.

The "subjective method" in sociology received independent support from a theory of development which concurrently conquered Russian economic thought. This was the famous doctrine of the "separate path," according to which the agricultural and industrial development of Russia would proceed along other than capitalist lines. I say "independent support" because the two theories, although often regarded as inseparable, had entirely different origins and did not depend on one another: the sociological theory came into being by way of philosophical deduction, the economic one by way of empirical induction. Yet the two reinforced one another inasmuch as both assumed the future to be

---

[5] Mikhailovsky distinguished between what he called "technical" and "social" division of labor. He objected only to the latter.

not predetermined but molded by the conscious actions of men; and for this reason it was not uncommon for Russians to subscribe to both.

The belief that Russians have a different destiny from other peoples derived from Slavophile ideas first formed in Poland and Bohemia at the beginning of the nineteenth century. Pressed by Germans, who with their superior power and more advanced economy threatened to engulf them, Polish and Czech intellectuals turned German Romantic nationalism around and claimed that their low state notwithstanding, the Slavs were inherently superior to the Germans and appointed by history to world leadership. The special Slavic virtue stressed by the founders of Slavophilism — Lelewel, Maciejowski, and Šafarik — was the communal spirit: the alleged ability of Slavs to live and work with each other in natural harmony uncoerced by state, law, property, and other repressive institutions necessary to peoples belonging to the German race. In the 1820's this doctrine spread to Russia, where it engendered a local variant of Slavophilism which identified these allegedly innate Slav virtues with Russian national and religious traditions. Like their Polish and Czech forerunners, Russian Slavophiles attached great importance to the spirit of communality or *sobornost'*, visible proof of which they believed to have found in the commune (mir) and artel'. "The communal spirit is the basis, the foundation of all Russian history, past, present, and future," Iury Samarin wrote in 1847, "the seed and the root of everything that appears on the surface lies buried in its fertile depths." [6] During the debates attending the emancipation of the serfs these ideas gained a wide audience. Among publicists who converted to them were Herzen and Chernyshevsky, radicals in other respects quite scornful of Russian reality.

These facts are well known and require no elaboration. What calls for comment is the influence that Slavophile ideas exercised on Russia in the decades that followed Emancipation. There exists a misconception that the belief in the peasant commune and in Russia's "separate path" of economic development, widespread during the years 1855–1890, owed its origin to the ideas of Herzen and Chernyshevsky. In reality, the influence of these two

[6] Cited in V. V. Sviatlovsky, *K istorii politicheskoi ekonomii i statistki v Rossii* (St. Petersburg, 1906), 103n.

thinkers on Russian opinion ceased to be significant after 1862–63 when Chernyshevsky was arrested and Herzen's *Bell* lost its audience because of its stand on the Polish uprising. From then until the 1905 Revolution censorship kept their writings out of the hands of Russian readers. The doctrine of the separate path was not a mere idea and owed relatively little to its intellectual antecedents. Its principal source was the realities of the Russian economy after the Emancipation. It represented a pioneering attempt to deal with problems which in the twentieth century have come to occupy the branch of economics concerned with questions of economic development.[7]

Any analysis of the Russian economy undertaken after 1861 had to begin with the fact that Russia was an overwhelmingly agricultural country in which more than nine out of ten inhabitants were officially still classed as peasants. Until 1890, when intense industrialization got under way, the economic problems confronting Russia were those of its agriculture, par excellence. The condition of Russian agriculture, in turn, was shaped by the Emancipation Edict, which had divided the bulk of the privately owned arable land into two nearly equal halves, one left in the hands of the gentry, its previous owners, the other transferred to the peasantry. From both the economic and legal points of view, land tenure in these halves rested on different principles. The land which the gentry were allowed to keep, as well as that which they subsequently sold to merchants and prosperous peasants, was private property. It could be mortgaged or sold, and as a rule it was cultivated not by its owners but by hired or tenanted labor. In Marxist terminology, this land constituted the capitalist sector of the Russian rural economy. The land which by the provisions of the Edict had been transferred to the peasants was held and exploited on a different principle, one which in Russian literature came to be known as "popular production" (*narodnoe proizvodstvo*). In this sector, every worker was assured (at any rate, in theory) of direct access to the means of production, a land allotment; but he was not free to dispose of it, because title to it belonged to the commune of which he was a member. The existence in Russia after 1861 of two different economic systems side by side, one considered Western and the other indigenous, permitted Rus-

[7] This point is made repeatedly in Mendel's *Dilemmas*.

sian economists to draw comparisons between them and to evaluate their respective merits.

The comparison did not favor the capitalist sector. Almost the instant the Emancipation Edict had been proclaimed, the gentry began to lose their share of the land. They mortgaged and sold estates at so rapid a rate that the government, alarmed by the prospect of losing a class on which it still relied heavily for internal security, took a number of remedial steps, such as the founding in 1885 of the Bank of the Nobility to make loans at rates below those available commercially. Government assistance, however, did not appreciably stem the economic decline of the gentry. Each year approximately 1 percent of the gentry estates was sold or foreclosed; had the process been allowed to take its natural course, the Russian gentry would have found themselves squeezed out of the land sometime before the middle of the twentieth century whether or not a revolution had taken place. (As it was, by 1916, 89.3 percent of all the arable land and over 94 percent of all the cattle in European Russia were in the hands of peasants.[8]) Evidence to this effect, carefully gathered by zemstvo statisticians and analyzed by professional economists, strongly suggested that capitalist agriculture had no future in Russia: if the gentry with their superior education, greater material means, and generous support from the government could not make a go of it, what chance had the peasant proprietor of a small or even medium-sized farm? On the tenth anniversary of the Emancipation, A. I. Chuprov, then a lecturer at the University of Moscow and subsequently the country's leading economist, expressed the conviction that if the communes were subdivided into private holdings, the peasantry would have no choice but to sell out and turn itself into a landless proletariat.[9]

Empirical evidence of this kind made the peasant commune attractive to Russians who subscribed neither to the conservative nationalism of the Slavophiles proper nor to the radical variant of Slavophilism formulated by Herzen and Chernyshevsky. Criti-

---

[8] A. N. Chelintsev, *Russkoe sel'skoe khoziaistvo pered revoliutsei,* 2nd ed. (Moscow, 1928), 10–11. This statistic, of course, disproves the commonly held view that until 1917 Russia was a "feudal" country.

[9] A. I. Chuprov, "Melkaia promyshlennost' v sviazi s artel'nym nachalom i pozemel'noi obshchinoi" (1871), in *Rechi i stat'i,* I (Moscow, 1909), 51.

cism of the commune came mainly from a few proponents of laissez faire, never very influential in Russia, such as I. V. Vernadsky and M. M. Kovalevsky. The dominant school of thought among professional economists, many of them pupils of Chuprov, held that under Russian conditions communal landholding was more viable than the capitalist system. This point was supported by numerous scholarly studies resting on a wealth of statistical data.[10]

But if the communal principle of land tenure was so well suited to Russia, why were the peasants so badly off? To this obvious question the defenders of the commune retorted that the admittedly miserable condition of post-Reform agriculture was due not to the communal system of land tenure itself but to faulty economic policies pursued by the government. In 1861 the government had allotted the peasant insufficient land to enable him to meet the taxes and redemption payments which it had concurrently imposed on him. Studies of family budgets showed that the peasant's fiscal obligations exceeded his income and left him no alternative but to fall into arrears on taxes and redemption payments. The situation would be readily improved once the government agreed to take two steps: to substantially increase peasant holdings at the expense of the gentry and the crown, and to reduce the peasant's fiscal obligations.[11] Easier credit and assistance in resettling peasants in Siberia were also urged. Once these things were done, the endemic agrarian crisis would resolve itself. Such was the conclusion of informed Russian opinion in the 1880's, shared by the majority of academic economists and professional statisticians.

No prominent economist or even publicist of this era was so naive as to believe that Russia was immune to capitalism, for signs of its penetration were visible everywhere. The question was not whether capitalism would conquer the Russian economy but whether it should be allowed to do so. The prevailing view held that Russia still had a mixed economy in which two systems

[10] For example, A. S. Posnikov, *Obshchinnoe zemlevladenie*, 2 vols. (Iaroslavl and Odessa, 1875–1878), and N. A. Kablukov, *Ocherk khoziaistva chastnykh zemlevladel'tsev* (Moscow, 1879). The ideas of the Moscow school of economists are discussed in N. K. Karataev, *Ekonomicheskie nauki v moskovskom universitete* (*1755–1955*) (Moscow, 1956).

[11] Such were the recommendations of a prominent statistician, Iu. E. Ianson: *Sravnitel'naia statistika Rossii i zapadno-evropeiskikh gosudarstv*, 2 vols. (St. Petersburg, 1878–1880).

— "capitalism" and "popular production" — were locked in mortal combat. The outcome of the battle depended on the government. If it left matters alone, popular production would triumph. If it persisted in promoting capitalism in agriculure and industry, as had been the case since 1861, capitalism would destroy the popular sector of the economy; but its victory would be a worthless one, for it would inherit a wasteland inhabited by a destitute mass of rural proletarians.

Such essentially empirical considerations suggested to Russian radical publicists the notion of the separate path. Combining evidence against capitalism in Russia furnished by economists and statisticians with their own objections to the capitalist system on moral grounds, they formulated a theory according to which Russian socialism of the future, like the most viable part of the Russian economy of their own time, would rest on popular production. In other words, socialism would evolve naturally from that sector of the Russian economy which already had proven its viability, rather than from the highly developed and centralized capitalist industry prevalent in England and Germany. This idea, apparently first advanced in 1872 by G. Z. Eliseev,[12] received its fullest statement in 1882 in *Fate of Capitalism in Russia,* by V. Vorontsov ("V.V."), one of the most influential books to appear in Russia in the second half of the nineteenth century.[13]

Vorontsov at the outset renounced models of economic development valid for all countries. In particular, he denied that the procedure which England followed in industrializing would be repeated in Russia. There were several reasons why this could not be done, the most important being Russia's late entry into the ranks of industrializing nations: as a rule, he wrote, "the later a country industrialized, the more difficult it was to do so by capitalistic means."[14] He rejected anticipated accusations that behind his view lay Slavophile sentiments:

To avoid any misunderstandings, we will add that in our opinion . . . Russia's deviation from the historic forms of the West

---

[12] *Sochineniia G. Z. Eliseeva v dvukh tomakh,* I (Moscow, 1894), especially pp. 127–188. See also N. K. Karataev in *Istoriia russkoi ekonomicheskoi mysli,* Vol. II (Moscow, 1959), Pt. 1, 424–425.

[13] V. V [orontsov], *Sud'by kapitalizma v Rossii* (St. Petersburg, 1882), a collection of essays first published separately in periodicals. The author (1847–1918) was a physician active in zemstva.

[14] *Ibid.,* 15.

occurred not as a result of any racial peculiarities of the Russian people. It is the natural consequence of the conditions in which various nations find themselves at the present time: the constriction of international trade which takes place as new nations enter the path of progress raises for young countries increasing difficulties that prevent their capitalist productivity from flourishing.[15]

Vorontsov conceded that in post-Reform Russia capitalism had made great inroads in agriculture and industry, but he ascribed these successes to government intervention rather than to the exigencies of the national economy. The imperial government persisted in aiding the capitalist sector despite ample evidence that in agriculture and industry alike the small, independent producer in control of the means of production (land, tools, and manufacturing equipment) was more efficient than the capitalist entrepreneur employing hired labor.

Two principal factors prevented Russian industry from expanding significantly by capitalist methods. One was excessive costs of production. Long distances and inadequate means of transport, the severity of the climate, the overabundance of cheap, unskilled labor, state monopolies, and a number of other factors combined to make Russian industrial products noncompetitive. The other was absence of markets. Foreign markets were already dominated by countries which had industrialized earlier. The domestic market was poor to begin with and deteriorating. The peasant, the principal consumer in Russia, depended heavily on the supplementary income which he derived from household manufacture. But as capitalist industry in Russia matured and saturated the domestic market, the outlets for the crude goods of peasant household manufacture diminished, with the result that the peasant had increasingly less money with which to buy industrial consumer goods. Russian capitalist industry was thus trapped in a vicious circle: "its progress demands a rich population, and yet every step it takes forward, toward development, is accompanied by the impoverishment of the population: the development of capitalist industry impoverishes the people, and this impoverishment undercuts capitalist productivity."[16] Fur-

---

[15] *Ibid.*, 274.
[16] *Ibid.*, 275. Essentially the same point was made by N. F. Danielson (Nikolai

thermore, Vorontsov argued, even under the most favorable conditions capitalist industry could not appreciably alleviate Russia's agrarian difficulties, because, owing to technological improvements, modern industry was able to keep on increasing productivity without hiring additional workers: hence it would not absorb the landless peasantry.

In sum, industrial capitalism in Russia was an artificial plant, grown in the hothouse climate of protective tariffs, government subsidies, and military procurements. Under Russian conditions it meant not improved productivity and increased employment but intensified exploitation.

The prospects of capitalism looked no brighter in agriculture. Statistics indicated the steady shrinkage of capitalist land and its passage into the hands of peasants. Intensified American competition, which bore much responsibility for this situation, would eventually drive all the Russian grain from the world markets and deliver the coup de grâce to what was left of Russian private agriculture.

The conclusion was obvious: the government must abandon its ill-advised and futile sponsorship of capitalism, and divert all its resources to the assistance of popular production. Those branches of industry which, because of heavy capital outlays and the necessity of central management, did not lend themselves to small-scale ownership — for instance, transport, mining, and machine building — should be nationalized. Such a measure did not call for outright expropriation: deprived of government support and left to their own devices, private businesses in these branches of industry would soon lose money and become bankrupt. Other industries, including those working for the consumer, should be entrusted to small enterprises organized on the artel' principle, under which associations of workers owned the means of production and dealt directly with the buyer. Such a reorientation of the nation's economic policy, according to Vorontsov, would create a new model combining the advantages of technical efficiency with the requirements of social justice. In agriculture, the government should in every way possible assist the small producer, assuring that the commune retain its cohesion and that all the land slipping out of the hands of capitalist owners come

-on) in "Ocherki nashego poreformennogo khoziaistva," *Slovo*, October 1880, 76–142. This article will be discussed in Chapter 4.

directly into those of the cultivators, by-passing the kulak middle-man and urban speculator.

Vorontsov's economic ideal bore some resemblance to that of German state socialism,[17] and came close to the New Economic Policy which Lenin inaugurated in 1921, under which the state controlled the "commanding heights" of the economy and turned over agriculture, consumer industry, and much of the trade to the small entrepreneur working alone or in associations. Marxist language and concepts were heavily in evidence, the capitalist economy as depicted by Marx on the English example being taken as the model of the capitalist economy in general.

The analyses of Russian agriculture by Chuprov and his disciples, and of Russian industry by Vorontsov, despite a certain lack of realism in the treatment of large-scale, centralized productivity, were by no means utopian. From the perspective of a century, they prove to have given an eminently realistic appraisal of the course of Russian economy. As a matter of historical record, Russia did not follow the capitalist path, it did not emulate Britain, but, short-circuiting capitalism, evolved a type of state socialism not unlike that envisioned by the radical opponents of capitalism in the nineteenth century. Those who held this view turned out to have been much closer to the truth than the Social Democrats who abused them as "utopians" and insisted that Russia had no choice but to emulate the West.

The theory of separate path was not, strictly speaking, voluntarist: its advocates did not claim that the government or the intelligentsia, by a sheer act of willing, could divert the country's economy in any direction they desired. Rather, like "subjective" sociology, it viewed history as the result of an interaction between objective realities and subjective aspirations. In this manner the two theories admirably complemented one another. The subjectivists and the proponents of separate path alike saw the future in terms of alternatives, of which the most humane were also the most realistic.

The two also had something else in common. So great was their fear of capitalism that they were willing to enter into collusion with the autocratic government to stop its further encroachments: Mikhailovsky, on grounds that capitalism by its division of labor

---

[17] The resemblance was noted by Struve: "My Contacts and Conflicts with Lenin," SR, XIII, No. 37 (July 1934), 66–67.

ruined man spiritually; Vorontsov, that it ruined Russia economically. Mikhailovsky was quite prepared to give up claims to
political and civil freedom for the sake of social justice: "By
giving social reform priority over political reform we renounce
only having our rights strengthened and our freedom enlarged,
[viewing the two] as instruments for oppressing the people and
magnifying our sin." [18] Vorontsov's economic program required
strong state intervention — taking over from the capitalists the
management of transport, mining, and much of the heavy industry. The logic of their views led the subjectivists and the proponents of separate path alike to political opportunism. This fact
must be kept in mind, for it provides an essential clue to the
emergence in Russia in the 1890's of a vigorous Social Democratic
movement dedicated to social equality *and* political liberty.

As stated earlier, Marxism was an intrinsic element of Russian
radicalism from the 1860's onward. If, nevertheless, in the 1890's
there arose in Russia under Struve's intellectual leadership a movement which challenged in the name of "Marxism" the radical
consensus outlined above, it is because "Marxism" can be used
in several distinct senses. These are: (1) an economic theory explaining the circulation of capital and the formation of profit in
capitalist economy; (2) a sociological theory which ties social,
political, and cultural phenomena to the basic processes of production; (3) a revolutionary theory which predicts the violent
collapse of the capitalist economy from mounting contradictions
between its economic base and social superstructure; and (4) a
political program (formulated not so much by Marx and Engels
as by their German disciples and canonized in the Erfurt Program)
which treats the attainment of political liberty as an essential
step in the proletariat's march to socialism. Like any ideology
which provides a general theory of history, Marxism need not be
taken in its entirety, but can be adopted selectively, à la carte,
as it were.

Russian radicals, both before and after the watershed decade of
the 1890's, adopted Marxism in such a selective manner, which
accounts for the confusion over the nature and even the chronol-
ogy of its influence on Russia. Marx's ideas became known as

[18] Mikhailovsky, *Sochineniia*, I, 870–871.

early as the 1860's, at the birth of the socialist revolutionary movement, and from then on never ceased to exert influence in Russia.
The socialist revolutionaries of the 1860's and 1870's studied Marx
and Engels attentively, translated them, and corresponded with
them to learn their opinions on Russian questions.[19] Although it
may be an exaggeration to say, as Struve did, that Marx was "the
main philosopher of the Russian Populists," [20] it is undeniably true
that no other Western socialist thinker enjoyed a comparable influence on pre-1890 Russian socialism. Marx's influence is strikingly in evidence in the fundamental distinction between capitalist
and popular modes of production drawn to justify the prognosis
of separate path. This distinction rested on the Marxian definition
of capitalism as a system separating the producer from the means
of production, and has no meaning unless related to it.

At first glance it may be difficult to see the reasons for Marx's
popularity in Russia, because the dominant mood among Russian
revolutionaries of pre-1890 vintage was anarchist. Marx himself
was doubly surprised by this following for he had never made a
secret of his loathing for both the anarchists and the Slavs. The
explanation is to be found in the particular use made in Russia
of Marx and his theories. To Russian radicals before 1890 Marx
was first and foremost an economist who had analyzed scientifically the capitalist mode of production and shown its method
of exploiting labor. They ignored his sociology, which, like Social
Darwinism, they disliked for its determinism and stress on social
conflict, as well as his politics, which they thought too parliamentary and placid. To them, Marx was a critic of capitalism par
excellence and as such a formidable ally in their effort to spare
Russia from its horrors. In 1880 — that is, some three years before
Plekhanov had founded in Geneva what is generally recognized
as the first Russian "Marxists" circle — Marx boasted to a friend

[19] The best edition of this correspondence is *K. Marks, F. Engel's i revoliutsionnaia Rossiia* (Moscow, 1967), henceforth referred to as MERR. Here as elsewhere
in this book the word "socialist revolutionaries" is used in the historically precise
sense to mean the Russian revolutionaries of the 1870's. The term "Populists,"
which is often applied to them in the historical literature, is a neologism coined,
as will be pointed out below, as a polemical device by the Social Democrats in the
1890's.
[20] "Na raznye temy," RM, March 1908, Pt. 2, 211. See also A. Martynov in OD,
II, Pt. 2, 296, and V. V. Vorovsky, *K istorii marksizma v Rossii* (Moscow, 1923),
15–17.

that his *Capital* had more readers and enjoyed greater acceptance in Russia than anywhere else in the world, and he was right.[21] His economic method and nomenclature were indeed widely adopted, and not only by revolutionary activists and writers, but also by academic economists of diverse political views, including many liberals and even some conservatives. Russians learned to view economic phenomena through Marxist categories long before they became aware of their social and political implications.

Marx and Engels not only did not frown upon such a perverse use of their theories, but encouraged it. When the Russian revolutionary movement was still in its talking stage they had few good words to say about the peasant commune and the theory of the separate path. In a sardonic essay directed against Tkachev, published in 1874, Engels ridiculed the idea of the Russians as the "chosen people" of socialism, destined to reach it by some private shortcut. The commune and artel' appeared to him relics of a primitive stage of economic development, better suited to a despotic than a socialist system.[22] In taking this position, Engels, and Marx along with him, were undoubtedly motivated in some measure by factional considerations, for they believed that Pan-Slav socialism (as they called it) was a child of the national messianism of Herzen and Bakunin, whom they detested as rivals. But they also had a more fundamental objection to the idea of separate path, namely the conviction that all societies had to pass through identical stages of economic development.

In the late 1870's, Marx and Engels changed their minds. Study of the economic and statistical literature received from Russian correspondents convinced them that the idea of separate path was not merely an expression of nationalist pride, but an earnest attempt to cope with an economy which in its fundamental features differed from the English. They began now to contemplate the possibility of different types of economies (for example, the "Asiatic" mode of production) and diverse models of economic development. They also had political reasons for shifting their position. In the late 1870's Western Europe was quiet. The sanguine hopes which Marx and Engels had had of an imminent

[21] Letter to F. A. Sorge of November 5, 1880, in Karl Marx and Friedrich Engels, *Werke*, XXXIV (Berlin, 1966), 477.
[22] Friedrich Engels, *Soziales aus Russland* (Leipzig, 1875).

social revolution waned as the Paris Commune became a memory: everything pointed to continued peaceful evolution in the West. Only Russia was seething. Beginning with 1874 and the first "going to the people" crusade, Russian youth became steadily radicalized, engaging the imperial government in a battle of mounting intensity. In 1878–79 the socialist revolutionaries went over to terror. The remarkable courage of the *narodovol'tsy,* their ability to stand up to the imperial police, and the possibility of their seizing power from a shaky autocracy aroused such admiration of Marx and Engels that they promptly dropped their earlier objections to the socialist version of Pan-Slavism. In 1877, in an open letter to Mikhailovsky, Marx denied holding the view which Mikhailovsky had attributed to him that all countries had to repeat the Western economic experience. He conceded that since 1861 Russia had been moving toward capitalism and that once capitalism took root there nothing could avert its familiar consequences. But only the consequences of capitalism were inevitable: the triumph of capitalism itself was not, he wrote. No law of history compelled Russia to emulate the West. "If Russia should continue along the road which it has pursued since 1861," he concluded, "then it would miss the best opportunity history had ever accorded a nation, and experience all the fateful misfortunes of the capitalist system." [23] With this "if" Marx threw his authority behind the proponents of the separate path in their battle against the Russian liberals.

Four years later, Marx faced the question again when Vera Zasulich, a disenchanted terrorist about to convert to Social Democracy, asked him for an unequivocal verdict on the future of the commune and the theory of the separate path. In his laconic letter of reply, he simply stated that the peasant commune could indeed constitute "the basis of support for the social regeneration of Russia," provided it was assured of normal development and

---

[23] MERR, 78. Marx did not dispatch this letter and it remained generally unknown in his lifetime. Engels discovered it in his papers in 1884, and sent a copy to Vera Zasulich, who then translated it into Russian. It was subsequently circulated in Russia in lithographed form. The first printed edition appeared in the organ of the People's Will, *Vestnik Narodnoi Voli,* in 1886; it was reprinted in 1888, in the juridical organ *Iuridicheskii vestnik,* published with the censor's imprimatur. Mikhailovsky's article to which it was a response was called "Karl' Marks pered sudom g. Iu. Zhukovskogo," *Sochineniia N. K. Mikhailovskogo,* IV (St. Petersburg, 1897), 165–206, especially p. 167–173.

protected from "baneful influences." [24] He did not go into the reasons for his belief but these can be found in the letter's three preliminary drafts. Here Marx committed himself more than ever before or after to the possibility and even the likelihood of a noncapitalist road to socialism in Russia:

> From the historical point of view, the only serious argument advanced as proof of the *inevitable dissolution* of the commune of the *Russian peasantry* is the following: Turning to the distant past, we encounter everywhere in Europe communal property of a more or less archaic type. With the progress of society, it has everywhere vanished. Why should it in Russia alone escape this fate? I answer: because in Russia, thanks to an extraordinary concatenation of circumstances, the peasant commune, still existing on a national scale, can gradually shake off its primitive qualities and develop directly as an element of collective productivity on a national scale. Precisely because it is a coeval of capitalist production, it is in a position to assimilate its positive achievements without going through all its horrors. Russia does not live in isolation from the contemporary world; at the same time, unlike the East Indies, it is not the acquisition of a foreign conqueror.
>
> If the Russian admirers of the capitalist system were to deny the *theoretical* possibility of such an evolution, I would ask them: must Russia, in order to introduce machines, steamships, railways, etc., like the West, go through the long incubational period of development of machine production? Let these people explain to me at the same time: how had Russia succeeded in introducing at once the whole mechanism of exchange (banks, credit societies, etc.), the working out of which in the West had required whole centuries?
>
> If, at the instant of the liberation of the serfs, the peasant commune had been at once placed in normal conditions of development, if, subsequently, the enormous state debt paid largely at the expense of the peasants, together with other vast sums presented through the intermediacy of the state (again at the peasants' expense) to the "new pillars of society" turned

[24] K. Marks, F. Engel's, *Sochineniia*, 2nd ed., XIX (Moscow, 1961), 250–251. The drafts which Marx wrote before dispatching the final version are given on pp. 400–421.

capitalist — if all these expenditures had been used for the *further development* of the peasant commune, then no one today would contemplate the "historical inevitability" of the commune's destruction: all would recognize in it the element of the regeneration of Russian society and the element of superiority over countries still enslaved by the capitalist yoke.[25]

Because of their admiration for the People's Will, Marx and Engels reacted with a coolness verging on hostility to the appearance of a Russian Social Democratic movement. Plekhanov, its pioneer, had originally broken with the People's Will because he disapproved of terror and coup d'état as an elitist tactic, incompatible with the fundamental tenet of the socialist revolutionary movement that the emancipation of the people had to be accomplished by the people itself. After he had left Russia and settled down in Switzerland, he immersed himself in Social Democratic literature. From this reading he quickly learned other, more basic objections to terror and power seizure. Acquaintance with the sociological and political writings of Marx, Engels, and their German disciples taught him that a socialist society had to rest on a mature economic base, and that such a base could be furnished only by capitalism. Even if the terrorists were to succeed in overthrowing the imperial regime and seizing power, he wrote in 1885 in *Our Disagreements*, they would not be able to organize the economy of Russia on socialist lines because of its primitive, precapitalist condition. The outcome of a successful coup d'état in Russia would be not socialism, but a "political abortion, like the ancient empires of China or Persia, that is, a revived tsarist despotism reposing on a Communist base." [26] Plekhanov urged Russians to abandon anarchism and Blanquism with their tactic of "direct assault" and to adopt a more sophisticated political strategy involving two distinct, successive phases: to begin with, an alliance between revolutionaries and all the social groups interested in abolishing absolutism (notably the bourgeoisie) and replacing it with a system guaranteeing political liberty. In this coalition, the socialists would arrogate for themselves the role of the "hegemon." (The latter point was worked out theoretically by

[25] *Ibid.*, 401.
[26] G. V. Plekhanov, "Nashi raznoglasiia," *Izbrannye filosofskie proizvedeniia*, I (Moscow, 1956), 323.

Paul Akselrod, Plekhanov's associate.) Once political liberty had been gained, the socialists would turn against their allies and initiate a class war, leading the proletariat to victory and socialism. Plekhanov regarded the penetration of capitalism into Russia as inevitable, and held out little hope for the peasant commune, although he acknowledged some of its advantages. The minuscule Emancipation of Labor Group which he founded in Geneva with Akselrod and Vera Zasulich adopted these principles as its program and dedicated itself to the task of destroying what was left of the People's Will, and replacing it with a Social Democratic party organized on the German model.

On the face of it, Marx and Engels should have embraced a Russian revolutionary movement that went beyond their economic teachings to assimilate the sociological and political essentials of their theory. In fact, however, they turned their backs on it. In the early 1880's they expected great things from the People's Will — the "vanguard of the revolutionary movement," as Marx called it[27] — and saw no point in backing a tiny group of Genevan émigrés determined to do it in. No, in Russia things had to be done differently, Marx was certain now. "Have you been following the juridical proceedings in St. Petersburg against the assassins?" he asked his daughter Jenny, alluding to the trial of the terrorists who had killed Alexander II, "they are decent people, through and through, *sans pose mélodramatique*, simple, business-like, heroic . . . they try to teach Europe . . . that their *modus operandi* is a specifically Russian, historically inevitable method of action which lends itself as little to moralizing, for or against, as does the earthquake of Chios." [28] In 1885 (two years after Marx's death), when Vera Zasulich, still hoping to win Engels' support for the Social Democratic cause, sent him a copy of Plekhanov's *Our Disagreements*, where Blanquism was condemned from the point of view of Marx's sociology, Engels replied in a manner which left no doubt his sympathy lay with the People's Will:

That which I know, or think I know, about the situation in Russia inclines me to the belief that the country approaches its

[27] MERR, 89. Maximilien Rubel of Paris is about to publish a collection of his informative essays on the whole subject under the title "Marx et Engels devant la révolution russe."

[28] Letter of April 11, 1881; Karl Marx and Friedrich Engels, *Werke*, XXXV (Berlin, 1967), 179.

1789. The revolution *must* erupt in the course of a definite period of time; it *may* erupt any day . . . This is one of the exceptional situations where a handful of people can *make* a revolution . . . If the Blanquist fantasy — to bring about the upheaval of a whole society by means of a small conspiracy — ever had some basis, then that is, of course, in St. Petersburg . . . In my opinion, the most important thing is that Russia be given a push, that the revolution break out. Whether the signal comes from one or another faction, whether it takes place under this or that flag, that is not so important to me.[29]

Thus, Plekhanov's attempt to apply to Russia the general theory of economic and social development of Marx and Engels did not receive the endorsement of either. To make matters worse for him, his writings were unknown in Russia before 1895, because censorship effectively prevented them from crossing the frontier.[30] So it happened that, until reinterpreted by Struve in the early 1890's, "Marxism" was generally understood in Russia to be an economic theory supporting the doctrine of separate path, whose founders, two eminent German scientists, admired the commune and approved of terror.

[29] MERR, 514. This statement strongly suggests that in October 1917 Engels would have supported Lenin and Trotsky rather than the Mensheviks, who insisted that a revolution could take place only when the conditions were exactly right.

[30] The question of Plekhanov's influence on the development of Marxism in Russia has been hotly debated by Russian and American historians. The weight of evidence clearly supports those who minimize that influence. For example, Voden says that in 1890 he could not locate a single publication by Plekhanov or by anyone else of his group in St. Petersburg (*Voden*, No. 3, 73). B. I. Nikolaevsky, on the basis of information supplied by A. N. Potresov, states that until 1892, when Potresov arrived in St. Petersburg from abroad with a supply of Liberation of Labor materials, these had veen virtually unknown in the city (*Potresov*, 16, 18). If such was the situation in the capital, Plekhanov certainly could not have been known at all in the provinces except as a name. His influence on Russian Social Democratic circles inside the country seems to have begun only in December 1895 with the legal publication in St. Petersburg of his *Monistic View* (see Chapter 6).

3. CONVERSION TO SOCIAL DEMOCRACY

In reading intellectual history it is not uncommon to find a writer explained in terms of firm and fixed beliefs: so and so, we are told, "believed" such and such, and this "belief" explains why he held certain political or social views. Undoubtedly, individuals of such constancy do exist, but they are rarely of sufficient interest to attract the attention of the intellectual historian. On close inspection, thinkers of quality usually turn out to be committed not to an idée fixe, but to two or more unrelated or even contradictory ideas; and it is precisely the divergent pulls which these exert, the tension which arises from the effort to fashion different elements into a single harmonious system, that underlies genuine intellectual activity. To identify these poles of belief is to locate the key to the mind of the serious and independent thinker.

In the case of Struve, two of these elements have already been noted: nationalism and liberalism. In the late nineteenth century, the relationship between them was by no means a natural one, because by then nationalism had become throughout Europe an illiberal, conservative ideology that glorified not the individual and freedom, but state and power. Struve had to exert a great deal of ingenuity to bring the two together. Much of his vacillation, which so puzzled contemporaries in the 1890's, was due to his stressing now the liberal at the expense of the national, now the national at the expense of the liberal. But to complicate matters further, he still owed a commitment to a third idea which in some ways vitiated the other two. This may be described as an extreme form of positivism: the conviction that the empirically verifiable alone was "real," and that consequently idealism, metaphysics, voluntarism, and everything else that could not be so verified had no existence except in the mind.

In itself, Struve's positivism was not surprising, for he grew up when it was the philosophy of virtually the whole Russian intelligentsia. But, as has been noted, Russian positivists seized upon Comte's late emendations of his system as grounds for diluting the doctrine: injecting into it a heavy dose of "subjectivism," they exempted, in effect, human history from the laws of positive science. Here Struve took an independent path: he refused to follow suit, and insisted on being a pure, uncompromising positivist. The difficulty of reconciling a positivism of such severity with liberalism is apparent: the latter rests on the concepts of natural law, inalienable rights, freedom, and other ideas which there is no way of demonstrating empirically and which, from the point of view of positivism, constitute metaphysical gibberish. As for nationalism, it, too, does not readily lend itself to being grafted on positivism, because it demands respect for authority and tradition, both of which positivism rejects. Wishing to be loyal to all three — liberalism, nationalism, and positivism — Struve was in constant intellectual turmoil until 1900–1901, when he decided, at last, to give up positivism. After that, his intellectual evolution became more straightforward.

The majority of Russian positivists were in matters of philosophy outright dilettantes. Indeed, positivism absolved them from the necessity of learning philosophy because it treated philosophy as fully dissolved in the sciences. Struve was different in this respect, too. He was the first prominent radical in Russia to acquire solid grounding in the history and vocabulary of philosophy, including logic. Although his philosophic writings are distinguished neither by clarity nor originality, his theoretical contributions on all subjects do at least show an awareness of the technical problems involved in making statements on such subjects as freedom, necessity, or the "dialectic", patently absent from the writings of a Mikhailovsky or Plekhanov.

In the philosophical currents of his time, he found the greatest affinity with Neo-Kantianism. Neo-Kantianism was not a philosophic movement in the ordinary sense, because it neither addressed itself to the traditional questions raised by philosophers nor tried to work out a comprehensive view of life and conduct. Its aims were more modest. It came into existence at a time (1860's–1870's) when the natural sciences were celebrating some of their most spectacular triumphs, and philosophic speculation seemed reduced to the status of a harmless but also useless pastime. The Neo-Kantians adapted themselves to this situation. They accepted, by and large, the claims of science and the positivist outlook based on it, but they saw some important uses still left for philosophy. They pointed out that a great deal of scientific theory rested on an uncritical use of words and an equally uncritical acceptance of knowledge acquired through the senses. They showed that science has not defined (and could not from mere empirical evidence) such freely used concepts as "matter," "energy" or "cause," and that it assumed the ability of the mind to perceive reality without allowing for the limitations of the mind's cognitive apparatus. The main intent of the Neo-Kantians was to deal with such methodological questions by means of logical critique. Their purpose was to strengthen science, to make it more truly "scientific," by providing it with a sound epistemological foundation.

The movement embraced a broad range of tendencies — historians have identified at least twelve distinct and contending schools — each associated with a particular German university. Some stressed the idealistic side of Kant, others the empirical. The best known Neo-Kantian school, that headed by Herman Cohen of the University of Marburg, was of the former persuasion. Struve did not like this variety at all. His preference was for the most positivist of the Neo-Kantian philosophers, Alois Riehl, the author of *Philosophical Criticism and Its Significance for Positive Science*.[1] Riehl viewed himself as a successor of a long line of Western thinkers running from Locke through Hume to Kant whom he called "critical" philosophers, the outstanding feature of whom was uncompromising hostility to metaphysics. "The "critical" philosophers were "realists" in that they acknowledged the fact that human perception of the external world depended on built-in categories of the mind, and drew a sharp line separating reality as it seemed from what it really was. "Critical" philosophy alone was compatible with science. Any philosophy which confused thought with the object of thought, or derived being from ideas and ideas from being, Riehl dismissed as "metaphysical." To him, Hegel was the "supreme metaphysician," and Kant, the "greatest realist." The task of modern philosophy was to demolish

---

[1] *Der philosophische Kriticismus und seine Bedeutung für die positive Wissenschaft*, 2 vols. in 3 (Leipzig, 1876–1887). The third part appeared in Russian translation in 1888.

both metaphysics (the "opium of the mind") and "uncritical materialism" (one that failed to distinguish ideas from objective reality), and in their place create a philosophic system worthy of modern science.

Riehl's *Philosophical Criticism* had for Struve's intellectual development a variety of important consequences: next to Aksakov and Marx no thinker did more to shape his mind. In particular, Riehl's work caused him to reject out of hand the whole "subjective method" and the theory of history based on it, on the grounds that it committed the cardinal sin of "uncritical materialism," namely confusing that which "is" with that which "ought to be," the *sein* with the *sollen*. Such a confusion was logically untenable. Causes of phenomena must be sought in other phenomena, not in ideas. Having rejected the "subjective method," Struve also rejected the whole edifice of philosophy of history and sociology erected on it: the notion that history could in some significant measure be influenced by the enlightened individual; that the intelligentsia as a collective body of such enlightened individuals constituted a prime mover of the historic process; and that society could be consciously shaped so as to satisfy the individual's striving for self-fulfillment. All this was "metaphysics." So was the corollary theory of radicalism espoused by the ideologues of the Russian intelligentsia, Mikhailovsky, Lavrov, and their followers.

Instead of "subjective sociology," Struve adopted a philosophy of history from which all ethics was exorcised. His earliest social theory was that very Social Darwinism which "subjective sociology" had been created to supplant. Under the spell of Darwin, Spencer, and their Austrian disciple Ludwig Gumplowicz, he came to regard history as a pitiless conflict which paid no heed to the individual and his aspirations. The intelligentsia's self-image as maker of history he always viewed as a self-delusion — comical when he was young, tragic as he grew older. Historical and social progress, in his view, followed their own laws, unmoved by man's desires and ideals.

Here we have one of the two reasons why Struve found the radical doctrine prevalent in Russia in the 1880's unacceptable (the other was dissatisfaction with its political opportunism). The search for a superior socialism led him straight to Social Democracy.

Struve's conversion to Social Democracy extended over a period of four years and involved two distinct phases: first (1888–1890), acceptance of the Marxist theory of history (economic determinism) in general, and its conception of the function of the capitalist phase of history, in particular; and then (1890–1892), recognition that what was occurring in Russia fitted not the theory of separate path, advanced by Marx's Russian disciples with his encouragment, but the classic scheme of how a capitalist society came into being, as described by Marx in his general economic writings. This evolution was not untypical of Struve's whole generation.

For Struve, the quintessence of Marxism was the thesis, succintly stated in the Preface to the *Contribution to the Critique of Political Economy*, defining the economic basis of social and political institutions:

In the social production of their life, men enter into definite relations that are indispensable and independent of their will, relations of production which correspond to a definite stage of development of their material productive forces. The sum total of these relations of production constitutes the economic structure of society, the real foundation, on which rises a legal and political superstructure and to which correspond definite forms of social consciousness. The mode of production of material life conditions the social, political and intellectual life process in general. It is not the consciousness of men that determines their being, but, on the contrary, their social being that determines their consciousness. At a certain stage of their development, the material productive forces of society come in conflict with the existing relations of production, or — what is but a legal expression for the same thing — with the property relations within which they have been at work hitherto. From forms of development of the productive forces these relations turn into their fetters. Then begins an epoch of social revolution.[2]

[2] Karl Marx and Frederick Engels, *Selected Works in Two Volumes* (New York, 1962), I, 362–363. Struve called the idea of this passage "the key to all of Marx's theoretical constructs" as well as "the quintesssence of what was new and original in [Marx's] contribution to political economy" (#40/112; also #35/664). Eduard Bernstein seems also to have regarded it in this light: P. Angel, *Eduard Bernstein et l'évolution du socialisme allemand* (Paris, 1961), 182.

A high proportion of Struve's writings from the 1890's is a gloss on the central propositions of this passage: that history is an inexorable process; that productive relations determine the content of institutions and ideas; that social changes are the unavoidable consequence of a temporary disparity between the economic base and the social superstructure. Struve considered that this view of history (not without some important correctives of his own, however) provided a scientific explanation as valid for the evolution of human society as Darwinism was for the evolution of biological forms. The theory met well the standards set by "critical" philosophy in that it did not confuse the *sein* with the *sollen,* as was the case with "subjective sociology." In 1890–91, in answer to a question from a friend as to what he considered the essence of Marxism, Struve replied: "that it contained not one ounce of ethics, that a consistent Marxist merely states what is and becomes." [3] So "scientific" did he believe Marx's system to be that he thought it possible to be a Marxist without becoming a socialist. [4]

Marxism for him had only one major flaw, and that was its philosophy. Struve from the beginning rejected the "dialectic" as an alien body of "metaphysics" in what otherwise seemed to him an admirably consistent "realistic" doctrine. He thought it superfluous and believed it could be ejected without great difficulty. As early as 1890 he confided to a friend that "in Marx and Engels the realistic point of view was unfortunately obscured by Hegelian phraseology," and that he "intended to round out this [realistic] point of view in the more adequate terms of the critical philosophy of Riehl." [5] It may be noted in passing that with his attempt to replace the Hegelian elements in Marxism with Neo-Kantian philosophy Struve pioneered, while still a university student, what later in the decade was to emerge as an important theoretical current in European socialist thought, namely "critical" or Kantian Marxism. [6]

---

[3] *Voden,* 74. The expression "Marx contains not one ounce of ethics" was coined by Werner Sombart: ASGS, V (1892), 490. Cf. #15/67 and #38/72.

[4] #15/69.

[5] *Voden,* 74.

[6] Karl Vorländer, who was unfamiliar with Struve's Russian writings, credits Konrad Schmidt with having made the earliest attempt, in 1896, to combine Kantian philosophy with Marxism: *Kant und Marx* (Tübingen, 1911), 157. Angel (*Bernstein,* 192) pushes the date back to August 1895, to Victor Adler's funeral oration for Engels. Struve, however, not only spoke of the desirability of fusing Kantian philosophy with Marxian sociology in 1890–91, but in 1894,

Marx, in fact, never succeeded in working out a philosophical theory to accompany his economics, sociology, and politics. He began as a Hegelian, then abandoned Hegel for Feuerbach, and finally rejected Feuerbach for a doctrine of his own making, which Plekhanov baptized "dialectical materialism." This doctrine Marx sketched only in its general outlines, which Engels later filled out in his *Anti-Dühring* and *Ludwig Feuerbach*. Marx's and Engels's philosophy rested on materialism; but their materialism was not of the ordinary kind, which was static and therefore unsuited to their thoroughly historical outlook. Theirs was a materialism made dynamic by fusion with the principle of the dialectic. Originally a device of logic (for example, in Plato), the dialectic became in the hands of Hegel and other German idealists a way of explaining change in the phenomenal world as progressing through negation, that is, through the transformation of an object into its opposite. The fusion of the dialectic with materialism permitted Engels to explain social change in terms of negation as well. The point was essential to his and Marx's sociology, in that it provided the logical grounding for the prediction that capitalism at an advanced stage of its development had to turn into its opposite, socialism. It gave the philosophical justification for viewing social change as inevitable in character and revolutionary in form.

As had been noted before, to Riehl, Struve's main authority in matters philosophical, Hegel was the "supreme metaphysician." And indeed the "dialectic" had all the earmarks of metaphysics, as Riehl defined it. In particular, it violated the logical principle of identity, which Riehl considered the key to causation. Drawing on analogies from mathematics and physics, Riehl showed that the cause always had to be transformed into effect directly and without loss: "As in a mathematical equation, the same quantity appears on the right side as on the left, so the cause reappears in the effect but in a different form." The identity of cause and effect, according to Riehl, manifested itself with particular clarity in the laws of conservation of matter and energy.[7]

---

in his book, expressed unmistakably his dissatisfaction with the philosophical foundations of Marxism (#15/46) and by frequent reference to Riehl and other Neo-Kantians indicated how he believed this flaw could be remedied. He was therefore justified in claiming later that he was a pioneer in the development of Kantian or "critical" Marxism: *Na raznye temy* (St. Petersburg, 1902), 5n.

[7] Riehl, *Kriticismus*, II, Pt. 1, 255–256. In another work Riehl defined causality

Translated into the language of sociology, the principle of identity meant that socialism could never come into being from a negation or denial of capitalism: if it was to be caused by capitalism (as Marx would have it) then it had to contain it. Struve concluded from this that "socialism owes its existence to capitalism not only in the historic but also in the logical sense: without it, it is a phantom devoid of flesh and blood."[8] Using Riehl's logic, he rejected early the whole concept of social revolution as utopian, and adopted in its place an evolutionary brand of socialism not unlike that of the Fabians. The critique of social revolution which Bernstein was to make in the late 1890's using empirical evidence, Struve carried out several years earlier by means of logical analysis.

In sum: between 1888 and 1890 Struve accepted the basic principle of Marx's theory, economic determinism, with the proviso that the transition from the precapitalist to the capitalist system would occur gradually and peacefully. Thus understood, Marxism gave him "scientific" proof that the autocratic regime in Russia would disappear. This was the main impetus behind his conversion to Social Democracy around 1888. As he later wrote: "Just as naturally as in 1885 I had become, by passion and by conviction, a Liberal and a constitutionalist, so about three years later I became, but this time *by conviction* only, a Social Democrat."[9] It was not in Struve's character to hold any conviction dispassionately, and there is no lack of evidence that his commitment to Social Democracy came from the heart as well as the head. But it is true that his attitude toward the two doctrines had a different quality. Liberalism was to him absolute good and the end of politics, whereas socialism was only the means. His feeling about social equality was and remained detached, and his talk about a new order that would some day abolish the exploitation of man by man has about it a hollow ring that is never present in his pronouncements on liberty. In a sense he reversed the classic conception of the relationship between liberalism and socialism established in Russian literature. To a Plekhanov or an Akselrod, po-

as a particular inference drawn from the principle of identity: *Philosophische Studien* (Leipzig, 1925), 202–218, esp. 209.

[8] #15/128.

[9] Struve, "My Contacts and Conflicts with Lenin," SR, XII, No. 36 (April 1934), 576–577; see also "Listki: Pamiati A. I. Skvortsova," RM, No. 2 (February 1914), Pt. 2, 164.

litical liberty was a stage on the road to class war; to Struve, class war was at best a way station on the road to political liberty. Socialism was to him an expendable item and for that reason it need not be treated as one of the basic elements of his thought.

Marx's sociology once accepted, it still remained to be demonstrated that capitalism could indeed gain a solid foothold in a country where nine-tenths of the population was classed as rural and the bulk of land was held communally, that is, could not be bought or sold. The issue could not be resolved with mere reference to statistics indicating the indisputable rise in capital investments and in the output of mines and heavy industry. Like most Russian economists, Struve defined capitalism in Marxist terms as a system characterized by the separation of the producer from the means of production. This separation, according to Marx, had to begin in agriculture, and manifest itself in the mass expropriation of the peasantry, on the pattern of the English Enclosure Acts.[10] Until it could be demonstrated that the communal system was actually disintegrating and peasants were abandoning the land to form a labor reserve, there could be no serious talk of capitalism triumphing in Russia.

Struve seems to have concluded that this process had indeed begun under the influence of two factors: the great famines of 1891–92 and the explanation given them by A. I. Skvortsov, a Russian economist whose writings exerted on Struve a major influence.

The terrible hunger which broke out in Russia in 1891 and then again in 1892 had a number of causes, among them a succession of poor harvests. Famines have occurred in Russia under every form of government, and there is no need to seek far-reaching political or social explanations for them. These particular famines, however, were widely regarded as something of a historical turning point and became the object of a heated debate. To radical publicists of the older generation they represented the corroboration of a diagnosis and the fulfillment of a prophesy: the government's fiscal and tariff policies had impoverished the peasantry to the point where it could no longer maintain even a subsistence level. Russia had to abandon the capitalist path or face ruin. This was said by Vorontsov, N. F.

[10] *Capital*, Vol. I, Chap. 26; "The Secret of Primitive Accumulation."

Danielson, and the other writers of the older radical school in the pages of *Russian Wealth* (*Russkoe bogatstvo*) and in books which will be discussed in the following chapter. To Struve, however, the famines signified the very opposite: unmistakable and welcome evidence that the Russian village was in the throes of class differentiation, and that capitalism at last was triumphantly on the march. The peasantry which the Emancipation Edict was to have assured of enough land for its needs was being divided into two broad classes, those who had more than they needed to feed themselves, and those who had less. The former, an emergent rural bourgeoisie, were buying up land and livestock on the open market (mostly from the gentry) and exploiting it with the aid of hired hands; those who lacked enough land for sustenance were becoming dispossessed and transformed into a proletariat. The advent of class differentiation in the village could mean one thing only: the process of primary accumulation of capital. Capitalism was incubating within the very womb of the national economy; it had ceased to be an "artificial" product of government policy and had acquired a life of its own.

"As far as I am personally concerned," Struve wrote in 1908, "the hunger of 1891–92 made much more of a Marxist out of me than the reading of Marx's *Capital*." [11] This can hardly have been so because the whole significance of the famines for Struve lay in the fact that they confirmed Marx's prediction. Rather the hunger reinforced Struve's Social Democratic tendencies. It persuaded him that the process which Marx described so eloquently in *Capital* was being repeated in Russia.

Why rural differentiation took place became clear to him from reading Skvortsov's *The Influence of Steam Transport on Agriculture*.[12] Skvortsov was one of those numerous Russian academic economists who in their work used Marx's methodology without in the least subscribing to his social or political philosophy. In

[11] "Na raznye temy," RM, No. 3 (March 1908), Pt. 2, 211.

[12] *Vliiane parovogo transporta na sel'skoe khoziaistvo* (Warsaw, 1890). After he met Skvortsov in 1894, Struve wrote to a friend: "He struck me as an intelligent man, as I had expected, and a perfectly decent sort. But *personally*, I did not like him. He is *not ours* at all, that is, he is a M[arxist] without being a C[ommunist]" (Struve to Potresov, June 22, 1894, first cited in *Potresov*, 20). Struve seems to have wanted to write "without being a S[ocialist]," but changed his mind, and by adding a perpendicular line to the letter "C" ("S" in Russian) he changed it into a "K," the first letter of "Kommunist." By this word he probably meant one who believed not only the economic side of Marx's teaching but also the political and social ones as expounded in the *Communist Manifesto*.

his politics he was a nationalist and no stranger, as Struve was later to discover, to anti-Semitic sentiments.[13] The purpose of his study was to determine the effects of steam transport on economic structure in general and on rent in particular. The introduction of steam transport on an extensive scale, he maintained, had undermined the old rent theories of writers like Ricardo and Thünen by destroying the isolated and self-contained economic entities which their theories had presupposed. In their place, it created a vast national and international market with a single price system, specialization, rationalization, and regionalism. By reducing to insignificance the factor of distance separating goods from the market, modern transport technology had created entirely new economic conditions.

In regard to Russia, Skvortsov showed that the 18,500 miles of railroad lines laid down since Emancipation shattered the walls surrounding Russia's sheltered and small agricultural communities. Railroads transformed agricultural produce from an item of consumption or barter into a commodity traded on the open market, and made the inefficient repartitional commune an anachronism. Struve later compared the impact of Skvortsov's book on him to that of Marx's *Capital*.[14] He entered with Skvortsov into what he described as an "old-fashioned scholarly correspondence . . . [exchanging] lengthy letters on theoretical subjects," [15] and long after he ceased being a Marxist he continued to regard him as one of Russia's most creative economists.[16]

If all these facts were true and if their interpretation was correct — and Struve was convinced of both — then the whole theory of separate path became a strange utopian dream, a modern version of old-fashioned Slavophilism. Struve arrived at this conclusion sometime in the early 1890's and from then on became the most implacable foe of this theory.

Although Struve expected capitalism to liquidate the autocracy, he did not expect this to be done by the bourgeoisie. He was well aware of the passivity displayed by the German middle class in the face of Bismarckian authoritarianism, and believed that the same would happen in Russia, where the industrial and business

[13] Struve to Potresov, June 22, 1894.
[14] "My Contacts and Conflicts with Lenin," 587; also #3/415.
[15] "Listki: Pamiati A. I. Skvorstova," 166.
[16] *Ibid.*, 164; also "My Contacts and Conflicts with Lenin," 587.

groups were even more dependent on the government for protection. "Personally I have always thought," he wrote in 1901,

> that [in Russia] the progressive force is not so much the nascent and rapidly growing bourgeoisie as it is those general conditions of economic and cultural life on the basis of which it grows. I continue now also firmly to adhere to the belief that our country will be moved forward in all respects by the capitalist system and not at all by the classes which command it.[17]

Impressed by the German experience, with which he became acquainted on his trips abroad, and by the writings of Plekhanov and Akselrod, he concluded that in Russia, too, the cause of political liberty would be advanced by that other child of capitalism, the proletariat; and that, as in Germany, the mission of spearheading the struggle would be taken on by Social Democracy: "It seems that henceforth the revolutionary political role [in Russia] will be assumed by the budding Social Democracy . . . It is precisely due to the economic backwardness of the country and the political backwardness of the industrial bourgeoisie that strivings which are at bottom political can appear [here] in a Social Democratic guise." [18]

The faith in the proletariat as the carrier of political liberty seems to have been firmly impressed on his mind by Rudolf Meyer's *The Struggle of the Fourth Estate for Emancipation*, one of the several books which later, in an effort to minimize the influence on him of Marx, he credited with his conversion to socialism.[19] A reader who removes Meyer's two volumes from the library shelves, and having blown away the dust, leafs through them, cannot fail to be astonished that this dry compendium of data on the international labor movement could have converted anyone to anything. However, the mass of ill-digested information does make a point, and that is that in the second half of the nineteenth century the "fourth estate" had become the ascendant class, about to replace the third. Struve found in it encouragement that what had happened in Germany was not an isolated incident but part of a

---

[17] #1110/xiv.

[18] #37/29. Voden says that Struve expressed similar sentiments in 1891: *Voden*, 76.

[19] Rudolf Meyer, *Der Emancipationskampf des vierten Standes*, 2 vols. (Berlin, 1874–75).

worldwide trend. The same economic developments which were already sapping the foundations of Russian autocracy were also certain to bring to the fore a class which, unlike the Russian bourgeoisie, could be relied upon to stay faithful to liberal and democratic ideals.

But political liberty did not exhaust the benefits which capitalism would bring Russia. It would also cure its other affliction, cultural backwardness. Like all Russian Westerners, Struve worshiped the West. ("I love European culture like the sun, like warmth and clean air; decaying carcasses and gray heads I cannot bear. *Und damit basta!* I will no more discuss my Westernism than a decent man discusses his morals." [20] Unlike Mikhailovsky and the older generation of radicals, he admired the West's material wealth, the endless variety of opportunities its more complex system of organization afforded the individual for self-fulfillment, the social discipline and civic virtues it fostered. All of this and much more that he liked about the West he attributed to "the general conditions of economic and cultural life" created by capitalism. First, by organizing productivity in the most efficient manner known, capitalism created unprecedented wealth and liberated man from want, without which cultured life was not possible. Second, it advanced culture — for example, by promoting mass education, civil rights, and legality — because it required them for its own proper functioning. Once it had finally established itself in Russia, it would exorcise from it that legacy of "Asianness" which, in common with other Westerners, he regarded as the country's curse.

In short, capitalism was panacea. It would bring both freedom and culture. No Russian thinker before or after Struve pinned such hopes on the capitalist mode of production as the solution to all of the country's ills. To him it was not merely a purgatory which society had to traverse as rapidly as possible if unable to bypass it altogether. It was a precondition of both socialism and civilized life. A revolution which would establish a higher social order on the ruins of capitalism was for him a contradiction in terms. revolutionary change had to be accomplished by evolutionary means, which, as it were, shifted the sum total of human culture from one side of the historic equation to the other.

[20] #79/186.

4. BEGINNING OF CONTROVERSY

In the autumn of 1889 Struve enrolled at the Faculty of Natural Sciences of the University of St. Petersburg to study zoology. That he should have chosen science as his field of concentration despite his attraction to the humanities and sociology is further evidence of his positivistic outlook. His choice of zoology as a scientific specialty attests to a commitment to Social Darwinism.

At first he was very happy. Mendeleev impressed him powerfully with the celebrated lecture opening the course on chemistry, in which he spoke of the distinction between "facts" and "appearances" and in the process took to task the classical system of secondary education institutionalized in Russia.[1] The zoologist V. M. Shimkevich impressed him also. With a fellow student (and future brother-in-law), V. A. Gerd, he prepared a digest of Shimkevich's lectures which Shimkevich afterward used as the basis for a textbook. Under his guidance, Struve and Gerd embarked on an ambitious program of study of German scientific literature.[2]

But Struve's ardor for science soon cooled. While Gerd went on with his studies, Struve became restless in the Faculty of Natural Sciences even before the first year was over. Chemistry, which had fascinated him as long as it dealt with questions of scientific methodology, paled as soon as Mendeleev passed on to more prosaic

[1] RiS, No. 231 (April 1934). Recalling Mendeleev's opening lecture many years later, Struve wrote that while listening to it he experienced a keen awareness of the "tragedy of Russian culture." " 'Professor' Shvarts i 'kurator' Melissino," *Rech'*, January 5, 1908; reprinted in Struve, *Patriotica* (St. Petersburg, 1911), 182. What he meant by this statement is suggested in his letter to Hans Delbrück of July 15, 1902 (in the Deutsches Bundarchiv, East Berlin): employed in the service of the police, classicism became disgraced in the eyes of Russian liberals. Mendeleev resigned his professorship in the spring of Struve's first year at the university (1890) after a political argument with the authorities.

[2] "Pamiati V. A. Gerda," *Voz*, No. 450 (August 26, 1926). The book was probably the textbook on vertebrate zoology (*Kurs zoologii pozvonochnykh*) which Shimkevich published jointly with N. N. Polezhaev in 1891–92.

subjects, such as the properties of water and hydrogen. Struve also had difficulty working in the laboratory because his eyes could not stand the strain of peering through the microscope.[3] At the end of the first year he decided, therefore, to give up science and transfer to the Faculty of Law, the curriculum of which embraced much of what today would be classified as social science. His brief encounter with zoology left on his thought no visible mark except, perhaps, that it enriched his scholarly vocabulary with some scientific terms drawn from ecology.

During the summer recess of 1890, he traveled to Germany and Switzerland. This trip was his first glimpse of the West since 1882 when, as a twelve-year-old boy, he had left Stuttgart to return home. What he now saw with the eyes of an adult stunned him. In Germany he at last had an opportunity to observe at first hand that "capitalism" which, like most Russian intellectuals, he spoke of on terms of familiarity but knew only from books. As he later recalled:

> When ten years ago I found myself abroad for the first time as a conscious and adult man, among other places, in Berlin, I was most of all overwhelmed by the intensity of Western material culture. These impressions, incidentally, were not entirely new for me, since I had partly grown up in Germany and was already familiar with the external order of Western European life. To a certain extent I also was not a stranger to the internal quality, or, to use an imported term, the "psychology," of German life. But all the same, at this time once again, the richness and intensity of material culture, and the astonishing, almost abject adaptability of Western man to it, made on me a tremendous and indelible impression.[4]

For all their importance for his intellectual development, however, these impressions were an incidental benefit of what Struve regarded as the main purpose of the trip, namely, direct acquaintance with the German Social Democratic movement. He could hardly have chosen a better time. Earlier that year the Reichstag let lapse Bismarck's antisocialist law, and the Social Democrats immediately emerged from the shadow world in which they had

[3] In an autobiographical sketch written in 1901, he said that he had abandoned zoology because of an eye disease (Pushkin House, Leningrad, Fond 377, No. 2633).

[4] #97/13; also #55/60.

operated for the preceding twelve years into the full light of day. There were frantic efforts to organize the scattered forces into a coherent party, and heated discussions of a party program to replace the one adopted at Gotha in 1875. The papers and journals were full of reports of these activities. Struve avidly read the pertinent literature, and perhaps even attended some of the open party meetings held in Stuttgart and Switzerland. What he saw and heard on this trip heavily contributed to his decision to become a Social Democrat.

In Switzerland he bought a large collection of Social Democratic literature which, with the help of one of his brothers, sent abroad by the government on a scientific mission, he smuggled via Germany into Russia.[5] Rather surprisingly he made no attempt to see Plekhanov. Later he explained this curious omission by lack of money and letters of introduction. But a more likely explanation is that he was discouraged from meeting Plekhanov by what he felt was the "doctrinal and simplist" quality of his writings.[6]

By the time he returned to St. Petersburg for the fall term, he was an acknowledged authority on Social Democracy as well as the possessor of an outstanding library of Social Democratic literature.

In Russia at this time interest in Social Democracy was visibly growing, the chief stimulant being the impressive victory which the German Social Democrats had won over Bismarck. Here and there Social Democratic study circles were beginning to form, usually on the initiative of foreign (Polish, Bulgarian, and so forth) students. None of these circles exerted much influence, however, partly because they operated in secret and partly because their members had only a vague notion of Marx's political and social theories.

Sometime in 1890 Struve formed a circle of this kind at the University of St. Petersburg. Its purpose was to find the "true" Marx, so perverted by his Russian disciples. This circle in a short time did more to spread Social Democratic ideas than all its forerunners put together, in part because it proselytized and in part because it had among its members youths of exceptional brilliance.

---

[5] "My Contacts and Conflicts with Lenin," SR, XII, No. 36 (April 1934), 578. Struve says his was the best and probably the only collection of German socialist literature in St. Petersburg.

[6] *Ibid.*, 578–579.

Serious penetration of Social Democracy into Russia began with this circle. It was Struve and his friends who first systematically injected Social Democratic interpretations into discussions of contemporary questions, and made the Russian public acquainted with the principles of Marx's social and political theory. If Plekhanov is rightly called the first Russian Social Democrat, Struve may be said to have been the first Social Democrat in Russia.

The group whose leader he became had a dozen or so members, all of them older than he; his intellectual precocity was exceptional even for the Russia of that time. They were self-righteous and arrogant, in the manner of young converts, but they were not doctrinaire. They believed they had found the "true" Marx and that this Marx furnished them with a key to the understanding of social anatomy and physiology. At the same time they did not regard every one of the master's opinions as validated for all eternity and therefore beyond dispute, as was to be the case with much of the provincial intelligentsia that converted to Social Democracy later. They were staunch Westernizers, discontented with the inactivity of the Russian liberals and radicals and skeptical of the philosophical and economic foundations on which the oppositional movement since the 1870's had reposed. Like Struve, they came from families belonging to the empire's social and professional elite. They were excellently educated and completely at home in Western Europe.

These youths were the first representatives of a new breed of students whose influence was to make itself increasingly felt as the century neared its end. The quality which most distinguished them from their immediate forerunners was their attitude toward learning. Russian radicals of the 1870's and 1880's held learning in contempt, because they regarded it as incompatible with a genuine dedication to revolution. The most ardent among them early abandoned the university for the "real" world, which, as often as not, turned out to be the world of factional polemics and intrigue. But even those who remained in school to cheer their colleagues from the sidelines had not been much interested in study. The intellectuals of the 1870's and 1880's were a generation of dilettantes. They discoursed on economics, sociology, history, and all other subjects with an authority that hardly suggested their knowledge came mainly from periodicals and pamphlets.

The new generation of radicals of the 1890's rejected the assumption that learning was incompatible with revolution or civic responsibility. The study of Marx and Engels and of their German disciples persuaded them that history was a rational and therefore a predictable process. To understand what lay ahead, to become a truly "scientific" revolutionary, one had to know the objective realities of the situation, especially economics. Social Democracy made knowledge an indispensable tool of revolutionary action. Its device read: *tantum possumus, quantum scimus* — loosely: knowledge is power.

N. V. Shelgunov, a leading figure of the old brand of radicalism, noted the appearance of this new breed in 1890, shortly before his death:

> Among the youth representing the future one can observe one intellectual quality that the generation of the eighties entirely lacks. The youth of the eighties did their thinking *from the top of their heads*, they thought in practical terms, being concerned only with the perils and dangers which surrounded them. They studied and read little, and, lost in the welter of resolutions and conclusions, ended up with the idea of social indifferentism. This lesson, apparently, was not lost. At any rate, present-day youth begins differently — not with generalizations and final things representing the conclusion and practical program of action, but with the particular: with the study of those social facts from which, as from a logical inference, there must follow of itself [the answer to]: what is to be done? At present, in St. Petersburg, a great deal of self-education is under way, as well as calm, serious scientific study of social questions . . . This movement, so far, is still in its embryonic phase, and as yet not fully organized. But should it continue to develop along the same lines, then there is reason to believe it will give us in the nineteen hundreds a generation of enlightened and educated active figures of public life such as Russia has never produced before.[7]

Struve's closest friend and associate among the Social Democrats was Alexander Nikolaevich Potresov, afterward a leading Men-

[7] N. V. Shelgunov, *Ocherki russkoi zhizni* (St. Petersburg, 1895), 1094–1095; cf. #55/56. See also I. M. Mogiliansky, "V devianostye gody," *Byloe*, No. 23 (1924), 151–152.

shevik.[8] Four years older than Struve, Potresov also began his university studies in the Faculty of Natural Sciences and then, together with him, transferred to the Faculty of Law. Potresov's mind was distinguished neither by erudition nor originality, but this did not prevent him from contributing more than anyone except Struve to the development of the Social Democratic movement in Russia. An energetic organizer and at the same time a man devoid of political aspirations, he provided an indispensable link uniting Social Democratic publicists at home and abroad — all of them, in varying degrees, vain, temperamental, or ambitious men — into a working partnership. Furthermore, having inherited from his mother an independent income, he was in a position to provide the first Social Democratic publications in Russia with much-needed subsidies.

Another member of the circle, D. V. Stranden, like Struve spent part of his childhood abroad. Upon his return to Russia he was enrolled at the Third Gymnasium in St. Petersburg, Struve's school, and graduated from it two years ahead of Struve. He left no writings, but is said by Struve to have come strongly under his intellectual influence.[9] V. S. Golubev was active in worker propaganda, and for a while served as representative of the socialist intelligentsia in the St. Petersburg Central Worker Circle. For this activity he had been expelled from the university in 1887. He was subsequently reinstated, then rearrested in 1891 and once more expelled, this time permanently.[10] The circle also counted among its members two natural scientists, Gerd and A. M. Voden, as well as N. D. Vodovozov, N. D. Sokolov, K. K. Bauer, R. E. Klasson, B. V. Nikolsky, N. P. Pavlov-Silvansky, and V. A. Obolensky.[11] Its

[8] The best biography of Potresov is that written by B. I. Nikolaevsky: *Potresov*, 9–90. In 1934 Struve said that Potresov had been close to him intellectually but not personally ("My Contacts and Conflicts with Lenin," 581). The letters which he wrote Potresov in the 1890's and which will be cited throughout this volume do not, however, bear out this statement.

[9] Born around 1868, at the university (1887–91) Stranden participated in worker propaganda, activity which soon brought him to the attention of the police: *Obzory*, XVII (1892–93), 275. Later he moved to London, where he became a vegetarian and married an English Theosophist: V. A. Posse, *Moi zhiznennyi put'* (Moscow and Leningrad, 1929), 254.

[10] After his release from prison, Golubev (1867–1911) joined the Constitutional Democratic party; on him, see Struve's obituary in RM, No. 2 (February 1911), Pt. 2, 188–189, and my *Social Democracy and the St. Petersburg Labor Movement, 1885–1897* (Cambridge, Mass., 1963), 136 and *passim*.

[11] V. A. Gerd was born in Zurich, the grandson of a British schoolmaster, James Heard, who had come to Russia at the beginning of the nineteenth century (see

sympathizers included the economist Michael Tugan-Baranovsky. Five years older than Struve, in 1890 he already enjoyed a professional reputation for his important essay on marginal utility. The young Marxists respected him for his learning, but they tended to regard him as somewhat naive. All through the 1890's he gave the Social Democrats valuable theoretical support without becoming engaged in their political activities.[12]

Struve's circle operated internally and externally: its members met in private to discuss Marxist theory and the history of revolutionary movements, and at the same time publicly propagated Social Democratic ideas among fellow students, industrial workers, the intelligentsia gathered in literary salons, and whomever else they could reach. Unfortunately, neither activity — self-study or proselytizing — is adequately documented.

The most influential papers read within the confines of the circle were given by Struve. His main purpose was to show that the ideas which until then had passed in Russia for Marxism in reality had little in common with it. As he presented it, Marxism was not merely a critique of the capitalist mode of production and, as such, a theory suitable for grafting on the subjective method and anarchist politics, but rather an integral system incompatible with

---

Chapter 7). Upon graduation from the university he was appointed to the faculty of the Novo Aleksandrovsky Institute as Professor of Agriculture. He later joined the Mensheviks. On him, see Struve in *Voz*, No. 450 (August 26, 1926). A. M. Voden (1870–1939) left Russia in 1891 to settle in the West. He published important memoirs on the origins of Social Democracy in St. Petersburg; see *Voden*. N. D. Vodovozov (1870–1896), the son of a prominent pedagogue, was active in the late 1880's as a student leader at St. Petersburg University. He was arrested in 1890, and the following year was expelled from the university, whereupon he moved to Dorpat. Struve reviewed his posthumous *Ekonomicheskie etiudy* (Moscow, 1897) in #55. N. D. Sokolov (1870–1928) later acquired fame as a public defender of political prisoners. In 1917 he played an active role in organizing the Petrograd Soviet and drafted the celebrated Order No. 1, issued in February 1917, which is generally held responsible for inaugurating the dissolution of the Russian Army. After the Revolution, he stayed in the Soviet Union. K. K. Bauer, whom Struve regarded as his only political disciple (see his "My Contacts with Rodichev," *SR*, XII, No. 35 [January 1934], 335) and a very close friend, went on his advice to work in the zemstva. Arrested and exiled in 1896, he came back a broken man. R. E. Klasson (born ca. 1886) graduated from the Technological Institute and earned a living as an electrical engineer. In the 1890's his apartment served the Social Democrats as one of their meeting places: *KL*, No. 13 (1925), 144–145. B. V. Nikolsky later became a conservative nationalist; he was executed by the Bolsheviks. The fame of N. P. Pavlov-Silvansky (1869–1907) as a historian rests on an unconvincing attempt to show that Russia had a feudal system similar to the Western one. V. A. Obolensky was a friend of Potresov.

[12] On Tugan-Baranovsky, see M. Golman, *Tugan-Baranovskii* (Leningrad, 1926), and Richard Kindersley, *The First Russian Revisionists* (Oxford, 1962), 52–59.

nearly everything that was regarded in Russia as socialism. He was
determined, in other words, to introduce into Russia Marxism in
its Social Democratic version as an independent theory and movement. In this task he succeeded. Voden, the only member of this
circle who published memoirs, attached particular importance to
a report on Marx's life which Struve delivered in the spring of
1890, that is, before his trip to the West. In it, he said, Struve for
the first time provided students of St. Petersburg interested in the
subject with an authoritative account of Marxist theory. "It was
this report, adapted to meet our immediate and most urgent need
— to acquire an idea of the basic facts of Marx's biography from
a Marxist point of view — that 'broke the ice.' It was the first
tangible step in that direction which afterwards became associated
with Struve's name." [13] The manuscript of this report circulated
among the students, enhancing Struve's reputation, but he himself
had a low opinion of it and dismissed it as weak and unoriginal.[14]
At another meeting of the circle, Struve read a report on the events
of 1848 in Germany in which he stressed the role played in them
by Marx and Engels. There were also lectures by Voden, who
spoke on French socialism, and by one B. L. Zotov, who reported
on the Decembrists.[15] In addition, a more select inner group held
closed sessions in the winter of 1890–91 to discuss Thün's *History
of the Russian Revolutionary Movement*, a copy of which Struve
had procured abroad.[16] All these activities, of course, were illegal
and participants in them risked arrest and long-term imprisonment
or exile.

The general as well as the restricted meetings of the circle seem
to have taken place at Kalmykova's apartment, which provided the
young Social Democrats with an ideal cover. After her husband's
death in 1889, Kalmykova was granted a pension by the government, the proceeds of which she used to open in her apartment
house a large book business that specialized in furnishing provincial libraries with all manner of "progressive" literature. Kalmykova distributed systematic bibliographies of books and other publications for the mass reader, and brought out two series of popular pamphlets under her own imprint, one dealing with nature, the

[13] *Voden*, 72.
[14] *Ibid.*
[15] *Ibid.*, 73.
[16] *Ibid.*, 75.

other with society. There was a constant stream of authors, librarians, publishers, and ordinary buyers coming and going in her shop; among them Pobedonostsev, a neighbor, who called her Deputy Minister of Education and ordered from her children's books; the novelist Leskov; and the painter Ge.[17] With all that traffic, a dozen or so students who gathered at her apartment from time to time did not attract the attention of the police. Kalmykova flourished in the atmosphere of intellectual excitement in which she suddenly found herself. Under Struve's influence, she was converted to Social Democracy; but the conversion seems to have involved less an acceptance of a particular socialist doctrine than initiation into a secret society of which her protégé was the guiding spirit.[18]

For external propaganda purposes, the most effective vehicle was the seminar on the theory of constitutional law taught by M. I. Svechnikov. An uninspiring and incompetent teacher, Svechnikov sought to ingratiate himself with students by the time-honored method of siding with them against the administrative and academic establishment. His seminars met in public and attracted a large crowd of auditors. His pupils in 1890–91 included Struve, Potresov, Pavlov-Silvansky, Sokolov, Voden, Vodovozov, and Nikolsky. In the course of class discussions, the members of this Social Democratic group took advantage of every opportunity to interpret social or economic questions in Marxist terms. Struve spoke in defense of or in opposition to virtually every paper presented in this seminar. On one occasion he delivered a scathing attack on non–Social Democratic socialism, describing it as a "utopian" doctrine. These, his first public appearances, were often greeted with storms of applause from supporters in the audience. Under police pressure, the university eventually closed down Svechnikov's seminar, but not before a considerable number of students had been exposed and converted to the new doctrine.[19]

Some members of the Social Democratic circle (for instance, Golubev and Stranden) also participated in worker propaganda, but Struve was not one of them. His activity was confined to the-

[17] A. M. Kalmykova, "Obryvki vospominanii," *Byloe*, No. 1/35 (1926), 72; Struve, "N. S. Leskov," RiS, No. 83 (June 29, 1930).

[18] "My Contacts with Rodichev," 351.

[19] *Voden*, 74; *Potresov*, 15–16; Mogiliansky, "V devianostye gody," 144; Kindersley, *Russian Revisionists*, 37–38; A. Meiendorf, "P. B. Struve," unpublished manuscript in the possession of Professor Gleb Struve, Berkeley, California; V. A. Obolensky, untitled reminiscences of Struve written in 1944, B. I. Nikolaevsky Archive, Hoover Institution, Stanford, California. See also #216.

ory. He never knew how to talk to common people, let alone pretend to be one of them, as the propagandists had to do. Golubev once brought him to a meeting of a worker circle, lending him a coat for disguise. But when soon after this escapade Golubev was arrested and took the coat to jail with him, Struve gave up this kind of activity.[20]

By the time he had completed his second year at the university (in the spring of 1891), Struve had acquired an enviable reputation for erudition and brilliance. He was the acknowledged leader of the small band of Social Democrats active at St. Petersburg University and the main spokesman for a fresh brand of radicalism.

And yet there was something unreal about his leading this or any other movement, for he had none of the personal qualities of a political leader. He was utterly incapable of exercising the intellectual discipline essential to all political activity, especially that conducted illegally. His mind worked so quickly and on so many simultaneous levels that even his most devoted admirers could never tell where he stood on any particular issue and what they, as his followers, were to believe. To cite but one example of many: Voden later recalled his astonishment at hearing Struve declare that the state performed a progressive historic function and would exercise authority even after the triumph of socialism.[21] Struve made this un-Marxist statement at the very time when he was trying to introduce his friends to the rudiments of Marx's sociology. He could, of course, have concealed such thoughts. But duplicity of any kind was alien to him. He always spoke his mind, sometimes in a disagreeably brusque manner, and never made the slightest attempt to adjust his ideas to the desires of the audience.

He puzzled most people. He had a habit — natural for the profoundly learned man that he was — of attempting to see every argument from different sides. He always drew a sharp line separating subjective wishes from objective realities. He could understand and even defend points of view which were unsympathetic to him. Others, however, saw not the subjective-objective distinction so dear to him but inexplicable contradictions. Arseniev, who had the utmost respect for Struve's intelligence, was heard to complain

---

[20] "My Contacts and Conflicts with Lenin," 583. The incident is also described by Golubev in *Byloe*, No. 12 (1906), 118.

[21] *Voden*, 74; Struve makes this point in his first book, #15/53.

that with him one never knew what he would say the following week.[22] Other contemporaries spoke of "Struvian *otsebiatina*," meaning a kind of intellectual capriciousness.[23] A man of such unpredictability, who insisted on obeying only the voice of his own subtle and restless mind, obviously was not suited to lead.

Moreover, his manner of public speaking was not calculated to win a mass following. Confronting an audience, he would pant and gasp for the words that lagged behind his rapidly flowing thoughts, flailing his arms in wild gestures which appeared to plead for help. One eyewitness who heard Struve speak in Arseniev's salon while he was still a gymnasium student had the impression of watching a man in a condition of utter helplessness, as he "energetically accentuated [the text of his speech] with sharp modulations of the voice and gestures of both hands which conveyed a sense of fidgety awkwardness, as if he were literally seeking assistance or fighting himself, and trying to convince himself rather than his audience." [24] Another eyewitness said that the sight of Struve on the public platform reminded him of a peasant girl drowning in cotton seeds.[25]

Nor was his physical appearance that of a man born to command. Obolensky, who saw him at the university around 1892 after a lapse of a couple of years, said that he found him grown somewhat more manly since school days; and notwithstanding his many freckles and cauliflower ears (about which he was very self-conscious), he was considered not unhandsome and apparently enjoyed success with women. Still his health was poor and his limp body could not withstand ordinary rigors or exertions. Like his mother, he constantly ailed from something or other, usually of a gastric nature. He was so sensitive that on cold winter days he would not leave the house. All work exhausted him, sometimes to the point of acute depression.[26]

He was always in a hurry to get somewhere, as if great events were about to happen where he was not. He never finished anything he began, and he began much.

And yet he had a mind of such extraordinary vigor, sweep, and

---

[22] *Voden*, 72, quoting Klasson; also, Meiendorf, "Struve."

[23] *Voden*, 72.

[24] I. V. Gessen, *V dvukh vekakh* (Berlin, 1937), 252; the recollection dates back to 1886–87.

[25] Meiendorf, "Struve."

[26] For example, Struve to Potresov, May 14, 1892.

integrity that all was forgotten: his intellectual gyrations, his comical manner on the speaker's platform, his hopeless lack of organization. The fascination which he exerted and the spell in which he held audiences is attested to by all who came in contact with him during these years. As long as Social Democracy remained a purely intellectual movement, that is, until approximately 1900, he was a political force of the first magnitude, the heir of Herzen, Pisarev, Chernyshevsky, and the then still living Mikhailovsky. The gathering Social Democratic forces had to have a leader and simply propelled him into that role. Kalmykova, who knew him best, seems to have been the only one to realize that there was some mistake in all this public adulation. Years later when Struve was accused of betraying the cause he had once led, she came to his defense: "He did not push himself to be leader of the Social Democratic Party: it was the conditions of Russian life that elevated him." [27] The judgment seems accurate.

In the spring of 1891, as the second year of Struve's university studies was drawing to a close, the Marxist circle which he had headed began to dissolve. Some members were expelled for participation in student riots; others went to jail for such offenses as indoctrinating workers with socialist propaganda or marching in Shelgunov's funeral procession. Struve for the time being somehow escaped trouble with the police, although he had been in the crowd that followed the Shelgunov cortege.[28]

Toward the end of 1891 he fell gravely ill with pneumonia.[29] Kalmykova nursed him back to health, and when he recovered he decided to spend the remainder of the academic year at the University of Graz in Austria. He was attracted to it mainly by the fame of Ludwig Gumplowicz, the Social Darwinist who with single-minded dedication advanced an interpretation of progress based on the scheme of evolving conflicts, first between races, then between states, and finally between social classes.[30] Struve

[27] Kalmykova to Potresov, August 26 [1903]. In her memoirs, Kalmykova says that in the 1890's she had warned against treating Struve as a Social Democratic leader: "[His] mind works so intensely that it is difficult to predict where it will lead; there is no point in calling him a leader so as to accuse him later of being a renegade": "Obryvki vospominanii," 66.

[28] Voden, 76.

[29] "My Contacts and Conflicts with Lenin," 583; "Pamiati Liudviga Gumplovicha," RM, No. 9 (September 1909), 159.

[30] Gumplowicz, a Polish Jew, was appointed to the Graz faculty in 1876 to teach

was strongly drawn to a man holding such antisubjectivist, Darwinian views, the more so because the "directness of [Gumplowicz's] one-sided thought approached cynicism." [31] Nothing was dearer to him at this point than more ammunition with which to puncture the ethical and sentimental socialism of the Russian intelligentsia.

At Graz he enrolled as an "extraordinary auditor" in Gumplowicz's course on administrative law and Richard Hildebrand's on political economy.[32] Gumplowicz was visibly surprised that anyone would come from Russia to Graz to study with him, and Struve soon found out why. The great man's lectures dealt with none of the broad sociological and historical questions which interested Struve; instead, they turned out to be a dreary catalogue of Austrian statistics and administrative legislation. Minutes after Gumplowicz had begun to speak, Struve decided he had nothing to learn from him.[33]

Although he stayed on as a registered auditor in Gumplowicz's courses through the summer term of 1892, he seems to have spent most of his time on independent study. He now deepened his knowledge of Neo-Kantian philosophy, and read a great deal of German economic literature. He was especially attracted to the socioliberal school of German economic thought, which combined a high level of professional competence with a sense of social responsibility. Outstanding figures in this school were Lujo Brentano and his pupils Heinrich Herkner and G. von Schulze-Gäwernitz. Struve liked particularly the central thesis upheld by these writers, that modern capitalism had no choice but to promote social reform because to function properly it required a prosperous working class. This approach, which suggested a steady diminution of class conflicts, accorded better with Struve's social philosophy than did the Marxist dialectic. In Brentano he also found support for his faith in the progressive function of rural capitalism.[34]

---

law and sociology. He committed suicide in 1909. See I. L. Horowitz's introduction to Gumplowicz's *Outlines of Sociology* (New York, 1963).

[31] "Pamiati Liudviga Gumplovicha," 159.

[32] Letter to the author from Dr. Walter Höflechner of the University of Graz.

[33] "Pamiati Liudviga Gumplovicha," 159. Struve's antipathy to Gumplowicz — caused at least in part by his habit of referring to Russians as "Asiatics" — is manifest in Struve's first publication, a review of Gumplowicz's book, written in 1892 (#1).

[34] See H. Herkner's *Die soziale Reform als Gebot des Wirtschaftlichen Fortschrittes* (Leipzig, 1891) and *Die Arbeiterfrage* (Berlin, 1894), and G. von

It was apparently during his stay in Graz that he decided to become a professional economist.[35] The decision had a variety of consequences affecting his entire life, one of which it is important to state now. Struve was a Marxist and a Social Democrat before he became an economist. At this time he perceived no conflict in this double commitment to a socialist doctrine and an academic discipline because, as pointed out, he thought Marxism to have virtually impeccable scientific credentials. Indeed, he considered it an asset to have mastered Marx in preparation for the study of economics since it made one aware of the social side of economic phenomena ignored by the classical economists. But as soon as he undertook to study economics in earnest, he became ideologically vulnerable. The more he deepened his knowledge of economics, the more conscious he became of the normative, nonscientific elements in Marx's theory. Here lay one of the seeds of his later Revisionism and his ultimate break with Marx.

Struve at this time also read much of the popular economic literature published in Germany and Austria. The nostalgia which he found in some of it for the vanishing precapitalist order reminded him of the views of the proponents of separate path in his own country. In Peter Rosegger, the poet of the Austrian peasant, he even believed to have identified the counterpart of a Russian Slavophile. An article which he wrote about him appeared in the *Messenger of Europe*.[36]

In May 1892, Kalmykova came to see him and they traveled to Venice. "The trip, on the whole, was successful," he wrote Potresov in June, after she had returned to Russia, "and I am satisfied with it, although it demonstrated once more, this time with particular

Schulze-Gäwernitz's *Zum sozialen Frieden*, 2 vols. (Leipzig, 1890). Using the example of England, Schulze-Gäwernitz showed how society acquired a political education and how peaceful evolution replaced the political violence forecast by the socialists. Struve, who greatly admired his work, arranged for the translation into Russian of two of his books: *Der Grossbetrieb* (in Russian, *Krupnoe proizvodstvo*, St. Petersburg, 1897), and *Volkswirtschaftliche Studien aus Russland* (in Russian, *Ocherki obshchestvennogo khoziaistva i ekonomicheskoi politiki*, St. Petersburg, 1901, translated by L. Krasin, the future Soviet Commissar of Trade). Schulze-Gäwernitz reciprocated the admiration, and in the second of these books complimented Struve (*Volkswirtschaftliche Studien aus Russland* [Leipzig, 1899], 106n, 344n).

[35] This is stated by Sergei Vodov, who may have heard it from Struve: "Petr Berngardovich Struve," *Studencheskie gody* (Prague), No. 1/18 (1925), 34; also, Voden, 74.

[36] #8.

vividness, how physically weak and helpless I am. Aleksandra
Mikhailovna astonished all the time with her strength. Of course,
she ate nothing, etc. There are such strange people!" [37] Shortly
after this vacation, he left Graz for Gräfenberg, a spa in Austrian
Silesia, where he took a water cure for his troublesome stomach.[38]
In the autumn he was back in St. Petersburg. He did not re-reg-
ister at the university, taking instead a job as librarian in the Ministry of Finance, a position which left him much time to indulge
in his latest passion, economic theory and history.[39]

These were the years of famine and of the great debates over
their causes and meaning. The discussions afforded the Social
Democrats their opportunity to challenge publicly the prevailing
views about the character of Russia's national economy. In the
process, they managed for the first time to disseminate their ideas
outside the narrow confines of student circles. During the immediate post-famine year (1892–93) Social Democracy in Russia became transformed from a secret doctrine into a distinct movement
of public opinion.

The position of the proponents of separate path was at this
juncture forcefully restated by N. F. Danielson (Nikolai -on) in
Outlines of Our Post-Reform National Economy, published in the
autumn of 1893.[40] Danielson had enjoyed for many years a reputation as Russia's leading exponent of Marxism. Indeed, he had closer
relations with Marx and Engels than any of his compatriots: he
corresponded with them for a quarter of a century, supplied them
with much of the statistical material on which they based their

---

[37] Struve to Potresov from Graz, June 13, 1892.
[38] Struve to Potresov from Vienna, July 29, 1892.
[39] Autobiographical sketch prepared for the editors of the Brokgauz and Efron
Encyclopedia, dated February 10, 1901, Pushkin House, Leningrad, Fond 377, No.
2633. Here Struve writes that he passed the state examinations as an extern in 1895.
His official post in the fall of 1892 was Assistant Librarian of the Scholastic
Committee (Kindersley, *Russian Revisionists,* 44). In April 1894 he was identified
in police reports as a university drop-out employed by the Chancery of the Ministry of Foreign Affairs (*Obzor,* XVIII [1894] 176–177). These jobs were probably fictitious. Throughout this period he seems to have been supported by Kalmykova.
[40] *Ocherki nashego poreformennogo obshchestvennogo khoziaistva* (St. Petersburg, 1893). There exist German and French translations published in 1899 and
1902, respectively. Danielson (1844–1918), by profession an accountant, worked
in St. Petersburg mutual credit associations. In his youth he had been an active
revolutionary.

views of the Russian economy, and translated all three volumes of
Das Kapital.[41] But he was more than a mere literary agent and
popularizer of Marx and Engels, for he also made an earnest if not
notably successful effort to apply their method of economic analysis to Russia in order to ascertain the consequences there of primary accumulation and transition to commodity production, which
Marx had traced on the example of England.

The first portion of his book appeared in 1880 as an article dealing with the effects of capitalism on Russian agriculture.[42] With
copious references to Marx, he argued that the imperial government had been pursuing since 1861 two mutually exclusive economic policies. In the Emancipation Edict, it laid down the foundations of a noncapitalist system of agricultural production which
assured every producer, the peasant, access to the means of production, the land. But in the two decades which followed it did
nothing whatever to promote the peasant's productive capacity.
All its efforts were exerted in the opposite direction, on behalf of
capitalism. By founding credit institutions and constructing railroads, it assisted the transformation of foodstuffs from articles of
consumption into commodities. Mastery over the village was passing to the grain merchants of St. Petersburg. With such help, capitalism was squeezing out the independent producers and impover-
ishing the mass of rural inhabitants.

The essay caused much stir on its appearance. Marx, to whom
Danielson had sent it for comments, congratulated him on its
originality and urged him to continue along the same lines.[43]

Danielson needed little encouragement. He doggedly kept on
gathering data and bombarding Marx, and, after his death, Engels,
with tedious letters full of statistics intended to prove the folly of
the government's economic policies. The famines of 1891–92 confirmed him in the soundness of his analysis. The next year he reprinted his 1880 essay in book form, appending to it a new study
dealing with the effects of capitalist industry on Russian agriculture. The purpose of *Outlines of Our Post-Reform National Economy* was to prove that in Russia capitalism performed a purely destructive function.

---

[41] The best collection of Danielson's correspondence with Marx and Engels is
MERR.
[42] Nikolai -on, "Ocherki nashego poreformennogo obshchestvennogo khoziaistva,"
Slovo (October 1880), 76–142.
[43] MERR, 437.

Struve's parents, Anna and Bernhard Struve

Struve as a child (center) with two of his brothers, ca. 1872

A. M. Kalmykova, ca. 1916

A. N. Potresov, 1925

Russian economic literature had concerned itself for some time with the crisis in household industry (*kustarnaia promyshlennost'*), the preservation of which was widely regarded as essential to a sound rural economy. Because the Russian climate restricted agricultural activity to a relatively brief season (in the Moscow area, less than six months in the year), Russian peasants customarily supplemented their income by turning out simple consumer goods, such as textiles, hardware, kitchen utensils, and musical instruments, which they sold in the villages and small-town markets. This industry was generally classified as belonging to the popular rather than to the capitalist sector of the national economy, because under it the manufacturer owned both the means of production and the finished product. The supplementary income derived from it was regarded by students of the peasant economy as indispensable for balancing the peasant's budget. To preserve household industry, however, it was necessary to restrain the growth of capitalist industry, whose more efficient production threatened to eliminate its primitive competitor. This consideration provided Russian economists and publicists of the 1870's and 1880's with yet another argument against the procapitalist policies pursued by the government.

These points had been made some time before Danielson published his book, most notably by V. Vorontsov. Danielson's argument caused a sensation because it made a causal connection between the growth of capitalist industry and the famines. It was his contention that in Russia, with its communal system of land tenure, any separation of industry from agriculture was ruinous both to the peasant and to capitalist industry itself.

Concentrating on evidence provided by the textile industry, Danielson showed that the emergence of giant mechanical mills lowered the price of cloth so much that it made unprofitable the spinning and weaving traditionally carried out in peasant households. Unable to compete with Moscow factories, the peasant in Central Russia rid himself of the spinning wheel and loom. By so doing he not only deprived himself of an important source of additional earnings: he also forced himself to buy on the market the cloth he had previously manufactured for his personal use. He simultaneously lost income and increased expense. The same held true of peasants employed in the other branches of household industry.

To replace the money he had lost and to earn the additional money he now needed, the peasant had no alternative but to exploit to the limit the only productive resource still left to him, his land allotment. Unable any longer to leave any of it fallow, he tilled it to the point of exhaustion. When in need of yet more money, he sold the grain set aside as seed or for domestic consumption. Next, he disposed of his cattle and implements. And finally, when he had nothing to sell, he abandoned the village to roam the country in search of employment. In this manner, capitalist industry brought about rural unemployment. And yet this industry was unable itself to absorb the unemployed it had created, because technological improvements permitted it to raise productivity without increasing the working force. The needs of European Russia for textiles, according to Danielson's calculations, were fully taken care of by 370,000 factory workers; these wage earners displaced tens of millions of independent part-time workers previously engaged in household textile industries. In sum:

In proportion as capitalism conquers the various branches of industry; in proportion as labor which cannot be utilized is released; in proportion as the producers themselves are expropriated from the means of production, the peasant has no alternative left but to draw all the means of subsistence from the land. But the soil, receiving nothing in return for what is exacted from it year after year, becomes increasingly exhausted. The concatenation of certain unfavorable natural conditions made inevitable what a whole series of socioeconomic conditions had prepared for little by little: the earth yielded nothing. Thus, the famine was a direct consequence of the inappropriate forms adopted by our industry over the past thirty years. Instead of adhering to our ancient traditions; instead of developing the inherited principle of maintaining a close connection between the means of production and the immediate producers; instead of using the inventions of Western science and applying them to develop industry based on peasant ownership of the means of production; instead of increasing the peasant's productivity by concentrating in his hands the means of production; instead of utilizing not the Western form of production but the Western organization of production, with its highly developed cooperation, division, and correlation of labor, machines, etc.; instead of developing the principle underlying peasant agriculture and applying it to peasant exploitation of land; instead of opening up for the peasant wide access to scientific knowledge and its application as a means to that end — instead of all this, we took the very contrary course. We not only failed to hinder the development of capitalist forms of production, although they rest on the expropriation of the peasant — on the contrary: we have done everything in our power to promote a fundamental break in our economic life, a break which led to the hunger of 1891.[44]

In the long run, according to Danielson, capitalist industry in Russia would not benefit from the misery it caused because by destroying household industry it impoverished the peasantry, who constituted nine-tenths of the country's population and therefore formed the main market for its goods. A peasant who could barely scrape enough money from the land for his obligations to state and landlord could hardly absorb the outpourings of modern factories. As for foreign markets, these had been seized by England and the other countries with advanced industrial economies.

Unlike Vorontsov, Danielson entertained no hope that household industry could be revived, for he thought capitalism had ruined it beyond recovery. Neither communal agriculture pursued in combination with household industry nor agriculture and manufacture based on capitalist principles had any future in Russia. The only solution to Russia's economic problems lay in the socialization of production. Through socialization, the proceeds of the economy could be diverted from the pockets of a small group of profiteers to the benefit of all society. Danielson apparently expected this socialization to be accomplished by the imperial government, but he did not say so explicitly.

Danielson's book delivered a severe blow to the young Social Democratic movement. Here was a writer, acknowledged as the country's leading Marxist, demonstrating in Marxist terms the destructiveness of capitalism in Russia and urging the immediate socialization of production. Inasmuch as the entire Social Democratic program posited the growth of capitalism and the emergence of an industrial proletariat as the precondition of a new political system, Danielson's thesis implied that Social Democracy in Russia had no future. The Social Democrats regarded as an "evil day"

[44] *Ocherki*, 322–323.

the day when his book appeared,[45] and during the next several years exerted great efforts to disprove its ideas. The impact of Danielson's book was reinforced by the publication in rapid sequence of three books by V. Vorontsov which, although not in accord with Danielson's positive recommendations, shared his pessimism about Russian capitalism.[46]

Reading the literature on the famine, Struve was struck by the similarity between the views of Vorontsov, Danielson, and Mikhailovsky and those of the pre-Marxist, "utopian" socialists of Western Europe. Both groups held that history was malleable, both idealized social cooperation and renounced class warfare, and both had an amateurish knowledge of economics. Sometimes the similarities were remarkably close; for example, Engels argued in 1845 (that is, before he and Marx had created "scientific socialism"), as did Danielson and Vorontsov in the 1890's, that capitalism could not flourish in their country, Germany, for want of domestic and foreign markets.[47] There were, of course, differences dividing Mikhailovsky from Vorontsov, and both from Danielson, but these paled into insignificance compared to the sociological and economic utopianism which they shared. So impressed was Struve by the parallels between Russian socialism of the 1870's and 1880's and Western "utopian" socialism of the 1830's and 1840's that he began to treat the two as historical analogues. The Russian variant of "utopian" socialism he now labeled "Populism."

This term, which is in common use today, owes its currency in large measure to Struve's early publicistic writings and not to the "going to the people" movement of 1874, as is commonly believed, even by some professional historians.[48] The Russian radicals of the 1870's and 1880's, as a rule, called themselves not Populists (*narodniki*) but socialists (or social) revolutionaries (*sotsialisty*

[45] S. Mitskevich, *Na grani dvukh epokh* (Moscow, 1937), 128. M. A. Silvin says that Marxists (read: Social Democrats) feared neither Mikhailovsky nor Vorontsov, but only Danielson, because he had personally known Marx and made use of Marxist terms and of statistics: KS, No. 1 (1934), 78.

[46] V. V[orontsov], *Progressivnye techeniia v krest'ianskom khoziaistve* (St. Petersburg, 1892); *Nashi napravleniia* (St. Petersburg, 1893), and, *Popytki obosnovaniia narodnichestva* (St. Petersburg, 1893). The last, a collection of articles originally published in *Russian Wealth*, gave new lease to the word *narodnichestvo*.

[47] #44/18.

[48] The evidence for my views on the history of the term "Populism" is given in my "Narodnichestvo: A Semantic Inquiry," SR XXIII, No. 3 (September 1964), 441–458.

or *sotsial revoliutsionery*). The word *narodniki* was coined in 1876 by a dissident socialist revolutionary faction which rejected the idea that had inspired the "going to the people" movement, on the grounds that it was presumptuous for intellectuals to teach the masses. These authentic narodniks were anti-intellectual and anti-socialist; they idolized the common man and wished to learn from him. Rather than go to the village to agitate or spread propaganda, they quietly settled down among peasants to share their lives. Later on, however, in the 1880's, the term came to be applied loosely to all kinds of movements professing love for the common people, whether anarchist, Jacobin, or conservative (for example, in the 1880's even Dostoevsky was occasionally referred to as a narodnik). In the late 1880's and early 1890's Vorontsov and Iuzov-Kablits tried to restore to the term a certain measure of precision by redefining it as an ideology that upheld folk institutions and rejected all attempts to impose socialism on the people; but the confusion persisted.

Among those who contributed to the confusion were the early Social Democrats. Plekhanov, eager to separate himself and his associates from all other Russian radical groups, began the practice of labeling as "Populists" all who, whatever their internal disagreements, held in common two views which he considered incompatible with "scientific" socialism: that the intelligentsia held the key to historical progress, and that Russia could attain socialism without going through capitalism.[49] Vera Zasulich also sometimes used the word in this sense in her correspondence with Engels.[50] But in the 1880's such use of "Populism" was still sporadic; there was then as yet no conception of Populism as an ideology performing a specific historical function.

Such a conception was first formulated by Struve in 1892–1894 in the writings which will now be discussed. From him it was quickly adopted by other Social Democratic writers, among them Lenin, and after 1917 entered the standard Russian and Western historical vocabulary. Although this usage is probably too deeply entrenched ever to be given up, one cannot stress too heavily that "Populism" used in this loose manner is not a scholarly but a polemical term, coined in the heat of struggles between two political

[49] E.g., G. V. Plekhanov, *Izbrannye filosofskie proizvedeniia*, I (Moscow, 1956), 173 and 392n.
[50] E.g., MERR, 508, 559. Engels was very skeptical of such usage: *Voden*, 91.

factions contending for influence over public opinion, and that as such it tells more about the environment in which it emerged than about the phenomenon it purports to define.

Struve viewed the famines of 1891–92 as a watershed in the history of Russia's economic development. In May 1892, he wrote from Graz to Potresov, who had gone to investigate the areas afflicted by hunger:

> You stand, so to speak, in the very midst of the materials bearing on the famine, and for this reason, I think, you are in a better position to assess its *economic* significance. Can the population recover from it, or will the national economy, under the impact of this blow, assume inevitably new forms, the triumph of which requires the ruin of the masses? I do not believe Russia will turn into a Palestine. But I am almost convinced that of the economic independence of the Russian peasant (even previously highly *questionable*) soon not even a trace will remain. And the famine will deserve much credit for this *service*.[51]

He was burning with impatience to present in print his own "Marxist" interpretation of the famine as the beginning of Russia's transition to mature capitalism. Sometime at the end of 1891, before he left for Graz, he told Voden that he intended to write a book criticizing the views of economic development prevailing in Russia and offering constructive proposals on how to end the agrarian crisis.[52]

But this was easier said than done. If he presented his views in a book, he had to contend with government censors, who had much experience in detecting political messages disguised as scholarship. If he broke the book up into articles he had to overcome a more formidable obstacle yet — unofficial censorship exercised by the "Populists," who controlled all the "progressive" monthlies.

This double censorship proved, for the time being, insurmountable, and he had to look for outlets abroad. In 1892, during his studies in Austria, he befriended Heinrich Braun, the editor of two German publications of a social-liberal orientation, one a theoret-

---

[51] Struve to Potresov from Graz, May 14, 1892; first cited in *Potresov*, 19.
[52] *Voden*, 76.

ical journal, the other a monthly newsletter devoted to the international labor movement.[53] In these periodicals, Struve reviewed between July 1892 and April 1893 six Russian books on agrarian topics, using the opportunity to develop with increasing boldness the interpretation of the Russian economy which he had formulated under Skvortsov's influence.[54]

What was wrong with Russian agriculture? Why had it been ailing for more than a decade, plagued by rising prices for land, declining prices for agricultural produce, and general impoverishment of the peasantry? In dealing with these questions, Struve wrote in one of the reviews,[55] it was essential to separate facts from wishes. Once this was done, it became apparent that the malaise of Russian agriculture stemmed not from mistaken economic policies pursued by the government since 1861, and in particular not from its failure to assure the peasant of adequate land allotments and to impose on him realistic fiscal burdens, but from the technical irrationality of the Russian rural economy. That economy was simply too primitive to support all those who wanted to live off it. The Emancipation Edict, which Russian economists and publicists so admired, bore heavy responsibility for this situation. In its eagerness to assure every peasant of land, the government had given him too little of it to enable him to concentrate on exploiting the productive soil, and too much to persuade him to give up hopes of attaining economic self-sufficiency. The Edict thus encouraged a greater proportion of the inhabitants to engage in agriculture than the land could support.

The peasant commune aggravated the malaise by artificially keeping on the land those who (from the economic point of view) had no business being there. It was a relic of a precapitalist, largely natural system of economy, elements of which still remained strongly imbedded in Russia's economic structure. The commune prevented capitalism, which was everywhere penetrating the coun-

[53] *Archiv für Soziale Gesetzgebung und Statistik* and *Sozialpolitisches Centralblatt* (later renamed *Soziale Praxis*). The *Archiv* had among its regular contributors Brentano, Sombart, Simmel, Schulze-Gäwernitz, and Herkner.

[54] #2–#7. Skvortsov first formulated his views on the agrarian crisis in a book-length essay called "The Economic Causes of the Famines in Russia and the Measures for Their Removal." Although completed early in 1892, it was published only two years later, under the title *Ekonomicheskie etiudy* (St. Petersburg, 1894) by Kalmykova. Struve, who maintained a regular correspondence with Skvortsov, undoubtedly knew this essay when he wrote his German articles. His line of reasoning follows Skvortsov's very faithfully.

[55] #5/175–176.

tryside, from organizing agricultural productivity on a higher, more efficient level. Inhibited by communal institutions, it turned instead into a brutal form of exploitation: the rural capitalist, or kulak, unable to become a genuine agricultural entrepreneur because of legal restraints on the sale of land, concentrated on squeezing money out of fellow peasants and hoarding.

The only realistic remedy lay in rapid industrialization. Struve's chain of reasoning, based on a combination of ideas taken from Malthus, List, Marx, Brentano, and Skvortsov, ran as follows: To improve the lot of the peasantry, Russia had to make its agriculture more rational, that is, more productive. Such rationalization required a stimulus in the form of an increase in the demand for agricultural produce. This increase of demand, in turn, called for a significant shift of the population from the countryside to the cities. Each peasant who abandoned the village and joined the labor reserve of industry became a potential buyer of foodstuffs and helped generate a demand which would solve Russia's agrarian woes.

The famines were certain to accelerate this population shift and in this sense they were economically progressive. They squeezed off the land marginal, inefficient producers, increased the demand for foodstuffs, and left the land in control of strong, economically viable peasants. Rural "class differentiation" undisputably brought suffering to its victims, but in the long run it was beneficial for all. Its long-term result would be to raise substantially the country's standard of living.

Struve dismissed as "superstition" the idea popularized by Herzen and Bakunin that the Russian peasant was by nature a socialist, and as "madness" the conviction, shared by radicals and conservatives alike, that all the peasants had to be kept on the land. In 1892 he happened to read the recently published Herzen-Turgenev correspondence from the 1860's. He was delighted to find in Turgenev's letters confirmation of his own views that the Russian peasant was by instinct not a socialist but a petty bourgeois, and that Russia would inevitably follow the Western path, not a separate one of its own making.[56] After becoming acquainted with this

---

[56] "The people before which you bow down is conservative, par excellence," Turgenev wrote Herzen, "it even bears the seeds of such *embourgeoisement* underneath its tanned sheepskin coats, within its overheated and filthy huts, inside its bellies forever stuffed to the point of heartburn, in its revulsion from all civic responsibility that it will exceed by far all those traits you have so accurately

correspondence he viewed the mounting conflict between the Social Democrats and their radical opponents not only as a historical counterpart of the conflict between Marx, Engels, and the "utopian" socialists, but also as a renewal of the old Russian controversy between Westerners and Slavophiles.

The destruction of the old agrarian order was unavoidable, he concluded. The peasant commune was breathing its last. Its survival depended on two conditions: a peasantry lacking in a sense of private property and an antiquated tax-gathering system. Neither of these conditions would obtain for much longer. The penetration of money into the countryside which the railroads had made possible awakened in the Russian acquisitive instincts and the desire to set up an independent farm. At the same time, with increased circulation of money, the government had to modernize its tax-gathering system. Russia was moving with giant steps into a phase of economic life dominated by the exchange of commodities. No one could prevent this process from taking its natural course: neither the government nor the intelligentsia. Given the existence of rural over-population, it was wasteful to pour more money into Russian agriculture, as the "friends of the people" advocated: more investments would merely prolong the misery. The best that could be done was to speed the inevitable, to "ease the birth-pangs of Russia's capitalist economy" by appropriate labor legislation and such other measures as would assure that the expropriation of the mass of small rural producers was accomplished with the least pain to those concerned.[57]

With these recommendations Struve made his debut as a publicist.

The six German reviews did not attract much attention. It was the seventh, a review of Danielson's book which Struve published in October 1893 in Braun's newsletter, that at last made the opposition sit up and take notice.[58] The review owed its impact to

---

identified in the letter depicting the Western bourgeoisie": *Pis'ma K. Dm. Kavelina i Iv. S. Turgeneva k Al. Iv. Gertsenu* (Geneva, 1892), 161. Turgenev's critique of Herzen's Slavophilism, Struve wrote, "constituted one of the most important determining influences" in his early intellectual development: "My Contacts and Conflicts with Lenin," 579–580; see also RiS, No. 225 (October 1933).

[57] #2/346 and #5/174, 175. The conception of the state as a midwife that lessens the birth-pangs of the new order echoes a similar remark by Marx at the beginning of *Capital*.

[58] #9.

the fact that Struve used Danielson's book as a springboard from which to launch a broad attack on the whole anticapitalist tendency in Russian radicalism, a tendency which he characterized, in the words that Marx and Engels had used in the *Communist Manifesto*, as "reactionary" and "utopian." [59] Here "Populism" was used for the first time to define an ideology and a movement of socialism in its pre-"scientific" phase. It was an early manifestation of that cleavage within Russian radicalism which a few years later was to lead to the formation of two rival radical parties, Social Democratic and Socialist Revolutionary.

"We are the philosophic contemporaries of our era without being its historic contemporaries" — with these words Karl Marx in 1843 characterized the attitude of the most advanced elements in Germany toward the whole spiritual and social life of their time. These words can be applied with full justice to the corresponding spiritual currents in Russia, especially since the emancipation of the serfs. Socialist ideas penetrated Russia when capitalism was, so to speak, *in statu nascenti*. These ideas, therefore, were from the beginning condemned to utopianism, and had no choice but to attach themselves to phenomena and institutions doomed by the progress of economic development. One needed only a certain dose of *idealism* in order to identify as closely as possible primitive economic forms with abstract socialist ideals, and a dose of *optimism* to trust in the triumph of these folkish forms, acting in association with the socialistically inclined intelligentsia, over the wicked forces of emergent capitalism. In this manner there arose in Russian social-political literature that movement whose spiritual fathers are Herzen and Chernyshevsky. Its adherents are known as "Populists" (*narodniki*), and its ideology represents an idealization of the peasant natural economy and of communal ownership. This national socialism was and remains decidedly utopian in character. What are the forces on which it relies — the much vaunted "communal spirit" of the peasantry and the socialist sympathies of a small band of representatives of the intelligentsia — compared to *those* forces that are released by the absolutely unavoidable transition from a natural economic organization to the money economy? On the side of capitalism stood and stands almost

[59] *Communist Manifesto*, Part III.

everything, namely that which counts the most: *economic progress*. The ruling classes and their representative, the state, are compelled by the whole social and political development to pave ever more decisively the way for capitalism. However, to the extent that capitalist development moves forward, the outlook described above must lose ground. It will either find itself reduced to a fairly pallid reform movement, capable of and eager for compromises, for which there are already hopeful seeds from previous times; or else it will have to become reconciled to the actual development as inevitable, and draw from it the inescapable theoretical and practical conclusions — in other words, it will cease being utopian.

Of course, the philosophical contemporaries of Karl Marx and Friedrich Engels were not able simply to ignore the results of the spiritual achievement of these great thinkers. Thus, the entire economic literature of Russian radicalism is permeated with the striving to reconcile somehow the utopian faith in a "unique" economic development of Russia with the insights of Marx and Engels. It has been clear for some time that this is a hopeless endeavor; proof of this is Plekhanov's brilliant polemical work against the Populists (*Our Disagreements*, 1885). Now, however, when the development of capitalism has incontrovertibly made giant strides forward, a position which, on the one hand, accepts Marx's teachings, and, on the other, consistently refuses to place itself on the base of capitalism, is so palpably utopian that its days must be numbered. It must give way to a more sensible, more realistic point of view.

After these introductory remarks, a kind of obituary for non–Social Democratic radicalism, Struve proceeded to deal with Danielson's thesis, which he described as a "Marxist body with a utopian face." After 1861, Struve asserted, nothing could have prevented the inroads of capitalism in Russia. Danielson's ideal — an economy based on the commune with the imperial government acting, through state planning, as the agent socializing industrial production — was fantastic. Danielson rejected large-scale industrialization because he did not appreciate the fact of rural overpopulation, for which capitalist industry was the only remedy. Once Russia industrialized, Struve predicted, its rural population would decline from over 80 percent to something like 50 or 40 percent, the proportion prevailing in the United States. As for markets, Russian industry, like American, would find them at home, especially in the country's vast hinterlands (Siberia, Turkestan, Persia). Capitalism was welcome and so were the government's measures to promote it:

> One may condemn Russia's protective policy from the point of view of social policy as vigorously as one will, but the system fulfills excellently its historic mission. However, by the time the agricultural population of Russia has been reduced from 80 to 50 or 40 percent, communal land property will have entirely lost any significant sociopolitical function, the natural economy will have declined beyond hope of salvation, and the modern state will have emerged from the twilight in which it still hovers in our patriarchal age (we refer to Russia) into the bright light of the overt class struggle. As for the socialization of production, one will have to look for other forces and factors.
> The regression of consumption and the general deterioration of the population's social condition, objectively speaking, are no argument against the viability of Russian capitalism. But, this aside, we are no doubt witnessing a transitional situation. For, as I have already pointed out earlier in the pages of this journal, "the positive, creative work of the capitalist process of development, as represented by industrial growth and rationalization of agriculture, will in Russia, as everywhere else, outstrip its negative, destructive work (proletarization of the rural inhabitants and the decline of small industry) . . ." Despite the contrary opinion of Mr. Danielson . . . I am no adherent of capitalism in the only conceivable sense of the term, and yet I do believe that *the development of capitalism, that is, economic progress, constitutes the first condition of the improvement of the lot of the Russian population.* When one contrasts *real* capitalism with an *imaginary* economic order that *ought to exist* simply because we *want* it — in other words, when one wants socialization of production without capitalism — then one only gives testimony of a naive, unhistoric outlook.

In addition to this brief polemical review of Danielson's book, Struve wrote a longer and more scholarly one for Braun's the-

oretical journal.[60] Here he called attention to numerous flaws in
Danielson's economic reasoning and attacked his view that the
growth of capitalist industry compelled the peasant to exploit
his land to the point of exhaustion. In Russia, he wrote, capitalism
was primarily a rural, not an urban phenomenon: industrial capitalism was of secondary importance. The roots of the agrarian
crisis had to be sought in the countryside, namely in overpopulation. If anything, Russia suffered from insufficient separation of
industry and agriculture, from too low a degree of division of
functions between city and village. He envisaged the future
development of the Russian economy along the following lines:

> further development of the social division of labor; progress
> in agriculture and, connected with it, the emergence of an
> economically strong peasantry adapted to the money economy;
> proletarization of a significant part of the rural population; a
> shift in the relationship between the agrarian and nonagrarian
> population to the advantage of the latter; growth of cities — in
> short, to use a well-known expression of Friedrich List, that
> herald of continental capitalism, Russia, will increasingly trans-
> form itself from an "agrarian state" into an "agrarian-man-
> ufacturing state." [61]

Danielson's book was the swan song of that sociopolitical orientation in Russia "which had wanted to reconcile the illusions about
the chosen people of social transformation" with the ideas borrowed from Marx and Engels. Rude reality has shattered these
illusions and opened the door to "a deeper penetration of . . .
Marxist teachings and an unprejudiced, scientific . . . objective
analysis of the facts. A different conception will and must break
a path for itself."

Struve's critiques of Danielson, especially those voiced in the
first and more polemical of the two reviews, instantly drew blood.
Before long, a major public controversy developed around the
themes they had raised.

The most shocking aspect of Struve's argument was its eulogy
of capitalism. For a Russian radical to praise capitalism was not

[60] #13.
[61] #13/354.

entirely without precedent. Belinsky, for example, as he lay dying in 1848, having heard the news of the outbreak of the revolution in Paris, wrote to a friend in his characteristically forthright manner:

> When, in our quarrels over the bourgeoisie, I called you a conservative, I was an ass, squared, and you were intelligent. The whole future of France rests in the hands of the bourgeoisie, all progress is entirely dependent on it, and the people here can only play a role of occasional passive helpers . . . It is now clearly evident that the internal process of civic development in Russia will begin no earlier than the minute the Russian gentry turn into a bourgeoisie.[62]

Dmitry Pisarev, disillusioned with socialism, toward the end of his brief life, predicted that capitalism would rationalize Russian agriculture and industry and "provide the best and the only possible school for the [Russian] people." [63] In words very reminiscent of those Struve was to use thirty years later he blamed Russia's backwardness on vestiges of serfdom and excessive dependence on agriculture.[64]

But these were afterthoughts, as it were, not systematic ideas. Struve went far beyond any Russian radical, including Plekhanov and his associates, in assigning capitalism a central place in Russia's political, economic, and cultural life. He was the first among them to regard it as the indispensable precondition of all further progress. In this respect he exceeded even Marx, who for all his willingness to admire the creative role of capitalism was prepared, when the occasion arose, to allow a country like Russia to bypass it.

Second, radical circles were outraged by the casual manner in which Struve dismissed the famine as a regrettable episode on the road to economic progress. Ever since Novikov had a century before organized public assistance to famine victims it had been

[62] V. G. Belinsky, *Polnoe sobranie sochinenii*, XII (Moscow, 1956), 468; letter dated February 15/27, 1848. It was almost the last thing Belinsky wrote before his death. In 1848 another Russian radical, M. V. Butasevich-Petrashevsky, also concluded that Russia required capitalism: L. G. Raisky, *Sotsial'nye vozzreniia Petrashevtsev* (Leningrad, 1927), 54.

[63] D. I. Pisarev, *Sochineniia*, III (St. Petersburg, 1894), 305–306.

[64] V. Kirpotin, *Radikal'nyi raznochinets D. I. Pisarev* (Leningrad, 1929), Chapter six.

an invariable practice of Russian intellectuals to commiserate with and, when possible, to come to the aid of the needy people. The outrage was compounded by incredible but true reports that in some areas struck by the hunger certain self-proclaimed "Marxists" refused to help feed the starving on the grounds that the worse the sufferings from the famine the better it was for the country's economic and social development.[65]

But perhaps the greatest resentment centered on Struve's use of the word "Populism." Shortly before Struve's review appeared, Mikhailovsky had quarreled with Vorontsov, and he was not amused at being told that whatever *he* thought, "objectively" speaking he belonged with opponent. Danielson, who regarded himself as a Marxist par excellence disliked being lumped with the other two. In the earliest response, S. N. Krivenko, an editor of *Russian Wealth,* called Struve's practice of pinning the Populist label on all defenders of the commune and all believers in separate path "indecent." He pointed out that the framers of the Emancipation Edict, certainly no "Populists," had also shown faith in the commune; and as for the separate path theory, it enjoyed the support of Marx himself.[66]

The issue, of course, was not the name alone. It lay in Struve's audacious claim that the then leaders of Russian radicalism were living on borrowed time, and that whatever they thought of themselves, they were in fact reactionaries. The charge exceeded any Plekhanov had dared to make; and the victims of the accusation reacted with understandable rancor.

Among the first to respond to Struve's review was Engels. He had watched the cleavage in Russian radicalism with displeasure, convinced that the tactics employed by the Social Democrats were unwise and dangerous to the Russian revolutionary cause. He no longer believed that Russia could by-pass capitalism; but he deplored the sharp assaults on the old radicals waged in the name of doctrinal purity.[67] On October 17, 1893, he wrote Dan-

---

[65] For example, V. I. Lenin; see my "The Origins of Bolshevism — The Intellectual Evolution of Young Lenin," in Richard Pipes, ed., *Revolutionary Russia* (Cambridge, Mass., 1968), 39.

[66] S. N. Krivenko, "Po povodu kul'turnykh odinochek," RB, No. 12 (December 1893), 184–192. According to N. Angarsky, Struve's review of Danielson first became widely known in Russia through Krivenko's and Danielson's articles: N. Angarsky, *Legal'nyi marksizm,* I (Moscow, 1925), 48.

[67] In view of their intrinsic interest, it is worth citing at some length the recollections of an interview which Voden, a one-time member of Struve's circle, had

ielson a letter which reflected the division existing in his own mind. Informing him that "a certain Mr. P. von Struve" had published in Germany a critique of his book, he went on:

> I must agree with [Struve] on one point: that for me too the contemporary capitalist phase of Russia's development seems an inevitable consequence of the historic conditions brought about by the Crimean War, of that method which had been applied in 1861 to change agrarian relations, and, finally, an inevitable consequence of the general political stagnation of Europe. But Struve is decidedly wrong when, in an effort to refute what he calls your pessimistic view of the future, he compares the contemporary situation in Russia with that of the United States. He says that the ruinous consequences

---

with Engels in London in 1893. Voden wrote: "Engels asked me to inform Plekhanov that he did not approve of the striving to exacerbate the conflict with the revolutionary Populists without there being an extreme need for it; that he (Engels) could not sympathize with the intention of creating in Russia at the earliest possible date an antithesis: here the 'Orthodox Marxists,' there the 'reactionary' mass, differentiated only by shadings. Such a *sharp* line of division was politically inexpedient for the Russia of 1893. I had to say that considerations of this kind were hardly likely to influence Plekhanov and even less the Social Democrats in Russia who found themselves directly provoked by the Populists . . . Engels inquired about Plekhanov's personal attitude to the question of the dictatorship of the proletariat. I had to confess that G. V. Plekhanov had often told me he was convinced that, of course, once 'we' had come to power, 'we' would grant freedom to no one else but 'ourselves' . . . In response to my question of whom one should understand more precisely as enjoying the right to this monopoly of freedom, Plekhanov replied: the working class, led by comrades who correctly understand the teaching of Marx and draw from it the correct conclusions. And in response to the query: what is the objective criterion for judging the correctness of one's understanding of Marx's teaching and of the conclusions flowing from it, G. V. Plekhanov confined himself to saying that all this, 'it seems, has been stated clearly enough' in his works. Having informed himself whether I would be content with such an objective criterion, Engels expressed the surmise that the application of such criteria could either transform Russian Social Democracy into a sect, with its inevitable and highly undesirable consequences, or engender in Russian Social Democracy, or at any rate among Social Democrats abroad, a succession of splits which might prove most disagreeable for Plekhanov himself." Calling Plekhanov a "Russian Hyndman," Engels went on to criticize his manner of waging polemics. He wished Plekhanov and his like would cease the use of "poisoned weapons" and told Voden that he not only "disapproved of treating all Populists as reactionaries, but wanted it to be known that, far from objecting personally to the proposed collaboration of the Avelings [Marx's daughter and son-in-law] with the Petersburg organ of the Populists [*Russian Wealth?*], he himself would collaborate with it if allowed by censorship to do so." In conclusion, Engels told his visitor that he hoped Russia itself would soon produce leaders inside the country capable of directing the movement, "that one could not, in general, lead a political movement from abroad, that he himself personally refrained from interfering in the 'internal affairs' of German Social Democracy." *Voden*, 94–95.

of contemporary capitalism in Russia will be overcome as easily as they have been in the United States. In so saying he completely forgets that the United States is contemporary, that it is bourgeois from its very birth, that it was founded by a petty bourgeoisie and a peasantry which had run away from European feudalism for the purpose of establishing a purely bourgeois society. In Russia, on the other hand, we have a foundation of a primitive communistic character — the tribal community — which antedates the era of civilization. True, this institution disintegrates now into dust, but it does still furnish that foundation, that material, with which the capitalist revolution operates and functions (because for Russia it is a true social revolution).[68]

Capitalism in Russia, Engels continued, would be much harder to bear than it had been in the United States. Nevertheless, Danielson was excessively gloomy: Russia was too great a country to be destroyed. In conclusion, Engels expressed agreement with Struve's main contention, the inevitability of capitalism in Russia.

Later on, when Danielson tried to secure Engels's help in his running controversy with Struve, Engels refused, ostensibly on the grounds that being inadequately informed on Russian conditions he could be misunderstood,[69] but in reality because he no longer agreed with his point of view. He praised Danielson's book and even arranged for its German translation,[70] but he was reverting to the position he had held in the early 1870's when he had denied the possibility of a separate path. Shortly before his death, he complained in a letter to Plekhanov, "It is quite impossible to debate with that generation of Russians to which [Danielson] belongs, a generation which continues to believe in the elemental communistic mission allegedly distinguishing Russia, the real Holy Russia, from the other, infidel nations."[71]

Danielson replied to Struve as well as his other reviewers in a two-part essay published in the spring of 1894 in *Russian Wealth*.[72] In dealing with Struve, he took great pains to show

[68] MERR, 660.
[69] *Ibid.*, 712–713.
[70] *Ibid.*, 695, 726–727.
[71] *Ibid.*, 723.
[72] Nikolai -on [Danielson], "Nechto ob usloviiakh nashego khoziaistvennogo razvitiia," RB, No. 4 (1894), Pt. 2, 1–34, and No. 6 (1894), Pt. 2, 86–130. Struve is discussed in the second installment, pp. 98–129.

that industrial growth could not alleviate Russia's rural over-population. Using statistical evidence, he argued that between 1865 and 1890 the industrial population of Russia had remained stationary, which meant that in terms of relative standing it had declined. His paradoxical conclusion was that in Russia capitalist industrialization diminished the percentage of inhabitants occupied in industry.

The most important response to Struve came from the pen of Mikhailovsky. Even before Struve's review of Danielson appeared, Mikhailovsky had tangled with the Social Democrats, whom he had accused of welcoming the destruction of the country's rural economy. This charge drew a response from a self-styled group of "Marxists" that sent him two letters accusing him of distorting their views. They desired neither the destruction of the rural economy nor the ruin of the peasantry: they were not procapitalist either, they wrote; they merely believed that the intelligentsia was unable to determine the course of economic development and that the remaining vestiges of the serf economy, such as the commune, had to disappear. The general line of argument advanced in these letters came so close to Struve's idiosyncratic brand of Marxism that they may be presumed to have been written either by him or by someone under his immediate influence.[73]

Early in 1894, Mikhailovsky resumed his debate with the Social Democrats in two lengthy articles in *Russian Wealth* in which he took up the issues raised both by his anonymous correspondents and by Struve's review of Danielson.[74] Sidestepping the economic questions, he went right to the philosophic heart of the controversy, the issue of historical inevitability. He gave Marx his due as a great sociologist, but went on to say that he could not accept much that passed for Marxism. There was no justification

[73] These letters were first published in full in 1924: *Byloe*, No. 23 (1924), 99–131. The editors of *Byloe* showed them to Lenin, who thought they had been written by N. D. Fedoseev, a Kazan Social Democrat, but the editors rejected this attribution. The ideas expressed in these letters resemble Struve's in several ways: the denial of the role of the intelligentsia in the process of economic development; the belief that the economic ills of Russia were due to the heritage of serfdom; the rejection of the dialectic; the stress on the need to separate ideals from objective reality. The style, however, does not seem Struve's. My guess is that they were written or dictated by Struve and edited by Potresov.

[74] N. K. Mikhailovsky, "Literatura i zhizn'," RB, No. 1 (January 1894), 88–123, and No. 2 (February 1894), 148–168. Mikhailovsky does not mention Struve by name, but he deals with his arguments.

for the distinction which Struve drew between "genuine Marxism" (his own) and "pseudo-Marxism" (Danielson's) on the grounds of their respective attitudes to the historical process, because Marx had never formulated a consistent theory of history. Marx had formed his historical ideas in the 1840's, before he had a chance to study history: these ideas were conceived "in the womb of the Hegelian metaphysic," not in reflection on the actual record of the past, and were not as consistent as Struve made them out to be. The concept of historical inevitability was so broad as to be useless: it could never satisfactorily explain why an event occurred in one way and not in another. Mikhailovsky restated his belief that individuals indeed influenced history, and at the same time rejected the view that history is an objective process, on which Struve had based his prediction of Russia's economic future.

Mikhailovsky's attack on Struve and other Social Democrats drew counterfire. Among the responses was one written by V. I. Ulianov (Lenin), an unknown young lawyer who had moved from Samara to St. Petersburg a few weeks before the appearance of Struve's review of Danielson. In the spring of 1894 Lenin wrote a book-length manuscript called "Who the 'Friends of the People' Are and How They Wage War on the Social Democrats." The political orientation of this work was not yet clearly defined, and may be said to lie about halfway between the ideology of Blanquism-Jacobinism and Social Democracy. In the course of criticizing Mikhailovsky (the "friend of the people") and the other contributors to *Russian Wealth,* Lenin came to Struve's defense.[75] This essay, reproduced in a minuscule edition by means of a duplicating machine, reached only a handful of readers, and memory of it would have survived only in specialized historical bibliographies were it not for its author's subsequent career.

In the spring of 1894, the split in the radical camp was out in the open. The conflict was not, as is often believed, over the subsidiary question of the peasant commune, but over profounder matters of considerable interest for our time. At issue were basic philosophical and economic questions: Was history an inexorable process, independent of human volition? Did all countries have to follow an identical route of historic development? Was capitalism

---

[75] "Chto takoe 'druz'ia naroda' i kak oni voiuiut protiv sotsial-demokratov?" *Lenin,* I, 53–222, especially 171–172 and 202–216.

in countries that industrialized late possible? desirable? inevitable? Was it likely to help reduce the rural population and raise the country's living standards? Struve, and with him most of the Social Democrats, answered these questions affirmatively and they did so without qualification. Their opponents had in common that they considered these questions open: they rejected historical inevitability in favor of a combination of "objective" and "subjective" factors, and believed in a variety of alternative forms of economic development, some of which they thought more suitable for Russia than others.

The controversy was not one between two hostile groups, one "Populist," the other "Marxist," but rather between two groups with differing conceptions of Marxism, one may say between two factions of Marxists. The older faction, headed by Vorontsov and Danielson, based its predictions on statistical evidence gathered by the zemstva and on Marx's specific pronouncements on Russia. It used Marx's writings to stress the negative functions of capitalism. The other, younger faction, represented by Struve, rested its case on Marx's general theory of capitalist development, as reinforced (or modified) by contemporary Western, mainly German and American, economic experience. It emphasized the affirmative side of Marx's evaluation of capitalism.

The Social Democrats were at first known either as objectivists (because they believed history to be an objective rather than a subjective process), or as Neo-Marxists (to distinguish them from adherents of Danielson's more familiar brand of Marxism). It was Struve and his friends, all youths in their twenties, against the middle-aged veterans of the radical movement of the 1870's. Confident that their hour had struck, the younger group demanded that the others — Mikhailovsky, Vorontsov, Danielson, Krivenko, Iuzhakov — clear the field. In the words of a ditty current at that time:

> The old "friend of the people" has gone his way
> And in his stead, von Struve now holds sway.[76]

[76] D. I. Gorev [Goldman], *Iz partiinogo proshlogo — Vospominaniia, 1895–1905* (Leningrad, 1924), 11–12. The verses are translated in Kindersley, *Russian Revisionists*, 239–241. Struve was in the habit of signing his German publications and correspondence "Peter von Struve" — an affectation his opponents exploited to depict him as a German who was indifferent to the plight of Russian peasants.

5. CRITICAL REMARKS

In the winter of 1893–94, in the wake of the storm which he had raised with his attack on Danielson and the "Populists," Struve wrote a series of articles systematically criticizing the theory of history and economics prevalent among the Russian left. He tried to place these articles in Russian periodicals, but they were rejected,[1] whereupon he decided to expand them into a book and try his luck with official censorship. The chances of securing the imprimatur seemed favorable at this time in view of the fact that late in 1893 the censors had passed a collection of essays by Skvortsov edited by Potresov.[2] Struve intended to follow this monograph, devoted to theoretical questions, with a second one that would trace the historical antecedents of large-scale capitalist production in Russia.[3] This plan accorded with the one which Voden says Struve had outlined to him three years earlier.[4]

Incapable of sustained work, Struve wrote in fits and starts, in a spirit which he himself later described as one of "possessed-ness."[5] "The writing of this book was on my part the fulfillment of some moral (as well as political) command and the realization of some call."[6] Kalmykova confirms in her memoirs that he worked in a "feverish temper"[7] — a statement which may be interpreted literally, since in her correspondence there are suggestions that he was sick.[8] The work was interrupted two times: first when he

[1] #15/viii; "My Contacts and Conflicts with Lenin," SR, XII, No. 36 (April 1934), 582. In #21/15 there is a hint that Mikhailovsky rejected these articles for *Russian Wealth*.

[2] A. I. Skvortsov, *Ekonomicheskie etiudy* (St. Petersburg, 1893). Cf. *Potresov*, 19–20.

[3] #15/274.

[4] See above, pp. 59, 71–72.

[5] "My Contacts and Conflicts with Lenin," 580–581.

[6] *Ibid.*, 581.

[7] A. M. Kalmykova, "Obryvki vospominanii," *Byloe*, No. 1/35 (1926), 66.

[8] Kalmykova to Potresov, undated letter, probably from early 1894.

was arrested and kept in jail for nineteen days on suspicion of belonging to a revolutionary organization,[9] and then again when he took some university examinations as an external student. At the end of June, the manuscript of *Critical Remarks on the Question of Russia's Economic Development* was completed. Before turning it over to the printer, he read parts of it to friends, on whose advice he eliminated some passages considered unnecessarily provocative, including one which praised the government's tariff policy.[10] Then, utterly exhausted, he left St. Petersburg to rest in the countryside.

He was not satisfied with his work. "I have butterflies in my stomach," he wrote Potresov from the country,

> so great are the flaws of my book, formal and other. I now see that you were right in advising me to skip examinations and concentrate on the book. I did not follow your advice, and, apart from *inevitable* flaws, the book bears terrible marks of exhaustion. I appear in it entirely *déshabillé*. Nothing can be done about that now, but it will make itself felt very strongly and *painfully* . . . Sometimes, my unhappiness over the book torments me terribly, literally *to the point of pain,* of complete despair . . .
>
> I now see more and more that the book will be torn to shreds and, in part, deservedly. It has many faults. But if those *to whom it is addressed* take it seriously, then it will have fulfilled its purpose, its faults notwithstanding. The sum total of ideas

[9] On April 19–20/May 1–2, 1894, the St. Petersburg police carried out a raid against students suspected of belonging to organizations of the Narodnaia Volia and Narodnoe Pravo. (The latter, founded by one-time *Narodovoltsy,* was a short-lived liberal party advocating a united antiautocratic front). According to police reports, Struve was believed to be a member of a subversive cell headed by one Maxim Keller; *Obzor,* XVIII (1894), 38. No charges seem to have been lodged against him and he was soon released. See also "My Contacts and Conflicts with Lenin," 581.

[10] "My Contacts and Conflicts with Lenin," 586. Struve had praised high tariffs in one of his German reviews, cited above (p. 92). Iu. O. Martov heard Struve read a chapter of his book in January 1894, during a visit to Potresov in St. Petersburg. His first and lasting impression was negative: "In the discussion that ensued, I formed a none too favorable opinion of the author's attitude. Somehow irrelevantly, with a strange smile, he alluded to the time when 'we made politics,' by which he probably meant the time when he played a leading role in the political movement among the students. But his sour smile and fastidious tone conveyed the impression of that 'practical wisdom' (*umudrennost'*) which usually accompanies an intellectual's rejection of all revolutionary activity." Iu. O. Martov, *Zapiski sotsial-demokrata* (Berlin, 1922), 221.

which it suggests or contains *only* potentially is great, but the development of this sum total of ideas into a useful and rounded sociophilosophic system calls for much time and effort not only of one or two persons but of such a number as to constitute a whole "movement." Either everything that occurs before our eyes is self-deception, or Westernism must enter a new phase of development. The old Westernism is disintegrating, the new one is not yet born. This accounts for the smell of carrion exuded by our progressive literature. . . . The task of interpreting the history of our social life from our point of view — a point of view that in the terminology of subjectivists like Mikhailovsky constitutes also a method — is great, immensely great. A broadly conceived historic study ought to proceed parallel with a publicistic struggle against the liberal-Populist idiocy in Russian literature.[11]

Critical Remarks was submitted to the censor's office at the end of August. Insofar as it took for its target the publicists of the left, and not only refrained from criticizing the government's economic policies but by implication approved of them, the censor found no grounds for turning it down. This was the first but not the last time the Russian Social Democrats were to profit from the fact that the government found useful their divisive tactics against other radical groups. At the beginning of September 1894 the book went on sale.

Critical Remarks bears the earmarks of Struve's intellectual strengths and weaknesses more clearly than any other of his works. The erudition is immense. To make his points, Struve draws on a vast body of economic, statistical, sociological, and philosophical literature, Russian and foreign (especially German), recent and old. This learning not only helps his arguments, but enables him to place the discussion of Russia's economic development on a broader basis than previous writers. He abandons the dichotomy "Russia and the West," fashionable since the 1840's, to treat economic phenomena comparatively, in terms of stages of growth. His book is a pioneering effort, the first serious attempt

[11] Struve to Potresov, letters dated June 22 and July 18, 1894. The examinations to which he refers are those taken by external students: see "My Contacts and Conflicts with Lenin," 581/11.

to interpret the economic development of Russia in the late nine-teenth century in other than national terms. In addition, it abounds in original insights, full of suggestions that Struve worked out more fully in later theoretical and historical writings.

But the lack of organization is exasperating. The exposition follows no apparent plan: discussions of basic economic and sociological questions are buried in the midst of polemical pas-sages; striking hypotheses are casually tossed out to float without supporting evidence; some matters are gone over time and again. The style is extremely sloppy. In sum, it is an important, seminal book, hastily put together, brilliant in content and chaotic in form.

The main purpose of *Critical Remarks* is to demonstrate that the transition to a money economy occurring in Russia is inevitable and progressive. In arguing this thesis, Struve takes issue with almost every accepted view of the country's economy, most of all with the anticapitalist spirit deeply rooted among the Russian left and right alike. Although the book is a Marxist tract, it is so only secondarily: it is first and foremost a treatise extolling the historic mission of capitalism, especially its role in organizing production in the most efficient manner known. Its near counter-part is Friedrich List's *National System of Political Economy* (1841). Struve frequently refers to this work, describing it in one place as "the victory hymn of triumphant commodity produc-tion, proclaiming to all its cultural-historical power and its relent-less advance" [12] — words which with equal justice can be applied to *Critical Remarks*. His book's celebrated closing sentence — "No, let us admit our lack of culture and enroll in the school of capitalism!" — which so intrigued contemporaries, really stands as a logical conclusion to the whole argument.[13] The book is about capitalism, about its creative function and the desirability of

[12] #15/124.

[13] To clear up the confusion which this phrase had caused, Struve explained later that he meant by it three things: that capitalism would educate Russians for a higher form of production which, in turn, would create conditions propitious for cultural progress and prepare them for a "higher economic formation," that is, socialism; that it would inculcate class consciousness, presumably in the working class; and that it would destroy "the phantom of an omnipotent, supraclass in-telligentsia which, in the main, still provides the foundation of the faith in the autochthonous economic development" of Russia (#21/15). The expression "to enroll in the school of capitalism" (*poiti na vyuchku [k] kapitalizmu*) must have been fairly current, for Vorontsov had used it twelve years before Struve without elaborating: V. V[orontsov], *Sud'by kapitalizma v Rossii* (St. Petersburg, 1882), 3.

Russia's experiencing all its effects in preparation for a higher stage of civilized life.

Woven into the analysis of the Russian economy is an exposition of the sociology of Marx, with stress on the relationship between productive forces and social structure. These sections of the book are intended to discredit the "subjective method" and to replace it with "economic materialism" as the only scientifically valid approach to history. But Struve does not accept Marx slavishly. "While adhering in certain fundamental questions to views fully formulated in literature [that is, Marxism]," he informs the reader in the introduction, "[the author] did not consider himself at all bound by the letter or code of any doctrine. He is not infected with orthodoxy, as long as by orthodoxy one does not mean the striving for consistency of thought." [14] True to his word, he criticizes (mainly in brief, casual asides) several basic tenets of Marxism. From the point of view of its place in the history of socialist thought, *Critical Remarks* may be said, therefore, to fulfill two functions: to provide a Marxist critique of the "subjective method" and the whole ideology of historic voluntarism dominant among the Russian intelligentsia in the 1870's and 1880's; and, at the same time, to make a pioneering contribution to European Revisionism.

The book is divided into six chapters, to which are appended statistical tables. Each chapter constitutes a self-contained entity. (This lack of structure may be due to the fact that it was composed of separate journalistic articles.) The only faintly discernible order is that of decreasing abstractness: from philosophy, through sociology, to economics.

The first chapter is devoted to demonstrating the existence of a "Populist" ideology. To compress into this category thinkers who in reality shared only certain negative attitudes, Struve refines the classification, dividing the genus "Populist" into two species, "Westerner" and "Slavophile." In the first, he places Mikhailovsky, Lavrov, and Iuzhakov, who held in common the belief that history is made by individuals. The ideology of this group he defines as "subjective idealism." The other, the Slavophile species, is distinguished by mistrust of the intelligentsia and submission to the communal spirit of the ordinary people. Here Struve places I. Kablits-Iuzov, V. S. Prugavin, and, above

[14] #15/viii–ix.

all, V. Vorontsov. "All these writers share although in varying degrees, the faith in the possibility of Russia's 'autochthonous development.' This faith joins writers of the most diverse make-up, from Mr. Mikhailovsky to Mr. Iuzov into a single movement to which *we assign* the name Populism." [15] Nothing is said about the fact that this faith (as Struve conceded on another occasion) [16] was shared by the majority of professional Russian economists; nor does Struve mention that on such important issues as the role of the intelligentsia in history or the future of small-scale economic productivity the so-called Populists were very much at odds with each other. The division of the Populists into Westerners and Slavophiles proved so unsatisfactory that Struve quietly dropped it in his subsequent writings.

Assuming that he had demonstrated the existence of a coherent "Populist" ideology, Struve undertakes in the second chapter an exposition of its antithesis, the theory of economic materialism. The passages in which this theory is summarized constitute probably the earliest account of the historical philosophy of Marx and Engels legally published in Russia. Except for an occasional polemical aside, the exposition here is lucid and systematic. Unlike subjective idealism, the theory of economic materialism, Struve says, "simply ignores the individual as a sociologically negligible quantity." [17] Men belong to social groups and classes, and cannot be conceived apart from them. Even the intelligentsia, which regards itself as a group apart, can be identified with concrete class interests. Struve takes issue with Mikhailovsky's philosophy of history, which defines progress as the maximum diversification of functions performed by each individual and the minimum diversification of society as a whole. Citing Georg Simmel's *Ueber soziale Differenzierung (On Social Differentiation)*, he argues that individualism is best promoted by a highly diversified social environment. The purpose of this particular argument is to depict the division of labor inherent in capitalism as conducive to the development of human individuality. (This point is restated and developed more fully in the fourth chapter.) Historic evolution does not depend on the aspirations of individuals. The "good" and the "bad" are determined by the objective factors of a given

[15] #15/29. Emphasis added.
[16] #3/415.
[17] #15/30. As noted before, the phrase originated with Herbert Spencer.

historical situation. Even as dreadful an institution as slavery may be progressive under certain conditions: in antiquity, for example, when (as pointed out by Marx) slavery made possible the great classical civilizations.

In this second chapter, Struve makes two major departures from Marx, one philosophical, the other political. Alluding to Mikhailovsky's critique of Marx's philosophy, he concedes "that the purely *philosophic grounding* of this theory has not yet been provided, and that it has not yet managed to cope with that mass of concrete material represented by universal history. Apparently, there is need for a *review of the facts* from the point of view of the new theory; there is need for a *critique of the theory* from the facts." [18] By frequent references here and in other parts of the book to Riehl, Simmel, and other Neo-Kantians, he leaves no doubt whom he considers his principal authorities in questions of philosophy. These remarks, their casual form notwithstanding, have considerable importance in the intellectual history of Russia, for they are harbingers of that Neo-Kantian idealism that was to revolutionize Russian thinking in the first decade of the new century. They also represent the earliest known instance of an effort to link Marx with Kant.

Second, Struve takes an unorthodox position in regard to the state. He defines it as "an organization of order" (*organizatsiia poriadka*) — an organization which *also,* under certain circumstances, *may* become an instrument of class domination. It is indispensable to every social system, from the classless society of primitive communism to the advanced one of postcapitalist communism: "One can conceive that, in a society in which the bases of production and distribution will differ from those prevailing in our own time, the domination of one social group over others will vanish, and the state will cease to function as an organization of [class] domination — and yet, at the same time, remain as an organization of order, of course *preserving its authority to compel.*" [19] In support of his conception of the state as an institution that exists apart and above class relations, Struve cites Lorenz von Stein, whom he credits with having discovered before Marx the "profound truth" that every social system strives to produce

---

[18] #15/46.
[19] #15/53. The belief that the state would survive into the mature socialist era had been voiced several years earlier by Bernstein: NZ, X, Pt. 2 (1891–92), 815.

its own political system.[20] He does not consider this view incompatible with the spirit of Marx's sociology, explaining Marx's hostility to the state partly by his dislike of it in its "bourgeois" form, and partly by the "genetic proximity of Marx's ideas to the *early* views of *Proudhon*." [21]

The third chapter discusses at greater length and more subtly than it had ever been done in Russian polemical literature the concept of capitalism as a historical and economic phenomenon. Struve rejects the antithesis between capitalist and popular (*narodnaia*) production. The real difference between the economic system prevailing in Russia and, for example, that in the United States (in Struve's view, two extremes) is not one of kind but one of degree: the degree of intensity of exchange relations. Some form of commodity exchange exists in all economies, even the most primitive, for although it is possible in theory to conceive of a pure natural economy, such an economy is not known to history. Struve argues that Russian household industry is not and never was a distinct form of industrial production, qualitatively different from large-scale, capitalist industry. It is the same capitalist production working for the market but of a low order of efficiency. (This thesis he was later to amplify in his essays on the history of household manufacture in Russia.)[22] Social inequalities also do not exist exclusively under advanced capitalism: they can be found even where capitalism is rudimentary, for example, in the Russian commune. Rejecting the antithesis capitalism — popular production, Struve interprets the progress of economic development as a continuum: at its lowest extreme the demand for goods is so weak it results in a low level of commodity production and distribution that gives the whole economy the semblance of being noncapitalist and "natural"; at its highest, it becomes "capitalism."

Capitalism is the antithesis neither of popular production nor of the socialist production of the future: it is merely the highest and most efficient form of exchange production. It comes into being when the demand for goods (whether agricultural or manufactured) exceeds productive capacities to such an extent that

[20] #15/53. Elsewhere, Struve defines state policy as the expression of "social resultants," i.e., as the sum of diverse social forces exerting pressure on the state. See also #46/48.

[21] #15/53.

[22] #63 and #72. They are discussed in Chapter 8.

the system of production becomes subordinated to the requirements of exchange. This can be brought about by a variety of causes, among which Struve singles out steam transport and overpopulation. Once the capitalist mode of production takes over, a whole chain of inevitable effects is set in motion: labor becomes specialized and differentiated; technology is vastly improved; inefficient, marginal producers are eliminated — in sum, the economic system becomes rationalized. The immediate and most visible result of this rationalization is an unprecedented increase in material wealth.

Beyond wealth, the rationalization of productivity accomplished by capitalism has very beneficial consequences of a social and cultural nature. Insofar as it can only thrive under conditions of labor mobility, that is, of social freedom, capitalism abolishes the vestiges of serfdom and slavery prevalent in economies with low levels of exchange. It also promotes private property, to which Struve assigns a great cultural role:

At the present time, when the ideas and principles of the eighteenth century are treated so lightly . . . [the] cultural-historical link connecting economic progress with the institution of private property, with the principles of economic freedom and the sense of individualism, is too often forgotten. Only by ignoring this link is it possible to expect that without the realization of these factors an economically and culturally immature society can attain economic progress. We feel no particular sympathy whatever for these principles and we understand perfectly well their historically *transitional* character; but at the same time we cannot fail to see their enormous cultural force, not only negative, but also positive . . . The example of the United States and our own economic reality beautifully demonstrate this dependence. The example [of the United States] is instructive in that in its case we have to do with a society the cultural level of which is, perhaps, the highest in the entire world.[23]

Discussing the eventual transformation of a capitalist society into a socialist one, Struve brushes aside the revolutionary element of Marxist sociology. The progression from capitalism, like that

[23] #15/91–92.

from natural economy to capitalism, must be evolutionary, moving
along a scale of stages, the higher system always beginning where
the lower one stops:

> Certain passages in Marx give grounds for the belief that Marx
> conceived the transition from capitalism to the new social order
> as involving a dramatic collapse, the collapse of capitalism
> under the weight of steadily mounting contradictions. But, at
> the same time, Marx was among the first to point out the socio-
> cultural significance of factory legislation and of the gradual
> economic and political unification of the laboring masses. From
> that time, his followers have unceasingly struggled, and con-
> tinue to struggle, for *reforms* serving the interests of the indus-
> trial proletariat. This policy implies recognition of the fact that
> it is possible, partially and gradually, to improve the condition
> of the working class on the basis of the capitalist system. Social
> reforms represent the links connecting capitalism with the
> order which will replace it, and regardless of the political char-
> acter of that closing ring which will mark the boundary be-
> tween the two socioeconomic forms *historically, one form will
> emerge from the other.*[24]

Such a conception of social change certainly owes more to the
Fabians and Brentano than to Marx and Engels.

Having dealt with production, Struve proceeds in Chapter 4
to distribution. Russian socialists, he says, have always attached
greater importance to distribution than to production, worrying
more about how to achieve a just social repartition of existing
wealth than about how to increase that wealth. Marx proceeded
on the opposite principle. He realized that social progress was
possible only as a consequence of economic progress and that the
latter required a quantum rise in productivity such as capitalist
rationalization alone could assure. Marx's view accorded with
the latest economic opinion. Struve cites Brentano and Schulze-
Gäwernitz to the effect that wealth created by the capitalist mode
of production everywhere leads to amelioration of the condition of
the working class, although he questions their optimistic assump-

---

[24] #15/130–131. The expression "the political character of that closing ring
which will mark the boundary between the two socioeconomic forms" is a classic
example of Aesopian language. Translated, it means: "whether socialism comes
peacefully or by a revolution."

tion that increased productivity automatically produces social improvement. (At one point he refers to Brentano and his school as a "reflection of Marx in bourgeois economic literature" [25] — a phrase Lenin was to borrow and turn against him in his review of *Critical Remarks*.) Increase in productivity, according to Struve, is a necessary but not a sufficient condition of social reform: words meant to convey the need for political action. The beneficent results of high productivity are to be sought neither in the good will of the capitalists nor in the alleged "harmony" of class interests, but in the exigencies of the capitalist mode of production. Referring to the American experience with high wages, he says: "Mass production is compelled to seek support in mass consumption; economic progress demands social reform." [26] Furthermore, capitalist productivity organizes the masses, pulling them into social and economic relations infinitely more complex than those prevailing under a more primitive economic order. Compared to Western workers, on whom the "Populists" lavish such pity, the majority of Russians lead "spontaneous and unconscious" existences. He concludes:

> Distribution, being closely connected with productivity and dependent on it, can progress in the direction of greater equality and the better fulfillment of human needs only by being based on rational productivity. The development of commodity production, flowing from the increase in human requirements, constitutes a necessary condition of further economic and general cultural progress. Only commodity production creates a genuine social or national economy. It lifts the productivity of labor and raises it to a level inconceivable under conditions of natural economy. Capitalism, as the acme of commodity production, socializes not only productivity but also the producer. It also makes man into a genuine social being, connecting individual existence with a thousand threads to the entire social organism.[27]

After a brief fifth chapter devoted to a critique of "Populist" economics and its idealization of the natural economy, Struve

[25] #15/138.
[26] #15/160.
[27] #15/159–160.

proceeds to the final topic, the future of the Russian economy. Here he restates the substance of his German articles. The conditions which had once led Marx and Engels to contemplate the possibility of Russia's by-passing capitalism no longer exist: Russia is in the very midst of a transition from a seminatural, semicapitalist economy to one dominated by full capitalism. This development is unavoidable. Sketching the antecedents of the Emancipation Act of 1861, Struve makes intriguing but unclear connections between the government's fiscal needs, the construction of railroads, and the abolition of serfdom — suggestions which he was later to work out more fully in studies on the history of the serf economy.[28] The real cause of the agrarian crisis is neither land shortage nor the large-scale capitalist industry. "The old expression *land shortage* is merely a colloquial way of describing that which science calls overpopulation." [29] The rural overpopulation of Russia is one of the legacies of serfdom: its symptom is a low level of productivity. Applying the demographic theory of Malthus, he argues that it is possible for the population growth to outstrip productive capacity, leading to a fundamental maladjustment between the economic and social systems. (Struve takes no notice of Marx's loathing for Malthus, whose *Essay on Population* Marx called "a libel on the human race.")[30] Marx, Struve blandly says, supplements Malthus without refuting him.[31] Russia's rural overpopulation can be overcome only by an expansion of capitalist industry. Reverting to the question of markets, he repeats his confident prediction that Russian industry will not lack outlets. He believes that Russia will follow the American rather than the British example, relying less on foreign trade and more on the domestic market.[32] Struve's vision of a Russia deriving its

[28] These were collected in *Krepostnoe khoziaistvo* (St. Petersburg, 1913).

[29] #15/186.

[30] Letter to J. B. Schweitzer: Karl Marx and Friedrich Engels, *Selected Works*, I (Moscow, 1962), 391.

[31] Struve always attached great importance to population growth as a stimulant of economic productivity. His principal work on the subject is an essay in a volume honoring the historian Kliuchevsky: "Problema rosta proizvoditelnykh sil v teorii sotsial'nogo razvitiia," *Sbornik statei posviashchennykh Vasiliiu Osipovichu Kliuchevskomu* (Moscow, 1909), 450–477. In a letter to Danielson dated January 9, 1895, Engels, referring to *Critical Remarks*, wrote that he "did not understand what Struve meant by saying that Marx allegedly *supplements* Malthus's population theory but does not *refute* it," inasmuch as in *Capital* Marx had unequivocally rejected Malthus's ideas": MERR, 715–716. See also #17a/424, #55, and #89/298n.

[32] In one of his reviews of Danielson, Struve gave Vorontsov credit for having

prosperity from a combination of highly paid industrial workers and prosperous independent farmers is closely modeled on the American experience, with which he was well acquainted from his reading.

It was a most idiosyncratic sample of Marxist analysis that the Russian readers received in *Critical Remarks*. The general conception of the operations of capitalist economy and of the manner in which this economy transformed society and its institutions derived from Marx. But Struve rejected so much else that was central to Marxism as a social theory, notably the concepts of pauperization and social revolution, that it is only with the greatest reservations that one can call *Critical Remarks* a Marxist book. Its orientation and spirit placed it somewhere between the right wing of German Social Democracy and Brentano's social liberalism. Struve repeatedly stated that although he regarded Marxism as a brilliant intellectual achievement, for him the ultimate authority in all matters was not doctrine, but empirical evidence and logical consistency. Any theory that contradicted either had to be discarded. That he conceived it possible eventually to renounce all of Marx on these grounds is implied in a passage of *Critical Remarks* that the reviewers overlooked: "Should it even happen some day that the critique of sociological knowledge demonstrates the one-sidedness of Marx's and Engels's historic-economic materialism, this theory will always have to its credit having provided a profoundly scientific, truly *philosophical* explanation of many historic facts of utmost importance." [33] Thus, even while proclaiming the birth of Russian Marxism, Struve acknowledged its mortality.

Critical Remarks was an instant success, far beyond Struve's modest expectations. By September 18, bookdealers had sold 750 copies, and soon they were out of the entire printing of 1,200. [34] Contemporaries agree that its appearance produced a sensation. It gave the Russian public the first more or less authoritative account of the new radical doctrine, which so far they had known

---

demonstrated that the English model of economic development was not applicable to Russia: #13/351.

[33] #15/50.

[34] Struve to Potresov, September 18, 1894. In "My Contacts and Conflicts with Lenin," 582, Struve says that the entire printing was sold in two weeks. Kalmykova ("Obryvki," 66) speaks of two months.

largely by hearsay, and the first analysis of the Russian economy from a Social Democratic point of view.[35] Its readers were not confined to the intelligentsia in the narrow sense of the word, for there was keen interest also in the highest bureaucratic circles. Baroness Uexküll, an aristocratic friend of Kalmykova, told her that Struve's book was "on the desks of all the ministers" and that in "their offices one talked of nothing else." [36] What fascinated these officials was the position taken by Struve in the continuing conflict between agrarian interests, championed by the Ministry of the Interior, and industrial interests, supported by the Ministry of Finance. The dominant school of radical publicists had always favored the policies of the Ministry of the Interior; the thrust of Struve's argument supported its rival. This book was the first indication of a shift in radical opinion, away from obsessive preoccupation with the rural economy toward support of the policies of intensive capitalist industrialization pursued by the Ministry of Finance.

In view of the great interest which the book had aroused, Struve's friends urged him to bring out a second printing. But he refused, saying that, having been hastily written, the book had too many shortcomings, and that in any event it had fulfilled its purpose, which was to stir controversy.[37] The book, therefore, was never reprinted. Nor did Struve ever write the projected second volume on the historic development of Russian capitalism. This was done five years later by Lenin, probably at Struve's instigation.

The reviews of *Critical Remarks* ranged from mildly favorable to highly critical. Nonpartisan critics were well disposed toward it by and large, tending to agree with Struve's conclusions while questioning his methods of proving them. A representative review of this kind appeared in the *Russian Messenger* over the signature of K. Golovin. This critic objected to Struve's arbitrary use of the word "Populist." He also wondered whether the "iron laws of economic determinism" were not in themselves a kind of meta-

[35] See the following testimonies: A. Lunacharsky, *Velikii perevorot* (St. Petersburg, 1913), cited in A. P. Mendel, *Dilemmas of Progress in Tsarist Russia* (Cambridge, Mass., 1961), 291n93, on the "colossal impression" which the book made on students in Kiev; M. Mogiliansky, "V devianostye gody," *Byloe*, No. 23 (1924), 156–157; and S. Mitskevich, *Na grani dvukh epokh* (Moscow, 1937), 184.

[36] Kalmykova, "Obryvki," 66.

[37] *Ibid.*

physical faith, and expressed surprise at Struve's indifference to the political side of Marx's teaching. On the whole he thought that Struve's ideas came closer to Manchester liberalism than to Marxism. He concurred, however, with Struve's assessment of Russia's economic development.[38]

Mikhailovsky, Danielson, and Vorontsov, the main targets of Struve's attack, responded in a fashion customary among Russian radicals, that is, by writing long-winded and acerbic replies which denied their opponent an ounce of either common sense or of decency.[39]

All three rejected Struve's usage of "Populist." "Under this label," Danielson wrote,

> which he treats as a pejorative one, [Struve] includes persons holding the most diverse views. He heaps them into a single pile and then, as the need arises, extracts from it those whom he can use to engage in a greater abuse of Populism. This is one of those "original" peculiarities of Mr. P. von Struve. It is, of course, self-evident that a considerable majority of the authors whom he cites share with Populism only the desire to uncover the causes of the deterioration in the peasantry's condition, and to indicate those remedies which, in the opinion of each, can change it for the better.[40]

Counterattacking, the three made the most of Struve's German ancestry. To Vorontsov, Struve was so ignorant of the Russian

---

[38] K. Golovin, "Dva novykh protivnika obshchiny," RV, CCXXXV (December 1894), 311–329, which also dealt with Skvortsov's *Ekonomicheskie etiudy*. Struve responded in #21/10–14. Golovin later brought out a book which dealt as harshly with the "Populists" as with the Marxists: *Muzhik bez progressa ili progress bez muzhika* (St. Petersburg, 1896). A long and hostile review by L. S[lonimsky] appeared in VE, No. 12 (December 1894), 875–882. J. von Keussler, in *Vierteljahrsschrift für Staats- und Volkswirtschaft*, IV (1896), 320–322, called Struve "obsessed" with Marx.

[39] N. K. Mikhailovsky, "Literatura i zhizn'," RB, No. 10 (October 1894), Pt. 2, 45–77, reprinted in his *Polnoe sobranie sochinenii*, VII (St. Petersburg, 1909), 885–924; Nikolai -on [N. F. Danielson], "Apologiia vlasti deneg kak priznak vremeni," RB, No. 1 (January 1895), Pt. 2, 155–185, and No. 2 (February 1895), Pt. 2, 1–34; Nikolai -on, "Chto-zhe znachit 'ekonomicheskaia neobkhodimost'"?" RB, No. 3 (March 1895), 44–58; V. V[orontsov], "Nemetskii sotsial-demokratizm i russkii burzhuaizm," *Nedelia*, No. 47 (1894), 1504–1508; No. 48 (1894), 1543–1547; and No. 49 (1894), 1587–1593; V. V[orontsov], *Ocherki teoreticheskoi ekonomii* (St. Petersburg, 1895), 208–318.

[40] RB, No. 2 (1895), Pt. 2, 17n. See also Mikhailovsky's objections in RB, No. 10 (1894), Pt. 2, 48. Vorontsov was the only self-styled Populist in the group.

economic literature, that only a "'visiting German' writing for Germans could be forgiven for appearing in print with such acquired equipment." [41] Mikhailovsky, repaying Struve for some sarcastic remarks he had made about his literary style, said that a "foreigner" had no business teaching him Russian — a point he saw fit to enliven with an anecdote about two Russian Germans arguing how to say "I had a haircut."

In the substantive parts of their reviews, Mikhailovsky and Danielson concentrated on what each knew best, philosophy of history and economics, respectively. Mikhailovsky accused Struve of misrepresenting the position of the Russian subjectivists. It was not true that they regarded the individual as the maker of history: they were well aware that man acted within limits set by the objective environment. Marx's assaults on idealism had made excellent sense in Germany in the 1840's, where the Hegelian notion of "being derived from consciousness" was deeply entrenched. But this was not the case in the Russia of the 1890's. To revive the arguments which Marx and Engels had once hurled against the German Hegelians was pointless. Mikhailovsky also questioned the uncompromising separation between science and ethics: without sympathy, knowledge was blind. Alluding to Marx's defense of ancient slavery, which Struve had cited, Mikhailovsky wrote that unless one also took into account the suffering of the slaves who had made classical civilization possible, one's view of the ancient world was bound to be partial and superficial.

Danielson on his part restated his familiar objections to Russian capitalism, and repeated his solution to the crisis: not industrialization but socialization of production, that is, the assumption by the government of control over industry and land for the benefit of society as a whole.

Mikhailovsky, Danielson, and Vorontsov agreed in denying Struve the right to call himself a socialist. As they saw it, he was a bourgeois who concealed his true identity behind the mask of socialism. Danielson explained the emergence of the kind of pseudo-socialism represented by Struve as follows: The famines of 1891–92 had inflicted on Russian capitalism a humiliating defeat by having revealed to all by its destructive effects on the economy. To justify failures of the past and to find an excuse for pursuing similar policies in the future, Russian capitalists now borrowed

[41] Voronstov, *Ocherki teoreticheskoi ekonomii*, 285n,

arguments from socialist literature. Their purpose was to persuade the country that the miseries they were inflicting on it were a necessary precondition to socialism. "Mr. P. von Struve" was really not a Marxist but an "ideologist of the plutocracy." Vorontsov for his part blamed the "bourgeois Marxism" of Struve and Skvortsov (in contrast to the "scientific Marxism" of Danielson) on the relative weakness of the Russian industrial proletariat. This weakness, he explained, enabled the Russian bourgeoisie to appropriate Marxism and pervert it for its own interests. These arguments set the tone for the whole subsequent response of the non-Social Democratic left to Struve and his party — including, as will be seen, that of Lenin.[42]

[42] Among critical appraisals stressing this point was that of I. Gofshtetter, *Doktrinery kapitalizma* (St. Petersburg, 1895), which accused Struve and his party of playing into the hands of the bourgeoisie (p. 11). In March 1895 Gofshtetter delivered a talk in the same vein criticizing Struve and others who "called themselves Marxists": NV, No. 6835 (March 10/22, 1895), 3. Forty years later, Struve agreed with those who had once depicted him as a bourgeois "apologist for capitalism": "My Contacts and Conflicts with Lenin, 581, and "Karl Marks i sud'by marksizma," *Segodnia* (Riga), No. 73 (March 14, 1933). But in the 1930's he wanted to minimize his early radicalism. In 1894 he certainly had not thought of himself in those terms. See the discussion of the split in the Russian Marxist camp between two schools contending for the title of "true" disciples in L. Slonimsky, "Karl' Marks v russkoi literature," VE, August 1897, 765–779, September 1897, 288–307, and October, 745–763.

PART TWO
THE UNITED FRONT

To satisfy one doubt, they give me three; it is the Hydra's head.
— *Montaigne*

6. ENCOUNTER WITH LENIN

In 1895, Marxism in its Social Democratic version suddenly caught on in Russia, and for the next three years it gripped minds and passions as ideas can do only in countries where they are a surrogate for political action. Its sudden popularity was due to a concatenation of several favorable circumstances.

From 1890 onward, Russian industry entered a stage of accelerated growth. All the indices of industrial output leapt upward, shattering the vision of a Russian economy anchored in small peasant holdings and household manufacture. In the decade of the nineties, the production of iron, coal, and petroleum tripled, and the length of the railroad network nearly doubled.[1] This spectacular expansion was achieved not by the popular but by the capitalist sector of the economy, that is, by large enterprises employing hired labor. An indication of the extent to which money (much of it foreign) penetrated the economy at this time can be seen in the statistics indicating that between 1890 and 1900 the capitalization of Russian corporations and partnerships issuing stock increased fivefold.[2] Russia, for better or worse, seemed certain to repeat the experience of England, Belgium, Germany, and the United States. Given these economic realities, with each passing year it appeared less and less realistic to think of Russia pursuing a "separate path." Political movements committed to such old-fashioned slogans, conservative and radical alike, now lost ground to those which posited accelerated industrialization and expanding capitalist productivity — that is, to Social Democracy, and somewhat later, Liberalism.

The growth of large-scale, capitalist industry altered the occupa-

---

[1] P. A. Khromov, *Ekonomicheskoe razvitie Rossii v XIX–XX vekakh (1800–1917)* (n.p., 1950), 456, 458, 459, 462.

[2] *Ibid.*, 463.

tional structure of Russia in favor of the Social Democratic position. Between 1887 and 1897 the number of industrial workers in Russia rose from 1.3 to 2.1 million, or by 59.0 percent.[3] If this rate could be sustained, Russia would have 3.2 million workers by 1907, and 5.0 million by 1917. That tendencies marked over one period of time need not, and, in fact, usually do not, carry into the future rarely disturbs those who look for trends. The Russian radicals were no exception. They saw a trend pointing to a swelling of the ranks of the industrial working class, and a corresponding increase in its influence. This was enough to persuade many of them of the soundness of the Social Democratic program.

And finally, there was the political news from Germany. The reemergence of the German Social Democrats in 1890 as a viable party after twelve years of semilegal existence and constant harassment had been impressive enough. But even more so was their ability to gain victory after victory in national elections: in 1890, 1.4 million votes and 35 seats in the Reichstag; in 1893, 1.8 million votes and 44 seats; and in 1898, 2.1 million votes and 60 seats. Their advance was so irresistible that the conservative Hohenzollerns had no choice but to acquiesce and adopt a policy of social reform (the Caprivi ministry, 1890–1894). The German experience indicated that absolutism was powerless to resist popular demands for political and social reform when these were voiced by the industrial working class organized and led by the Social Democratic party. Such evidence persuaded many Russian radicals of the advantages to be derived from political freedom and helped convert them to Social Democracy.

The ease with which Struve's book had navigated censorship and its success with the public suggested to Potresov that the time had come to attempt a more ambitious publishing effort. He conceived a plan to bring out a series of books that would present an authoritative account of Social Democratic theory and break the monopoly on periodicals enjoyed by the older radicals. Beyond this enlightening mission, Potresov also had in mind a political aim. He envisaged the undertaking as a device that would bring together the scattered Social Democratic forces at home and abroad and fuse them into a nucleus around which, in time, would

[3] A. G. Rashin, *Formirovanie rabochego klassa Rossii* (Moscow, 1958), 24–25.

form a Russian Social Democratic party.[4] In order to reach and
influence the largest possible number of intellectuals, he intended
to operate strictly within the law, by clearing all his publications
with censorship. The method of spreading legally camouflaged
revolutionary propaganda was based on confidence in one's ability
to circumvent censorship by the use of coded or "Aesopian" language. It was modeled on the practices first developed by the
Russian radicals of the 1860's.

The literary movement which Potresov conceived, organized,
and financed, and which Struve furnished with intellectual leadership, is ordinarily known as "Legal Marxism." The term would be
unobjectionable were it used in a precise sense for one of the
several techniques which Russian Social Democrats employed between 1894 and 1899 to spread their views. The books and periodicals which Potresov and Struve brought out during these five years
can be properly labeled "legal" in the sense that they were issued
with the censor's imprimatur. But unfortunately, as is the case with
many other terms relating to the history of the Russian revolution,
"Legal Marxism" has been long ago perverted for polemical purposes by being assigned political content. A good example of
such improper usage can be found in a standard Soviet reference
work, where "Legal Marxism" is defined as an "ideological-political
movement of the Russian bourgeois intelligentsia" espousing a
program, originally formulated by Struve in *Critical Remarks*, that
rejected class war and revolution, denied economic materialism,
and extolled capitalism.[5] In a variety of forms, this definition has
found its way into works written in the West.[6]

Now while it is true that Struve himself espoused an evolutionary, liberal brand of Social Democracy, and extolled the historical mission of capitalism, it is not true that his ideas created a
movement, for he had virtually no intellectual following (though
he had a personal one). There was at no time a "Legal Marxist"
tendency or faction, and no trace of either can be found in documents originating in the 1890's; there was only a "legal" propa-

---

[4] *Potresov*, 20–23; N. Angarsky, *Legal'nyi Marksizm*, I (Moscow, 1925), 135–
137.
[5] *Sovetskaia istoricheskaia entsiklopediia*, VIII (Moscow, 1965), 519–521.
[6] A happy exception in this, as in many other respects, is Leonard Schapiro's
Communist Party of the Soviet Union (London, 1960), where such usage is
called "inappropriate" (p. 14).

ganda technique. This technique was employed by all prominent Russian Social Democratic theorists, the majority of them dedicated revolutionaries, economic materialists, and foes of capitalism. Among them was Lenin: until the launching of *Iskra* in 1900–1901, he published nearly all his writings in books and journals cleared by the censors, most of them edited by Struve.

Like "Populism," the term "Legal Marxism" goes back to factional struggles in the radical movement, the latter having been coined by Lenin in the polemic against Struve. Its earliest usage goes back to the years 1900–1901, when Lenin, disenchanted with one-time friends and allies, decided to break with them.[7] Ashamed of having collaborated with those whom he now came to despise, he retrospectively divided the Social Democratic movement of the 1890's into two hostile factions: a "revolutionary" one, best represented by himself, and a "legal" one, represented by his archenemy, Struve. The more he viewed himself as the only genuine revolutionary, the more prone Lenin was to project the conflict between "true" and "false" revolutionaries into the past and to assign the term he had coined a precise ideological meaning. After 1917 the usage, derived from his writings, passed into the standard Soviet vocabulary. Potresov on one occasion tried to discourage it: in a letter sent to the editors of the Soviet historical journal *Red Chronicle* in 1925, he wrote that Lenin had incorrectly used the term because "there was no group of 'Legal Marxists.'"[8] But his corrective was not heeded then and has not been since.

An unfortunate consequence of the belief in the existence of a "Legal Marxist" movement is a widespread misconception of what happened between 1894 and 1899: and that was not a division of Russian Social Democracy into two camps, "revolutionary" and "legal," but a joining of Russian Social Democrats of all persuasions into a united front.

As soon as *Critical Remarks* came off the press, Potresov left for Switzerland to deliver a copy to Plekhanov, with whom he had been in contact since 1892. In Geneva he learned that Plekhanov had gone to London, so he followed him there. Displaying tri-

---

[7] The subject is discussed more fully in my *Social Democracy and the St. Petersburg Labor Movement, 1885–1897* (Cambridge, Mass., 1963), 74n–75n.
[8] KL, No. 2/13 (1925), 146–147.

umphantly the first Social Democratic book legally published in Russia, he invited Plekhanov to join in his projected publishing venture. Plekhanov, however, hesitated, for he had serious doubts about the feasibility of conducting genuine Social Democratic propaganda with the censor's imprimatur. The sample that Potresov had brought did nothing to dispel these doubts: Plekhanov's ultra-orthodox antennae were quick to detect the heresies perpetrated by Struve. He was cross and negative: if *Critical Remarks* was any indication of what Potresov had in mind, he wanted no part in it. But Potresov kept on arguing, and in the end he persuaded him. Plekhanov gave him three manuscripts for publication: a book-length treatise criticizing Mikhailovsky's philosophy of history, called "In Defense of Materialism," and two shorter essays. For the sake of maintaining a united front against the "Populists," he also agreed to refrain from voicing publicly any criticism of Struve's book.[9] He was true to his word; the few opinions about *Critical Remarks* which he subsequently made in print may be described as moderately friendly.[10]

Potresov returned to St. Petersburg in mid-October 1894, and proceeded to make arrangements for the publication of Plekhanov's book. It, too, cleared the censors without difficulty, and came out in December bearing a less provocative title, *On the Question of the Monistic View of History*.[11] A lucid, well-organized exposition of Marxist philosophy of history, it gave Russian readers a much better idea of "historical materialism" than Struve's book had done. It was the first of Plekhanov's works to circulate widely in Russia and make his views known — though as yet not his name, since the identity of the author was concealed behind the pseudonym Beltov.

Plekhanov's book provided the occasion for Struve's first meeting with Lenin. The encounter, which began a relationship of consid-

---

[9] Angarsky, *Legal'nyi Marksizm*, 68, 70. See below (p. 257) Plekhanov's complaints in 1900 that five years earlier he had been told, presumably by Lenin and Potresov, "not to shoot at Struve."

[10] E.g., G. V. Plekhanov, *Sochineniia*, VII (Moscow, 1925), 268–288 and 314–318. Plekhanov justified Struve's "incautious" statements eulogizing capitalism on the ground that they arose from the "noble passion of a Westerner" and compared them to Belinsky's statement of 1848, cited above (p. 94).

[11] Beltov [G. V. Plekhanov], *K voprosu o razvitii monisticheskogo vzgliada na istoriiu* (St. Petersburg, 1895).

erable importance to both men, occurred either in December 1894 or January 1895 at an informal gathering assembled to discuss the *Monistic View*.[12]

Struve and Lenin came from vastly different social and cultural backgrounds. Both were born in families of civil servants, but whereas Struve's father belonged to its very uppermost stratum, and his uncles held high diplomatic and educational posts, Lenin's father had been a run-of-the-mill provincial official. Struve grew up in a highly cultivated milieu: at home, at Kalmykova's, in Arseniev's salon, he had rubbed shoulders with the country's foremost writers and artists. He had been raised partly abroad and partly in St. Petersburg, Russia's most Europeanized city, and spoke fluent German. Lenin lacked such cultural advantages. His knowledge of literature, philosophy, or art was and remained throughout his life rudimentary. His attitude toward knowledge unrelated to revolutionary action was that of a typical radical intelligent of the 1870's and 1880's, that is, contemptuous. He went abroad for the first time at the age of twenty-five, and then he not only found everything new and strange, but realized to his dismay that he understood not a word of spoken German.[13] The two men embodied, as it were, two strains in nineteenth-century Russian culture: the cosmopolitan culture of the metropolis and its service aristocracy, and the narrower culture of the provincial middle class. How the representatives of the latter group looked at the former may be gathered from the testimony of two of Lenin's friends of that era, L. B. Krasin and M. A. Silvin, who came from backgrounds similar to his:

As provincials, we were, of course, incomparably less educated, and even plainly ignorant, compared to such representatives of St. Petersburg University youth as N. V. Vodovozov, P. B. Struve, N. D. Sokolov, the brothers Gerd, V. V. Bartenev, and many others. Many members of that group had not only studied systematically the social sciences and history, but also knew foreign languages and read in the original books, which either

---

[12] The meeting took place in R. E. Klasson's apartment. Klasson's brief recollections appeared in KL, No. 2/13 (1925), 144–145. Struve says the meeting occurred in the "autumn or winter" of 1894: "My Contacts and Conflicts with Lenin," SR, XII, No. 36 (April 1934), 590. Potresov dates it December 1894 or January 1895: KL, No. 2/13 (1925), 146.

[13] V. I. Lenin, *Pis'ma k rodnym* (Moscow, 1934), p. 58.

were not available in Russian translation or which were prohibited by contemporary censorship. We, on the other hand, had come from dark Siberia, where, apart from the "fat" journals, there was no literature.[14]

Our theoretical preparation as Marxists was weak. We worked hard, read, but mostly unsystematically, haphazardly, in response to questions which happened to arise in our minds. . . . It must be added also that Marxist literature of that time was not rich, at any rate in Russian; as for foreign languages, we knew them poorly. I heard . . . that there were in St. Petersburg educated Marxists: the names of Struve, Klasson, Potresov were mentioned, but it was said that they kept to themselves as a kind of spiritual aristocracy estranged from revolutionary circles; that they worked a great deal theoretically, knew foreign languages well, and even published in German journals. I formed a prejudiced ill-feeling against this company — Russian Marxists unwilling to write for Russians! I made no attempt to approach these people, being embarrassed to face them with my meager theoretical equipment.[15]

The different social and cultural backgrounds influenced the political outlooks of Lenin and Struve as much as did their different temperaments. At the time they met, they both believed themselves to be "Marxists" and both assumed Russia would and should go through capitalism. But they understood "capitalism" to mean quite different things. To Struve it meant an intricate network of institutions and habits, many of them not economic at all, which commodity production fostered and which in turn created an environment favorable to it, such as existed in Germany and the United States. It meant wealth, freedom, and culture, in contrast to an agrarian economy which had to be, by its very nature, poor and backward.[16] Lenin — at any rate until his first foreign

---

[14] M. N. Liadov and S. N. Pozner, ed., *Leonid Borisovich Krasin* (Moscow and Leningrad, 1928), 95–96. Krasin refers here to himself and his brother Herman. They belonged to the circle of worker propagandists recruited in the Technological Institute which Lenin joined in 1893 on his arrival in St. Petersburg.

[15] M. A. Silvin, *Lenin v period zarozhdeniia partii* (Lenin, 1958), 37–38. Silvin, too, belonged to the circle of Technologists.

[16] In an encyclopedia article on the agrarian state in 1894, Struve described a society in which agrarian pursuits predominate as necessarily backward and poor (#17a/425).

trip in 1895 — knew capitalism largely from Russian radical literature. Like Vorontsov and Danielson, he saw it as a purely destructive force and a particularly vicious mode of exploitation. How
little notion he had of its true dimensions may be gathered from
the fact that in 1892–1894 he believed Russia was already fully
in the grip of the capitalist economy[17] — Russia, a country in
which 87 percent of the population belonged to the peasantry! He
was in a great hurry to overcome this capitalism and make revolution, not only because he was by temperament a man of action but
also because he had no idea of the complicated social and cultural
environment which a mature industrial civilization requires. This
he realized only many years later as dictator of Russia, when he
found his ambitious plans for the country's reorganization wrecked
by what he had sadly to concede then was its lack of "culture."[18]

Lenin became a revolutionary rather late in life and then more
by accident than by design. In school he was a model student —
obedient and conscientious in all respects. Unlike his elder brother
and sister, both of whom were involved with the People's Will,
he carefully steered clear of all politics. At the University of Kazan,
which he had entered in the fall of 1887, he was approached by
members of a local People's Will cell, who had recognized him as
the brother of a recently executed terrorist. He apparently joined
their organization, but before he could get into deeper trouble,
the university expelled him for participating in a student riot.
Even though the misdemeanor was of a minor disciplinary (rather
than political) nature, Lenin was not permitted to reenter this or
any other university, his requests for readmission being turned
down by the police, who liked neither his family's political record
nor the information about his university associates which came to
their attention.

For the next four years (1888–1891) Lenin lived in complete
idleness, from his mother's pension and income from her estate. His
resentment toward the political system and society which punished him so cruelly and apparently closed to him forever the possibility of any career grew into an obsessive hatred. During these

---

[17] The evidence concerning Lenin's early development on the pages which follow
is provided in my *Social Democracy* and in "The Origins of Bolshevism: The Intellectual Evolution of Young Lenin," in Richard Pipes, ed., *Revolutionary Russia*
(Cambridge, Mass., 1968), 33–66.
[18] See, for example, his bitter remarks about the "semi-Asiatic Russian lack of
culture" (*beskul'turnost'*): *Lenin PSS*, XLV, 364; also *ibid.*, 390.

years he steeped himself in radical literature and became a revolutionary. His revolutionary passion, however, had as its root less the vision of a better world than the thirst for vengeance. Lenin wanted to destroy, and committed all the energy which he had previously put into his studies to finding an effective revolutionary strategy.

In his political views during these years (1887–1892) Lenin adhered to the ideology of the People's Will. He believed in the feasibility of a coup d'état that would topple the imperial government and bring to power a socialist dictatorship. He thought Russia could by-pass capitalism as experienced by the West and build socialism on existing rural foundations. He treated the "exploiters" — landowners, bourgeoisie, and bureaucrats alike — as a compact, undifferentiated mass, the "enemy." During these four years he associated with clandestine revolutionary organizations of the People's Will, displaying a particular affinity for that party's most radical, Jacobin wing. There is no indication that he had any connection with the Social Democratic study groups that sprang up around 1890 in the Volga region, where he lived with his family. In 1889, he read Marx's *Capital,* but he did so as part of his socialist revolutionary education, that is, primarily to obtain evidence against capitalism. He shared none of Marx's admiration for capitalism's historic accomplishment. He hated it in all its forms and manifestations: the bourgeoisie, liberalism, parliamentary democracy, plurality of parties, and social reforms. All this was part of "their" world, the world of the enemy which had to be destroyed.

The theoretical premise on which Lenin's radicalism had rested was shaken by the famines of 1891–92. Like many of his contemporaries, Lenin suddenly realized that all was not well in the village, that the economic and social foundations on which the new system was to have been built were crumbling. As soon as he had passed the external examinations for the law degree, to which he had been at last admitted in November 1891, he undertook a systematic analysis of the voluminous statistical material on the rural economy compiled by zemstvo boards. It did not take him long to conclude from this evidence that the Russian peasantry had lost its social homogeneity and become differentiated into three classes, of which the uppermost, that of kulaks, constituted a rural "bourgeoisie," and the lowest, a landless "proletariat." The expropriation of the agricultural producer was proceeding apace,

throwing an increasing number of peasants into the labor reserve
and transferring control of the Russian countryside to a peasant
middle class. In reaching these conclusions Lenin was particularly
influenced by the work of the statistician V. E. Postnikov, which
indicated that in some southern provinces as much as one-fifth of
the peasantry hired workers to help till their land.

Impressed by such evidence, around 1892–93 he broke with the
People's Will and became a "Marxist." But it was a curious kind
of Marxism that he adopted. Like Danielson, Vorontsov, and the
other pre–Social Democratic Marxists in Russia, he believed that
capitalism in Russia was wholly destructive, that it had undermined beyond recovery the old economic system based on peasant
self-sufficiency, and that the only solution lay in nationalization
of the means of production. But unlike them, he did not believe
that the nationalization could be accomplished by the imperial
regime. Russia was ready for a socialist revolution, to be achieved
by terrorism and a coup d'état. In reading Marx, he was most profoundly impressed by the notion that all ideas stood for concrete
economic interests. He explained to himself the political opportunism of the proponents of separate path by the fact that they
represented the interests of the small rural producer. For this
reason he was against the Danielsons and Vorontsovs, who sought
compromise with the autocracy. But he was also hostile to Social
Democracy: he rejected political liberty, a constitution, and parliament, and saw no advantages to be derived from an alliance
with the "progressive bourgeoisie," which he viewed as firmly tied
to the autocratic regime.

In St. Petersburg, where he had settled in the autumn of 1893,
ostensibly to practice law but in fact to engage in subversive
activity, Lenin joined a circle formed by students and recent
graduates of the Technological Institute to bring socialist propaganda to workers. This circle, like many others of its kind, supplied tutors and literature to autodidactic groups formed by the
skilled workers so as to awaken in them a sense of class consciousness. Lenin had little confidence in such activity, which seemed
to him to breed only an inactive labor intelligentsia, and he participated in it rarely and without great enthusiasm. His own interests at this time were mainly literary. He followed with keen
interest the controversy between the Social Democrats and the
contributors to *Russian Wealth,* which had broken out shortly

after his arrival in St. Petersburg. In 1894, as has been noted, he wrote a long essay criticizing Mikhailovsky and his collaborators. In the controversy, while in general siding with Struve and his point of view, he took a somewhat independent position, for he disliked in both parties their liberalism and renunciation of revolutionary methods.

When introduced to Struve, Lenin had already gone through *Critical Remarks* with his customary thoroughness and had even written a lengthy review.[19] It was agreed that he would present a summary of it to a small gathering of his and Struve's friends. Subsequently, he also held numerous private meetings with Struve in which he read to him its full text and discussed topics of common interest.[20]

Unfortunately, the original version of Lenin's critique of Struve has not survived, and our knowledge of it derives solely from recollections of N. Valentinov, to whom Struve described it in 1918, nearly a quarter of a century later.[21] In this first version, Lenin seems to have objected mainly to Struve's timetable of Russia's capitalist development. "Lenin indicated that capitalism had already conquered the country," Struve recalled, "and that I had failed adequately to appreciate that fact by depicting capitalism not as a factor already manifest in all its vigor but as something lying in the future." [22] To Social Democrats, the capitalist timetable was of course of critical importance for their political strategy: on it depended whether one joined the "liberal bourgeoisie" against the autocracy or fought it in the name of socialism. Struve carried away the impression that at the time of their en-

---

[19] Lenin's original draft is said to have been called "The Reflection of Marxism in Bourgeois Literature." The only evidence for this title is Lenin's own statement made many years later (*Za 12 let — Sbornik Statei*, St. Petersburg, 1908; cf. *Lenin*, I, 499, and *Lenin*, IV, 374n). As noted, the phrase was taken from Struve's book (#15/138). If the original draft indeed bore that title, it is indicative of Lenin's sympathy for Danielson and Vorontsov, who also regarded Struve's socialism as "bourgeois."

[20] "My Contacts and Conflicts with Lenin," SR (April 1934), 591. Struve says the original version was briefer than the printed one. Lenin repressed in his memory these private meetings, as he did much else involving his relations with Struve, and recalled only meeting Struve in the company of others: *Lenin*, XII, 59. Struve says that in 1895–96 he and Lenin "passed innumerable evenings together discussing economic and political questions": "Le Bolchévisme et Lénine," in M. G. Klutchnikoff, ed., *La Russie d'aujourd'hui et de domain* (Paris, 1920), 124.

[21] N. Valentinov, "Iz proshlogo: P. B. Struve o Lenine," SoV, No. 8–9/673–674 (1954), 169–172.

[22] *Ibid.*, 171.

counter Lenin in his heart believed in the possibility of separate path, and that that was the reason he was so insistent on Russia's already being capitalistic.[23] Potresov had similar impressions. He was unfavorably struck by Lenin's "one-sided, insistently simplified" approach to the complexities of life, and by his tendency to regard "the emergent capitalist society as a homogeneous reactionary mass." [24] Struve, however, was not overly distressed by Lenin's views, being certain they would change as soon as Lenin had an opportunity to see with his own eyes what Western European capitalism really was like.[25]

Struve left extensive recollections of Lenin. They are undoubtedly very much colored by the loathing he felt toward him at the time of writing (1933–34) and must be read with caution. They nevertheless deserve citation because they furnish the most complete picture of Lenin in his youth drawn by someone intimately acquainted with him at that time but outside his immediate family:

. . . The impression which Lenin at once made on me — and which remained with me all my life — was an unpleasant one.

It was not his brusqueness that was unpleasant. There was something more than an ordinary brusqueness, a kind of mockery, partly deliberate and partly irresistibly organic, breaking through from the inmost depths of his being, in Lenin's way of dealing with those on whom he looked as his adversaries. And in myself he sensed at once an adversary, even though then I stood still fairly near to him. In this he was guided not by reason, but by intuition, by what hunting people call "flair."

[23] *Ibid.* In memoirs written sixteen years after his 1918 talks with Valentinov (who had virtually total recall), Struve contradicts Valentinov's account by saying that "until his very advent to power, Lenin held a jump from 'Capitalism' to 'Socialism' to be utterly impossible": "My Contacts and Conflicts with Lenin," SR, XIII, No. 37 (July 1934), 71. But Struve supports this assertion with citations from Lenin's works from 1905–1911, rather than from the 1890's. In 1895 Lenin characterized as "nonsense" the proposition that all countries have to go through capitalism: *Lenin,* I, 262.

[24] *Potresov,* 23. Elsewhere, Potresov wrote of Lenin's 1895 critique of Struve that "behind the Marxist mode of expression one could detect the traditional view of capitalist society as a reactionary mass, an attitude characteristic of the underpinning of all revolutionary-utopian movements": A. N. Potresov, "Lenin — Versuch einer Charakteriesierung," *Die Gesellschaft,* No. 11 (1927), 407.

[25] Valentinov, "Struve o Lenine," 171.

Later on I had much to do with Plekhanov. He, too, had a brusqueness verging on mockery in dealing with people whom he wanted to strike or to humble. Yet, compared with Lenin, Plekhanov was an aristocrat. The way in which they both treated other people could be described by the untranslatable French expression *"cassant."* But in Lenin's *"cassant"* there was something intolerably plebeian and at the same time something lifeless and repulsively cold.

A great number of people shared with me that impression of Lenin. I shall mention only two of them, and very different they were: Vera Zasulich and Michael Tugan-Baranovsky. Vera Zasulich, the cleverest and subtlest of all the women I have ever met in my life, felt an antipathy for Lenin verging on physical aversion — their subsequent political quarrel was due not only to theoretical or tactical differences, but to the profound dissimilarity of their natures.

Michael Tugan-Baranovsky, with whom for many years I was on very close terms, used to tell me with his wonted *naïveté* for which many people unjustly thought he was simply stupid, about his irresistible antipathy for Lenin. Having known, and even been on close terms with Lenin's brother, Alexander Ulianov . . . he used to point out, with amazement which verged on horror, what a different man Alexander Ulianov had been from his brother Vladimir. The former, with all his moral purity and firmness, was an extremely gentle and tactful man, even dealing with strangers and enemies, while the latter's brusqueness really amounted to cruelty.

Truly, in his attitude to his fellow-men Lenin breathed coldness, contempt and cruelty. To me it was clear even then that in those unpleasant, even repulsive, qualities of Lenin, lay also the pledge of his power as a politician: he always had in view nothing but his objective towards which he marched, firm and unflinching. Or rather, there always was, before his mental eyes, not one objective, more or less distant, but a whole system, a whole chain of them. *The first link in that chain was power in the narrow circle of his political friends.* Lenin's brusqueness and cruelty — this became clear to me almost from the outset, from our first meeting — was psychologically indissolubly bound up, both instinctively and deliberately, with his indomitable love of power. In such cases it is, as a rule, difficult to determine which is at the service of which, whether the love of power is at the service of an objective task or a higher ideal that a man has set up for himself, or on the contrary, that task or that ideal are mere means of quenching the insatiable thirst for power.

I have just described the most striking feature in Lenin which was revealed to me from the very first time I met him. It was cruelty in that most general philosophical sense in which it can be opposed to gentleness and tolerance for men and for everything human, even when it is inconvenient and unpleasant or even repulsive to us personally. Lenin was absolutely devoid of any spirit of compromise in that Anglo-Saxon moral or social sense, such a striking expression of which is to be found in John Morley's famous treatise *On Compromise*. . . .

In accordance with this dominant feature in Lenin's character, I at once perceived that his principal *Einstellung* — to use the now popular German psychological term — was hatred.

Lenin took to Marx's doctrine primarily because it found response in that principal *Einstellung* of his mind. The doctrine of the class war, relentless and thoroughgoing, aiming at the final destruction and extermination of the enemy, proved congenial to Lenin's emotional attitude to surrounding reality. He hated not only the existing autocracy (the Tsar) and the bureaucracy, not only the lawlessness and arbitrary rule of police, but also their antipodes — the "Liberals" and the "bourgeoisie." That hatred had something repulsive and terrible in it; for being rooted in the concrete, I should even say animal, emotions and repulsions, it was at the same time abstract and cold like Lenin's whole being. Once, in the late nineties, Potresov was talking to me about Lenin and drew my attention to the enormous self-discipline which that man, full of cruelty and pervaded with hatred, showed in some trivial things of everyday life. "Out of asceticism he will refuse an extra glass of beer," said Potresov then. And I thought there and then, and somehow expressed it, I think, to Potresov, that it was precisely this that was terrible. The terrible thing in Lenin was that combination in one person of actual self-castigation, which is the essence of all real asceticism, with the castigation of other people as expressed in abstract social hatred and cold political cruelty.[26]

Lenin left no comparable description of Struve (or, for that matter, of any other friend or political associate). Still, even without positive evidence, it seems certain that he promptly realized Struve's total unfitness for any revolutionary work. Well endowed with what Etienne Leroux called "the ability to penetrate the worst side of human nature," he must not have taken long to see a fundamental contradiction between Struve's talk and his behavior. Struve had the moral sensitivity of the typical Russian intellectual, a sensitivity that vitiated his intellectual acquiescence to violence and suffering. Struve was aware of that quality: he once confessed to Potresov that the sight of human suffering drained him of all capacity to act.[27] He bandied about clichés like "class struggle" and "survival of the fittest," praised the progressive function of ancient slavery, welcomed the "service" performed for modern Russia by the famines. But this was in the abstract only. He could not have calmly witnessed any of these things, let alone abetted them. For Lenin, friendship with a man like Struve was entirely out of the question: he was too soft, too intellectual, too "professorial"; he had too many qualms.

But not an alliance. Lenin, even then, was consumed with political ambition, the fulfillment of which required him to keep personal feelings under tight rein. A lawyer without a practice (incidentally, still continuing to live off his mother at the age of twenty-five), a would-be writer with not one printed word to his

---

[26] "My Contacts and Conflicts with Lenin," April 1934, 591–593. Struve's impressions of Lenin bear a striking resemblance to Madame de Staël's impressions, formed a century earlier, of another dictator on the make: "I had a confused feeling that no emotion of the heart could act upon him," she wrote of her first encounter with the young Napoleon. "He regards a human being as an action or a thing, not as a fellow creature. He does not hate more than he loves: for him nothing exists but himself; all other creatures are ciphers. The force of his will consists in the impossibility of disturbing the calculations of his egoism. He is an able chessplayer, and the human race is an opponent to whom he proposes to give check-mate. His successes depend as much on the qualities in which he is deficient as on the talents he possesses. Neither pity nor allurement, nor religion, nor attachment to any idea whatsoever could turn him aside from his principal direction . . . His discourse indicated a fine perception of circumstances, such as a sportsman has of the game he pursues . . . Yet nothing could triumph over my invincible aversion for what I perceived in him. I felt in his soul a cold sharp-edged sword, which froze the wound that it inflicted." *Considerations on the Principal Events of the French Revolution* (London, 1818), Pt. III, Chap. 26, 197–199.

[27] See below, p. 173.

name, a revolutionary leader with a following of a dozen part-time tutors, he had to form "alliances" even with persons and parties he did not like because this was the only way of obtaining a power base of some kind. Such activity occupied a great deal of his time. One day he would sign a contract with a People's Will organization for the use of their clandestine printing press; another, he would negotiate with Martov for the merger of their respective minuscule organization; a third, he would try to formalize relations between the Social Democratic intelligentsia and the workers in charge of mutual aid funds. He treated Struve as merely another link in what Struve called his "chain of power." Having concluded some time earlier that Mikhailovsky, Vorontsov, Danielson, and other publicists of the "Populist" camp (usage he had promptly adopted from Struve) represented the interests of the small agrarian and industrial producer (the "petty bourgeoisie"), he decided they were class enemies who had to be mercilessly fought. In this struggle Struve could prove of great value. Whatever his attitude toward revolution, he was sincerely and passionately opposed to the "Populists" and could be a useful ally in the campaign against them. Lenin very much wanted Struve to devote himself fully to the task of "unmasking" the "Populists," and he was heard to complain that Struve wasted his time at the university on "scholasticism." [28] The key word in Lenin's relationship to Struve during the five years when they collaborated closely (1895–1900), was "use." The uncontrollable rage with which Lenin turned against Struve in 1900–1901 was due to his sudden conviction that instead of being the manipulator he himself had been the object of manipulation.

To Struve, his association with Lenin was also a utilitarian political arrangement, even if devoid of the manipulative quality that always loomed so large in Lenin's personal relations. He was interested in abolishing autocracy and replacing it with a liberal government. To attain this end, he favored the broadest coalition of groups and parties interested in political freedom. He repressed within himself an instinctive aversion for Lenin because he saw his great political gifts and single-minded devotion to the political struggle. As he recalled later, he "used to drive away" his hos-

---

[28] M. A. Silvin, "V. I. Lenin v epokhu zarozhdeniia partii," KS, No. 1 (1934), 82–83. This hostility to scholarship is another bit of evidence of Lenin's closeness to the traditions of the People's Will as late as the spring of 1895.

tile thoughts and images of Lenin, as "mental checks and complications to the intercourse, which, for the sake of its potential political utility, I regarded both as morally obligatory for myself and
politically indispensable for our cause." [29]

In the winter of 1894–95, at the time of Lenin's encounter with
Struve, Potresov was preparing another Social Democratic volume,
a symposium built around the two essays which Plekhanov had
given him in London. He invited Lenin to submit to it his review
of *Critical Remarks*, but in a revised form from which particularly
offensive passages (and, possibly, some he regarded as un-Marxist)
had been removed. Lenin hesitated, for, eager as he was to make
a literary debut, he was loath to give in on matters of principle. He
was also subject to pressures from members of his circle, activists
with little grounding in theory and therefore considerably suspicious of it, who preferred not to become too closely involved with
the university intellectuals.[30] On Potresov's urging, he agreed in
the end to submit the issue to the arbitration of N. E. Fedoseev, a
Kazan Social Democrat whose judgment he valued highly; and he
complied when Fedoseev advised him to make the requested
changes.[31] The review appeared in the symposium in a revised and
expanded version called "The Economic Content of Populism
and Its Critique in Mr. Struve's Book." [32]

There exists a widespread impression that in this, his first
printed work, Lenin excoriated *Critical Remarks* as an un-
"Marxist" book.[33] This, however, was not the case, as can be readily
ascertained by anyone who takes the trouble to read it. While it
is true that Lenin repeatedly points out where and how Struve
departs from Marx, it must be kept in mind that in the introduction to *Critical Remarks* Struve had openly stated his intention to
do so. It required no sleuthing to discover Struve's unorthodoxy.

[29] "My Contacts and Conflicts with Lenin," 593. In an interview with Boris
Nikolaevsky held on August 8, 1926, at Juan-le-Pins, Potresov stated that Struve
from the beginning had a strong antipathy for Lenin: Boris I. Nikolaevsky Archive,
Hoover Institution, Stanford, California.
[30] L. Martov, *Zapiski Sotsial-Demokrata* (Berlin, 1922), 258–259; Silvin, "V. I.
Lenin," 82–83; Angarsky, *Legal'nyi Marksizm*, 58; L. B. Krasin, cited in *Potresov*,
15.
[31] Valentinov, "Struve o Lenine," 172. On Lenin and Fedoseev, see my "Origins
of Bolshevism," 32, 42.
[32] *Lenin*, I, 223–362.
[33] This view, mandatory in Soviet historiography, is also widespread outside
Russia. For example, Gérard Walter in his *Lénine* (Paris, 1950), 43, speaks of
Lenin's having accomplished a "démolition radicale" of Struve's book.

In reality, Lenin's aim was not to pillory Struve but to correct and amplify him. The tone which he assumed was that of a teacher, not that of a prosecutor, and his strictures were friendly and constructive. Noting that Struve had admitted to being "uninfected with orthodoxy," Lenin took it upon himself to restate Struve's theses — with which he expressed complete agreement[34] — in a more "Marxist" way. "As the reader sees," Lenin said at one point, "I merely have to dot the i's in Mr. Struve's theses, to give them a different formulation — 'to say the same thing in a different way.' " [35]

Lenin directed the brunt of his critique at Struve's "objectivism," by which he meant his habit of testing the validity of any idea against objective reality. Though Struve at one point said that, like the intelligentsia in general, the "Populists" represented the interests of a definite social class, he did so in passing, without bothering to analyze what that class and these interests were. By and large, his book was an exercise in the history of ideas, not in their sociology. To Lenin, confronting ideas with reality was a waste of time: it was a "professorial" occupation. What really mattered was the relationship of ideas to class structure. Laying bare the class content of any idea was the quintessence of Marxism: "Materialism involves, so to say, a party commitment (*partiinost'*) which demands that every evaluation be accompanied directly and explicitly by reference to a definite social group." [36] Marxism had nothing in common with the ideas ascribed to it by Struve: "Hegelian metaphysics, the belief that every society must go through the capitalist phase of development, and other such nonsense." [37] Lenin here articulated an interesting conception, the implications of which seem to have escaped his contemporaries. Although all Marxists acknowledged that ideas were bound up with class interests, it never occurred to any of them before Lenin to interpret this relationship as meaning that what really mattered was not whether a given idea was true but whom it benefited. One of the several corollaries of this notion was the readiness to transform every intellectual disagreement into a personal one, and to insert every personal quarrel into an ideological framework. The

[34] *Lenin*, I, 362.
[35] *Ibid.*, 303.
[36] *Ibid.*, 280.
[37] *Ibid.*, 262.

basic ingredient of thought control and a great deal of totalitarianism besides was clearly implied in it.

In line with his own conception of Marxism, Lenin undertook to supplement Struve's "objective" evaluation of "Populist" theory with a socioeconomic analysis of its class content. The "Populists," according to Lenin, represented the petty bourgeoisie: they were not, as Struve claimed, apologists for the natural economy, but for the small producer.

Lenin missed no opportunity to demonstrate his unwavering loyalty to Marx, at any rate as he understood him. To Struve's boast of intellectual independence, he proudly countered that he accepted "all" of Marx.[38] He criticized Struve for discerning in Marxist philosophy metaphysical elements, but he did so in a manner that cast doubts on his own grasp of the difference between materialism in its "dialectical" and plain, or "vulgar," forms. "According to Marx and Engels," Lenin stated, "philosophy has no independent existence and its material is distributed among the positive sciences."[39] He also took Struve to task for his views on statehood and overpopulation. In his analysis of the agrarian crisis, Lenin sided with Danielson. Russia's overpopulation, he wrote, was indeed due to capitalism, which reduced the number of industrial workers and thereby caused unemployment — not, as Struve maintained, to an insufficiently capitalized agriculture.[40] Lenin also agreed with Danielson that capitalism ruined the peasant.

The critique throughout was dogged, precise, and deliberately unoriginal. "Orthodoxy" was assumed to be a supreme moral virtue, intellectual independence a symptom of spiritual corruption. The whole discourse was conducted in the tone of a sympathetic but firm divine, admonishing a fellow Christian for being attracted to heresy.

The conversations between Struve and Lenin which began in January 1895 and continued until the summer exercised a strong

[38] *Ibid.*, 226.
[39] *Ibid.*, 290. This assertion seems to be a simplification of Engels's statement in the Preface to his *Anti-Dühring* that all that had survived of philosophy was logic and dialectic, the remainder having been dissolved in the positive sciences, natural and historical.
[40] *Lenin*, I, 327–329; see also "My Contacts and Conflicts with Lenin," April 1934, 594.

if transitory influence on both men. Under Lenin's prodding,
Struve moved leftward, away from liberal socialism toward a
more orthodox brand of Marxism, while Lenin, under Struve's
pressure, moved to the right, away from the mixture of Jacobinism
and Social Democracy which he had espoused since 1892 toward
Social Democracy proper.[41] In the course of these talks, the two
entered into something like a political alliance, based (according
to Struve's memoirs) on common opposition to "Populism," the
acceptance of the necessity of capitalism for Russia, and the assignment of the highest priority to the struggle for political freedom.[42]

Struve's leftward evolution can be discerned in the essay "To
My Critics," which he wrote in the spring of 1895 and published
in Potresov's symposium.[43] The essay was a reply to the reviewers
of *Critical Remarks*. Here he no longer tried to improve on Marx.
Apart from briefly expressing dissatisfaction with Marx's philosophy, he professed agreement with all of his basic doctrines. In a
lengthy discussion of overpopulation, he refrained from citing
Malthus;[44] nor did he repeat statements about the positive function of the state or the value of social reforms. He defined the
"Populists" as representatives of the "petty bourgeoisie" and
throughout laid great stress on that class commitment or partiinost'
which had formed the substance of Lenin's critique of his book.
Even his definition of capitalism here seems narrower and closer
to that held by Lenin. In explaining the closing sentence of the
book, he emphasizes the function of capitalism in developing class

[41] Unfortunately, none of the letters exchanged between Struve and Lenin are
available. Lenin's letters to Struve have probably perished (V. I. Lenin, *Pis'ma k
rodnym, 1894–1919* [Leningrad, 1934], 74, 151, 183, 208). Struve's letters to
Lenin have not been published and probably repose in the Institute of Marxism-
Leninism. That the two did correspond is corroborated by Krupskaia: Istpart, *O
Lenine*, I (Leningrad, 1925), 26.

[42] "My Contacts and Conflicts with Lenin," July 1934, 66; Lenin mentions in
his recollection only agreement on a joint struggle against the "Populists": *Lenin*,
XII, 59.

[43] #21. Struve did not react to Lenin's critique of his book, by far the most
extensive that appeared, because he was adhering to the policy of establishing a
united front against the "Populists": Angarsky, *Legal'nyi Marksizm*, 68.

[44] In an essay published two years later, Struve even spoke of the class content
and class appeal of Malthusianism: #55/57–58.

consciousness more than its role in creating culture.[45] All of which indicates that Lenin did not exaggerate a decade later, when, trying to justify his one-time partnership with Struve, he said that it had had the effect of pushing Struve "leftward," that is, toward greater orthodoxy.[46]

Struve, for his part, was instrumental in causing Lenin to rid himself of the vestiges of the ideology of the People's Will, and to embrace the basic principle of Social Democracy: cooperation with all oppositional groups, including the bourgeoisie, for the purpose of fighting the absolutist regime and winning political freedom for Russia.[47] By the time he left for Western Europe in the summer of 1895, Lenin was already well inclined in this direction. In Geneva, he was won over. Akselrod explained to him the ideology of the proletarian "hegemony," according to which the Social Democrats were to organize and lead all the forces in Russia interested in overthrowing the autocratic system. Hearing his and Plekhanov's arguments, Lenin acknowledged he had erred in his "abstract, bookish" attitude toward the bourgeoisie.[48]

On his return to Russia in the autumn of 1895 Lenin declared himself a full-fledged Social Democrat. The earliest evidence of his new political attitude is an obituary of Engels in which for the first time in his life he publicly praised constitutions and parliaments.[49] A few months later he went further yet. In the draft of a program for a future Russian Social Democratic party he depicted the autocracy (rather than capitalism and the bourgeoisie) as the main enemy of the working class, and called for a coalition with "all the strata of the bourgeoisie" against the monarchy: "The struggle of the Russian working class for its liberation is a political

[45] #21/16.

[46] *Lenin*, XII, 59.

[47] "It is characteristic that V. Ilin [Lenin], after his critique of my book, veered away from Orthodoxy rather than move toward it"; Struve to Potresov, February 2, 1899; first printed in *Potresov*, 33.

[48] Lenin admitted this much to his sister Anne. See her "Kak ne sleduet pisat' istoriiu," *Izvestiia*, No. 72 (2405) (March 29, 1925), 4. See also *Perepiska G. V. Plekhanova i P. B. Aksel'roda*, I (Moscow, 1925), 271; and N. Valentinov, "Chernyshevskii i Lenin," NZh, No. 27 (1951), 225. A Soviet historical journal states that after meeting Lenin in 1895, Plekhanov wrote Struve a letter expressing a very favorable opinion of him: BK, No. 8–9 (1933), 47. This letter, if it ever existed (which is doubtful, because the two men are not known to have corresponded in the summer of 1895), has not been found.

[49] *Lenin*, I, 415–416.

struggle, and its goal is the attainment of political liberty." [50] There was nothing in these sentiments that Struve could not have subscribed to.

However, Lenin's commitment to the struggle for political liberty and alliance with the "liberal bourgeoisie" does not seem to have rested on deep conviction. Whenever Lenin made a genuine intellectual leap — and he was prone to making them — he invariably went through a prolonged spiritual crisis in the course of which he intensely appraised the facts of the situation and engaged in feverish soul searching. This happened around 1888 when he became a revolutionary, in 1892–93 when he abandoned the People's Will for his peculiar brand of Marxism, and again in 1900–1901 when he broke with Social Democracy and laid the bases of Bolshevism. Only in the case of his conversion to Social Democracy is there no evidence of any spiritual crisis. In the spring of 1895 he was heatedly assailing capitalism as a destructive force; a few months later, he was calling for an alliance with the capitalists. It is highly probable, therefore, that what attracted him to Social Democracy was not the vision of a free society as a precondition of socialism, but rather the prospect of the strategic advantages to be derived from an alliance with the bourgeoisie implicit in Akselrod's theory of hegemony. What makes this supposition even more plausible is that when in 1900–1901 Lenin lost faith in the idea of Social Democratic hegemony (under conditions which will be detailed later) he immediately lost interest in Social Democracy as well.

But this was concealed for the time being. In 1895, owing largely to Potresov's efforts, a Social Democratic coalition was forged; and Lenin and Struve, for all their differences, became political allies.

The symposium, *Materials for the Characterization of Our Economic Development*,[51] was submitted to the censor's office in May 1895. This time, the censorship committee did not prove accommodating. Charging that the book contained seditious appeals to revolution and class struggle, especially in Lenin's essay, the censors refused for a long time to approve the volume for distribution, and, finally, in March 1896 ordered the entire printing seized and

[50] *Ibid.*, 426, 444.
[51] *Materialy dlia kharakteristiki nashego ekonomicheskogo razvitiia*, with the imprint St. Petersburg, 1895.

burned.[52] Potresov managed to save a hundred copies, which subsequently circulated among Russian readers. Despite this defeat, Potresov did not lose heart, and the following year he brought out two more Marxist volumes with the official imprimatur.[53] But by then the book series had lost some of its importance, because the Social Democrats had found better outlets to spread their ideas.

[52] The censor's report is reproduced in KA, No. 4 (1923), 308–316. See also N. Iakovlev, "Lenin v tsenzure," KL, No. 2/11 (1924), 19–34; and *Lenin,* I, 499.

[53] They were: I. Gurvich, *Ekonomicheskoe polozhenie russkoi derevni* (St. Petersburg, 1896), a translation of the American original — I. A. Hourwich, *The Economics of the Russian Village* (New York, 1892), reviewed by Struve in #10; and A. Volgin [G. V. Plekhanov], *Obosnovanie narodnichestva v trudakh g-na Vorontsova* (St. Petersburg, 1896).

7. SOCIAL DEMOCRATIC CHAMPION

The years 1896 and 1897 marked the apogee in the fortunes of Russian Social Democracy. The movement now penetrated society at large, polarizing it to an extent unequaled since the controversy between Westerners and Slavophiles half a century earlier. "Wherever one happened to show up," recalls the historian A. A. Kizevetter, "the first question posed was: Are you a Marxist or a Populist?":

At all the higher institutions of learning, students, male and female, ranged themselves in hostile camps, Marxists and Populists, and the two engaged in steady verbal cannonade. In accord with a foolish Russian custom, the arguing parties defended their positions not so much by means of convincing proofs as by accusations, charging their opponents with political cowardice and, while at it, with all manner of other political sin as well. The Marxists thundered that the Populists sabotaged the unification of the proletariat into a mighty force capable of serving as a weapon against the existing regime. The Populists accused the Marxists of simply playing into the hands both of the capitalists, by preaching the inevitability of heavy industrial development, and of the agrarian interests, by opposing the enlargement of peasant holdings and a new redistribution of land. These mutual compliments were always delivered to the accompaniment of whistling and hissing directed against the enemy accused of treachery, toadying to the authorities, etc. Nearly every public appearance of a scholar or public figure associated with one of the warring parties, even when connected with a subject far removed from the burning issue of Marxism and Populism, was accompanied by noisy demonstrations, a battle pitting applause and whistles against hissing.[1]

The factor that more than any other contributed to the success of the Social Democrats at this particular juncture was the unexpected surge of Russian labor. One of the difficulties the Social Democrats had encountered in their proselytizing up to that time was the statistical insignificance of the Russian industrial working class: what weight could be assigned a social group which constituted less than 1 percent of the population, compared with the peasants, representing 86 percent? Even if one acknowledged the rapid growth of the industrial working class after 1890, and assumed that it would be sustained in the years to come, the grounds for arguing that so small a minority could significantly influence the course of history were still tenuous. This objection lost much of its validity when in May 1896 and then again in January 1897 the textile workers of St. Petersburg organized the two greatest strikes the country had ever known. The thirty thousand striking cotton spinners and weavers displayed such a degree of initiative and discipline that many of the skeptics on the left became convinced sheer numbers were not quite as important as had been generally assumed. The workers' ability to organize the strikes and to formulate (with a minimum of help from the socialist intelligentsia) a set of broadly conceived demands indicated that industrial labor indeed possessed that class consciousness which the Marxists ascribed to it and which the more numerous but amorphous peasantry had shown itself time and again as lacking. When in June 1897 the government capitulated to the strikers and agreed to an eleven-and-a-half-hour working day, it no longer seemed unrealistic to pin hopes for Russia's political liberation on the working class, small as it still was in the country's total population.[2]

The Social Democrats, whom the scent of first victories had drawn closer together, felt acutely frustrated by the absence of an organ through which to spread their views. Struve was furious

[1] A. A. Kizevetter, *Na rubezhe dvukh stoleti* (Prague, 1929), 214, 216–217.
[2] The story of these strikes is told in my *Social Democracy and the St. Petersburg Labor Movement, 1885–1897* (Cambridge, Mass., 1963), Chapter 6.

at his inability to respond to the polemical barrage laid down against him and his friends by the subjectivists after the appearance of *Critical Remarks,* and he spoke of the acquisition of a publication of its own as the most urgent task facing the movement. Together with Potresov he made several attempts to break into the periodical press, but he was frustrated each time. In the summer of 1894, while *Critical Remarks* was still in press, for example, he had learned of a weekly newspaper that was for sale. Greatly excited, he sought and found a financial sponsor, one N. A. Reitlinger, and even assembled a provisional editorial board, but in the end all these exertions came to naught.[3] A year later he received an invitation to contribute regularly to the *Stock Exchange News* (*Birzhevye vedomosti*), a St. Petersburg daily which, its name notwithstanding, was less of a financial organ than a literary-political one. Potresov advised him against accepting the offer on the grounds that by writing for such a paper he would play right into the hands of Mikhailovsky, furnishing him with irrefutable evidence that Social Democrats were capitalist flunkies. Struve, however, saw nothing wrong in using a capitalist organ to propagate Marxism.[4] He published in the *Stock Exchange News* one or two articles,[5] after which, for some unknown reason, he ceased to contribute.

In 1896 he and his colleagues tried to start a new monthly. Assured of financial backing, Struve formed with Potresov's help an editorial board, consisting, in addition to themselves, of Tugan-Baranovsky and his wife (the daughter of a prominent St. Petersburg publisher), Kalmykova, V. A. Obolensky, and several sympathizers. To conceal from the authorities the true political orientation of the projected journal, the group named Obolensky publisher, and designated as formal editor a shady figure of St. Petersburg café society who, in return for a fee, took on himself the legal responsibility. Actual editorial functions were to have been assumed by Struve. When these preparations were completed, Obolensky petitioned the Main Publishing Office for a

---

[3] Struve to Potresov from Montreux, September 23/October 5, 1895, and October 6, 1895.

[4] Struve to Potresov, September 23/October 5, 1895, October 4, 1895, and October 2/14, 1895, all from Montreux.

[5] One of these articles dealt with the agrarian question, the other with the writings of V. Vorontsov. From Struve's correspondence with Potresov it appears that at least one of them was published, probably toward the end of October 1895.

license; but the authorities, neither impressed by his illustrious name (he was a prince) nor deceived by the political innocence of the pro forma editor, turned the request down, and there the matter rested.[6]

While these efforts failed, the first Social Democratic periodical in Russia made its appearance in the provinces. In October 1896 a circle of Social Democrats in Samara headed by P. P. Maslov gained control of the local newspaper, *Messenger of Samara* (*Samarskii vestnik*), and transformed it into an organ of Social Democratic opinion. The editorial committee promptly invited Struve and Tugan-Baranovsky to become contributors. So famous had the two become that the paper accorded them special prominence by setting their names on the masthead in large type. (This practice was soon dropped, however, when another contributor threatened to quit because of it.) Struve published in the *Messenger* two, possibly three, articles.[7] It was good at long last to have an outlet for Social Democratic articles in Russia, but the *Messenger* did not satisfy the craving for an organ of one's own; for this Struve had to wait yet another year.

In the meantime, he and his friends in St. Petersburg had to be content with speeches at the Free Economic Society. The country's most venerable and prestigious private institution, it had been originally intended by its founder, Catherine II, to disseminate knowledge of practical rural economics; but in the second half of the nineteenth century it quietly evolved into a forum of open discussion of most diverse national questions, including public finances and tariffs and even such noneconomic subjects as corporal punishment and mass education. The Society published

---

[6] The incident is described by V. A. Obolensky in "Na ekrane moei pamiati," PN, January 10, 1928. The other members of the proposed editorial board were Reitlinger, Bauer, A. A. Nikonov, and V. V. Vodovozov.

[7] #41 and #42. According to N. Samoilov PR, No. 7/30 (1924), 99, Struve published in the *Messenger of Samara* a third (unsigned) article on household industries, called "K voprosu o kustarnykh promyslakh" (SaV, Nos. 62ff for 1896). Lack of access to these issues of the paper prevents me from verifying this information. Lenin's first printed publication, a brief article on secondary education, appeared in the *Messenger* in November 1895, that is, before it had been taken over by the Social Democrats: *Lenin*, I, 401–406. The contributor who objected to the prominence accorded to Struve and Tugan-Baranovsky was P. N. Skvortsov (not to be confused with his namesake, A. I. Skvortsov): A. Sanin in PR, No. 12/35 (1924), 263. According to Sanin (p. 270), the *Messenger of Samara* carried in Nos. 59 and 60 for 1897 an article by P. N. Skvortsov criticizing Struve's views.

abstracts and monographs, and held regular monthly meetings divided into three sections: (1) rural economy, (2) rural industry, and (3) agricultural statistics and political economy. Open to members and their guests, these meetings enjoyed great popularity with zemstvo deputies from the provinces and civil servants.

In March 1895, the Society elected a new president, Count P. A. Geiden (Heiden), a Baltic German of liberal views. Under his direction, the Society's stated meetings became livelier than ever before and the discussions encroached steadily on areas of current government policy. The bureaucracy tolerated this development for five years, and then, in 1900, closed the Society down. Until that happened, however, between 1895 and 1900, the debates held in its venerable halls were conducted in so free and uninhibited a spirit as to earn the Society the title "Russia's Parliament." They attracted large audiences, including university students.

Struve was elected to membership in the third section on March 2/14, 1895, at the very beginning of Geiden's tenure.[8] With the assistance of Tugan-Baranovsky, he at once injected a tone of stridency into the previously decorous meetings of the third section. He deliberately politicized the meetings, transforming what had been technical debates into exciting public spectacles. He minced no words attacking any speaker in whose presentation he detected the faintest trace of "Populism" (defense of the natural economy, resistance to economic rationalization, and so forth), whether delivered from a radical or from a conservative position. Sometimes he became so excited that the chairman was forced to intercede and call him to order. Besides criticizing "Populism," he also availed himself of every opportunity to familiarize the audience with Marxist sociology and economics. In a debate on peasant associations, for example, he called attention to the class differentiation occurring in the Russian village;[9] while arguing against bimetallism, he noted the benefits agrarian interests would derive should silver become legal tender;[10] and more than once he challenged as fallacious the belief, shared by both the right and the left, that Russia possessed and would do well to preserve

[8] *Trudy* IVEO, No. 4 (1895), Pt. 2, 4. His sponsors were K. K. Arseniev, P. A. Korsakov, and P. A. Kostyshev: *ibid.*, No. 2 (1895), Pt. 2, 93.

[9] #26.

[10] #27. See also #52/217–221.

a system of popular, or natural, economy.[11] Tugan-Baranovsky seconded him in these polemics, compensating with his economic erudition for a certain blandness of delivery.

Word of these exchanges soon spread in the city and students flocked to see Struve, a youth in his mid-twenties, duel with established academic authorities. It is difficult today to picture those excited scenes, for under any other circumstances the subjects treated could only have agitated (and at that, mildly) audiences of professional economists.[12] Whenever Struve was expected to take the floor, the halls of the Free Economic Society so overflowed with students that the regular members had difficulty finding seats. They cheered and clapped their approval at every point scored by their idol, encouraging him to assume even more extreme positions than he was already predisposed to take by his own impassioned temperament. Female students worked themselves into frenzy over Struve's remarks on bimetallism, and collapsed in dead faints hearing him discourse on cereal prices. The excitement was generated in the first place by the sheer novelty of hearing at open and legally convoked meetings frank discussion of national policies. Simply to be present when a speaker publicly criticized the government was enough to electrify an audience. When the speaker was an exceptionally brilliant youth conversant with the latest foreign authorities who tore to shreds every current belief about Russia's future, heads swam and knees buckled.

One of the sharpest of the exchanges in which Struve was involved occurred in the two-day session of March 1/13 and 2/14, 1897, devoted to a recent book on the effect of low cereal prices on the national economy.[13] On this occasion two contrary schools of thought on Russian economic development, one established, the other aspiring, clashed for the first time directly and in the open. It was a contest between youth and age: Struve and Tugan-Baranovsky, champions of the St. Petersburg Social Democrats, against A. I. Chuprov and the traditionalists espousing the separate path doctrine. The hall was filled to the rafters.

[11] For example, #58.
[12] There are descriptions in NV, No. 7206 (March 21/April 2, 1896), 3; Obolensky, "Na ekrane"; and O. Lepeshinskaia, "Iz moikh rannykh vospominanii ob Il'iche," SB, No. 5/8 (October–December 1933), 166.
[13] A. I. Chuprov and A. S. Posnikov, *Vlianie urozhaev i khlebnykh tsen na nekotorye storony russkogo narodnogo khoziaistva*, 2 vols. (St. Petersburg, 1897).

The book which provided the occasion for the debate had been prepared by a group of eminent economists and statisticians headed by Chuprov, at the behest of the Ministry of Finance, and was intended to furnish authoritative evidence refuting the charge of radicals and conservatives that the Ministry's proindustrial policies ruined the peasantry. In dealing with low cereal prices and their consequences, Chuprov and his colleagues proceeded on the assumption that Russian agriculture in the main functioned within a natural mode of production, under which the farmers themselves consumed the bulk of foodstuffs. They based this assumption on evidence indicating that no more than one-third of the country's agricultural produce reached the market. This being the case, they concluded that low cereal prices benefited the peasants, since those among them who had dealings with the market tended to come as buyers rather than as sellers.

The glorification of Russian rural backwardness implied in this analysis was more than Struve could bear, and he attacked the book in a language intemperate even for him. To begin with, the premise on which Chuprov and his colleagues rested their case was fallacious:

> I fully understand the sharp critique voiced here of the allegedly statistical conclusion that because in Russia between one-fourth and one-third of the annual harvest of cereals reaches the market and the remainder is consumed within the confines of the [producers'] households, Russia is a country with a predominantly natural economy. I consider this conclusion utterly fantastic. It is perfectly analogous to the following conclusion: Supposing that we know the quantity of butter produced and consumed per capita in a given locality, for instance, in Denmark. By multiplying both these quantities by the number of inhabitants of this locality we will arrive at a certain surplus of production over consumption. But are we entitled on the basis of this fact to conclude that every inhabitant of Denmark is an independent producer of butter? With such a method one can prove that the United States operates under a system of natural economy.[14]

[14] #58/20.

From this false premise, Chuprov drew wrong practical conclusions. It was not true, Struve exclaimed, that the majority of peasants grew enough food for their needs, or that they benefited from low prices: "low grain prices . . . hindered the economic culture and the social progress" of Russia. He shouted in his excited, high-pitched voice:

Yes, we are indeed in the grip of a natural economy, but it is not the idyllic one that Mr. Chuprov depicts . . . It is a natural economy closely tied to the sale of the labor force. The labor force is bound to the natural economy, and for that reason it suffers and is degraded when the latter is strengthened and preserved. Labor sells its services for the lowest price; it is shackled by the bonds of serfdom. All these phenomena are the incontrovertible fruits of the natural economy and the vaunted "economic independence" [of the peasant] established by our opponents themselves. This "economic independence" is tantamount to the vilest form of economic exploitation and legal humiliation of the individual. Even today, gentlemen, from this very forum, you have heard very eloquent speeches about the humiliation of the individual and the importance of elevating him. We merely go further: we study the foundations on which this humiliation of the individual rests. And we conclude that it is tied with unbreakable threads to the economic relations prevailing in our society, that it rests on the celebrated "natural economy." The *fantastic* conclusion of Mr. Chuprov holds that in Russia the dominant form of the economy is natural. The *factual* conclusion which we owe to that glorious monument of Russian thought, zemstvo statistics, holds that what prevails in Russia is the natural exploitation of peasant labor, or, what amounts to the same thing, the condition of semiserfdom. A solid rise in grain prices will promptly sweep away these relations. And *for this reason* and in *this* sense, long live high grain prices! [15]

The correspondent for the conservative newspaper *New Times,* who witnessed these debates and reported them over the signature of "Old Gentleman" (he was A. V. Amfiteatrov), could not pass

[15] #58/82–83; also #52/223–225.

over the violence of the tone adopted by Struve and Tugan-Bara-novsky, the latter of whom he dubbed a "licensed doctor among the 'Struvists.'" Of Struve he said that "between him and the ability to speak in public lies, unfortunately, an insurmountable obstacle in the form of extreme nervousness, which transforms his speech into a succession of hysterical shouts accompanied by com-pletely epileptic motions." [16]

The debate over cereal prices received wide coverage in the press, the *Messenger of Samara* included. Maslov, its leading spirit, a Marxist so rigid that one of his friends compared him to a fanatical Old Believer, was appalled by the argument advanced by Struve and Tugan-Baranovsky. To defend capitalism and to assess economic phenomena from the point of view of national prosperity rather than that of class warfare appeared to him a travesty of Marxism, and he said so in a long personal letter to Struve.[17] Struve sent the letter on to Lenin. Lenin himself was not entirely happy with all that Struve had said in his debate with Chuprov,[18] but he unhesitatingly took his side. In part, he did so because he had come to share Struve's general economic outlook. According to Martov, who describes this incident, Lenin at this time "retained no trace of his earlier mistrust of Struve's capitalist apologetics, an attitude to which he adhered also during the ensu-ing years when he was much occupied with agrarian problems." [19] But above all he wanted to forestall any split in the united front against the "Populists." He therefore asked Martov and several other friends to support Struve,[20] and did so himself in a letter to the Samaran Marxists, in which he defended Struve's and Tugan-Baranovsky's position "fully and without qualifications." [21] This

[16] NV, No. 7554 (March 9/21, 1897), 2–3.
[17] L. Martov, *Zapiski Sotsial-Demokrata* (Berlin, 1922), 330. According to another source, the letter of the Samarans had been provoked by Struve's editorial in the first issue of the *New Word* (*Novoe slovo*) under his editorship (#44): Sanin, PR, No. 12/35 (1924), 275. The two versions do not necessarily contradict one another, since in the *New Word* article Struve restated his belief in the progressive function of high cereal prices (#44/19–20).
[18] The Houghton Library at Harvard University has a copy of the volume of the Proceedings of the Free Economic Society (*Trudy* IVEO) with the discussion of Chuprov's book annotated by Lenin. Lenin approved of much that Struve said on this occasion, but questioned some passages, including the closing sentence: "And *for this reason* and in *this* sense, long live high grain prices!"
[19] Martov, *Zapiski*, 329.
[20] *Ibid.*, 329–330; N. Angarsky, *Legal'nyi Marksizm*, I (Moscow, 1925), 100–107.
[21] Martov, *Zapiski*, 330. The letters from the Samarans to Struve and Lenin's

episode, not very significant in itself, illustrates how closely Lenin had moved by this time to Struve, and to what lengths he was willing to go to preserve the recently-formed Social Democratic alliance.

The debates at the Free Economic Society, being widely reported in the press, greatly increased Struve's reputation. He became an intellectual star of the first magnitude, and even something of a legend.[22] Arseniev called him "the ruler of thoughts" (*vlastitel' dum*) and compared him to Pisarev.[23] Indeed, it would have been necessary to go back to Pisarev and the sixties to find an intellectual enjoying so much influence over his contemporaries at so early an age.

Struve would have been even more famous had it been known that he was the author of an anonymous open letter addressed to Nicholas II, in which opposition to the new ruler was for the first time publicly voiced.

Alexander III died in November 1894. The accession of Nicolas II, who for some reason enjoyed the reputation of a liberal, aroused hopes in society that the government would revert to the reformist course abandoned in 1881, and seek to bridge the wide gulf which had come to separate the rulers from the ruled. These hopes were cautiously expressed in some of the messages of congratulation adopted by zemstvo assemblies in the winter of 1894–95 in honor of the new monarch. Several of the zemstva, along with tendering the customary assurances of loyalty, took the liberty of asking the new ruler to restore to them powers curtailed by his father, restrain the bureaucracy, and safeguard civil liberties. The boldest of these was the address edited by F. I. Rodichev and submitted in the name of the Tver zemstvo.[24]

---

letters to them have not been published and may be lost. In a letter to his mother dated May 18/30, 1897, Lenin spoke of waging "war" against the Samarans: V. I. Lenin, *Pis'ma k rodnym* (Leningrad, 1934), 41; also p. ix.

[22] Among the tales that circulated about his performances at the Free Economic Society was a story that he cited from memory long passages from *Das Kapital*: it is reported as a fact by Harold Williams (SR, IV No. 10 [1925], 20), although there is nothing in the Society's Proceedings to substantiate it.

[23] A. Meiendorf, "P. B. Struve," unpublished manuscript, 1944–45, in the possession of Professor Gleb Struve, Berkeley, California.

[24] These resolutions are summarized in S. Mirnyi [D. Shakhovskoi], *Adresa zemstv, 1894–95, i ikh politicheskaia programma* (Geneva, 1896). The Tver address can be found in translation in Struve's article "My Contacts with Rodichev," SR, XII, No. 35 (January 1934), 349–350.

Nicholas lost not time in disabusing these expectations. Despite his liberal reputation, his temperament was conservative, and he regarded the institution of autocracy as a sacred trust which he was duty-bound to bequeath to his successor inviolate. He made clear this intention (for though his political acumen, to put it mildly, was of a low order, he was an honorable man) in a speech from the throne delivered on January 17/29, 1895, to a gathering of zemstvo deputies:

> I am glad to receive representatives of all the estates assembled to give expression to their sentiments of loyalty. I believe in the sincerity of these sentiments with which every Russian has been imbued since time immemorial. But it has come to my knowledge recently that in certain zemstvo assemblies voices have been raised by people, lured by senseless dreams of the participation of zemstvo representatives in domestic government. Let it be known to all that devoting all the strength at my disposal to the cause of national well-being, I shall safeguard the principle of autocracy as firmly and as steadfastly as did my unforgettable late father.[25]

These remarks, with their insolent paternalism, at once set a good part of public opinion against the new ruler. His speech was widely interpreted to mean — as events were to show, correctly — that the new administration intended neither to curb the bureaucracy nor to provide society with a voice in the making of policy, but to govern as before by means of a police-bureaucratic apparatus. The sense of anger and frustration spread beyond radical and liberal circles. Many conservatives, too, were dismayed by the tsar's statement; for while they rejected constitution and parliament, they did want Russian government to function in an orderly and lawful manner, and this required some curb on the bureaucracy and the police. The "senseless dreams" speech of 1895 helped forge the first link in that radical liberal conservative alliance which ten years later, in the guise of the "liberational" movement, precipitated the first revolution.

Struve at once sensed the implications of Nicholas's remarks, and in a state of white fury sat down to compose an open letter to him. He predicted in it that if the tsar were to persevere with

[25] V. Burtsev, ed., *Za sto let, 1800–1896*, I (London, 1897), 264.

the political program hinted at in his speech, he would drive Russian society into the arms of revolutionaries and cause the fall of the dynasty:

> If autocracy identifies itself by word and by deed with bureaucratic omnipotence, if its existence is possible only on the condition of complete silence of society and the de facto permanent validity of the supposedly temporary regulations concerning increased security — then the game is up. Autocracy digs its own grave, and sooner or later, but in any event in the not too distant future, it will fall under the pressure of living social forces. By your words and by your behavior you yourself have put to society such a question, a clear and open posing of which in itself constitutes a terrible threat to autocracy. You have flung a challenge to the representatives of the zemstva and with them to Russian society as a whole. They will have no choice now but to decide deliberately whether to move forward or remain loyal to autocracy.[26]

Struve read his letter to several friends and then, with their help, reproduced it on a duplicating machine in Kalmykova's shop. On the night of January 19/31, these sheets were posted from a mail-box at a railroad station to chairmen of all the zemstvo assemblies as well as to leading editors and other notables.[27] The open letter circulated widely, everywhere attracting attention by its sharp and uncompromising tone. The public attributed it to Rodichev, who shortly after its appearance was relieved of his post as chairman of the Tver zemstvo. The police, on the other hand, equally mistakenly believed it to have been written by émigrés associated with the Free Russian Press in London.[28] The letter was later reprinted several times abroad.

The open letter added nothing to Struve's already formidable reputation, for its authorship remained unknown at the time, but it did bring him one valuable side benefit. The small circle which was privy to its secret included Prince Dmitry Shakhovskoi, a liberal prominent in the zemstva and in the cooperative movement.

[26] #20/266. An English translation of the text in full is in Struve's "My Contacts with Rodichev," 352–354.
[27] "My Contacts with Rodichev," 351.
[28] *Obzory*, XIX–XX (1895–96), 312.

Shakhovskoi gave a copy to Rodichev and other liberal leaders, whom it impressed favorably.[29] In this manner, Struve established connections with the constitutional wing of the zemstvo movement, whose principal theoretician he was to become after being ejected from the ranks of Social Democracy.

In the autumn of 1895 Struve once again went abroad. His first destination was Switzerland, where he wanted at long last to meet Plekhanov and the rest of the Liberation of Labor Group.

The encounter with Plekhanov went badly from the start. Plnekhanov, an extremely vain person, was very rude to anyone in whom he saw a possible rival to his claim to being the founder and head of Russian Social Democracy. Russian Social Democrats who made the pilgrimage to Geneva often were terribly disappointed at the suspicious manner in which they were received there. Notwithstanding their sincere respect and even adulation, Plekhanov treated them sullenly, for unwittingly they made him aware of how much estranged he had become from his country after many years of exile, and of how little influence he really wielded there. In the case of Struve, he had particular reasons to be unfriendly: not only had Struve's fame eclipsed his own, but it was gained in the name of a reformist, liberal brand of socialism which he detested. The two quarreled at their first meeting,[30] and from then on eyed one another with a reserve that needed slight cause to turn into open hostility. Vera Zasulich at first also took a dislike to Struve, but she soon changed her mind and became both a personal friend and political supporter. Struve all but fell in love with her: he considered her the finest person in the movement and spoke of having feelings toward her "verging on the religious." [31]

From Switzerland he proceeded to Berlin, where he remained until the end of December 1895. His intention was to devote himself to intensive study of German economic literature. But he had also undertaken to write an article on Marx for the Russian

---

[29] "My Contacts with Rodichev," 358. Struve had known Shakhovskoi at least since 1889 (RiS, No. 83, June 29, 1930), and Rodichev since approximately 1890 ("My Contacts with Rodichev," 348).

[30] Writing to Potresov on August 26, 1903 Kalmykova reminded him of Struve's "sharp theoretical disagreements with Plekhanov from the time of their first encounter." Lydia Dan, Martov's sister, confirmed in conversation with me that Plekhanov always felt a strong personal aversion to Struve.

[31] Struve to Potresov, undated letter, probably from early November 1896.

Encyclopedic Dictionary of Brokgauz and Efron, and in this connection he carried out research on Marx's life. He began with the obscure chapter in the prehistory of "scientific socialism," the 1840's, when Marx and Engels first formulated the principles of their theory. The subject held for him a particular fascination, for, as noted, he viewed the Marxist-"Populist" controversy of his own time as a historic counterpart of the conflict waged fifty years earlier in the West between "scientific" and "utopian" socialisms. He soon became so engrossed in this subject that he abandoned the original plan of study and devoted himself fully to the early history of socialism. In the course of these researches, he made a stunning discovery: the earliest traces of the "young Marx," the left Hegelian exponent of "alienation," previously unknown and even unsuspected.

While going through issues of the *Westphalian Steamboat* (*Das Westphalische Dampfboot*) for 1846–47, a journal published by German radical exiles in Belgium, he came upon two articles that attracted his attention. Neither was signed, but so confident was he of his familiarity with Marx's style that without hesitation he attributed both to Marx.[32] The mere fact that Marx should have written for this journal was curious, because it was the organ of the "true socialists," a group which Marx and Engels were savagely to attack in the *Communist Manifesto* as petty bourgeois apologists. But what was said in these articles was even more noteworthy. Pursuing the clue, Struve was led into the uncharted waters where "scientific socialism" had had its origins.

"True socialism" (*der wahre Socialismus*) was an ephemeral socialist movement inspired by two of Feuerbach's disciples, Moses Hess and Karl Grün. Its theoretical basis derived from Feuerbach's concept of "true man," the true *ens realissimum,* concealed beneath the web of "projections" which man had produced in the process of imbuing external objects with his emotions. In his seminal *Essence of Christianity* (1841), Feuerbach applied his theory of psychological projections to religion. He explained the concept of God as resulting from transferrence onto a fictional image of all that man either desired for himself or feared in others.

---

[32] #85/xxvii–xxviii. The discovery had to be made sometime between the end of October 1895, when he arrived in Berlin, and December 8–9 (NS) when he reported it to Plekhanov: *Literaturnoe nasledie G. V. Plekhanova,* IV (Moscow, 1939), 292.

It was not God who created man in His image, but the reverse: man created God in his image. By so doing, however, he alienated qualities proper to his nature, and thereby impoverished and diminished himself. The task of philosophy was to emancipate man from the tyranny of his fetishes, and put him once more in the center of the universe where he belonged: anthropology was to replace theology. In this manner alone would man realize his full potential, and unite with the rest of humanity in a brotherhood of equals. Hess and Grün applied the method devised by Feuerbach to various social and economic institutions, such as money, interpreting each in terms of "projections," "fetishes," and "alienation."

It is obvious that the basic premise of Feuerbach and his disciples — that of an immutable "true man" reposing underneath actual man — was unacceptable to Marx and Engels in their mature years. The classic Marx and Engels considered it axiomatic that all phenomena, man included, must be viewed in a historic setting, never abstractly. For them, there was no such thing as "true man," there was only concrete man, historically conditioned. It was on these grounds that in the *Communist Manifesto* they heaped abuse on the "true socialists."

Today it is a matter of common knowledge that before formulating the theory which bears their name, Marx and Engels had gone through a transitional phase during which they had been close to Feuerbach and his school. But in 1895 this chapter in their biography was unknown even to specialists, for neither Marx nor Engels had written about it and that which today is known as Marxological scholarship did not yet exist. Then it was believed that in 1843, when he settled in Paris, Marx broke with Hegel and the Hegelians, and began to formulate his own theory. *The Holy Family*, which he had published in 1844 to discredit Bruno Bauer, a leading left Hegelian, was regarded as proof that by this time he had decisively rejected "philosophical idealism." [33]

The articles in the *Westphalian Steamboat* which Struve had discovered and, as it turned out, correctly attributed to Marx, were polemical essays directed against Grün and the "true socialists." In them Marx settled accounts with his one-time friends and intellectual associates, and for the first time enunciated the principles of "scientific socialism." From an internal analysis of these

---

[33] See, for example, the anonymous biographical sketch of Marx (written by Karl Liebknecht) in NZ, I, No. 10 (1883), 442.

articles, Struve deduced that Marx, too, had once been within the Feuerbachian orbit, and that his journey from philosophical socialism to economic materialism had taken a longer and more circuitous route than was generally assumed. In a letter written to Potresov shortly after he had discovered Marx's articles, Struve expressed his initial thoughts on the subject:

I am becoming convinced that the Hegelianism of M[arx] and E[ngels] can be historically depicted in the shape of a curve:

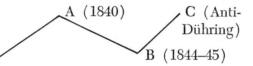

A (1840)   C (Anti-Dühring)

B (1844–45)

In "A" they are Hegelians à la Bruno Bauer, in "B" they are Feuerbachians, i.e., *non-Hegelians.* Then there occurs the anti-Hegelian reaction in Germany, and they, from a counterreaction, again accept Hegel. (Important here also was the formal coincidence of *evolution* and dialectic.) The spirit of the *Holy Family* is not Hegel's but Feuerbach's. I think E[ngels] would have rejected this scheme, but this would not have persuaded me in the least.[34]

Struve announced his discovery in *Die Neue Zeit,* the theoretical organ of the German Social Democrats.[35] In addition to summarizing Marx's articles he gave a brief appraisal of Marx, in which he depicted him as a successor of the great German metaphysicians and a member of the long line of thinkers seeking all-embracing philosophic systems.[36] Before long he had the satisfaction of having his attribution confirmed by Eduard Bernstein, the executor of the Marx-Engels estate, who reported in *Die Neue Zeit* that the articles Struve had found in the *Westphalian Steamboat* were indeed by Marx and had been located at one time in

[34] Struve to Potresov, December 2–3, 1895.

[35] #28.

[36] "With [his] penchant for philosophical unity, his 'instinct for philosophic construction' (*philosophischen Bautrieb*), to use a well-known expression of F. A. Lange, Marx identifies himself as an heir of the great German metaphysicians" (#28/54). (In the printed text, the word used is *Baustil,* not *Bautrieb,* but this was a mistake which Struve corrected in a letter to Karl Kautsky, the journal's editor, dated April 1/13, 1896.) Struve subsequently elaborated on this point in the first installment of #48.

Marx's archive, but at Engels's request were not republished.[37] As learned subsequently, one of these was an installment of a major work called *German Ideology,* the complete text of which became known only in 1932.[38]

Elated by his find, Struve delved deeper into the prehistory of Marxism. The subject was then a virtual *terra incognita.* At that time, only a handful of Marx's and Engels's early writings were still in circulation: *The Holy Family, The Condition of the Working Class in England,* and some journalistic fragments.[39] With the assistance of German librarians and book-dealers, Struve located runs of rare socialist publications from the 1840's, among them Marx's *German Brussels Newspaper* (1846–47), a complete set of which no scholar had previously inspected.[40] He also reread with a fresh eye the familiar writings of Marx and Engels from before 1847, searching for other traces of "true socialism." On the basis of these investigations, he wrote three essays which represent a pioneering insight into the intellectual evolution of the young Marx.[41]

Illustrating his analysis with passages from *The Holy Family, The Condition of the Working Class,* and *German-French Annals,* Struve called attention to frequent recurrences in these works of terms and ideas characteristic of "true socialism." This evidence, though long available, had been overlooked, he explained, because alongside statements typical of philosophical idealism, Marx and Engels also expressed views that anticipated "scientific socialism." Marx and Engels, he concluded, were in 1843, 1844, and early 1845 "true socialists": they belonged to the circle of Feuerbach's followers, and like Hess or Grün based their vision of a good society on the concepts of "true man" and "humanity." In this sense, they too had once been utopians. Struve regarded this chapter in the intellectual evolution of Marx and Engels as of more than biographical significance: he believed that elements of Feuerbachian thought remained imbedded in the mind of the mature Marx, and

[37] "Marx und der 'wahre' Sozialismus," NZ, XIV, Pt. 2, No. 33 (1895–96), 216–220.

[38] *Marx-Engels Gesamtausgabe* (MEGA), I, Vol. 5 (Berlin, 1932), 471–516; it was the only installment of the work to appear in Marx's lifetime. The other essay, directed against Hermann Kriege, is reprinted *ibid.,* I, Vol. 0, 1–21.

[39] See, for example, the bibliography of Marx's available writings compiled by Engels for *Handwörterbuch der Staatswissenschaften,* IV (Jena, 1892), 1133.

[40] #39.

[41] #38.

pointed to the concept of commodity fetishism in Marx's analysis of capital as an example.

The anti-Grün essay in *Westphalian Steamboat* shed light on another obscure aspect of Marx's early intellectual evolution, namely, his attitude toward the Prussian conservative writer Lorenz von Stein, the author of *Socialism and Communism in Contemporary France*. First published in 1842, this book anticipated some of the theories of "scientific socialism," including the conception of the proletariat as a social class. The parallels were so striking that Werner Sombart ascribed to Stein an important influence on the young Marx;[42] however, since he could adduce no proof that Marx had even read Stein, his hypothesis was not taken seriously. The anti-Grün articles which Struve had now discovered contained such explicit references to Stein's book that they not only dispelled all doubts about Marx's familiarity with it, but even indicated that Marx treated Stein with a measure of respect. From this evidence, Struve felt entitled to conclude that the question of Stein's influence on Marx was settled affirmatively once and for all.[43]

The German Social Democrats were not pleased by the link which Struve drew connecting Marx and Engels with the "true socialists" or by his conclusion that the founders of "scientific socialism" had once been "utopians." They disliked even more his assertion that Marx had been influenced by Stein, for Stein was a Prussian monarchist whose ideas anticipated the social policies of Bismarck, whom they despised above all men. After the first installment of Struve's three-part essay had appeared in *Die Neue Zeit*, Franz Mehring, the party's historian, promptly made the establishment's displeasure known. In an unsigned editorial,[44] he flatly denied any connection between Stein and Marx, and, referring to Struve as a "Marxist" (in quotation marks), dismissed all talk of such a connection as completely groundless. He also

[42] *Sozialismus und soziale Bewegung* (Jena, 1896), 70.

[43] Struve dealt with Stein at greater length in an article which he published two years later (#48/161–164). G. Salomon, the editor of Stein (*Geschichte der Sozialen Bewegungen in Frankreich*, I [Munich, 1921], xxii) gives Struve credit for having been the first to demonstrate Stein's role in Marx's intellectual development. See also Ernst Grünfeld, *Lorenz von Stein und die Gesellschaftslehre* (Jena, 1910), 239.

[44] "Politik und Sozialismus," NZ, XV, Pt. 1 (1896–97), 449–455. Mehring dealt with the "true socialists" in another article, "Nochmals Marx und der 'wahre Sozialismus'," NZ, XIV, Pt. 2 (1895–96), 395–401, in which he defended them as advanced social thinkers.

dropped hints that Struve performed a disservice to the socialist cause by airing such matters in public.

Responding to Mehring's challenge, Struve devoted the second and third installments of his essay (these appeared only after a six months' delay) to a defense of his views on Stein and Marx. The proof of Stein's influence on Marx, he replied, was to be found in Stein's book itself. Stein was an "idealist," true, but his idealism concealed a hard inner core of realistic thinking. Treating political conflicts in terms of underlying social and economic conflicts, he discovered the existence of the proletariat. For all his admittedly "bourgeois" inclinations, he was more advanced in his thinking than either Hess or Grün, who remained captives of philosophic idealism. In freeing himself from the "true socialists," who hated Stein, Marx fell under Stein's spell. Precisely how much influence Stein exercised on him could not be determined; that he influenced him was incontrovertible.

Struve's hypothesis concerning the Feuerbachian period in the lives of Marx and Engels passed, for the time being, virtually unnoticed. Mehring continued to minimize Feuerbach's influence on Marx even forty years later, in his standard biography of Marx.[45] The matter was finally settled with the publication of the full body of the writings of Marx and Engels after World War I. Here Struve's conjecture received brilliant vindication. The appearance in 1932, under the title *Economic and Philosophical Manuscripts*, of a loose collection of papers written by Marx in 1843–44 proved his Feuerbachian phase beyond doubt and located it almost precisely during the years Struve had posited.[46] Today, the existence of this phase is not only acknowledged by all serious scholars, but is regarded by some as the most interesting period in Marx's life.[47] Indeed, among the general public, the "young Marx," the exponent of psychological "alienation," has all but eclipsed the mature Marx, the theorist of economic exploitation. This shift in emphasis is probably due to the fact that, after the passage of a century, the economic and social ideas of Marx are of interest mainly to the intellectual historian, whereas the Feuerbachian ideas with which he toyed in his youth retain their

[45] Franz Mehring, *Karl Marx* (New York, 1935).
[46] *Marx-Engels Gesamtausgabe*, I, Vol. 3 (Berlin, 1932), 33–172.
[47] The literature on this subject is vast; Jean-Yves Calvez, *La pensée de Karl Marx* (Paris, 1956) is representative of the genre.

relevance today by virtue of their closeness to modern psychology and philosophy. Whether the theory of alienation reflects the views by which Marx wished to be known and on which his fame rests, and whether the credit for it belongs to him rather than to Feuerbach, is another matter.

As for the influence of Stein on Marx, the question remains unresolved.[48] In 1902 Mehring, with characteristic intolerance, dismissed all attempts to link the two thinkers as unworthy of serious consideration.[49] Some modern scholars, on the other hand, regard it as amply demonstrated.[50]

Struve's findings on the early history of Marxism represented a superb example of his ability to grasp intuitively the answer to a problem without laboriously tracing all the stages lying between hypothesis and conclusion. He was better, however, at understanding than at demonstrating.

Although aware of the value of his discoveries, he felt guilty at having allowed himself a diversion from the "cause" to indulge his curiosity. "But what is to be done, since knowledge in itself is so attractive?" he wrote, apologetically, to Potresov; "One must know how to reconcile [life and knowledge]. The question here is not one of intellectual orientation, but of temperament. And, fortunately or not, my temperament is not professorial, for which reason I stand in no danger from pure knowledge." [51]

His Marxological studies soured somewhat his relations with the German Social Democrats. Even if intellectually more tolerant than their Russian counterparts, they resented what they considered his irresponsible probing into aspects of the movement's history which everyone would rather have left forgotten. After the essays on the young Marx, Struve never again appeared in *Die Neue Zeit*.

On his return to Russia in the last days of December 1895, Struve found the Social Democratic ranks decimated by arrests. To depict the circumstances under which these arrests took place,

[48] The subject is discussed at length in the introduction to Stein's *History of the Social Movements in France, 1789–1850* (Totowa, N. J., 1964), 25–33, by the editor of this translation, K. Mengelberg.

[49] Franz Mehring, ed., *Aus dem literarischen Nachlass von Karl Marx, Friedrich Engels und Ferdinand Lasalle*, I (Stuttgart, 1902), 186–187.

[50] Robert Tucker, *Philosophy and Myth in Karl Marx* (Cambridge, 1961), 114–117.

[51] Struve to Potresov from Berlin, December 2–3, 1895.

something must be said about worker agitation and the Union of Struggle for the Emancipation of the Working Class, an organization dedicated to its practice.

As used by Russian revolutionaries, the word "agitation," and its corollary "propaganda," went back to the 1870's and stood for two distinct methods of inciting the masses to revolutionary action. The propagandists concentrated on educating the working man, whether peasant or proletarian. They sought to enlighten him about the forces of nature and society in the hope that he would draw in time from such knowledge practical conclusions and turn against the existing order. The agitators believed such intellectual preparation superfluous. To them every working man was a latent rebel: all that was needed was a spark to ignite what Bakunin had called the "evil passions" of the masses. The purpose of agitation was to provide that spark, to urge the "toiler" to rebel or at least stop work. While the propagandists taught, the agitators incited. These techniques, developed originally by the socialist revolutionaries, were subsequently adopted also by the Social Democrats.

In the late 1880's and early 1890's, the socialist intellectuals in Russia engaged almost exclusively in propaganda. This involved mainly staffing self-formed worker study circles with tutors, whose task it was to steer the worker's essentially pacific educational effort in a radical direction. The circle of Technologists which Lenin had joined on his arrival in St. Petersburg in 1893 was one of many dedicated to activity of this kind.[52]

In the autumn of 1895, when he returned to Russia from his first trip to the West, Lenin's head was full of ambitious political plans designed to lay the groundwork for a Russian Social Democratic party. At this time he met Martov. Martov considered worker propaganda old-fashioned and useless, and urged Lenin and his colleagues to abandon it in favor of a new technique of worker agitation which he and his Jewish friends had tested in Vilno. Because the Vilno workers failed to respond to political propaganda, and indeed resented it, the local Jewish socialist groups decided to give up preaching socialism and to concentrate instead on inciting workers to strike. Their hope was that the strikers would promptly discover that the autocratic government was not an impartial arbiter standing above all the classes, as it claimed and they believed it to be, but an ally of the capitalists. Once the soldiers and Cos-

[52] Pipes, Social Democracy, 46–56.

sacks appeared to crush them on behalf of the owners, the strikers would come to realize that they could not fight for the satisfaction of their economic grievances without recourse to political action, without transforming a government serving the exploiters into one serving the working people. Thus conflicts originating in specific economic grievances would lead to a politization and radicalization of the working class in Russia; and once this happened, the Social Democrats would be able to organize an effective political party.

In order to allay the suspicions of the workers that the agitators were bent on getting them into trouble, the Vilno agitators incited on the basis of "legal" demands. In their agitation they urged the workers to ask not for higher wages or shorter hours (demands forbidden by law) but only for the strict fulfillment by the capitalists of the empire's existing (even if rudimentary) labor legislation. By means of leaflets, they acquainted the workers with their rights under the law, and exhorted them to lay down their tools until the employers gave evidence of respecting them. This technique proved surprisingly effective, because it tied the regime's hands: the authorities could not very well repress a strike based on such legitimate demands without risking the charge of abetting lawlessness on the part of the employers. Drawing on the experience gained in Vilno, Martov and his friend L. Kremer formulated a theoretical justification of agitational action, which they outlined in the pamphlet *On Agitation*.[53] On Martov's urgings, this technique was adopted by the circle of Technologists.

The Martov-Lenin organization (as yet unnamed) was conceived on an ambitious scale: in addition to initiating worker agitation in St. Petersburg, it was to publish a newspaper, *The Worker's Cause* (*Rabochee delo*), of which Lenin was to be editor-in-chief, and to enter into contact with the embryonic trade union organizations formed by workers in the skilled trades of St. Petersburg over the preceding decade. Their organization, however, realized few of its aims. In December 1895, its members, all of them intellectuals, as well as some workers from affiliated circles, were arrested after scattering a few agitational leaflets in several factories. By the end of January 1896, both Lenin and Martov were behind bars. These arrests notwithstanding, the Martov-Lenin organization, baptized (after Lenin's arrest) Union of Strug-

[53] *Ibid.*, 58–64.

gle for the Emancipation of the Working Class, continued to function sporadically with a skeleton membership, in which Potresov
played a leading role until his arrest at the end of the year.

In jail, Lenin at once began work on a historical study dealing
with the growth of the internal capitalist market in Russia. Its
purpose was to prove the fallacy of Danielson's market theory by
demonstrating the strong native roots of Russian capitalism.
Through one of his sisters, Lenin established regular contact with
Struve, with whose help he borrowed books necessary for his research from the rich collection of the Free Economic Society.[54]
Struve must have helped Lenin and his jailed friends in other ways
also, for, according to Martov, "he performed for the [Union of
Struggle] all kinds of services."[55]

Even though the Union of Struggle bore no responsibility for the
outbreak of the textile strikes of 1896 and 1897, which had occurred spontaneously, it received much credit for them.[56] In this
it was unwittingly helped by the police, who, eager in their reports
to depict the workers as staunchly loyal to the throne, ascribed all
labor troubles in the Empire to socialist agitation.

The textile strikes of 1896–97 marked something of a watershed
in the evolution of Russian socialism. They not only greatly enhanced the self-confidence and the prestige of the Social Democrats, as already noted, but made them more conscious of labor
and trade unionism. During these two years of disturbances, Social Democrats tended to regard the nascent movement as the
vanguard of Russian socialism and to assign themselves the more
modest function of helpers or servants of labor. Even a man as politically minded as Lenin was so impressed by these strikes, the
details of which he learned in jail, that he began to envisage the
main task of Social Democrats as not leadership of the working
class but assistance to it. He also became persuaded that Martov
and Kremer were correct in predicting that economic strife,
whether spontaneous or caused by agitation, would automatically
radicalize the proletariat.[57]

In this atmosphere of euphoria the Union of Struggle decided
to send a delegation consisting of Potresov and Struve to the Con-

[54] Lenin, Pis'ma k rodnym, 14–15; A. I. Elizarova, "Vladimir Il'ich v tiurme,"
PR, No. 3/26 (1924), 113–114, 123.
[55] Martov, Zapiski, 303.
[56] Pipes, Social Democracy, 104–106.
[57] Lenin, I, 426, 438–439, 440, 441.

gress of the Socialist International, scheduled for August in London. It was the first delegation ever sent to an international socialist congress from Russia, Russian socialism having been previously represented by émigré delegates exclusively. The plan entailed grave risks because the police, aware of the connections between Potresov, Struve, and the arrested members of the Union, kept a close watch on the two. Kautsky thought Struve foolhardy to go under these circumstances: "I must confess," he wrote Plekhanov, "that I consider this an act of reckless daring, because London will be full of Russian agents, and Struve is already under a cloud of suspicion." [58] As a single concession to security, the names of Struve and Potresov were omitted from the official roster of delegates.

Struve left Russia in July 1896, six weeks before the opening of the Congress, to consult with Plekhanov and his friends in Switzerland and to prepare with them the report of the Russian delegation. Plekhanov took upon himself the responsibility for the main report (except for the part dealing with the recent textile strike, entrusted to Potresov); Struve was to write a supplement explaining the agrarian policy of Russian Social Democrats. During his Swiss stay, Struve also wrote two articles on the textile strike and its implications.

In the agrarian report,[59] Struve argued that the Russian peasants were so backward and so lacking in class consciousness that there was no point in devoting much attention to them for purposes of propaganda or agitation. Although conceding that it was possible occasionally to incite them to rebellion, he saw no likelihood of systematic agitation's producing a response in the village. The peasantry would be seized by the revolutionary spirit only after shown the way by a class-conscious Russian proletariat. Struve's whole report was permeated with that scorn and suspicion of the peasant that Russian Social Democrats of this period had in common.

In the articles on the labor disturbances in St. Petersburg,[60] Struve expounded the central dogma of Social Democratic poli-

---

[58] *Gruppa Osvobozhdenie Truda*, V (Moscow and Leningrad, 1926), 222.
[59] #31.
[60] #37 and #60; the latter came out the following year (1897) but appears to have been written during Struve's stay in Switzerland or shortly afterward.

tics: that the proletariat would liberate Russia from absolutism. The proletariat could not avoid fulfilling the mission which history had assigned to it, he wrote. Russia was the only European country in which large-scale capitalist development took place under an autocratic regime. That fact assured that Russia's industrialization would produce significant political side-effects. Capitalism greatly increased the number of industrial workers and at the same time made it necessary to provide them with a rudimentary education (since an industrial economy required a literate population), thereby unwittingly undermining the autocratic system. Workers who knew how to read were bound sooner or later to realize how lawless was the regime under which they lived: and once this happened, they would be driven to fight the regime which stood in the way of their self-improvement: "The Russian working class needs political freedom in order to wage a united economic struggle for better working conditions, in order to educate itself without hindrance — in a word, in order to live better." [61] The two main concerns of the workers as revealed by their activities in the 1890's in St. Petersburg — the desire for education and the drive to form trade unions — pushed them toward a head-on collision with the autocratic regime. "The Russian revolution has at last found the people," [62] Struve exclaimed.

Struve wrote his articles on peasants and workers in the radical spirit which seized him whenever he was near professional revolutionaries like Plekhanov or Lenin. But as soon as he found himself in London, away from the stultifying air of the Russian underground, his fundamental liberalism at once reasserted itself. He read avidly the reports which the other delegations submitted to the Congress, and was particularly impressed by that presented by the Fabian Society with an elaborate exposition of evolutionary socialism.[63] The Fabians stated as their aim the gradual, piecemeal attainment of political democracy and social justice by means of exerting pressure on the national legislature. A dramatic confrontation between capitalism and socialism (that is, revolution) was ruled out. Capitalism would imperceptibly shade into socialism, they predicted: society, presently divided into classes, would

[61] #60/xii.
[62] #60/xv.
[63] *Report on Fabian Policy and Resolutions Presented by the Fabian Society to the International Socialist and Trade Union Congress* (London, 1896).

transform itself into a classless society. Compromises were essential: socialism would not solve all human problems.

This was sweet music to Struve's ears. He believed all these things and suppressed them within himself only because Russian autocracy, by its stubborn refusal to share any power with society, forced liberals like him to become radical. During the Congress and after it had closed he had long talks with Vera Zasulich. He must have argued very persuasively in favor of the Fabian positions because even she temporarily fell under their spell.[64] He also talked with Bernstein, whom he found equally impressed by the Fabian Report.[65] Three years later, when Bernstein came out publicly against the idea of social revolution, Struve reminded Vera Zasulich of their "English conversations," [66] and in a review of Bernstein's celebrated "revisionist" book flatly attributed its basic ideas to the Fabians.[67]

For reasons which will be spelled out below, Struve was in no hurry to return home. After the adjournment of the Congress, he rested a few days at the seaside resort of Bournemouth in the company of the other Russian delegates; and after they had departed, he settled down in London. He remained here until the end of October, spending most of his time on research in the library of the British Museum.

The literature which occupied him during the two months in London was the collection of Blue Books issued by a Parliamentary commission on unemployment. Going through these materials, he experienced his first doubts about the Marxist explanation. In an article written on the basis of these researchers, he stated that the theory of "capitalist overpopulation," advanced in Volume I of *Capital*, more than any other teaching of Marx "required revision and critique utilizing the enormous quantity of accumulated new factual data." [68] The causes of unemployment were very complex, involving, among other things, seasonal and cyclical factors. Although capitalism was indeed responsible for it in considerable measure, unemployment was intrinsic to economic progress: even a phenomenon otherwise as progressive as trade unionism could

---

[64] Vera Zasulich to Plekhanov from London [1896]: *Gruppa Osvobozhdenie Truda*, V (Moscow and Leningrad, 1926), 157.

[65] *Gruppa Osvobozhdenie Truda*, V, 158.

[66] See below, p. 219.

[67] #83/739.

[68] #54/92. See also his remarks in #18.

contribute to it. These critical observations were the first evidence of a conflict in Struve's mind between socialist theory and economic scholarship.

Struve found the atmosphere of English politics more congenial than Russian and German sectarianism. He retained to the end of his life a warm sympathy for England, which he looked upon as having approached more nearly than any other country the ideal of political perfection.

The events recounted in this chapter took place against the background of an intense personal drama. Struve lingered so long in Britain and Switzerland (nearly half a year in all) not only in order to draft socialist reports and study Blue Books, but also to get away from a painful dilemma that had arisen in his relations with Kalmykova.

Sometime after he moved into Kalmykova's apartment he became her lover. Such a relationship was bound to produce complications if only because of the difference in age — Struve was then in his twenties, Kalmykova, in her forties — but their temperaments assured its becoming tortuous. As a youth, Struve had (and readily admitted to having) a soft and vacillating character. He was as incapable of making a firm decision of any kind as of seeing a decision through to the end. His frequent acts of intellectual defiance, his temperamental outbursts, and his notorious penchant for shocking statements were symptoms of this personal quality, for like many indecisive people he could assert himself only spasmodically, saving himself in this manner the necessity of making a deliberate choice. During the years they spent together, he had come to depend on Kalmykova to provide him with all his needs. She was his mother and mistress. Because he had a strong sense of moral responsibility, he felt terribly guilty about this unnatural liaison and tried to put an end to it, but he saw no honorable way out. He twice proposed marriage, but Kalmykova refused. Because he could not bring himself to move, he stayed on, feeling ever guiltier and more tortured.

Kalmykova, too, could not decide on a break. She needed Struve's affection (she seems to have had a strong craving for young men); she also believed that without her he would not manage in life. In the summer of 1895, having settled him in the vicinity of Samara to take a cure of mare's milk for his ailing stomach, she wrote Potresov:

> During the five days which we traveled, I talked with him a great deal, and reflected even more. *I have become more than ever convinced of his helplessness and lack of courage.* Lately, in St. Petersburg, the desire has often made itself felt that all *this* should finally happen and come to an end. But once you reflect, you clearly realize that *this* will not be the end but the beginning of a long, difficult, and *unsuccessful* life. Everything persuades me of the latter, and this awareness arouses a burning sensation of pain and responsibility. And if I realize this, I must protect.[69]

So the strange liaison dragged on, upheld on one side by the fear of hurting a proud middle-aged woman and, on the other, by the desire to protect a helpless youth. Struve believed his relationship with Kalmykova to have left him "incurably maimed." [70]

The affair might have gone on indefinitely, were it not that sometime before June 1896, when he departed for Switzerland, Struve fell in love with Antonina (Nina) Aleksandrovna Gerd, the sister of one of his university friends. She was two years older and very plain. (Their friends joked that it was only fair for Struve to have chosen an unattractive woman because, being a Marxist, he believed *chem khuzhe, tem luchshe* — "the worse, the better.") She won him with her gentleness and kindness, which contrasted sharply with the character of the domineering Kalmykova, whose "soothing good nature," as Struve later wrote, concealed "true spiritual hardness." [71] Nina's family background was remarkably like his, being both foreign and academic. Her grandfather, the Irishman James Heard, a specialist in the Lancaster method of instruction, had first visited Russia in 1817 at the invitation of Count Rumiantsev and then returned and stayed. Alexander, his son and Nina's father, a distinguished educator, was appointed tutor in the imperial household and taught the future Nicholas II.

Torn between the two women, Struve left Russia in a condition

---

[69] Kalmykova to Potresov, June 11, 1895.
[70] See below, p. 173.
[71] "Vremena," *Voz,* No. 537 (November 2, 1926).

close to a breakdown. In London, after painful soul searching, he decided to break with Kalmykova and marry Nina. He sent Kalmykova several hysterical letters in which he implored her to meet him in Germany to hear out his explanations. This she refused to do, and at the end of October he proceeded to Montreux to meet Nina, who was awaiting him there. He now told her everything about his past relationship with Kalmykova, and asked her to marry him; she consented. His joy was tempered only by the knowledge that he had still to straighten out matters with Kalmykova. In a desperate effort to extricate himself from the predicament, he sought Potresov's assistance. In November 1896 he wrote him two long letters which merit extensive citation because they permit an unusual insight into the private life of a man who, as a rule, jealously guarded it from outsiders:

In London I have experienced the most difficult moments of complete spiritual collapse, verging on despondency. Of this condition A[leksandra] M[ikhailovna] [Kalmykova] has certainly informed you; I had sent her quite senseless letters while in this unbearably difficult mood. Now I see that the cause of this mood lay in that anarchy in my private life which only here I have cut short. I arrived here with an empty and ravaged soul — I depart with a soul full of faith, eager for work and action. It was necessary to find a way out from that impossible situation which had dragged on for some three years, and I think the one I have chosen is the *only correct* one. You yourself have advocated it so recently and so convincingly that I believe I have you on my side. I am happy now, insofar as a man in my situation can be happy, that is, a man with a tortured soul, shattered nerves, and an infirm body. Help me, dear friend, with all the power at your disposal to terminate the old relationship, which becomes more pernicious the longer it lasts. And the new life is good with its astounding harmony. It carries with it new and heavy cares, but these will not oppress me — they will rather give me a fresh lift. That which I have gone through during the seven years of my first youth was *worse* than material cares; it drained my nerves more severely and inflicted on my soul countless wounds. Peace to the past! I shall always retain in my soul the feeling of profound gratitude for those happy minutes which lay in that past, but one must not sacrifice to it the present and the future. It is enough that I am already in many respects incurably maimed. I am not simply infatuated. I have had enough time to test my infatuation with calm thought. I am spiritually much too shattered to become simply infatuated. For me this solution is a genuine salvation, and not merely a more convenient way of life . . .

What is my relationship to A[leksandra] M[ikhailovna]? I have not ceased to love her without end. But I felt and still feel that these relations simply destroyed my strength, and their liquidation was prompted by an instinct of self-preservation. That this liquidation should have lasted three years, that, of course, is my misfortune; but in return I found N[ina] A[leksandrovna]. And this is a remarkable fortune . . .[72]

To Struve's dismay, Potresov sided with Kalmykova, who was hurt and furious at the manner in which he terminated their affair. The following is Struve's reply to Potresov's letter (unfortunately, lost), written from Montreux on November 23, 1896:

My failure to reply immediately to your letter *was due not to negligence;* on the contrary, it was deliberate and intended to postpone writing an answer. The point is that your letter had struck me most disagreeably, and I did not want to reply while under its immediate impression. Moreover, I did not want to be unfair, valuing highly fairness in all relations and realms of life. Now I am able to do so calmly.

You write that I acted like a *weak* man, and thereby tormented A[leksandra] M[ikhailovna]. You are correct in ascertaining that fact, but you take the facts without considering the soul of the man whom they concern. I could not have acted differently because I am not only a person with a weak will (I readily confess this) but I am also particularly powerless when confronted with the suffering of others. The suffering of others, especially involving persons close to me, drains me of the last ounce of that will power which, in such situations and conflicts, alone perhaps produces good results. The question here is not one of fault, for I have twice taken the firm decision which A[leksandra] M[ikhailovna] had only to confirm. And the noth-

[72] Struve to Potresov, undated letter, probably from early November 1896, and apparently from Montreux.

ing that happened would have happened. Now, of course, it is [too] late, but if my and her well-being are there, in that past which could have been the present and the future, it is not my fault that this did not occur. I was weak, but who was strong? The question is now settled for me once more by the suffering of a third, completely innocent person. I mention this quality of mine — powerlessness in the face of the suffering of others — not to boast of it. But in it lies the main explanation of my whole conduct, now as then. Aleksandra Mikhailovna does not understand this (and there is much in me that she never has understood and never will — after all, you yourself know what a *subjective* person she is), but others, and you above all, should have grasped and understood.

I hesitated because I loved much and strongly, and I suffered much, infinitely much, from someone else's suffering, transforming it into my own and placing myself thus in the midst of insoluble conflicts between feelings and obligations. . . . Were it not for that quality I would not have gone to Montreux but long ago returned to St. Petersburg. . . . If in speaking of this weakness of mine, you are hinting at the mood which had induced me to request Aleksandra Mikhailovna to come and meet me in Germany then I shall tell you: I do not like to have recourse to neuropathology, but for me, now, as it was then (in lucid intervals), it is obvious that my spiritual condition, for some immediate, concrete causes which are not entirely clear to me, was really quite abnormal. My awareness of the abnormality, of the pathological nature of my condition, of course did not make matters easier for me. You are right that this is a weakness, but it is a weakness that excludes subjective guilt in *my own* eyes, that is, in the eyes of that individual for whom it is most difficult and painful to state his own abnormality.

In considering that my weakness "lowered and debased" me in the eyes of Aleksandra Mikhailovna, you may be (and even certainly are) correct, but after all that I have told you, perhaps you will not find strange my own admission that this weakness has always personally *elevated* me in my own eyes. I may regret this *weakness* from the point of view of time lost and spiritual energy expended, but had it not existed there would also have been none of our spiritual conflicts, that is, there would have been absent that which constituted the essence of my relations with A[leksandra] M[ikhaidovna] and lent them their specific coloring. She, a strong person, pushed on my shoulders, the weak one, the whole burden of the decision. Given the conditions in which I have lived these past three years, *I* could *only have hesitated* . . .

The following spring, Struve and Nina left St. Petersburg for Vienna and there, on May Day of 1897, they were married.

8. *THE NEW WORD*

In the winter of 1896–97, after three years of trying in vain, the St. Petersburg Social Democrats at last acquired a journal of their own. Its name — *Novoe slovo, The New Word* — was coined not by them but by the journal's founders, but it well reflected the task which they had in mind for it: spreading the new Westernizing gospel to counteract the ideologies of nationalism entrenched on both the right and the left.

The involved story of the passage of the *New Word* into Social Democratic hands can be briefly told.[1] The journal, a "fat" monthly, had been founded in 1893 as an organ of middle-of-the-road liberal opinion. It fared poorly, and two years later was sold to the wealthy wife of a St. Petersburg publisher, Olga Popova, who consigned it to a board of socialist editors headed by S. N. Krivenko. This move, however, failed to attract new subscribers, and by the end of 1896, Popova, having lost on the journal nearly fifty thousand rubles and tired of bickering with the editorial staff, was looking for a way to rid herself of the troublesome property. At this point she was approached by the journalist V. A. Posse, a recent convert to Social Democracy. Posse proposed that she turn over the ailing journal to him and his friend M. N. Semenov, a prosperous landlord, with the understanding that they would gradually buy her out from the proceeds of sales. In the event that these did not come up to expectation, Semenov pledged his estates as security. Popova, who stood to lose nothing, agreed, and

---

[1] The history of the *New Word* is told in the following studies: V. Poliansky, "Marksistskaia periodicheskaia pechat'," 1896–1906," KA, No. 2/9 (1925), 240–263; V. A. Posse, *Moi zhiznennyi put'* (Moscow and Leningrad, 1929), 111–136; V. Evgenev-Maksimov, *Ocherki po istorii sotsialisticheskoi zhurnalistiki v Rossii XIX veka* (Moscow and Leningrad, 1927), 223–229; N. Angarsky, *Legal'nyi marksizm*, I (Moscow, 1925), 113–35; and Richard Kindersley, *The First Russian Revisionists* (Oxford, 1962), 82–92.

in February 1897 the *New Word* passed to Posse and Semenov. Krivenko and his associates loudly protested their eviction, and even took the dispute with Popova before a board of arbitrators, but to no avail.

The new owners were confident that they could resuscitate the ailing monthly, having sensed that there existed in Russia a sizable untapped market for Social Democratic publications. This was indicated by the favorable reception given the books published by Potresov and the impressive circulation figures of the *Messenger of Samara*.[2] The first decision they had to make was to select an editor, and here the choice was obvious. Struve was by then not only the leading spokesman for Social Democracy in Russia, but also Posse's relative by marriage. After consulting Kalmykova (with whom he remained on good terms), Struve accepted the proffered position. An editorial committee was then established: Struve, editor-in-chief; Tugan-Baranovsky, coeditor; Posse and Semenov, editors in charge of foreign and domestic news, respectively; and Kalmykova, literary editor. As a precaution against police harassment, Popova's husband was listed officially as editor-in-chief.

The *New Word* was Struve's journal from beginning to end. He edited it magnificently, transforming it at once into Russia's liveliest monthly. He was a born editor, one of the greatest the country has ever produced, and the best of his generation. The very qualities which repeatedly frustrated his political ambitions — insatiable curiosity and sympathy for the most disparate points of view — enabled him, throughout his long editorial career, which now began, to fashion every journal placed in his care into an outlet for the best informed and most advanced opinion of the time.

This intellectual breadth and vitality were particularly striking in the *New Word* in that it was intended to be the organ of an as yet unformed but very real political party. About its orientation there could be no mistake. Martov, who was in exile in Siberia when the first issue edited by Struve came out, later wrote of the joy with which he and his friends greeted its appearance: The *New Word*, in his words, became "in the fullest sense of the word

[2] The *Messenger of Samara* was shut down on orders of the Ministry of the Interior in March 1897, that is, one month after the *New Word* had passed under Posse's and Semenov's control.

an organ of the nascent [Social Democratic] party." [3] Lenin, too, had nothing but praise for the journal, which conformed to his notion of partiinost' ("partyness"),[4] Most of the contributors were dedicated Social Democrats and treated political and socio- logical, as well as historical, literary, and artistic subjects from the party's point of view. But Russian Social Democracy at this time had not yet ossified into dogma. It was young and self- assured, and therefore reasonably open-minded. Its adherents did not hesitate to dispute one another, confident that they had on their side objective truth, which a frank airing of disagreements would only serve to bring out. Mikhailovsky rejoiced over every incon- sistency he spotted in the *New Word,* but in vain: these did not trouble Struve in the least. As he informed the readers: "Contra- dictions in the opinions of contributors to the *New Word* exist and will continue to be . . . We shall not polemicize with each other for the benefit of our adversaries. But if, in the course of things, such polemics should become necessary in the interest of our readers, we will not hesitate to initiate them." [5]

Like the other "fat" monthlies, the *New Word* consisted of two parts, one literary, the other scholarly and political. In the lit- erary part, Kalmykova printed novels and stories written in the "realistic" manner. The only outstanding contributor to this sec- tion was Maxim Gorky, then still an unknown, who published there his first important story, "Konovalov." [6] (Posse had great difficulty securing his collaboration, because Gorky at that time hated the Marxists, probably for what he considered their anti- humanitarian attitude toward the recent famines.)[7] The journal's literary criticism was also Marxist in approach. In a perceptive review of Chekhov's "Peasants" ("Muzhiki"), Struve stressed the story's value as a social documentary. He praised in particular Chekhov's skill in contrasting the semiurbanized, semicivilized hero, Nikolai Chikildeev, with his relatives, who remained sunk

[3] L. Martov, *Zapiski Sotsial Demokrata* (Berlin, 1922), 306.

[4] *Lenin,* XXVIII, 30, and III, 156n; V. I. Lenin, *Pis'ma k rodnym* (Moscow, 1934), 32.

[5] #65/185.

[6] NS, No. 6 (March 1897), 1–41.

[7] Posse, *Zhiznennyi put',* 126; I. Gruzdev, *Maksim Gorkii* (Moscow, 1926), 28–29. Struve had a low opinion of Gorky's talents: "As I see it, there is in him much strength, but at the same time also a great deal of *mannerism* and *preten- tiousness.* I am afraid that he appeals to Russian intellectuals mainly because of his mannerism, not his strength" (Struve to Potresov, July 11, 1898).

in the idiocy of rural life.[8] From favorable remarks about Zola,[9] it may be concluded that at this time he sympathized with the naturalistic school of literary criticism.

It was the second, theoretical half of the journal that had the heavy guns. All leading figures of Russian Social Democracy were represented here: Plekhanov, Struve, Vera Zasulich, Martov, Lenin, Tugan-Baranovsky, Victor Chernov (later a leader of the Socialist Revolutionary party), the historian Eugene Tarlé, and others.

It attests to both the quality of the journal and the sophistication of the Russian readership that a monthly of such size (it averaged five hundred pages an issue) and of so high a theoretical level could attract a large number of subscribers. Its circulation, which under Krivenko had averaged 1,500 copies, climbed rapidly after Struve took over, reaching 4,000 copies with the sixth issue (August) and 5,600 with the ninth (November). The demand was so great that the October number was reprinted.[10]

As if editing a monthly were not enough to occupy him, Struve concurrently assumed editorship of a book series published by Popova under the title "Educational Library." It consisted of scholarly works on natural science, philosophy, psychology, sociology, and history. In this position, which he held from 1897 to 1901, he arranged for both original books and translations, among them a new edition of Volume I of *Capital*, and the first Russian book on Spinoza.[11] The post permitted him to assist impecunious friends, from whom he commissioned editorial and translating jobs.

Struve contributed to the *New Word* two regular columns. One, "On Various Themes" ("Na raznye temy"), consisted of informal

---

[8] #50/46–47.

[9] #50/43.

[10] Evgenev-Maksimov, *Ocherki*, 223, 235, 239; Posse, *Zhiznennyi put'*, 133–134. The reprinting of the October issue is announced on the cover of the November issue.

[11] Among books edited by Struve during this period were: Pol' de Ruz'e (Paul de Rousiers), *Professional'nye rabochie soiuzy v Anglii* (St. Petersburg, 1898) (cf. #75); G. Giggs (H. Higgs), *Fiziokraty* (St. Petersburg, 1899); S. i B. Vebb (Sidney and Beatrice Webb), *Teoriia i praktika angliiskogo tred-unionizma*, 2 vols. (St. Petersburg, 1900–1901), the first volume translated by Lenin; I. Lippert, *Istoriia kul'tury* (St. Petersburg, 1901); and G. Shultse-Gevernits (G. von Schulze-Gävernitz), *Ocherki obshchestvennogo khoziaistva i ekonomicheskoi politiki Rossii* (St. Petersburg, 1901) (cf. #110). The book on Spinoza was by V. Bolin. On the new edition of Marx, see #81.

essays on literary and theoretical subjects. The other, "Current Questions of Domestic Life" ("Tekushchie voprosy vnutrennei zhizni"), dealt with the internal affairs of contemporary Russia. In order to escape liability, Struve, like the other contributors, signed his articles with pseudonyms, using "Novus" for the former and "P.B." for the latter.

But even without the author's name it was not difficult to identify Struve, for the quality of his mind was impressed like a signature on everything he wrote. The range of topics touched upon and the wealth of information brought to bear on them exceeded the competence of any other Russian writer of the period. Struve could discuss with a depth appropriate to a scholarly journal such diverse subjects as labor legislation in Russia and Western Europe, the intellectual and social antecedents of German socialism, Russian Romanticism, and the philosophical implications of the antinomy of freedom and necessity. He could also review authoritatively a recent novel and a historical study of ancient Greece. The erudition revealed in these articles and in his other writings was particularly impressive because it was never paraded for the sake of impressing.

During the year he edited the *New Word,* Struve was more orthodox in his Marxism than at any other time in his career. In dealing with ideological subjects in the journal, he stressed more than ever before, or after, the class content of ideas and the economic interests of their advocates — a practice he was to find most repugnant later on. Consciously or not, in his contributions to the *New Word* he adopted Marx's manner of debating, and frequently used a tone of biting sarcasm which suggested that anyone who did not agree with him was a fool or a hypocrite or both. Although he retained some of his earlier reservations about particular features of Marx's system, notably its philosophy, he had a high degree of confidence in the system as a whole. The connection which Marx had established between economic and social phenomena seemed to him to possess a scientific validity which Marx's specific misjudgments did not vitiate. As far as he was concerned, the "metaphysical" elements that Marx allowed to creep into his philosophy and sociology no more disproved historical materialism than Newton's religiousness or Darwin's inability to account for genetic changes invalidated the laws of gravity or of natural selection. The obscure or weak sides in

Marx's theory, Struve at this time confidently believed, were certain some day to be clarified or improved upon by a logical critique of Marxist methodology and an open-minded analysis of fresh evidence.

At the same time, however, he remained loyal to his fundamental liberal convictions and in all his contributions treated freedom as the ultimate good.

Struve's most outstanding contributions to the *New Word* took the form of monthly essays under the general heading "Current Questions of Domestic Life." Modeled on Arseniev's "Internal Surveys" in the *Messenger of Europe,* which Struve had so much admired in his school days, they gave critical analyses of social, economic, and political developments taking place throughout the Russian Empire. But these essays were more than topical journalism. For all their apparent casualness, they were bound by a common theme, and, read in sequence, provide a remarkable insight into the anatomy of the imperial regime at an advanced stage of decomposition.

The theme was stated in three words in the opening article of the series: "Narodnaia zhizn' uslozhniaetsia" — "The nation's life is growing complex." [12] Russia was becoming so diversified in all aspects of its life that it was bursting from the institutional and legal strait jacket forced on it by the imperial government. The purpose of the series was to demonstrate through examples taken from everyday experience (often in the form of citations from the conservative press) that the liberty and democracy which the opposition groups demanded were not impractical ideals but necessities of modern life. Struve was, in effect, using evidence drawn from the contemporary scene to demonstrate the very contention which twelve years earlier had converted him to liberalism: Russia had outgrown its government.

As his first illustration he took the legislation pertaining to the peasantry. Russian local government from the 1860's onward had assumed that the country's population was divided into well-defined legal estates, among which the peasantry formed a single homogeneous entity. But in the time which had elapsed since, the peasantry in fact had become economically and socially so differ-

---

[12] #45/157. This is also the theme of Struve's editorial for the newspaper *Severnyi kur'er* in 1899, discussed below, Chapter 10.

entiated that it ceased to constitute a true social unit. The needs
and interests of the various subgroups of the peasantry were no
longer identical; nor could the peasantry be quite so sharply distinguished from the other estates as had once been the case.
These economic and social facts demanded a reform of the rural
administration which would replace the class principle with the
territorial one. The idea of *vsesoslovnaia volost'* — an all-class
administrative unit embracing not only villagers but also all the
inhabitants of a given district — was not merely a liberal slogan,
but a requirement of contemporary life.

Similar observations could be made about the gentry. Commenting on a recent imperial pronouncement expressing concern over
the decline of the gentry, Struve argued that efforts to save that
class were futile.[13] The gentry had been declining economically
since 1861, despite all the attempts made to rescue them. Between
1861 and 1892 they had lost 23 percent of their land, and the rate
of attrition showed no sign of abating. The reasons for the gentry's
economic decline lay deep in its historic past. The serf system
had not prepared the Russian landowning class for modern, rational agriculture based on the calculation of profit. The gentry
were therefore unable to benefit either from the vast sums they had
received as part of the Emancipation settlement or from the subsequent rise in rents. Unaccustomed to a money economy, the
gentry did not invest their capital productively in land, but spent
it on personal consumption. Whenever they ran out of cash, they
mortgaged or sold their estates. Thus, the gentry grew poorer,
and when, in the 1890's, rents and land prices suddenly declined,
they faced disaster. A further cause of the gentry's decline as a
rural class was the great demand in post-Reform Russia for personnel with higher education. As the principal educated class, the
gentry found strong inducements after 1861 to leave their estates
and seek employment with government and private business, as
well as to enter the free professions. Struve estimated that approximately one-fifth of the Russian gentry were lost to agriculture in
this manner. The decline of the gentry which the emperor la-
mented was due not to causes capable of being removed by legislation or some extraordinary effort from above, but to factors
deeply imbedded in the country's economy and culture. Life again
triumphed over law. The privileged social and political status of

[13] #52/207–217.

the gentry had become incompatible with their actual economic position. Having lost the bulk of the land, the gentry could no longer rule the zemstva. It was utopian to try to recapture for them the authority which they had enjoyed in the countryside before the Emancipation.

Struve argued in a similar vein in articles on the labor movement,[14] on the bourgeoisie and corporation laws,[15] on trials by jury,[16] and on censorship.[17] In each case he used an incident from life or a quotation from the right-wing press as the text for a sermon on the hopeless inconsistency between the content and the form of Russian reality. Each event was interpreted as a symptom of the inexorable, though still invisible, force pressing against the outwardly rigid forms of autocracy: "The future historian of our age will some day note its curious quality: in small clashes over the most trivial causes he will uncover the slow but irresistible action of powerful historical currents." [18]

Struve also gave a prominent place to the Polish question.[19] In articles on this subject he wrote with surprising candor about the follies of Russification, about the brutality with which the western provinces had been "pacified" after the 1863 uprising, about the rights of the Poles to a national culture. Anyone inclined to think of late nineteenth-century Russia as a country of muzzled opinion would do well to read these passages, published at the height of reaction in a legally certified journal.

The mood of these surveys, six in all, was optimistic. Struve viewed the reactionary policies of the government as either follies or acts of desperation. They could be pursued for another year or two, but eventually life had to triumph, and life was on the side of liberty. He laid great stress on human rights and dignity, not only as valuable in themselves but as indispensable to the proper functioning of law and the economy.[20] Russia must be Westernized:

[14] #56.
[15] #47/235–240.
[16] #53/201–209.
[17] #47/231–235.
[18] #53/190.
[19] #47/230–231; #64/246–260.
[20] Struve ascribed British economic leadership to the high productivity of the English worker, and explained this high productivity by the sense of self-respect which law and democracy inculcated in the country's citizenry. He deduced from this premise that Russia would not be able to compete effectively on world

There can be no doubt that the node of all the problems confronting the Russian Empire lies in the level of development
and culture of the Russian center, of the heartland of Russia
(*korennaia Rossiia*). We would say that it lies in Moscow.
The Europeanization of that center which gravitates toward
Moscow, the creation in it of Russian culture — not the "true
Russian" culture [of the reactionaries], but first and foremost
a fundamentally European culture — here lies the solution of
all the burning problems of the Russian Empire without exception . . .[21]

Among Struve's theoretical contributions of this period, the most
important took the form of a debate with Sergei Bulgakov over
the question of freedom and necessity raised by Rudolf Stammler
in his recent book *Economics and Society*.[22]

Stammler, a German Neo-Kantian, subjected the concept of
causality in Marx's sociology to a thoroughgoing analysis. Accepting Marx's premise that ideas and social institutions — the
superstructure — depended on underlying economic factors, he
nevertheless found that this dependence could not be adequately
explained in causal terms. The economic base was never sufficiently distinct from the superstructure to permit one to state
unequivocally that one "caused" the other. The legal institution
of property, for example, which Marx assigned to the superstructure, was at the same time part of the economic base, insofar as
the concept of property implied a particular arrangement of the
productive forces. The relationship of "base" and "superstructure," according to Stammler, was better understood in terms
not of cause and effect, but of content and form. He proposed
that sociology take as its object of study "society," approaching
it once from the economic, and then again from the legal (super-
structural) point of view. This explanation was an important
modification of the Marxist method and had far-reaching implications, which Struve, however, drew fully only several years
later in his critique of Marx's theory of social development.

Stammler furthermore questioned whether in the historic proc-

---

markets until it had granted its working class basic civil and political rights.
#56/241–42.

[21] #64/249.

[22] *Wirtschaft und Recht nach der materialistischen Geschichtsauffassung* (Leipzig, 1896).

ess there existed a single causal chain, since such a conception made no allowance for purposeful, forward-oriented human activity. Satisfied neither with the standard Marxist solution of the freedom-necessity conflict ("freedom means recognition of necessity") nor with that provided by Kant (there is no conflict because freedom and necessity belong to different realms of explanation), he proposed a different solution. Parallel with the causal chain, established by the mind, he posited a "teleological" one, determined by the will. Causation answered the question "why?" teleology the question "what for?" Will was motivated not by that which had happened, but by that which was desired — not by antecedent events but by goals lying in the future. Once the will attained its object, this object became part of the inexorable causal chain itself; until then, however, the will was free to want. This interpretation saw history as a result of interaction between necessity and freedom.

Stammler's book was coolly received by such critics as Max Weber[23] and Plekhanov.[24] The young Russian Marxist Bulgakov, however, found its thesis attractive and wrote on it a long essay entitled "On the Subjection of Social Phenomena to Laws," published in the journal *Problems of Philosophy and Psychology.*[25] With some reservations, he accepted Stammler's argument that alongside the causal factor in history, guided by necessity, there existed also a teleological one, determined by the exercise of the will.

To Struve, Stammler's argument was not entirely new, for he had encountered it previously in the writings of Mikhailovsky and the American sociologist Lester Ward. He had already had occasion to reject the latter's suggestion that social science allow for the teleological (or "telic") factor, citing the authority of Riehl, who held that goals and will also belong to the category of causality.[26] In response to Bulgakov's essay, Struve published in the same periodical a lengthy critique of Bulgakov and Stammler, "Freedom and Historical Necessity." Bulgakov replied in the

---

[23] Max Weber, "Rudolf Stammlers 'Ueberwindung' der materialistischen Geschichtsauffassung," ASS, XXIV (1907), 94–151.

[24] G. V. Plekhanov, *Izbrannye filosofskie proizvedeniia,* I (Moscow, 1956), 491.

[25] Sergei Bulgakov, "O zakonomernosti sotsial'nykh iavlenii," VFP, No. 5/35 (1896), 575–611; reprinted in Sergei Bulgakov, *Ot marksizma k idealizmu* (St. Petersburg, 1903), 1–34.

[26] #15/54n–55n.

pages of the *New Word,* and Struve concluded the debate with a
final rebuttal.[27]

Struve continued to adhere to the Kantian view of freedom and
necessity:

> The whole edifice of social idealism which Stammler erects in
> no way competes . . . with the materialist conception of his-
> tory. We can leave social idealism entirely in peace. If that
> edifice is constructed in the spirit of Kant, then it bears on the
> realm of the "thing in itself," which, as Kant persistently taught,
> is inaccessible to understanding and explanation: "Where de-
> terminism in accord with the laws of nature ends, there all
> explanation ceases as well . . ."
>
> Inevitability (*zakonomernost'*) is unthinkable outside its mat-
> ter, outside phenomena. The materialist conception of history
> — and this cannot be overstressed — is a construct referring
> entirely to the realm of experience. For this reason, even if
> the social teleology of Stammler were impeccable, its existence
> would in no way affect the economic conception of history — at
> any rate, from the point of view of those who accept the
> Kantian theories of knowledge and experience . . .
>
> Thus, freedom is subject to no laws [*bezzakonna* or *gesetzlos*].
> Besides, *philosophically,* the word *freedom* has no other mean-
> ing than that of denying necessity or inevitability.[28]

While rejecting Stammler's solution, he praised him for having
raised the problem of the relationship between freedom and necessity, which the Marxists largely ignored:

> The merit of Stammler, as I see it, lies among other things in
> a clear formulation of the contradiction between freedom and
> necessity. Such a formulation was important for the critique,
> and, if you will, for the self-critique of the materialist concep-
> tion of history. Until now this conception was satisfied with
> Hegel translated by Engels into the language of materialist
> metaphysics, which, as is well known, furnished Engels with his
> philosophical foundations. Engels transforms Hegel's absolute

---

[27] #43. Sergei Bulgakov, "Zakon prichinnosti i svoboda chelovecheskikh deistvii,"
NS, No. 8 (May 1897), 183–199; reprinted in his *Ot marksizma,* 35–52. Struve's
answer: #49.

[28] #43/122–123, 132.

necessity, which is at the same time freedom, into the ordinary necessity of the empirically real world, and, having accomplished this transformation, explained freedom as the "recognition of necessity."

This is correct as long as one does not assign freedom the only definite meaning, which consists in the denial of necessity or of causality. Engels could philosophize in this manner because, being a complete stranger to the critical point of view, he failed to notice that no dialectic can remove epistemological contradictions — contradictions which themselves actually constitute one of the foundations and justifications of the dialectical point of view.[29]

What then of freedom? Whence come our ideals and what force do they exert? They are essentially psychological facts:

It is said — I used to say so myself — that scientific collectivism derives its ideal from the socioeconomic reality. This is true and at the same time false. The ideal, of course, grew out of real conditions, as is always the case with all ideals, but for every acting subject who consciously formulates the ideal and for the masses who strive toward this ideal spontaneously, or even consciously, the ideal represents a psychological *prius* in relation to reality and the forces active in it. In the scientific investigation of this reality, the ideal seeks for itself only recognition of its reality and inevitability. Such was the actual course of the progress of modern collectivism from utopia to science. The ideal (of course, in its main outlines) remained unchanged — only the view of the condition under which it could be realized changed. The ideal itself, however, stands outside science, or, if you will, above it, although it does require scientific sanction . . .

We repeat, the necessity of the ideal with which we are dealing here refers to the future and, in particular, to future human actions. And I assert that in this realm of the empirically real world it is not possible to paint any kind of an integral conception of the future completely in the hue of necessity. Logically, of course, the whole future is as predetermined as the past is determined. But, in that predetermined future in which

---

[29] #43/132.

our actions participate, there is always a blank spot which volition and free activity can color according to their desires. Psychological consciousness, actively oriented toward the future, always operates with that compound of freedom and necessity which the logical consciousness finds intolerable. This compound is an unavoidable expression not merely of the inadequacy of scientific knowledge, but of that deeper and more fundamental fact that neither human life nor human consciousness are fully exhausted in cognition, in experience, in science. "World and life," as Riehl beautifully puts it, "can never tracelessly dissolve in science." The very possibility of life and action rests on two orientations of consciousness.[30]

Struve concluded this argument with the assertion that the "materialist conception of history does not pretend to answer the question: what is to be done? This question is resolved on another level, that of interests and ideals. It tells only how to act." [31]

After Bulgakov's reply, Struve wrote a second article on the subject, "Once More Freedom and Necessity," in which he restated his psychological view of freedom:

From the point of view of experience, [freedom] is an indubitable illusion; but from the point of view of the activity of the live individual, it is an equally indubitable *reality*. The contradiction between cognition and life exists for those who want to express all of life in terms of cognition. This is impossible, because for cognition freedom is only a "bare idea," whereas for life freedom is an irrefutable fact, and the idea of freedom is an enormous effective force.[32]

This was a remarkable concession for a Marxist and Social Democrat to make. For all its abstruseness, the import of the argument was clear: first, moral values exist prior to and therefore independently of the economic and social environment; and second, real life is not entirely held in the grip of the laws of necessity. "Economic determinism" was thus doubly assailed: as an explanation of how things were determined and as an exposi-

[30] #43/136–137.
[31] #43/139.
[32] #49/207.

tion of why they had to be determined. The debate with Bulgakov uncovered for a brief instant one side of the evolution which Struve had been quietly undergoing since the writing of *Critical Remarks*. It showed him well on his way toward philosophical idealism, which he was openly to embrace three years later. He himself later regarded the debate as marking his break with Marx's view of freedom and necessity.[33]

Plekhanov was very unhappy with Struve when he read his exchanges with Bulgakov. A great admirer of Engels and a rigid economic determinist, he had difficulty suppressing his rage when he saw Struve refer to Engels's philosophy as "materialist metaphysics" and voice opinions clearly incompatible with Marxism. Plekhanov's wife complained in private that under Struve's influence St. Petersburg youth had gone mad over Kant.[34] But, to preserve the "united front," Plekhanov continued to keep quiet.

The first issues of the *New Word* under Marxist management had no difficulty getting by the censors, at least partly because Semenov regularly bribed them.[35] The trouble began with the November issue, from which an overzealous censor ordered removed several articles, including Struve's "Current Questions" dealing with recent labor legislation. The December number was impounded and was not allowed to go on sale.[36]

By this time, the authorities had second thoughts about the *New Word*. The question of renewing its license was taken up on December 10/22, 1897, by the Council of Ministers. The Council ordered the journal suspended on the grounds that it carried seditious materials and, owing to its wide distribution, was likely to

[33] #102/19. From the philosophical point of view, the answer given by Struve here and in his later writings to the problem of freedom and necessity differs from that of Mikhailovsky and the other "subjectivists" in that it insists on sharp ontological and epistemological distinctions between the two. How this solution differs in application from Mikhailovsky's it is difficult to see. The matter will be treated at greater length in Chapter 12.

[34] Angarsky, *Legal'nyi Marksizm*, 71n; *Literaturnoe Nasledie G. V. Plekhanova*, I (Moscow, 1934), 297.

[35] Posse, *Zhiznennyi put'*, 134.

[36] According to Kindersley (*Russian Revisionists*, 86), the December issue was pulped. Struve later reprinted the column "On Various Themes" from this issue in his book *Na raznye temy* (St. Petersburg, 1902), 170–186 (see bibliography, #65). The installment of "Current Questions of Domestic Life" removed from the November issue has not been republished to this day; it dealt with labor legislation (apparently continuing #56) and bore the title "Pravila i instruktsii 20 sentiabria o proizvoditel'nosti i raspredelenii rabochego vremeni"; Lenin, *Pis'ma k rodnym*, 84.

cause unrest in the country.[37] Ten months after the Social Democrats had taken control of it, the *New Word* was dead.

Deprived of editorial work, Struve at once diverted his restless
energies to scholarship. Before turning to these studies, however,
it is necessary to recount an important episode which briefly interrupted them in February 1898.

In the winter of 1897–98, a number of clandestine Social Democratic organizations active in Russia agreed to hold a national
congress for the purpose of founding a Social Democratic party.
Who actually took the initiative in this matter is disputed by
historians: some credit the Kievan group connected with the
Workers' Newspaper (*Rabochaia Gazeta*), others the Jewish Bund
of Vilno, and still others the St. Petersburg Union of Struggle for
the Liberation of the Working Class.[38] These were the organizations which agreed to meet on March 1/13, 1898, in Minsk.

In making preparations for the congress, the organizers thought
it proper to issue a manifesto pithily summarizing the party's principles and aims. The Kievans submitted a draft written by a member of their group, but Stepan Radchenko, the representative of
the St. Petersburg Union of Struggle, did not like it and it was
set aside.[39] Radchenko then proposed to commission Struve to
draft a different text. The Kievans hesitated, for they preferred
that the task be entrusted to Plekhanov, but Radchenko swung
the Bundists behind him, and sometime in February 1898 he was
authorized to invite Struve to compose the party's official manifesto. Struve accepted.

The assignment was a difficult one, because the document had
to satisfy two disparate factions which had emerged within the
Russian Social Democratic movement. One faction, to which belonged the movement's leading theoreticians, including Plekhanov, Struve, and Lenin, remained faithful to the political
orientation. It saw as the movement's primary mission the trans-

[37] The minutes of the Council session at which the fate of the *New Word* was
decided are in *Osv*, No. 4 (August 2/15, 1902), 52–55. See also Evgenev-
Maksimov, *Ocherki*, 240–241.

[38] N. Nevsky, "K voprosu o pervom s"ezde RSDRP," PR, No. 1 (1921),
82–110, "Materialy k istorii pervogo s"ezda RSDRP," PR, No. 3/71 (1908),
152–169; V. Makhnovets (Akimov), "Pervyi s"ezd S-D R. Partii," MG, No. 2
(1928), 128–168; Leonard Schapiro, *The Communist Party of the Soviet Union*
(London, 1960), 29–30.

[39] The Kievan draft is reproduced in Nevsky, "K voprosu," 94–95.

formation of Russian labor into an organized force that would fight first for political freedom for all and then for political power for itself. The other faction, soon to be known as "Economist," agreed that the attainment of political freedom and power were the ultimate goals of the movement, but wanted to reach these goals by a circuitous route. Intimate and continuous contact with industrial workers (of a kind that Plekhanov, Struve, or Lenin had never had) persuaded these men that the workers were not interested in politics, preferring to occupy themselves with improving their economic and social conditions. From this premise they concluded that Social Democrats would do better to concentrate on helping labor fight for what it wanted, and trust that with time labor would come to realize that a significant improvement in its economic and social condition required a basic change in the country's political system. This strategy, implicit in the agitational method, was originally conceived not as a new theoretical orientation but merely as a new technique. As noted, during the strike years of 1896–97 the notion that one reached politics by way of economic conflicts appealed even to such staunchly "political" men as Struve and Lenin. But by the autumn of 1897 what had originated as a technique became an orientation. In October of that year a circle of St. Petersburg workers and intellectuals jointly launched a labor newspaper, *Worker's Thought* (*Rabochaia mysl'*), dedicated to the proposition that the workers' struggle for economic improvement constituted the essence of socialism, and that socialists should let political activities recede into the background. Political freedom was to be won "in passing." [40] During the next two years, this Economist tendency came to dominate the Russian Social Democratic movement at home and abroad, engendering its first major crisis.

The division between the two Social Democratic factions was not yet sharply drawn in February 1898, but it was beginning to cause trouble. The Jewish Bund, by far the strongest Social Democratic organization in the Russian Empire and the only one enjoying a certain measure of mass support (the others still consisted exclusively of intellectuals), inclined toward Economism.

---

[40] The editorial of the first issue of *Rabochaia Mysl'*, stating its general position, is translated in my *Social Democracy and the St. Petersburg Labor Movement, 1885–1897* (Cambridge, Mass., 1963), 129–131.

The Kievans, on the other hand, with their close links to the traditions of the People's Will, tended to emphasize political action. The three cells of the Union of Struggle represented at the conference took a middle-of-the-road position.

Struve not only had to accommodate the two points of view on politics, but he also had to overcome his own reservations about a number of Social Democratic doctrines. His unorthodox views on such issues as state and revolution could not very well be voiced in a document intended to speak for the party as a whole. Many years later, he claimed that in drafting the manifesto he sought to express not so much his own beliefs as "the traditions of the Social Democratic church," adding: "I did my best to avoid putting into it any of my personal views, which would have either seemed heretical or been incomprehensible to an average Social Democrat. The manifesto . . . did not in the least correspond to my personal and more complex views of the period." [41] This self-appraisal deserves to be taken with a grain of salt, inasmuch as the central thesis of the manifesto — that the working class would win liberty for Russia — certainly did correspond to his political outlook at that time. But on many other issues he probably spoke without personal conviction.

The document, as it finally emerged, was a compromise designed to please the different groups. Lack of access to the original draft precludes a textual analysis of its evolution. We do know, however, that some of the participants at the Minsk congress were dissatisfied with the text which Struve had submitted. The strongest objections came from Kremer, the representative of the Bund and coauthor (with Martov) of *On Agitation*, who disliked Struve's strong emphasis on political struggle as the means and political freedom as the goal of the movement. But on this point the St. Petersburg representatives were adamant, and Kremer gave in. In the final version of the manifesto, economic struggles and industrial strikes were given their due, but were subordinated to political goals. The Kievans, in turn, insisted on linking the Social Democratic movement with the Peo-

---

[41] Struve, "My Contacts and Conflicts with Lenin," SR, XIII, No. 37 (July 1934), 75. Makhnovets says that Struve was already talking of the "traditions of the Social Democratic church" in 1898: "Pervyi s"ezd," 159. He adds that Struve took the assignment so seriously that he spent "an entire evening" writing the manifesto.

ple's Will. This concession was made, though in a qualified manner. Struve, on his part (he was not present at the congress and communicated through Radchenko), urged the participants to include in the title of the new party the adjective "labor" (*rabochaia*). This had not been intended originally, because the party as then constituted had no workers. His suggestion was adopted (although not without resistance from Kremer and his group, who thought it gave a misleading impression), and the organization was christened the Russian Social Democratic Labor party, a name it retained until 1919.[42]

The complete text of the manifesto in the form in which it was publicly released read as follows:

Fifty years ago the vivifying storm of the 1848 revolution passed over Europe.

The modern working class appeared for the first time on the stage as a mighty historic force. Utilizing the power of this class, the bourgeoisie succeeded in sweeping aside many anachronistic feudal-monarchical regimes. The bourgeoisie, however, quickly sensed in the new ally its worst enemy and handed itself, the proletariat, and the cause of freedom into the hands of reaction. But it was too late: the working class, suppressed for the time being, reappeared on the historic stage ten or fifteen years later with redoubled strength, with a developed self-consciousness, as a fully matured fighter for its final liberation.

All this time Russia apparently remained outside the highroad of historic progress. There was in Russia no visible class struggle, but it existed, and, what is most important, it matured and grew. The Russian government itself, with praiseworthy zeal, planted the seeds of the class struggle by robbing the peasants, protecting the landlords, and feeding big capitalists at the expense of the laboring population. But the bourgeois order is not thinkable without the proletariat, or working class.

---

[42] Makhnovets, "Pervyi s"ezd," 147–149, 157–161; Struve, "My Contacts and Conflicts with Lenin," 75. Kremer's objecting to the word "labor" as misleading: Makhnovets, "Pervyi, s"ezd," 153. The émigré Union of Russian Social Democrats, in which the Economist tendency was well entrenched, refused to endorse Struve's manifesto: *Perepiska G. V. Plekhanova i P. B. Aksel'roda*, II (Moscow, 1925), 86.

The latter is born together with capitalism, grows with it, strengthens itself, and, as it grows, increasingly comes into conflict with the bourgeoisie.

The Russian factory worker, bonded and free alike, has always waged a covert and overt struggle against his exploiters. The magnitude of that struggle grew in proportion to the development of capitalism, embracing ever wider strata of the working population. The awakening in the Russian proletariat of class consciousness and the growth of the spontaneous worker movement coincided with the final development of international Social Democracy as the carrier of class struggle and the class ideal of the conscious working people of the whole world. All modern Russian worker organizations, consciously or not, have always acted in the spirit of Social Democratic ideas. The strength and significance of the labor movement and of Social Democracy, which leans on it, has been most clearly revealed in a whole series of recent strikes which have occurred in Russia and Poland, especially the celebrated strikes of the St. Petersburg weavers and spinners of 1896 and 1897. These strikes compelled the government to issue the law of June 2, 1897, regulating the duration of the working day. The law, whatever its shortcomings, will remain forever memorable as evidence of that mighty pressure which the united efforts of workers exert on the legislative and other activity of the government. But the government imagines in vain that concessions will pacify the workers. Everywhere, the more the working class obtains, the more it demands. So it will be also with the Russian worker. Until now, he has been given anything at all only when he has *demanded* it; and so in the future he will be given only that which he *will demand.*

And what is it that the Russian working class does not need? It completely lacks what its foreign comrades enjoy freely and securely: participation in the administration of government, freedom of speech and press, freedom of association and assembly — in short, all those weapons and means which the Western European and American proletariat uses to improve its condition and at the same time to struggle for its final liberation, against private property and capital — for socialism. The Russian proletariat needs political liberty as the lungs require pure air for healthy breathing. Such liberty is the basic condition of its free development and successful struggle both for partial improvements and for final liberation.

But the freedom the Russian proletariat requires it can win only by *itself*.

The further east in Europe one proceeds, the weaker, more cowardly, and baser in the political sense becomes the bourgeoisie and the greater are the cultural and political tasks that devolve on the proletariat. The Russian working class must and will carry on its powerful shoulders the cause of political liberation. This is an inevitable but only an initial step toward the realization of the proletariat's great historic mission, the creation of a social order which will allow no room for the exploitation of man by man. The Russian proletariat will itself throw off the yoke of autocracy in order to continue with greater energy to fight against capitalism and against the bourgeoisie to a full victory.

The first steps taken by the Russian labor movement and Russian Social Democracy could not help but be uncoordinated, in a certain sense haphazard, devoid of unity and plan. Now the time has come to merge the local forces, groups, and organizations of Russian Social Democracy into a single "Russian Social Democratic Labor party." Aware of this, the representatives of the "Unions of Struggle for the Liberation of the Working Class," the group publishing the *Rabochaia Gazeta,* and the "All-Jewish Labor Bund in Russia and Poland" have convened a conference, whose resolutions are given below.

Merging into the party, the local groups realize the full importance of this measure and the full significance of the responsibility flowing from it. By this measure they finally complete the transition of the Russian revolutionary movement into the new era of conscious class struggle. As a socialist movement and tendency, the Russian Social Democratic party carries on the cause and traditions of all the preceding revolutionary movements in Russia. By placing the conquest of political freedom at the head of the immediate aims of the party as a whole, Social Democracy moves toward the goal clearly charted by the glorious fighters of the old "People's Will." But the means and the paths chosen by Social Democracy are different. Its choice is determined by the fact that it consciously wants to be and remain the class movement of the organized laboring masses. It is firmly convinced that the "liberation of the working class can only be achieved by its own efforts" and it will undeviatingly guide all its actions by this basic principle of international Social Democracy.

Long live Russian and international Social Democracy! [43]

The Siberian exiles, to whom the text of the manifesto had been sent by mail, received it jubilantly. Martov in his memoirs wrote that he and his fellow exiles toasted it with homemade liquor. Such scenes were repeated in other places. Lenin and Plekhanov also welcomed it warmly.[44]

The Minsk congress did not realize any of its organizational plans because the instant the participants had completed their deliberations they were seized by the police and jailed. Nevertheless, it has always been officially recognized as the first held by the Russian Social Democratic party. The manifesto which Struve wrote for this occasion is accordingly acknowledged (although usually without his receiving credit for it)[45] as the first formal pronouncement in the party's history.

Struve drafted the Social Democratic manifesto in the midst of a period of intense and productive scholarly work that began with the suppression of the *New Word* and occupied him for the three years that followed (1898–1900). The subject was the history of Russian agriculture.

Struve became interested in agrarian history in the course of reflections on the economy of Russia in his own time. Pondering the developments in the rural economy since 1861, he experienced great difficulty finding a formula capable of defining its character and explaining its peculiar problems. It was not a natural economy, because money played in it too large a part; and yet it was not a capitalist one either because it lacked such features as mobility of labor and complete freedom in disposing landed property. The more he thought the matter over, the more he wondered whether the Emancipation Edict was as significant a watershed

---

[43] #70. The text translated above is taken from *KPSS v rezoliutsiiakh i resheniiakh,* I (Moscow, 1953), 11–14.

[44] Martov, *Zapiski,* 397–398; Struve, "My Contacts and Conflicts with Lenin," 75.

[45] E.g., the official handbook of documents of the Communist party of the Soviet Union, *KPSS v rezoliutsiiakh i resheniiakh,* 11.

in the country's economic development as was commonly believed.

The explanation of the causes of the Emancipation Edict current at that time held that serfdom was abolished because it had ceased to be profitable. It was given as early as 1847, when serfdom was in its heyday, by a conservative agrarian specialist,[46] and it was subsequently adopted and elaborated upon by Russian economists and publicists, often buttressed with arguments taken from Marx and Engels. According to the prevailing view, the imperial government, having in the 1850's recognized the unprofitability of serfdom and decided to abolish it, had two options. It could have thrown all the arable land open to free competition, even at the risk of seeing a large part of the rural population expropriated (the capitalist option). Or it could have withdrawn from the market that part of the land which was necessary to sustain the peasantry, and given it to the peasants, in order to assure them of economic independence (the "popular" or "folkish" option). The government wisely chose the second alternative and all would have been well had it adhered to its decision. Unfortunately, at the same time it actively sponsored capitalistic agriculture and industry, and thereby undermined the "popular" sector of the economy.

Even while working on *Critical Remarks* Struve had doubts about this whole interpretation, and in particular about the assumption that the Emancipation marked a watershed between the old economy, based on the exploitation of serf labor and the new one, based on self-sufficient productive units run by peasants. The first hint of what was to be his most noteworthy contribution to economic history comes in a letter to Potresov written in the spring of 1894, shortly after he had completed *Critical Remarks*.

Certain points only touched on in the book assume for me better and better shape, acquiring, as it were, a scope that calls for monographic treatment. Here arises, above all, the question of the "serf economy" (*krepostnoe khoziaistvo*) and the peasant population. It will be necessary to address oneself to this subject and to work it out as comprehensively and thor-

[46] A. P. Zablotsky-Desiatovsky; see his *Graf P. D. Kiselev i ego vremia*, IV (St. Petersburg, 1882), 281–284. See also A. A. Kornilov, *Krest'ianskaia reforma* (St. Petersburg, 1905), 10–11.

oughly as possible. In my opinion, the solution of this question is of the utmost importance for the understanding of our entire economy, post-Reform as well as pre-Reform.[47]

What the solution could be, he had suggested in the introduction to the book:

In order to understand our post-Reform economy, it is above all necessary to study the economy we had before the Reform. The view of our entire pre-1861 economic order prevailing among the public and not uncommon in literature and, in particular, the view of the condition of the pre-1861 peasantry — this cannot withstand the slightest touch of historical criticism . . . Only an understanding of the economic order whose liquidation *began* on February 19, 1861, can fully illuminate the economic phenomena of our time. Such a study will perhaps reveal that the calamities which it is now common to view as specific products of capitalism, are a historical legacy of "popular production" — an economic category which, translated into generally recognized legal language, means the law of serfdom (*krepostnoe pravo*).[48]

Approaching the subject in a Marxist manner, Struve distinguished two aspects of serfdom, the economic and the legal — the system of production utilizing bonded labor, and the set of laws institutionalizing that bondage. The former he christened *krepostnoe khoziaistvo* ("serf economy") to differentiate it from the familiar *krepostnoe pravo* ("serf law").[49] After he had delved into materials bearing on the condition of the rural economy in the decades immediately preceding Emancipation, he concluded that the Emancipation Act affected only the legal superstructure of serfdom and barely touched its economic base. The serf economy survived 1861 fairly intact and began to disintegrate slowly and gradually only afterward, largely owing to extensive railroad construction. The agrarian crises of the 1880's and 1890's were symptoms of its agony; they completed the process of peasant emancipation on the economic level.

[47] Struve to Potresov, June 22, 1894.
[48] #15/ix–x.
[49] M. Pokrovsky, GM, No. 3 (1914), 299, credits Struve with having coined the expression "krepostnoe khoziaistvo."

To prove this hypothesis, Struve had to analyze the Russian rural economy before the Emancipation. Was it indeed true, he asked himself, that serfs had been freed because it had become apparent by the middle of the nineteenth century that working land with them was no longer profitable? In other words: was the Emancipation forced by economic exigencies? An affirmative answer would have indicated that 1861 did mark the beginning of a new economic era; a negative answer would have confirmed Struve's hunch that it marked nothing of the kind. It is to find answers to such questions that in the first three months of 1898 he carried out research in the library of the Free Economic Society, concentrating on primary literature dealing with Russian agriculture from the middle of the eighteenth century to 1861.[50]

The preliminary results were highly encouraging. They indicated that on the eve of Emancipation the rural economy of Russia not only was not declining but was just beginning to approach the highest levels of productive efficiency. Serfdom, it therefore appeared, was not abolished for economic reasons at all. Indeed, from the economic point of view, Emancipation was a regressive move. In April 1898 Struve communicated his preliminary conclusions to Potresov:

The abolition of serfdom and the liquidation of the serf economy occurred at the peak of their economic flowering. In itself, the agricultural serf economy was by no means *internally* ripe for abolition, although for other, external, reasons, its liquidation had become economically imperative. The decline of post-Reform agriculture showed that the serf economy was not yet ready to be done away with. As you can see, somewhat unusual views. Incidentally, the contemporary organization of the landlord economy furnishes evidence that by 1861 the serf economy had not yet outlived itself. Its true *internal* liquidation is occurring only now.[51]

So excited was he by these findings that toward the end of March 1898 he spoke of writing a "big book," almost certainly on this subject.[52]

[50] Nina Struve to Potresov, April 10, 1898.
[51] Struve to Potresov, April 5, 1898.
[52] *Ibid.*; Kalmykova to Potresov, undated letter from 1898.

He continued to work on this project throughout the year and, in December 1898, he announced his findings in two public lectures at the Moscow Juridical Society.[53] The first of these lectures provided Social Democratic students with an occasion for one of those noisy demonstrations which had by then become a familiar feature of Russian academic life. A. Kizevetter, who was present, left the following account:

> The serf economy in the first half of the nineteenth century! Of what interest could this have been to the mob of students who filled the assembly hall of the university so densely that the audience stood pressed shoulder to shoulder? Of course, they were not interested in the serf economy. But the speaker was the apostle of Marxism, a man whose name sent some into such raptures and others into such fits of anger. How could one help taking a look at him, even if with one eye only? The hall on this particular occasion seemed crowded with the speaker's admirers, representatives of Social Democratic youth. These Social Democratic gents and maidens conducted themselves in a very excited fashion. For some reason they shouted to each other across the vast auditorium in very belligerent voices, as if literally wishing in this way to say: "This is our gang, we are Marxists, we will show you." Finally, the impatiently awaited speaker appeared on the podium. The hall burst into a frantic storm of applause and excited shouts. The storm raged on and on. Professor Komarovsky, the chairman of the meeting, exhausted himself ringing the bell, but one could not even hear it. Finally, having let off steam, the audience calmed down. Struve began to read his report. His admirers expected from him a political speech, but he read a specialized scholarly report with a preliminary outline of the ideas which he later developed in a book on the serf economy. I looked around and noticed that the Social Democratic ladies were gone, and the gentlemen sat with knitted brows. After all, they had not come for the sake of scholarly enlightenment, but to witness the same verbal brawl familiar from daily experience.[54]

[53] Accounts of these lectures can be found in RV, No. 279 (December 9/21, 1898), and No. 280 (December 10/22, 1898).

[54] A. Kizevetter, *Na rubezhe dvukh stoletii* (Prague, 1929), 218–219. L. Akselrod reported to Plekhanov that the audience was disappointed with Struve's talk: *Literaturnoe nasledie G. V. Plekhanova*, I (Moscow, 1934), 303.

Struve later published expanded versions of both these lectures,[55] and continued his research until 1913, when he published his collected papers on the subject in a volume called *The Serf Economy*.[56] Had he written nothing else, this book alone would have won him a secure place as one of Russia's greatest economic historians. His interpretation of the character and evolution of the rural economy of modern Russia represented a bold departure from prevailing views; and though he raised a number of questions which he could not answer and which remain unanswered to this day, his contribution accomplished a quantum leap in the historiography of Russian rural life.

The substance of Struve's views, as provisionally formulated in 1898 and refined in subsequent works until 1913, can be summarized as follows:

In Russia the peasantry never owned land but tilled land belonging to others. For this right it paid either with labor (corvée, or *barshchina*) or rent (*obrok*). Until the middle of the eighteenth century, the prevailing form of payment was rent, for two reasons: (1) the landlords, required by the government to render perpetual service and often absent from their estates, could not personally supervise the peasants, which had to be done for serf labor to be productive; and (2) because Russia had few cities and industries, and the state did not yet make significant purchases, the market for agricultural produce was too small to encourage production beyond immediate needs.

In arguing these points, Struve assumed that corvée represented a more efficient (as well as more onerous) form of exploitation than rent. To prove the validity of this premise he showed that whenever landlords in Muscovite Russia either were able personally to supervise the peasants or found markets for their produce, they promptly switched from rent payments to payments in labor. This was the case in the monastic establishments, whose personnel, being exempt from state service, were in a position to supervise their labor force; and among private landlords at the beginning of the seventeenth century, after a protracted civil war had substantially driven up prices of foodstuffs. The reason for corvée's superiority to rent lay in the Russian peasant's low level of entre-

[55] The first gave a general description of the serf economy in the first half of the nineteenth century; it was published as #87. The second was an investigation of attempts by serf owners to organize peasant labor and it appeared as #77.
[56] *Krepostnoe khoziaistvo* (St. Petersburg, 1913).

preneurship. Required to turn over most of the money he made to the landlord and the state, he had no incentive to accumulate, and failed to develop either habits of disciplined work or acquisitive instincts. The Russian peasant became relatively efficient only when closely supervised by astute managers.

Until the middle of the eighteenth century, the serfs living on private estates were fairly well off because their masters had neither the opportunity nor the inducement to subject them to intense exploitation. Struve cites accounts of eighteenth-century travelers indicating that the Russian serf was better off than his German or Baltic counterparts.

The first changes in this situation occurred in the reign of Peter the Great. At that time, the establishment of a large standing army compelled the government to start making purchases of commodities grown or manufactured on private estates by serf labor. Thus emerged an internal market. The situation was completely altered in the 1750's and 1760's with the passage of a series of laws whose effect was to transform the Russian landlord from a state servitor into an agrarian and industrial entrepreneur. The key act, of course, was the decree of 1762 which freed the gentry forever from the obligation of bearing service. This law enabled landlords for the first time to settle down on their estates and there to undertake in earnest the exploitation of their serfs, the kind of exploitation the monasteries had been carrying out since the Middle Ages. Among lesser items of legislation having the same effect were laws abolishing internal tariffs in the Empire, permitting free trade in cereals (1762), and authorizing the gentry to supply the military with foodstuffs and manufactured goods. The founding of the Free Economic Society in 1765 testified to the intense interest in agricultural improvement which these legislative acts had aroused.

Responding to their new opportunities, some gentry settled on the land and began to rationalize their estate economy. A good indication of this phenomenon, according to Struve, was the steady shift from the collection of rent to the exaction of corvée which occurred on private estates between 1775 and 1850. Struve cites numerous statements by landlords from this period to the effect that corvée yielded them greater profit than rent — sometimes three times as much. Some landlords were so carried away by the possibilities inhering in agricultural rationalization with serf labor that they had visions of vast utopian communities not unlike those found in the writings of Western Communists of that era.[57]

By such steps there came into being in Russia between the middle of the eighteenth and middle of the nineteenth centuries the economic system which Struve labeled *krepostnoe khoziaistvo,* the serf economy. Its defining quality was production for the market employing bonded rather than free labor. It was a system especially suitable for a money economy at a low level of development, because it offered some of the advantages of the large-scale productive organization of capitalism:

> Corvée was triumphing over quit-rent . . . owing to the fact that it represented an economically more coordinated and therefore more convenient organization of production. To put it more precisely, the corvée economy excelled the rent economy by virtue of the general and recognized advantages of the large-scale economy over the small one in matters of production and marketing of goods, and, on top of that, because of the historic unreadiness of the Russian peasant tiller for commodity production.[58]

As was observed at the time, Struve's conception of the serf economy in Russia bore close resemblance to that of the economic function of slavery in the ancient world advanced concurrently by the German historian Eduard Meyer. Meyer denied that slavery was an inferior, more primitive form of labor organization, invariably antedating free labor, by showing that it had been employed in Greece and Rome during periods of economic expansion side by side with the latter.[59]

So relentlessly was Russian agriculture rationalized before 1861,

[57] These projects are discussed in #77. Incidentally, long before I knew anything of Struve's views on the subject I arrived at a similar interpretation of the military colonies of Alexander I: Richard Pipes, "The Military Colonies, 1810–1831," *Journal of Modern History,* XX, No. 3 (September 1950), 205–219.

[58] #87/271–272 (December 1899 issue).

[59] Eduard Meyer, "Die Sklaverei im Altertum," lecture delivered in Dresden on January 15, 1898, that is, at the very time when Struve began his researches on the history of Russian agriculture: Meyer, *Kleine Schriften,* 2nd ed., I (Halle, 1924), 169–212, especially 196–197. See RV, No. 279 (December 9/21, 1898), which reports a remark made during the discussion of Struve's paper by someone in the audience comparing Struve's views with Meyer's.

according to Struve, that, had the process not been cut short by Emancipation, the Russian gentry might eventually have ejected the serfs from the land, and transformed itself into a class of Junkers employing only hired hands. The serf economy run by the gentry was the most dynamic sector of the pre-Reform Russian economy — it was a "moneyed wedge" buried in the body of a predominantly natural economy. The growing indebtedness of the Russian gentry in the decades immediately preceding Emancipation did not vitiate this thesis, for it was accompanied by rising prices on land and produce. Furthermore, Struve believed, many of the loans and mortgage moneys were invested in agrarian improvements.

If the serf economy was so healthy, why was serfdom abolished? In answering this question Struve could have had recourse to familiar political and social explanations: the fear of peasant revolution and the widespread realization after the Crimean debacle that Russia had no choice but to change.[60] But such explanations would not do for him, because as a Marxist he had to locate a central economic cause. Since, by his own analysis, the economy (that is, the demands of productivity) required not the abolition of serfdom but its retention, he had to seek economic causes resting in the future rather than in the past. The device of retroactive causality permitted him to argue that serfdom conflicted with forces lying just beyond the historical horizon, above all, with the incipient railway boom. Such reasoning was severely criticized by his contemporaries and remains the most controversial feature of his theory of serfdom.[61] Yet the thought that the "future casts its shadow on the present" is not as outlandish as it may seem at first glance. A great deal of Marxist historiography is based on the assumption that the present responds to forces lying in the next immediate phase of historic development.[62] That some observers of the pre-Reform era realized the potential effect of railway transport on Russian agriculture before the rail-

---

[60] This national-political explanation was used by another student of the subject, I. Ignatovich: RB, No. 12 (1900), Pt. 1, 92–93. Struve partly accepted it in his earlier writings, e.g., *Critical Remarks*; see #15/195–196, where the Emancipation is explained by the treasury's need for revenue and the monarchy's fear of social revolution.

[61] See, e.g., Jerome Blum, *Lord and Peasant in Russia* (Princeton, 1961), 615–616.

[62] As will be noted later, Struve explained in a similar manner the phenomenon of protective tariffs: #80/224–233, discussed in the next chapter.

way boom actually got under way is attested to by remarks which the Prussian land expert Haxthausen made in 1847.[63]

Because Emancipation was not brought about by a crisis in the economy of serfdom, it is not surprising that this economy outlived serf law. Its decomposition began only later, with the penetration of railways into the countryside. The fiscal and other obligations imposed on the liberated peasant and the retention of the repartitional commune prevented the peasantry from evolving into a genuinely free rural class. The peasant still had to pay his one-time master and work his land, he still could not consolidate his strips into an independent farmstead, he still lacked incentives to accumulate. In effect, he remained a semi-serf. Such was the legacy of serfdom Russia had to cope with nearly four decades after Emancipation, and such was the root of its endemic agrarian crises. The celebrated "popular" system of production was in reality nothing but a euphemism for the serf economy in decline.

In the course of investigating the history of Russian agriculture, Struve also directed his attention to household industry. This system of manufacture, as has been noted, was generally considered in Russia to be related to "popular" production, for unlike "capitalist" production, it left in the worker's hands the tools and the finished product.

Struve had already voiced skepticism about this interpretation of household industry in *Critical Remarks*,[64] but he did not pursue the matter further until 1897–98, when given an opportunity to do so in a polemic with Paul Miliukov.[65] He now concluded, and said so with his customary peremptoriness, that Russian household industry had never been "natural" or "popular" but had always been capitalist. To prove this contention, he had recourse to the nomenclature of Karl Bücher, who devised a system of classification of productive systems using as a criterion the distance between the producer and the consumer. In the most elementary type, household economy, no distance at all exists because the producer is also the consumer. In the next, intermediate type, the urban economy, the distance is of moderate length, the producer manufacturing on order from the consumer and delivering to him

[63] August Fr. von Haxthausen, *Studien ueber die innern Zustände . . . Russland's* (Hanover, 1847), II, 104, 305.

[64] #15/97–105.

[65] #63 and #72. The latter was originally delivered as a lecture at the St. Petersburg Historical Society on March 26/April 7, 1898.

directly. In the system which Bücher called "national economy" commodities circulate: before reaching the consumer they undergo a complicated routing. The Western guilds, according to Bücher's scheme, belonged to the urban stage insofar as they produced on order. Using these terms, Struve classified Russian household industry in the third category, that of national economy, inasmuch as it had always produced goods for a large and uncertain market. More primitive than the factory system, it was nevertheless cognate to it. In the tradition of household industry Struve saw a guarantee that large-scale capitalist industry in Russia would encounter less resistance from entrenched forces created by an earlier productive system than had been encountered in some Western countries.

Struve did not pursue further his pioneering studies on the history of Russian industry because that was the specialty of his friend Tugan-Baranovsky. When in 1898 the latter brought out his *Russian Factory*, a major historic study disproving the "artificiality" of big industry in Russia, and the existence of the alleged conflict between "popular" and "capitalist" production, Struve hailed it as the last nail driven into the coffin of "popular" production.[66]

Looking back on Struve's works devoted to the history of serfdom and household manufacture, one is struck by the exuberance that characterizes so much of his intellectual achievement. Even if it is true, as he says, that the serf economy was not declining but expanding on the eve of Emancipation, it is difficult to believe that pre-Reform Russia had as many Turnip Townshends as his analysis suggests. Even if the Russian *kustar'* did manufacture for an indeterminate and distant market, did he thereby in any meaningful sense resemble a capitalistic industrialist? The insights which Struve provided into the history of the modern Russian economy would have been even more convincing had the evidence been more patiently weighed and the conclusions more temperately worded.

And yet, even with these flaws, his confident prediction of 1898 that scholarship some day would accept his findings, notwithstanding their apparent paradoxicality,[67] has been vindicated. Modern research on the history of pre-Emancipation agriculture

[66] #74.
[67] Struve to Potresov, April 5, 1898.

in Russia has shown the correctness of his basic hypothesis of an expanding rural economy under late serfdom.[68] Similarly, his theory of the capitalist character of old Russian household manufacture has become accepted and elaborated upon by economic historians from Tugan-Baranovsky onward.[69] He thus made a major contribution to Russian economic history at a time when the discipline was still in its embryonic phase. Considering both his youth and the rapidity with which he conceived and formulated these discoveries, the sheer brilliance of the achievement is astounding.

[68] See, e.g., two recent studies, one by a Western, the other by a Soviet historian: Michael Confino, *Domaines et seigneurs en Russie vers la fin du XVIII siècle* (Paris, 1963), 194–201, and N. L. Rubinshtein, *Sel'skoe khoziaistvo Rossii vo vtoroi polovine XVIII v.* (Moscow, 1957), 127–130.

[69] Struve claimed merely that Tugan-Baranovsky adopted his system of classifying household industry (#74/458), but Miliukov went further and gave Struve credit for having provided the first systematic account of Russian household industries: P. N. Miliukov, *Ocherki po istorii russkoi kul'tury*, 3rd ed., I (St. Petersburg, 1898), xi.

9. REVISIONISM

During the first half of 1898 Struve was busy and excited by his historical research, which had yielded such seminal results in so short a time. But as the year drew to a close, his mood changed, and he appeared increasingly withdrawn and irritable.

The tension was caused in part by financial worries. The income which he derived from editorial work for Popova and occasional journalism was so meager that it required astute management to provide for the needs of the family, especially after April 1898 (OS), when Nina gave birth to her first son, Gleb. Struve could not manage finances carefully and neither could Nina; if anything she was even more disorganized and helpless in practical matters than he. Having no place to live, the young couple moved in with Kalmykova, and spent the first year of married life in her apartment. Common life in the very rooms where Kalmykova and Struve had been lovers did not make for a relaxed domestic life. Kalmykova saw her worst fears confirmed: "He shows no concern for settling down at all," she complained to Potresov, "and since the main responsibility for running the household falls on him, I really don't know what will happen. There is so little money, and therefore such need for great energy. And where is it, who has it?" [1] After Gleb was born, the Struves moved to an apartment of their own on Malaia Italianskaia 47. But money was in even shorter supply now, and Struve had to ask Potresov for a small loan to pay the expenses of moving his family to the countryside for the summer holidays. [2]

But the main cause of Struve's anxious state was intellectual, not financial, namely the outbreak in Germany of the controversy between Orthodox and Revisionist Marxists. The reading of Bern-

[1] Kalmykova to Potresov, undated letter, probably from 1898.
[2] Struve to Potresov, July 11, 1898.

stein and of the polemical literature which Bernstein had provoked
stirred in him the many doubts that he had felt about Marxism at
various times, doubts which so far he had usually suppressed for
the sake of Social Democratic unity. Now they floated to the surface, setting off agonizing conflicts between his conscience and his
loyalty to the movement and his friends in it. Kalmykova, was one
of the first to sense these conflicts and to grasp their significance.
"I have observed," she wrote Potresov in March 1899,

> a most intense intellectual process undoubtedly taking place
> deep within P[eter] B[erngardovich] during the past year. On
> the outside, it expresses itself very capriciously, mostly in irri-
> tated attacks on *something* and someone. Depending on the
> moment, it is you, and the Samarans of blessed memory, and I,
> and "our oldsters." You know how difficult it is to talk to him.
> I cannot do so at all, but he also won't talk to others, which
> greatly annoys many people. I once said in the presence of M. I.
> [Tugan-Baranovsky] and a third person, in response to M.I.'s
> statement that I view them with suspicion, as if expecting them
> to take a wrong turn: "No, I have no such suspicions, but I know
> Peter well, and for that reason I can say with certainty that he is
> in an *incubational period*, the result of which will make itself
> felt in literature in a very noticeable fashion. I anticipate this
> with fear, because I know his manner of *"sharing thoughts."*
> For some, these are *only thoughts* — for others, the destruction
> of their inner world.[3]

Revisionism, in its historically precise meaning, describes the un-
successful effort, formally launched by Eduard Bernstein in 1898,
to revise the Erfurt Program of the German Social Democratic
party. But since Bernstein's ideas had both their antecedents and
their sequel, Revisionism may be defined more usefully as the ideology of that faction of socialism which occupies the indeterminate
zone separating the doctrinaire component of socialism from the
pragmatic, or, what is the same thing, the ideological from the political.

[3] Kalmykova to Potresov, March 28, 1899. The "Samarans of blessed memory"
are the editors of the *Messenger of Samara*; "our oldsters" are Plekhanov and
the Liberation of Labor Group.

Criticisms of the Erfurt Program began from the instant of its adoption. In the summer of 1891, Georg von Vollmar in the famous "Eldorado" speeches delivered in Munich questioned the concept of social revolution on the grounds that in history, as in nature, changes occurred not by leaps but by steps. In 1894, Bruno Schoenlank, another German Social Democrat, criticized the Marxian theories of pauperization and concentration of landed property. By the mid-nineties doubts about these and other articles of Social Democratic theory as embodied in the Erfurt Program were widespread and openly voiced.

The extent to which the social and political progress achieved by the countries of Western Europe in the second half of the nineteenth century affected socialist thinking may be best illustrated by the example of Engels himself. In March 1885, shortly before his death, in a new introduction to Marx's *Class Struggles in France*, Engels acknowledged that history had followed a different course from the one he and Marx had foreseen. In 1850, when Marx wrote the book, the revolutionary upheavals of 1848 were still fresh in memory, and it was reasonable to assume that new waves of social violence of mounting intensity would occur before long. Now, nearly half a century later, it became apparent that these expectations had been too sanguine. During the intervening period, the worker had acquired the democratic franchise, a new weapon of far greater potency than any he had ever possessed. Socialist strategy had to be adjusted accordingly:

> The insurrection of the old type — street fighting with barricades — which in 1848 had everywhere played a decisive role, has become significantly outdated . . . The era of surprise attacks, of revolutions in which small, conscious minorities lead the unconscious masses, is over . . . The irony of world history stands everything on its head. We — "revolutionaries," "destroyers" — have succeeded far better with the help of legal means than with that of illegal means and the coup d'état.[4]

Although Engels conceded that the idea of revolution remained too dear to the hearts of socialists to be altogether abandoned,

[4] First published in a slightly bowdlerized version in *Die Neue Zeit*, Nos. 27 and 28 for 1894–95. The integral text can be found in Karl Marx and Friedrich Engels, *Werke*, XXII (Berlin, 1963), 509–527. The passages quoted are on pp. 519, 523, 525.

and allowed for the possibility of violence and social upheavals occurring here and there even under modern conditions, the drift of his analysis pointed in another direction: socialist society would come into being peacefully, by imperceptible progress in which the voting booth replaced the barricade. These statements by the cofounder of Social Democracy may be regarded as inaugurating Revisionism in the more narrow and historically precise sense of the word.

After Engels's death, Bernstein, his closest collaborator, continued to develop this evolutionary idea. In various theoretical essays published in official Social Democratic organs, he subjected to a systematic critique the whole body of ideas underlying the theory of social revolution, among them the dialectic, the concentration of land ownership, and the "withering away" of the state.[5] In this critical work he was assisted by Werner Sombart,[6] Paul Kampffmeyer, and a number of other German theorists. The journal *Sozialistische Monatshefte*, founded in 1897, served as the organ of German Social Democrats of this evolutionary persuasion. Although Struve did not contribute to it, he clearly was among its sympathizers. His early criticisms of some features of Marxist doctrine may be viewed as a Russian reflection of this current of German Social Democracy.

The uproar into which Bernstein threw the party in 1898–99 was due not to the novelty of his ideas — these had been in circulation for some time — but to his insistence that the party adjust its official program to them. With his October 1898 letter to the Stuttgart Congress of German Social Democracy, in which he urged the party to disassociate itself from the theories of pauperization and social revolution, Bernstein shifted the ground of Marxist critique from the realm of speculation to that of politics. The party's leaders panicked. To them, pauperization and social revo-

[5] "Probleme des Sozialismus," NZ, XV, Pt. 1, and XV, Pt. 2 (1896–97). A recent account of Bernstein's intellectual development and of the origins of Revisionism is Pierre Angel's *Eduard Bernstein et l'évolution du socialisme allemand* (Paris, 1961).

[6] Werner Sombart, *Sozialismus und die soziale Bewegung im 19 Jahrhundert* (Jena, 1896), reproducing lectures delivered in Switzerland the preceding year. Sombart called dialectical materialism a "mystification" and, like Struve, asked for a critical reappraisal of the philosophical foundations of Marxism. There are many parallels between the two men, who seem to have been acquainted with one another: *Arhiv za pravne i društvene nauke* (Belgrade), No. 1–2 (July–August 1938), 182.

lution were not mere ideas to be adopted, adjusted, or abandoned in conformity with the latest word of science, but articles of faith needed to keep together a radical movement functioning in what had become a stable and prosperous society. They did not object to a critical review of any or all of Marx's doctrines as long as it remained confined to theoretical journals. But revision of the party program was another matter entirely. Here the instinct of the professional Social Democrat was not different from that of any other politician: to stick by any slogan required by the party's interests, whether it was "realistic" and "true" or not. In this instance, the innate conservatism of the political organization worked, paradoxically, in favor of retaining a revolutionary pose.

The theoretical grounding of Bernstein's views, which he prepared at the party's request and published in 1899 as *Preconditions of Socialism* (in English: *Evolutionary Socialism*), became the subject of animated discussions inside Germany and abroad. Ultimately, the German Social Democrats rejected Bernstein's proposals, and so did the Socialist International. But — and this fact is worth remembering in view of what subsequently happened to Struve — Bernstein was allowed to retain his party membership. Together with his followers, he found a peripheral but secure place on the right flank of German Social Democracy, and had the satisfaction of observing the party practicing the kind of evolutionary socialism which it had refused to preach. Characteristically, the shrillest demands for the expulsion of the Revisionists from the International came from Eastern Europeans like Plekhanov, Parvus (Helphand), and Rosa Luxemburg.

Following closely the controversy in the German party, Struve had no difficulty deciding where his own sympathies lay.[7] He at once sided with the Revisionist faction, although he had only slight regard for its leader's intellect. He thought Bernstein "philosophically poor, something of a philistine, not very lucid in his theoretical reasoning,"[8] altogether an unoriginal thinker, heavily dependent on borrowings from the Fabians, the Webbs particularly.[9] Bernstein's critique of Marxism appeared to him superficial,

---

[7] Struve was in Stuttgart in the autumn of 1898 and may have witnessed the Stuttgart Congress.
[8] Struve to Potresov, February 2, 1899.
[9] #83/739.

because it treated Marxism as if it were a mere "empirical construct" instead of a "grandiose philosophical system" which required philosophical analysis.[10] But, these reservations notwithstanding, he greatly admired Bernstein for his civic courage. He
also had no doubt that the cause which Bernstein championed
would ultimately triumph, being truer to life and more "realistic"
than Marxist Orthodoxy.[11]

He was therefore incensed by the harassment to which the party
stalwarts and especially Plekhanov subjected Bernstein. Not content to dismiss out of hand the substance of his arguments, Plekhanov impugned Bernstein's personal integrity. Employing freely
those "poisoned weapons" which Engels had found so distasteful
in his polemical methods, Plekhanov launched a systematic campaign in the Russian and German press to discredit the Revisionist party. When Kautsky, the leader of German Orthodox Marxists, in rejecting Bernstein's arguments had the courtesy to thank
him for having "made the party think again," Plekhanov did not
hesitate to assail Kautsky as well.[12] The viciousness of Plekhanov's
counterattack was at least in part induced by injured vanity, for
Bernstein had mortally offended him in the *Preconditions of Socialism,* saying that he and his followers represented a minority in
the Russian Social Democratic movement.[13] But at bottom it derived from a kind of Old Believer fanaticism: the conviction that
the faith must stand inviolate in all its particulars or fall.

Struve was convinced that behind Plekhanov's anti-Revisionist
campaign lay intellectual dishonesty. He would have been willing
to tolerate Plekhanov's dogmatism if he felt that Plekhanov really
believed Bernstein to be wrong. In that case, one could have questioned Plekhanov's judgment but not his morals. But Struve was
certain that deep in his heart Plekhanov knew Bernstein had a
good case. By rejecting Revisionism from pure political calculation,
Plekhanov placed considerations of party interest above truth and
conscience and, in effect, deliberately lied:

[10] #82/701–702.

[11] In the spring of 1899, in a note to Bernstein recommending Tugan-Baranovsky, Struve wrote: "I take this opportunity to congratulate you on your brave
critical challenge of Orthodoxy, so pregnant with consequences. Despite all attacks
[on you], I believe that you will be proven right in essential matters." Struve
to Bernstein, May 28/June 9, 1899.

[12] Samuel H. Baron, *Plekhanov, the Father of Russian Marxism* (Stanford, Calif.,
1963), 176–177.

[13] *Ibid.,* 177.

Objectively, a lie can be harmless or useful, but only so long as it is not perceived as a lie. When a person upholds something which he knows to be untrue, the lie turns into noxious poison. So it is with Orthodoxy. To believe in it is harmless, but once one has ceased to believe one must cast it away as a lie . . . otherwise it will corrupt thought.[14]

The intellectual corruption caused by conscious lying found expression in the tendency, so pronounced in Plekhanov, to substitute for a rational discussion of the issues a "proletarian-revolutionary investigation" of motives and loyalties.[15] To Struve, Plekhanov's treatment of Bernstein carried with it ominous portents of inquisition and the police. It shocked him and aroused fears about the future of the movement, fears which were to grow to alarming proportions with each year that followed.

So certain was Struve of the inevitable triumph of reality over myth that at first he thought it an easy matter to isolate Plekhanov and lead Russian Social Democrats into the Revisionist camp. Tugan-Baranovsky and Bulgakov were already with him, and in some respects even ahead of him. Vera Zasulich seemed a likely convert; and so did Lenin.[16]

The experience he had trying to convert Potresov should have given him pause. In lively exchanges of letters carried out in the early months of 1899 (Potresov was then under administrative exile in the provinces), Struve worked hard to win him over. But he had no success, and the correspondence grew acrimonious, carrying hints of a personal break. "I began with critical doubts," Struve wrote in one of these letters,

then I went through an extremely productive and useful phase of fascination with Orthodoxy, and now I have conclusively reverted to criticism, yielding to the pressures of irrefutable internal conviction, which have caused and continue to cause much anxiety to my spiritual life . . . I do not know whether you will be cured of utopianism or I will abandon realism, but if neither happens, a deep difference will emerge in our views.[17]

[14] Struve to Potresov, February 2, 1899.
[15] Struve to Potresov, July 26, 1899.
[16] See below, p. 240.
[17] Struve to Potresov, January 16, 1899.

"I was saddened by your letter," Potresov replied,

> saddened because I feel we have ceased to understand one another and begun to speak different languages. And yet how many personal and other recollections we share in common, you and I, how much have we lived through together! *Once* you used to understand my mood from half a word — *now* all the shafts of your letters pass by, missing their goal. It is a bad omen! [18]

The exchanges became so heated that Kalmykova destroyed one of Struve's letters to Potresov to prevent an open break between them.[19] By August 1899, Struve decided it was useless to engage in a further exchange of ideas. Potresov eluded Struve. Later, he pointedly chose as his pen name "Starover" — "Old Believer."

At this juncture, Struve was given an opportunity to edit a second Social Democratic journal. This time, the initiative for founding the journal — of course, unknown to him — came from the police. Observing the emergence of the Russian labor movement and eager to be better informed about its connections with the intelligentsia, the Ministry of the Interior decided at the end of 1898 to infiltrate Social Democratic circles. Its strategy was to sponsor a Social Democratic periodical and to place on its board a police agent. The police had available for the job a suitable agent provocateur in the person of M. I. Gurovich, an ex-pharmacist who had served time in Siberia for revolutionary activity and since his return from exile had gone on its payroll as an informer. Gurovich's personal habits were not exactly those of a Russian intellectual, since he associated with ladies of the demimonde and even was reputed to play the stock market. But the doubts which this behavior aroused in some were stilled by his generous support of philanthropic and civic organizations and by the personal endorsement given him by V. Ia. Iakovlev-Bogucharsky, a trusted revolutionary and a fellow exile from Siberia. Gurovich made many acquaintances among the St. Petersburg intelligentsia, on whom he regularly informed to his superiors.[20]

---

[18] Potresov to Struve, August 27, 1899.
[19] Struve to Potresov, February 10, 1899.
[20] On Gurovich: L. Kleinbort, "M. I. Gurovich-Kharkovtsev'," *Byloe,* No. 16 (1921), 86–107; V. M. Abramkin and A. L. Dymshits, *"Nachalo" — marksistskii*

What made Gurovich particularly suitable for the particular job
the police had in mind was that his common law wife, A. A.
Voeikova, owned a publishing business. The police took advantage
of this fact, and on December 19/31, 1898, issued Voeikova authorization to publish a monthly journal. Whether Voeikova knew
to whom she owed this gift and where her husband had obtained
the money which he offered to finance the publication cannot be
established. In any event, she decided to benefit from the good
fortune, and in January 1899 invited Struve to assume editorship
of the monthly, with the understanding that he would run it along
the lines of the *New Word,* that is, as an organ of "economic materialism." The journal was to be named *Nachalo — The Beginning.* Struve promptly put together an editorial board consisting of
his trusted associate Tugan-Baranovsky (associate editor), Kalmykova (literary editor), Iakovlev-Bogucharsky and Maslov (contributing editors).[21] Voeikova being the publisher, Gurovich was
in a very advantageous position to secure information.

Struve had been dissatisfied with the literary side of the *New
Word.* Hoping to improve on it, he established contact with the
leading Symbolists, whose poetry was just beginning to attract attention, offering to place *The Beginning*'s literary section in their
charge.[22] Nothing came of this idea, however, and only when he
took over *Russian Thought,* his greatest journal, in 1907 did he
succeed in winning the collaboration of the literary avant-garde.
His hope of publishing Chekhov also came to naught. Chekhov
agreed to contribute to the *Beginning,* but being ill and near death
was unable to keep his promise.[23] Of the writers better known in

zhurnal devianostykh godov (Moscow, 1932), 22–27; and V. Totomiants, "Zhurnal
'Nachalo' i provokator Gurovich," NZh, XLIII (1955), 264–266.

[21] The story of *The Beginning* is told in the following studies: Abramkin and
Dymshits, *Nachalo;* V. Poliansky, "Marksistskaia periodicheskaia pechat', 1896–
1906 gg.," KA, No. 2/9 (1925), 264–268 (based on censors' reports); V. Evgenev-
Maksimov, *Ocherki po istorii sotsialisticheskoi zhurnalistiki v Rossii XIX veka*
(Moscow and Leningrad, 1927), 230–265; and Richard Kindersley, *The First
Russian Revisionists* (Oxford, 1962), 92–104. The enterprise was originally con-
ceived as a daily newspaper based in Moscow, but that plan was abandoned in
favor of a monthly brought out in St. Petersburg: *Frank,* 19, 21, and summary
of an interview with S. Frank by B. I. Nikolaevsky in the Nikolaevsky Archive,
Hoover Institution, Stanford, California.

[22] Abramkin and Dymshits, *Nachalo,* 112–113.

[23] The original of Struve's invitation to Chekhov, dated January 12, 1899, is at
the Manuscript Division of the Lenin Library, Moscow, Arkhiv Chekhova, Fond
331, Karton 59, Ed. khr. 67. Chekhov's letter to Gorky indicating willingness to
collaborate is reprinted in A. P. Chekhov, *Polnoe sobranie sochinenii i pisem,*
XVIII (Moscow, 1949), 24.

Russia, only Merezhkovsky and V. V. Veresaev published there. Gorky did not contribute, although he apparently belonged to the staff, because he appears in the formal photograph of the editorial board, sitting in the middle, next to Kalmykova and in the shadow of Gurovich.

The fact that both the editor-in-chief and his deputy were Revisionists assured that *The Beginning* would adopt a policy friendly to the "critics." In early 1899, however, Revisionism was not yet a formal heresy, at least in Russia, and Struve therefore had no difficulty securing the collaboration of all the leading Social Democratic publicists, most of them adherents of orthodoxy. Plekhanov alone would collaborate with Struve no longer, and refused to participate.

The first number of *The Beginning*, a double issue, came out in February 1899. Struve built it around a programmatic article by Potresov, "The Heritage and the Heirs." Replying to the "Populist" charge that the Social Democrats had betrayed the great traditions of Russian democracy, Potresov maintained that in fact it was they who carried on the "democratic" traditions of the 1860's.[24] The issue also had a chapter from Lenin's forthcoming history of Russian capitalism. Struve contributed two articles, both dealing mainly with peasant questions, neither of which contained as yet any hint of Revisionism.[25] The only "critical" article was Bulgakov's review of Kautsky's *Die Agrarfrage* (*The Agrarian Question*). In the space of three pages, Bulgakov managed to accuse Kautsky of serious mistakes in treating agrarian problems, and altogether to assume a most irreverent attitude toward the coryphaeus of international Social Democracy.[26]

Apparently the channels of communication between the police and the Main Censorship Office were not all they should have been, for the censors took one look at the first number of *The Beginning* and ordered it suppressed. Goremykin, the Minister of the Interior, hastily interceded to overrule this verdict. The

[24] "O 'nasledstve' i 'naslednikakh'," in A. N. Potresov, *Etiudy o russkoi intelligentsii* (St. Petersburg, 1906), 73–109.

[25] #77 and #78.

[26] Sergei Bulgakov, "K voprosu o kapitalisticheskoi evoliutsii zemledeliia," *Nachalo*, No. 1–2 (1899), Pt. 2, 1–3. According to Kindersley, Bulgakov's essay was the first in which "any Russian Marxist had raised his voice against a German contemporary of comparable standing" (*Russian Revisionists*, 98).

journal finally received the imprimatur, but on condition that Potresov's programmatic essay be removed.

The Beginning aroused none of the enthusiasm of *The New Word*. Marxism was no longer a novelty, the Marxist-Populist controversy had grown stale, and too much of the new journal was taken up with technical economic literature. It made, therefore, only a minor splash. Plekhanov alone seems to have considered its appearance a significant event. He was the first Russian Social Democrat to detect in it a Revisionist tendency and to sound the alarm. After reading the first number, he wrote Akselrod: "The struggle against Bernsteinianism in Russia is the most urgent task of the moment. *The Beginning* is wholly on Bernstein's side. We must oppose to the influence of our *Marxists of the academic chair* (*Kathedersocialisten*) our influence, that of *Marxists-revolutionaries*." [27]

Plekhanov's warnings were vindicated in the second (March 1899) issue. Here, in an essay on the young and then still unknown writer V. Rozanov, Struve inserted a statement denying the possibility of serious class warfare in Western Europe. The homogeneity of its culture, he wrote, immunized the West against a revolt of the barbarized masses of the kind that Herzen and Dostoevsky had prophesied. There class distinctions were not cultural in character, and did not affect the essential quality of culture, the spirit of individualism. Where class conflicts did not assume cultural forms, they had limits beyond which they would not go.[28] In another article, Struve dismissed as "vulgar" the contention that protective tariffs were enacted in the interest of the class in power: in reality, they served the interests of the class or classes whose power lay still in the future.[29] He had said such things before, but now, against the background of Bernstein and the raging controversy over Revisionism, they acquired a very different connotation.

The censors held up the third number, printed in April, mainly on account of an article by Potresov which they correctly interpreted as a continuation of the article removed from the first

---

[27] Letter dated April 21, 1899: *Literaturnoe nasledie G. V. Plekhanova*, V (1938), 297.

[28] #79/187–188.

[29] #80/229–230.

issue. They further objected to Struve's "Domestic Survey" dealing with Finland and labor disturbances.[30] April came and went, the staff was readying for the printer the next, May, issue, and authorization to distribute the April number was still not forthcoming. Struve lost patience and, entrusting editorial responsibility to Tugan-Baranovsky, left for a spa in Austrian Silesia. From there he sent Vera Zasulich a feeler:

> Journalism, with all the cares that it brings, has completely exhausted me: it calls for major physical effort that requires one to give up all thinking. Yet thoughts assail me, and fundamentally the joy of work — really big and fully satisfactory — is the main charm of life . . .
>
> Our English conversations [of 1896] came back to me now that the party is in turmoil over "Bernsteinianism." As you undoubtedly guess and perhaps know, I do not, by any means, side with the opponents of Bernsteinianism. Looking at the matter from the point of view of Bernstein's opponents themselves, I regret that they have assumed from the very beginning of the conflict an incorrect tone and have thereby damaged their cause. After all, it was obvious that sooner or later the ideas of the party would come under review, partly because, as Heraclitus says, "everything flows," and partly because every, even the soundest, system *must* have its weak sides: the richer a system's content, the more, relatively speaking, weak sides in it. And, therefore, the "critics," regardless of how weak their forces, had to raise the question of a review, lest they be guilty of intellectual insincerity or dishonesty. To speak in this instance of opportunism is to put the question quite incorrectly — incorrectly from the logical as well as the *moral* point of view. Bernstein's book is weak, much weaker than the previously published pamphlet of Kampffmeyer. In Bernstein, the philosophic and abstract economic parts are particularly poor. But this does not mean in the least that the movement which he has inaugurated is no match for the Orthodox counterreaction. Truly, this Orthodoxy evokes feelings of pity, now that it has

[30] *Potresov,* 31. Struve's article, under the general heading "Domestic Survey" ("Vnutrennee obozrenie") — the successor of his "Current Questions of Domestic Life" in the *New Word* — has not been reprinted; on it, see Abramkin and Dymshits, *Nachalo,* 39–40.

been joined by Luxemburg, Parvus, and Schoenlank; and that which is being said, for example, by Zetkin, comes not from the intellect but from passion. Of course, passion is a great thing, but you cannot feel enthusiasm for something in which you do not believe. For that reason the absence of "enthusiasm" not only does not deserve condemnation but, on the contrary, calls for full recognition and respect. One ought to criticize lack of faith, but one ought not to suspect intentions and motives. And the opponents of Bernstein have greatly sinned in this respect, whereas Bernstein replied with great dignity that this question concerns not his person but the interests of the party . . . (P.S. I won't argue this with G. V. [Plekhanov], for it would be quite useless to do so.)[31]

During Struve's stay in Silesia (he came back at the end of May, when Nina gave birth to Alexis, their second son), *The Beginning* ran into increasing difficulties with censorship. After protracted deliberations, the censors finally refused to allow distribution of the April issue. They authorized the May issue, but by then Goremykin had decided to abandon the experiment with a police-sponsored radical journal. On June 22, 1899, *The Beginning* was suspended. Libraries and reading rooms were instructed to remove back issues from their shelves; for good measure, copies of the *New Word* were included in the proscription.[32]

After losing *The Beginning*, the Social Democrats still had three outlets in which to publish: *God's World* (*Mir Bozhii*), *Scholarly Review* (*Nauchnoe obozrenie*), and *Life* (*Zhizn'*).[33] None of these publications, however, functioned as a party organ. The absence of such an organ was due mainly to stringent censorship; but it was also symptomatic of the diseased condition of

[31] Letter dated May 10, 1899, in the B. I. Nikolaevsky Archive, Hoover Institution, Stanford, California.

[32] Kindersley, *Russian Revisionists*, 104.

[33] *Mir Bozhii* had been founded in 1891 as a journal for youth, but shortly afterward was transformed into a regular monthly dealing with social problems. Its founder and publisher, A. A. Davydova, was Tugan-Baranovsky's mother-in-law. *Nauchnoe obozrenie* came into being in 1894 and lasted for one decade. Its editor was M. M. Filippov. *Zhizn'* began in 1896 as a family journal, but it was taken over by Posse and turned into an organ of socialist opinion. On these three periodicals, see Poliansky, "Marksistskaia periodicheskaia pechat'." Gurovich hovered in the background of these publications and reported their staffs' activities to the police. He was finally unmasked by Socialist Revolutionaries in 1901, whereupon he became an overt Okhrana official.

Russian Social Democracy, whose "united front" had by now disintegrated into several warring factions.

The remarkable feature of Struve's Revisionist theory is that it sprang from his head fully formed. The instant he decided to align himself openly with the Bernsteinians (at the beginning of 1899), he came out with a systematic critique of Marx: there were no hesitations, no gropings, no attempts to doctor the Marxist doctrine by removing or reformulating some particular elements in it. Once he had launched his critique, he went straight for the fundamentals: the theory of value, central to Marx's economics, and the theory of revolution, central to his sociology of politics. A critique so well thought out must have required years of gestation — and yet the years immediately preceding his Revisionism (1895–1898) were the ones when Struve professed the most loyal adherence to Marxism. Because in his case conscious duplicity is out of the question, one must assume that he carried in his mind all along two contrary ideologies, one positive, the other critical. Such intellectual schizophrenia is not easy to understand, especially since Struve upheld first Orthodoxy and then Revisionism with equal sincerity and passion. His life offers no better illustration of his extraordinary ability simultaneously to assume divergent intellectual positions.

Why did he wait for Bernstein's signal before spelling out fully his own reservations about Marx's economics and sociology? The answer is hinted at in a letter to Potresov from the summer of 1899. In it Struve explained that as long as the Social Democratic movement had been united he had felt duty bound to keep his doubts to himself. But once Orthodoxy was publicly challenged and the critical objections had been exposed to the eyes of the bourgeoisie, once its theoretical and organizational unity began to disintegrate, silence no longer served any useful purpose. At that point the good of the movement required not the suppression but the open airing of critical thoughts.[34]

In launching his critique of Marxism, Struve conceded at the outset that he did not expect from it consistency of thought:

It is impossible to conceive of a scientific system distinguished by profundity and wealth of ideas that is free of contradictions.

[34] Struve to Potresov, July 26, 1899.

The richer in content the system, the greater must be the diversity of intellectual motives behind it, and the greater the likelihood of conflicts among them . . . No intellect, not even that of the greatest genius, has the strength to create an integral scientific edifice and at the same time to occupy itself with the task of subjecting to critical scrutiny the individual stones used in its contruction. The creator must follow a plan which he has formed in his head freely and without critical *arrière-pensée*. He constructs according to criteria which to later criticism appear to be largely aesthetic.[35]

Great creators of science in general are never distinguished by methodological clarity. And bless them for it: such methodological clarity always constrains the sweep of creative thought; it is always inspired by a certain skepticism which is nothing else but theoretical cowardice.[36]

The trouble with Bernstein was that instead of subjecting Marxism to a general philosophical critique he tried to give it the appearance of consistency by "amputating" from it the doctrines of pauperization and social revolution, and by reformulating the sociology to make it appear a trifle less deterministic. A critique of this kind was inadequate. Marxism required a thoroughgoing critical analysis of its individual elements:

My approach . . . foregoes consciously and a priori the attempt to assign Marx's intellectual structure a consistent meaning. It strives much more to lay bare the rich play of the diverse intellectual motives and tendencies in it. The contradictions not only should not be removed from the system but, on the contrary, they ought to be revealed as psychologically necessary and logically interdependent. This done, the critique can assign the individual intellectual motives the *limits of their validity*. Such, after all, is the most proper task of epistemological criticism of all scientific achievement.[37]

Marxism is not an empirical construct, of which there are dozens. It is a grandiose philosophical system built under the

[35] #85/xxxii–xxxiii.
[36] #86/178.
[37] #83/730.

influence of thinkers like Hegel, Feuerbach, Saint-Simon,
Fourier, Proudhon. All such systems, no matter how much
permeated they are with empirical matter, must be examined
in their philosophical fundamentals, that is, they must be taken
apart epistemologically and logically.[38]

This approach, in which the critique of method was an intrinsic
feature of scientific investigation, was typically Neo-Kantian.

In the spring of 1899 Struve wrote a major essay on Marx's
social theory in which he made a persuasive case against the
theories of class struggle and social revolution.[39]

As the basic test for his analysis, Struve took the *locus classicus*
of Marx's social theory, the celebrated passage from the *Critique
of Political Economy* in which Marx asserted that "the mode of
production of material life determines social, political, and
spiritual life," that at certain historic periods the mode of production and the social relations of production resting on them enter
into contradictions, and that, when this occurs, the conflict is
resolved by means of social revolution. Referring to this statement, Struve asks: if it is indeed true that the mode of production
"determines" social relations, how it is possible for social relations
ever to "enter into contradictions" with the mode of production?
How can the effect elude its clause? Why should it require a
social upheaval to establish the kind of relationship between productive and social factors that, according to the basic premise of
the theory, must prevail by the very nature of things? Because
these questions cannot be answered, Marx's theory of social
revolution stands in direct contradiction to his basic principle of
economic determinism.

The only valid conclusion to be drawn from the principle of
economic determinism, Struve continues, is that productive forces
and the social structure are in a state of "constant partial collisions
and adjustments": as soon as social institutions fall behind changes
in the mode of production, a readjustment takes place which rights

[38] #82/701–702.
[39] #82. This article came out in the late summer of 1899. In a letter to Hans
Delbrück dated July 9, 1902, Struve described it as his most important publication. There is a Russian translation of the article of inferior quality, which Struve
disowned: *Marksovaia teoriia sotsial'nogo razvitiia* (Kiev, 1905). A French translation appeared in *Etudes de Marxologie* (Paris), No. 6 (1962), 105–156.

the balance. The discrepancy between the two can never be large or significant enough to allow a social upheaval. Hence, in the historical process there occurs not an intensification of social conflicts (because this would contradict the principle of economic determinism), but their steady diminution. An illustration of that fact can be found in the manner in which capitalist society had gradually accommodated itself to the emergence of labor and Social Democracy. Social progress is more typically achieved by the erosion of resistance than by mounting contradictions leading to a social revolution:

> The concept of social revolution, as a theoretical concept, is not only worthless and useless — it is actually misleading. If "social revolution" is intended to mean a complete upheaval of the social system, then the modern mind can conceive of it only as a protracted, continuous process of social transformations. Even if political revolution should furnish the capstone to that process of development, the element responsible for the upheaval in this process does not in the least depend on the political revolution, and can be very well conceived without it.[40]

It is, of course, always possible to proclaim the "dictatorship of the proletariat" by means of a coup d'état, as the Jacobins and Blanquists advocated. Such Jacobin-Blanquist elements were strong in Marx's thought, for Marx believed "in the miracle of the political prime act of the proletariat." [41] But to seize power is not yet to achieve a revolution:

> [The dictatorship of the proletariat] is either entirely superflous for a social transformation or it is totally insufficient. The closer society approaches socialism, owing to the strengthening of the working class, the less it is either possible or necessary to think in terms of the dictatorship of that class. The greater the distance separating society from socialism, the less can the forceful remedy of the "dictatorship" overcome this immaturity and assist the arrival of socialism.[42]

[40] #82/673.
[41] #83/726.
[42] #82/685n.

Insofar as economy and society (or law) exist in a condition of "constant partial collisions and adjustments," their relationship is not one of cause and effect, but of content and form. Struve now accepts Stammler's formulation. He concedes that the economy constitutes the content in this relationship and has primacy because it is always real, whereas law need not be. (There has never been a "paper" economy, he notes, while there have been many paper laws.)[43] But precisely because it is the content, the economy can never be conceived in isolation from its form, society. This peculiar bond precludes their developing at a different pace, and provides yet another argument against social revolution. If the economy were able to pull in one direction and society in another, then body and soul could be said to lead separate existences. Such a belief Struve calls "historic utopianism."

Socialists would do well to shed vestiges of this utopianism and recognize that capitalism imperceptibly transmutes itself into socialism. Historical significance lies not in what differentiates the two systems from one another, but in what unites them. Socialism will come into being when, and only when, class conflicts diminish to the point of total cessation.

From revolution, Struve proceeds to pauperization. He defines it as intensified exploitation of labor, and says it can take place in two principal ways: by a lowering of wages or by a rise in the rate of surplus value. Because empirical evidence conclusively shows that wages in capitalist countries are not declining, the first possibility disappears, leaving the second, the rise in the rate of surplus value. A rise of this kind can be achieved also in one of two ways: either by an extension of the working day or by intensification of labor productivity. But the working day is in actual practice becoming shorter, not longer, so that this explanation must be precluded as well. We are then left with intensification of productivity. Although it is true that such intensification is taking place, it is usually accompanied by a rise in wages which absorbs the potential accrued surplus value; and in any event, intensification of production has natural limits beyond which it cannot be pushed. For all these reasons pauperization is not taking place and will not take place, and the working class, instead of declining, will steadily gain political and economic power.

But even if one were to posit some *deus ex machina* that would

---

[43] On this point, see also #90/372–373.

pauperize the working class, pauperization would furnish the strongest possible argument against socialism. Where would a pauperized — that is, impoverished, brutalized, and dehumanized mass of workers — find the moral and intellectual resources to build a socialist society?

> One must not forget that for Marx socialism meant very broadly the flourishing of culture. He claimed for his socialism all the cultural achievements of the bourgeoisie. As long as the progressive pauperization of the masses was an indisputable fact and conceived as an unchangeable, immanent tendency of the dominant economic order, there simply could be no socialism that would take over all the cultural achievements of bourgeois society and develop them further. A realistic viewpoint simply precluded the simultaneous occurrence of pauperization and of the sociopolitical maturing of the working class that would qualify it to set in motion the greatest conceivable social transformation . . . The more oppressed one conceives the proletariat to be, the more one demands of it in the task of creating a new social order, and the less one can realistically expect from it.[44]

Although adducing these arguments against an intensified class struggle culminating in social revolution, Struve in his closing remarks nevertheless allows (as Engels had done before him) that Social Democracy need not altogether give up faith in revolution. He speaks of Social Democracy as a religion whose adherents require a social ideal. Marx believed in socialism before he began the scientific research that furnished him with proof of its inevitability. From this faith he derived great strength. Every political system, every mass movement, requires a dose of utopianism; Social Democracy also has a right to it.[45] The essential thing is not to confound the scientific with the utopian by insisting that Marxism is a consistent scientific theory. Eventually, like all religious movements, Social Democracy will become secularized, and when that happens, its utopian dogmas — class struggle and revolution — will quietly fade away.

[44] #82/661–662.
[45] Struve had already observed in 1896 that although Marxism as a scientific theory had "not one grain of ethics," the same could not be said of the modern proletarian socialist movement (#38/72).

In his critique of Marx's *economics*, Struve concentrated on the crux of the system, the theory of value. His procedure, as in the case of Marx's sociology, was to lay bare the theory's logical flaws.

According to Marx's analysis in Volume I of *Capital*, the exchange value of commodities is determined by the labor necessary for their manufacture. The capital expended on the purchase of this labor, Marx called "variable," to distinguish it from "constant" capital, used to buy raw materials, equipment, buildings, and so forth. "Variable" capital alone creates surplus value, the object of capitalist exploitation, because it is only by pocketing the difference between the wage paid the worker and the price obtained for the good produced by that worker that the capitalist makes money. The capitalist's "rate of profit," in Marx's terminology, is determined by the ratio of surplus value to the total capital, variable as well as constant. Other things being equal, the greater the proportion of variable to constant capital, that is, the more spent on labor, the higher the profit rate.

Even before Marx died economists had noted inconsistencies in his theory of profit. Böhm-Bawerk pointed out forcefully that Marx's theory contradicted the well-known fact that under the capitalistic system the rate of profit tended to be uniform — in other words, that it was not significantly affected by the "organic composition" of capital, the proportion of constant and variable capitals contained in it. If this was the case, then in what sense could it be said that the value of commodities and the level of the profit rate were determined by the quantity of labor used in production?

Engels promised a solution to this riddle in the third, posthumous, volume of *Capital*, which he was preparing for publication. But when that volume finally appeared in 1894, it caused widespread disappointment. Conceding the constant rate of profit, Marx here abandoned the view that commodities were exchanged on the basis of their labor value. Instead, he accepted the old-fashioned view that the value of commodities was determined by the "costs of production," of which labor constituted only one. In order to reconcile the two views of value, Marx suggested that even if individual commodities could not be shown to trade according to the labor value inherent in them, they still did so if one treated them in the context of the whole "social product."

Böhm-Bawerk promptly pointed out in his *Karl Marx and the Close of His System* that this explanation was tautological, and concluded that Marx, after all, had not resolved the fundamental contradiction of his value theory.

The appearance of Volume III and its inability to dispose satisfactorily of what had come to be recognized as the central problem of Marxian economics was a powerful stimulus in the development of Revisionism. (Bernstein himself acknowledged that this had been a decisive moment in his own break with Orthodoxy.)[46] The contradiction between Volumes I and III of *Capital* also played an important part in Struve's intellectual evolution. At first, he was enthusiastic about Volume III. Having read it shortly after its publication, while he was in Switzerland, he reported to Potresov that all talk of contradictions in Marx's value theory was "nonsense." [47] He was still defending it as late as December 1896, in a review of a new translation of *The Critique of Political Economy*.[48] It is quite remarkable how slow he was in publicly criticizing any aspect of Marx's economic theory. Both Tugan-Baranovsky and Bulgakov anticipated him in this respect,[49] but then they were far less deeply involved in the movement than he and stood to lose less.

But once Struve admitted to doubts, he proceeded to demolish the system thoroughly and mercilessly. When he finished, not much more was left of his Marxism than a personal admiration for the mind of its creator.

In the winter of 1898–99 he decided that Marx's acceptance of "costs of production" as the determinant of prices proved that Marxist economic theory was eclectic:

> Until the appearance of Volume III of *Capital*, it was thought by many — among these many I must confess to having belonged — that with his analysis of value, surplus value, and capital, Marx had finally destroyed the venerable "vulgar" (according to the popular derisive terminology of Marx himself) theory of "costs of production" as the basis and measurement of value. But, in reality, Volume III of *Capital* showed that in

[46] G. Zaidel, *Ocherki po istorii vtorogo internatsionala (1889–1914)*, I (Leningrad, 1931), 156.
[47] Struve to Potresov from Montreux, October 4, 1895.
[48] #40/112.
[49] Their writings are discussed in Kindersley, *Russian Revisionists,* 157–163.

dealing with this bourgeois theory, too, Marx's intention was not to destroy. The third volume of *Capital* merely provided a sociological foundation work for the vulgar theory of costs of production.[50]

Reflecting on the contradictions between Volumes I and III, he decided that they derived from Marx's unconscious confusion of sociological and economic points of view:

Altogether, it seems to me, one must not exaggerate Marx's achievement in the realm of analysis of purely economic phenomena (phenomena of the market). Marx accomplished a revolution in the science of political economy by ascertaining their sociological foundations. But undoubtedly he himself remained unclear about the relationship of these sociological foundations (the theory of capital, as a social relationship) to the analysis of the market — an analysis which aims at entirely different tasks from the sociological grounding of political economy. The lack of clarity in the understanding of the relationship between the sociological foundations and economic analysis appeared most sharply in the inner contradiction which indisputably exists in the theory of value, as expounded in Volumes I and III of *Capital*. On the other hand, this lack of clarity led Marx in Volume III, perhaps in large measure unconsciously but therefore more expressively, to rehabilitate classic-vulgar political economy, insofar as it provided an analysis of market relations. In my opinion, the critique of Marx — this most important task of our time in the realm of theoretical economics — should be to separate clearly the sociological bases of Marx's political economy as such from his analysis of market phenomena. Such a critique ought first of all to direct itself to the concept of value . . .[51]

The task was to break up Marx's value theory: to subject to a "critical dismemberment that creation of genius in which sociological and economic problems and solutions are not separated but woven into an aesthetically harmonious but scientifically uncoordinated whole."[52]

[50] #90/362.
[51] #76/48–49. Published in January 1899.
[52] #86/178.

Marx, without being aware of it, had several theories of value:

He treated as one *homogeneous problem,* namely that of value, two entirely different problems: the sociological problem of exploitation in general and of capitalist exploitation in particular, and the economic problem of value [in general] and of exchange value in particular. Thus, in Marx's theory of value there intertwine two different points of view: that of sociological observation, which treats the capitalist mode of production as a specific, historically conditioned form of exploitation of the producer and of the appropriation of surplus value; and the point of view of economic observation, to which belong the phenomena of exchange and therefore also the proper problem of value. As we have said, Marx never kept these two points of view clearly separated. And, added to this, there came in his case still a third point of view, which culminated in the *mechanistic-naturalistic* conception of *value as a substance* (*Wertsubstanz*). This conception provides an allegedly objective foundation for value. This objectivity, however, defies all comprehension, and, on closer investigation, dissolves into subjective elements . . . There is no objective *substance of value,* whose quanta are fully comparable and measurable. One can ascribe objectivity to value only insofar as one contrasts subjective value judgments with the objectivization of value judgment accomplished by judgments of social value, that is, by the phenomenon of prices. But the objective here, in the final analysis, flows from the subjective and can be deduced only from it.[53]

The more Struve reflected on Marx's value theory, the more struck he was by its inconsistencies. In the autumn of 1899, in an essay called "The Basic Antinomy of the Labor Theory of Value,"[54] he took up the so-called falling rate of profit doctrine, earlier criticized by Tugan-Baranovsky. According to Marx, the maturation of the capitalist mode of production led to a steady decline in the rate of profit, because mechanization increased the proportion of constant capital, and constant capital brought no

---

[53] #83/727.
[54] #89. Tugan-Baranovsky's essay, "Osnovnaia oshibka abstraktnoi teorii kapitala Marksa" (1899), is discussed in Kindersley, *Russian Revisionists,* 160–163.

profit. This assertion, so sharply at variance with observable facts, Struve blamed on Marx's tendency to establish between surplus value, constant capital, and variable capital a purely "mechanistic" relationship. In the Introduction to a new Russian translation of *Capital* published under his editorship in 1899, he stated that Marx had borrowed the concept of value from the classical economists and endowed it with metaphysical substance:

> Marx was to a far greater extent than is commonly believed a successor of Anglo-French "classical" political economy, defined as the whole scientific movement beginning with Quesnay and ending with Ricardo. From the Physiocrats and their English successors, he adopted that mechanistic-naturalistic viewpoint which is so clearly manifested in his theory of labor as the substance of value. This theory is the crowning of all *objective* theories of value: it directly materializes value, transforming it into an economic substance of economic goods on the example of physical matter, the substance of physical things.[55]

Finally, in the spring of 1900, Struve published in two installments a long article in which he outlined the first principles of his own economic theory.[56] This article will be discussed in its proper place in the chapter devoted to his economics (Volume II), for in it the constructive elements begin to take precedence over the critical ones. In 1900 he still thought it possible to reconcile non-Marxian economics with Marx's sociology. He spoke of the desirability of inserting the theories of the great "realists" — Ricardo, Gossen, Walras, Jevons, Menger, Wieser, and Böhm-Bawerk — into the "broad and grandiose framework of Marx's sociological generalizations,"[57] much as he had once wanted to replace the dialectical materialism of Marxist philosophy with Neo-Kantian positivism. But he soon concluded that such hybridization was not feasible. Having abandoned the labor theory of value, he toyed for a while with the idea of marginal utility, but in the end

---

[55] #85/xxxi.
[56] #9. This article was left uncompleted. Struve had intended it to be part of a major treatise on political economy: Struve's letter to the editors of the Brokgauz and Efron Encyclopedic Dictionary, February 10, 1901, Pushkin House, Leningrad, Fond 377, No. 2633.
[57] #89/305.

he entirely abandoned value as an economic category, substituting for it the concept of price.

Because in 1899 and even for several years afterward, Struve still thought of himself as a socialist, it is legitimate to inquire in what sense this was the case.

In the first place, he continued to believe in the increasing concentration of industry:

> From the point of view of socialism, in my opinion, the only important thing is whether in the course of development the *owners of the means of production* constitute an ever smaller proportion of society. In capitalist society, this question is settled. The general rise in living standards not only does not contradict this fact, but in large measure depends on it, because the concentration of the means of production as private property is at the same time the concentration of these means of production as such, and embraces both the growth of social productive capacity and the conditions for a successful class conflict.[58]

This meant that the socialization of the means of production was progressing apace and that it would ultimately lead to a socialist society.

Second, he continued to believe that as a result partly of this concentration (which increased the number of wage earners), and partly of industrial technology (which raised the level of skill of these wage earners), the working class was steadily gaining influence. It was socially the most dyamic element of the modern age, the "fourth estate" destined to dominate modern society. The rise of the proletariat — in wealth, numbers, and political power — further assured the advent of socialism.

This vision of the future was not dissimilar to the "industrial democracy" of the Webbs. It viewed socialization as an inevitable accompaniment and consequence of technological advance, as an inherent feature of economic modernization.

Finally, Struve retained admiration for Marx as the creator of a new and seminal approach to economics. Marx's greatest achieve-

---

[58] #83/731. Struve believed that a similar concentration was occurring in agriculture.

ment was to interpret all economic phenomena and concepts (value, capital, rent, and so forth) as expressions of relations into which men enter in the process of production.[59]

We have here as yet no real turning away from Marx or from socialism. This occurred later, after the Revolution of 1905, when Struve not only abandoned certain specific theories of Marx, but on moral and philosophical grounds rejected the socialist outlook in its entirety. As he once put it, he broke with Marx twice, first superficially, and then profoundly.[60] For the time being, his attitude toward socialism was best defined in the words which he used in 1902 in a letter to the German historian and political writer Hans Delbrück: "I am a socialist, but socialism for me has long ago transformed itself from a solution into a *problem*." [61]

[59] E.g., #83/729–730 and #85/32.
[60] *Rossiia*, No. 26 (February 18, 1928).
[61] Struve to Hans Delbrück, July 9, 1902.

10. END OF THE UNITED FRONT

As 1899 drew to a close, it became apparent that Struve's optimistic estimate of the prospects of Revisionism in Russia had been wide of the mark. A few Social Democratic theorists did abandon Marxist Orthodoxy, but Revisionism caught on in Russia neither with the professional revolutionaries nor with the rank and file of the intelligentsia. In the end, instead of converting others, Struve found himself expelled from the movement.

It is difficult to see how it could have been otherwise. In Germany, the Social Democrats had a legitimate party organization, functioning in the open, with a large following that included half of the country's trade unionists. As Robert Michels noted long ago, in countries where it was legalized, Social Democracy provided the bright worker with opportunities for moving upward socially, such as the Church had traditionally offered the peasant and the petty bourgeois.[1] The larger its membership and the more complicated its administrative apparatus, the less inclined was a party of this kind to allow itself to be guided by ideological considerations. The leaders of German Social Democracy, as practicing politicians, were interested not in ideological purity but in preserving their party's cohesion and inner discipline. To achieve this end, they had to show a minimum of intellectual tolerance. For this reason (as well as because of the clear preference of the trade unions for Revisionism), rather than expel the Revisionists, they let them remain in the party.

In Russia, the situation was different. There, all political activity was illegal and carried the risk of severe penalty. By a process of natural selection it attracted individuals whose motives were primarily ideological or emotional. Like all politically active people in Russia, the Social Democrats were bound to one another

[1] Robert Michels, *Political Parties* (Glencoe, Ill., 1949), 278–279.

not by political interests (the prospect of coming to power through a socialist revolution was too remote at this time to influence their attitudes) but by political ideals and the codes of behavior of their own group.

The conception of the party as a body of men held together by a common ideology rather than by common interest was deeply ingrained in Russian radicalism and helps explain its bigotry. Plekhanov, whose intolerance was notorious and was later exceeded only by Lenin's, defended it as a virtue which kept the party intact: "Freedom of opinion in the party can and must be limited, precisely because the party is a union, freely made up of *people with common ideas;* once unanimity disappears, a split becomes inevitable." [2]

If police persecution encouraged in Russian radicals intellectual intolerance, the lack of mass following bred in them an instinctive antipathy to social reformism. In the 1890's, Russian Social Democracy was an elite movement composed wholly of intellectuals, most of them from the gentry or the middle class. Deprived of daily contact with the party organizer or union functionary, and free of electoral pressures, its leaders lacked that moderating influence which in Germany a few years after legalization transformed Social Democracy from a revolutionary party into a reformist one. In Russia, the movement developed an esprit and a code all its own. Russian Social Democrats owed responsibility only to each other, and in their relations adhered to a code of ethics in which undeviating commitment to revolution served as the touchstone of integrity. For them, revolution was less a means for bringing about a better world than a symbol of group loyalty. Evidence that society was in fact unwilling to follow the revolutionary path they took as a warning not that their premises stood in need of reappraisal, but that society required more radicalization. Demands for the abandonment of revolutionary slogans emanating from within socialist ranks they interpreted as symptoms of a sickness: the cure was surgical treatment in the form of an excision or "purge" of the morbid elements. This was the instinctive reaction of Plekhanov and, following him, Lenin to Economism and Revisionism.

[2] G. V. Plekhanov, *Sochineniia*, XII (Moscow, 1925), 455, cited in Samuel H. Baron, *Plekhanov, the Father of Russian Marxism* (Stanford, Calif., 1963), 177. Emphasis added.

Struve seems not to have been aware of these facts when he counted so confidently on life triumphing over dogma. "Life," in this case, was not the social reality of Russia, from which the Social Democratic leaders were isolated, but the reality of the personal relations established within the self-contained circle of the party faithful. To his colleagues, the "cause" was not merely or even primarily a means of fighting for freedom and national greatness (which it was to him) and as such an undertaking infinitely flexible in its means, but a bond that kept them together and gave meaning to their existence. There was no room for doubters here. Conceived as an end in itself, apart from the human beings whom it was intended to serve, the "cause" loomed supremely large in the mind of the revolutionaries then, when they were outcasts, and later, when they came into power.

Struve's defeat and subsequent expulsion from Social Democratic ranks in 1900–1901 was a portent of things to come. He was the first victim of that commitment to revolution for revolution's sake which after 1917 was to become in Russia the policy of the Bolshevik government and to find application on a national scale, claiming victims by the millions.

The campaign to expel Struve was inaugurated by Plekhanov. He had refused to collaborate with *The Beginning* even before he had seen a single issue; having seen it, he at once declared war on the journal as the organ of Russian Bernsteinians. Later, in the summer of 1899, in a speech delivered in Switzerland, he said that Struve had never been a materialist, that is, by implication, a Marxist.[3] As far as he was concerned, the instant Bernstein came forth with his heretical proposals, the "united front" forged in 1895 by Potresov dissolved. The danger to the movement now came not from the "Populists" but from the Revisionists, and he therefore no longer felt under obligation to refrain from attacking deviant fellow Marxists.

Akselrod also thought Struve lost to the cause, but he reacted to the loss more in sorrow than in anger. Early in 1900 he wrote Kautsky: "I must confess frankly to you that Struve's break with Marxism saddened me more than did Bernstein's. I felt for him a special tenderness and entertained for him great hopes. Perhaps when the first articles of Bernstein appeared I was too busy with

[3] *Literaturnoe nasledie G. V. Plekhanova,* V (Leningrad, 1938), 163.

other things, but they did not put me into such a state of agitation by far as have Struve's writings." [4]

Potresov, as has been noted, resisted Struve's urgings to abandon Orthodoxy, but he remained personally friendly to him. The same held true of Vera Zasulich. Lenin vacillated, but at this time he was prepared to make important concessions to keep Struve in the movement. Had these three stood fast, Struve might have been allowed to stay, despite Plekhanov. But this was not to be, because in the winter of 1900–1901 Lenin turned against Struve, and from a supporter turned into his deadliest enemy.

In the spring of 1897, when he left for his three-year Siberian exile, Lenin was Struve's political ally and even something more, what in party language was called *Genosse*, a comrade in arms. As mentioned, one of his final acts before departing for Siberia had been to defend Struve from the rigidly Orthodox Samarans in the dispute over cereal prices. At this time, his views on major political issues did not significantly differ from Struve's. In particular, like Struve, he had come to regard the struggle for political freedom — that is, for a constitutional and parliamentary order — as the most important immediate task of the movement. Struve's influence was noticeable in Lenin's greatly changed attitude toward capitalism: after having rejected it in an unqualified manner, in 1897–1899 he came to acknowledge it as a creative and progressive force.[5] He still disapproved of Struve's "improvements" on Marx, but at this time he tended to deprecate theory unrelated to political action. As long as Struve remained committed to the essential point, which to Lenin was that organized Social Democracy should displace "Populism" and direct the national struggle for the overthrow of autocracy, he was willing to overlook his ideological peccadilloes.

This friendliness and tolerance gave no signs of waning through most of Lenin's stay in Siberia. The two men were in constant communication with each other on a variety of matters either directly, by correspondence, or indirectly, through members of

[4] Akselrod to Kautsky, February 24 [1900], in the B. I. Nikolaevsky Archive, Hoover Institution, Stanford, California. This letter was brought to my attention by Prof. Abraham Ascher.
[5] *Lenin*, II, 305, 315. Lenin also adopted Struve's view that Russia's agrarian troubles were the heritage of serfdom: *Lenin*, II, 519. See also Martov's testimony, cited above, p. 152.

Lenin's family. Much of these exchanges concerned literary matters, for during these years Struve acted as something like Lenin's literary agent: he placed Lenin's articles in periodicals, found publishers for his books, read his proofs, and obtained for him paid literary assignments. In 1898, at Lenin's request, he arranged for the publication of a collection of his papers called *Economic Essays and Articles*.[6] Struve played a particularly active role in the publication of the history of Russian capitalism which Lenin had been working on since his arrest in December 1895. In this case he not only helped Lenin obtain the necessary source materials, made all the publishing arrangements, and did the proofreading, but also gave the book its title. Lenin originally intended to call it *The Process of Formation of the Internal Market for Heavy Industry*, but Struve objected on the grounds that this title was unappealing, and suggested instead *The Development of Capitalism in Russia*. After brief resistance (Struve's title was "too bold and broad, and promised too much") Lenin eventually gave in, and his main contribution to scholarship has been known ever since by the name which Struve gave it.[7] But it was not only business that kept them corresponding. Their exchanges had personal touches, too, one of which Krupskaia records in her memoirs: a letter to Lenin from Nina Struve describing their baby (presumably Gleb): "every day we carry him up to the portraits of Darwin and Marx, and say: 'bow to Uncle Darwin, bow to Marx,' and he does it most amusingly."[8]

Struve also helped Lenin find translating jobs. The eight rubles a month which the government had allotted Lenin to pay for his upkeep sufficed for essentials, but not for additional expenses, such as books and periodicals. Lenin was usually short of money and at one point owed Kalmykova a hundred rubles.[9] To provide him with spending money, Struve arranged for him to translate *Industrial Democracy* by Sidney and Beatrice Webb for Popova's series. Lenin completed the translation of the first volume in an incredible six months, while working on his own book as well.[10]

[6] *Ekonomicheskie etiudy i stat'i* (St. Petersburg, 1898). Lenin's reliance on Struve as literary middleman is documented in his *Pis'ma k rodnym, 1894–1919* (Leningrad, 1934), 87, 104–105, 109, 143.

[7] Lenin, *Pis'ma k rodnym*, 123n, 166, 169, 185, 209.

[8] N. K. Krupskaia, *Vospominaniia o Lenine* (Moscow, 1933), 32.

[9] Lenin, *Pis'ma k rodnym*, 48, 147, 186.

[10] *Teoriia i praktika angliiskogo tred-unionizma*, trans. V. Ilin [V. I. Lenin], Vol. I (St. Petersburg, 1900), in the Economic Library series issued by the pub-

Industrial Democracy charted the process by which trade unions and cooperative associations forced modern society to assume increasing responsibilities for social services and in this manner pushed it peacefully in the direction of socialism. According to the Webbs, socialism would come into being not through direct political action but through the steady accretion of imperceptible administrative changes. The aim was a democratic and egalitarian society managed by the state. These sentiments must not have been entirely alien to Lenin at this time, for in April 1899 he praised the Webbs as representatives of "one of the most advanced currents in English political thought." [11]

In 1897 and in 1898 Lenin's esteem for Struve was not qualified in any noticeable way, if one excepts his annoyance with Struve's unreliability as a correspondent.[12] He continued to regard highly Struve's ability as a publicist: "in the realm of journalism, [Struve] reveals himself as an even better writer than in the realm of pure economics," he wrote to Potresov.[13] He voiced no displeasure with any of Struve's unorthodox economic and social opinions, including his openly stated rejection of the philosophical foundations of economic materialism and the idea of social revolution. He raised no objections to Struve's lecture on Russian household industries, in which Struve employed Bücher's non-Marxist typology;[14] nor to his explanation of serf emancipation, which denied the existence of an economic cause. The latter elicited from Lenin only a laconic query whether "it made sense to present such novel views in a brief talk." [15] In April 1899, Lenin received the first two issues of *The Beginning*. He was furious at Bulgakov for the review of Kautsky: its tone struck him as one of "professorial pretentiousness" and its argument as "utter nonsense." [16] But "in general," he wrote his family, he liked *The Beginning*

---

lishing firm of O. N. Popova, under the general editorship of Struve. Although the second volume of this book, published in 1901, also bears Lenin's name on the title page, it was in fact mostly translated by E. Smirnov (Gurevich): Lenin, *Pis'ma k rodnym*, 99n–100n, 209.

[11] *Lenin*, II, 389. While in Siberia, Lenin also translated Kautsky's book criticizing Bernstein, *Sbornik statei* (St. Petersburg, 1905): *Lenin*, II, 590.

[12] Lenin, *Pis'ma k rodnym*, 143, 202, 206–207; Lenin, XXVIII, 19–20.

[13] *Lenin*, XXVIII, 19. Lenin refers to #67.

[14] #72. (See above, pp. 205–206.) *Lenin*, XXVIII, 19. In his *Development of Capitalism in Russia*, however, Lenin objected to Bücher's terminology and Struve's use of it: *Lenin*, III, 430–431.

[15] Lenin, *Pis'ma k rodnym*, 166.

[16] *Ibid.*, 202.

"very much." [17] To appreciate the full significance of this remark it must be borne in mind that these were the very issues which caused Plekhanov to declare war on Struve and Russian Revisionism.[18]

In view of this record, it is not surprising that Struve viewed Lenin as a likely convert to Revisionism. In February 1899 he wrote Potresov: "I think that, in regard to the *Zusammenbruchtheorie* [theory of collapse of the capitalist system], [Lenin] has not yet abandoned orthodoxy, but I hope that this will happen sooner or later. Because faith in this theory requires a conservative or an unthinking mind, whereas [Lenin] has a lively and progressing mind, and genuine intellectual integrity." [19]

Lenin's slowness in reacting to Revisionism, his lack of sensitivity to the Marxist criticisms of Struve and his associates, had several causes. One was the delay with which books and journals reached him in exile. In the summer of 1899 he still had not seen Bernstein's book and had to ask Potresov whether it was indeed true that the Revisionists denied class warfare.[20] Poorly informed, he was for a long time simply unable to appreciate the full extent of Bernstein's challenge to Orthodoxy. In the second place, his total disinterest in speculation unrelated to politics caused him to ignore such harbingers of Revisionism as the Neo-Kantian critiques of Marx's philosophy. He had bothered to read neither Stammler's *Economics and Society* nor the Struve-Bulgakov controversy generated by it. By the time Plekhanov's anti-Kantian writings alerted him to their significance, Revisionism had progressed far beyond the stage of philosophic critique. And, third and perhaps most significant, in the spring of 1899 Lenin still believed it a matter of overriding importance to preserve the united front against the "Populists." In his exile, he did not realize that the old conflicts had receded into the background, and that the new political alignments were crystallizing within the

[17] *Ibid.*, 202, 209. These compliments, sent to his family, may have been intended for Struve's eyes. Lenin was somewhat more critical of *The Beginning* in letters to Potresov: *Lenin*, XXVIII, 30.

[18] Lenin contributed to his reputation as a Revisionist sympathizer with an essay in which he treated Skaldin (F. P. Flenev), a publicist of the 1860's generally considered by radicals a "bourgeois liberal," as a forerunner of the Social Democrats: *Lenin*, II, 306–315, 659.

[19] Struve to Potresov, February 10, 1899; first published in *Potresov*, 33.

[20] Lenin, *Pis'ma k rodnym*, 212, 227; *Lenin*, XXVIII, 31, 42. Bernstein's *Preconditions of Socialism* finally reached Lenin at the end of August, 1899: *Lenin*, *Pis'ma k rodnym*, 230.

Editorial board of *Nachalo*; top row, third, fourth, and fifth from right: V. Ia. (Iakovlev)–Bogucharsky, M. I. Tugan–Baranovsky, M. I. Gurovich; bottom row, first four from right: V. A. Posse, P. B. Struve, A. M. Kalmykova, M. Gorky.

Struve, ca. 1905

Social Democratic movement itself. He still worried that Mikhailovsky might exploit the quarrels among the Social Democrats.[21] In February 1899, when Struve invited Lenin to review a book by another contributor to the *Beginning*, Lenin hesitated: he did not like the book and yet he felt it improper to criticize a fellow Social Democrat in public. He resolved the difficulty by devoting four-fifths of his review to an attack on the "Populists." [22] "It is, after all, possible, while polemicizing among ourselves, to stipulate common solidarity against the Populists," he wrote apologetically to his family, after he had made up his mind to assail Bulgakov.[23] These "diplomatic" considerations were decisive in Lenin's long delay in joining Plekhanov in opposition to Struve.

Lenin first became alarmed by Revisionism in the spring of 1899. His initial reaction was a compound of distrust and disbelief. On April 27 he wrote to Potresov that he was "extremely suspicious" of the "new critical tendency" which so fascinated Struve and Bulgakov. He also "disliked" Struve's statement[24] that Marx's theory of value, as presented in Volumes I and III of *Capital*, "suffered from a contradiction" — not because the appraisal was necessarily incorrect, but because Struve called it "indisputable," whereas for Lenin it was "controversial." [25] When Potresov, who kept in closer contact with Struve, assured him that Struve was indeed gravitating toward Revisionism, Lenin was depressed: "If P. B. [Struve] is really such a passionate defender of Bernstein that he all but 'swears' by him, then this is very, very sad, because [Bernstein's] anticatastrophic 'theory' — exceedingly narrow for Western Europe — is altogether unsuited and dangerous for Russia." [26] (It may be noted that when he wrote these words, Lenin had not yet seen Bernstein's book.)[27]

That spring, Lenin had a minor altercation with Struve, the first since 1895 when they had become acquainted and had

---

[21] In the winter of 1898–99, Lenin still thought it worthwhile to write a long essay criticizing the "Populists": *Lenin*, II, 305–338. Cf. Lenin, *Pis'ma k rodnym*, 210.

[22] Lenin, *Pis'ma k rodnym*, 182; *Lenin*, II, 381–382.

[23] Lenin, *Pis'ma k rodnym*, 210; letter dated May 1/13, 1899.

[24] #76/49.

[25] *Lenin*, XXVIII, 31.

[26] *Ibid.*, 32; written on April 27, 1899.

[27] Lenin, *Pis'ma k rodnym*, 212: "I have seen neither [Bernstein's] book nor anything written about it (except for casual remarks in *Frankfurter Zeitung*). Too bad." Written on May 9, 1899.

argued over *Critical Remarks*. Then, their disagreement had re-
sulted in a meeting of minds and a political alliance: now it led
to estrangement.

The occasion was Lenin's intervention in the debate between
Bulgakov and Tugan-Baranovsky over the perennial issue of markets.[28] Lenin sent an article to Struve on the subject, requesting
him to place it in a journal. Struve did as asked, but appended to
it a note of his own in which he criticized Marx's theory of value.
In the opening paragraph, he made known his delight that Marxism was increasingly being subjected to critical scrutiny: "The
dominant sound heard, of course, is still that made by the Orthodox, chanting by rote, but that cannot silence the new critical
current, because in scientific questions true strength lies always
on the side of criticism, not of faith." [29] Lenin received the journal
containing his and Struve's articles at the beginning of March.
He was pleased that in his dispute with Bulgakov and Tugan-
Baranovsky Struve sided with him more than with them, but
he was angry over what he considered to be either Struve's
misunderstanding or perhaps his deliberate misrepresentation of
Marx. He immediately sat down to write a reply.[30] Its tone was
acerbic. Once again, as he had four years earlier, he assumed
the stance of a teacher, but this time he showed less sympathy for
the erring pupil. To Struve's call for an unrestrained critique of
Marx, Lenin responded: "No, we prefer to remain 'under the
banner of Orthodoxy,'" adding that, as he understood it, Orthodoxy committed one neither to blind faith nor to a renunciation of
constructive criticism.[31]

This disagreement, for all its insignificance, disappointed Struve
greatly. He seems to have been genuinely puzzled over his inability to persuade friends by sheer logic: "Even the most knowl-
edgeable and keenest of Marxists," he commented, "are capable
of avoiding conclusions which follow with absolute necessity
from the basic theoretical assumptions of their master." [32] Writing
to Potresov in the summer of 1899, he no longer spoke of Lenin's
"lively and expanding mind." Quite the contrary: Lenin's *Development of Capitalism*, which he was preparing for publication,

[28] The literature on this controversy is given in *Lenin*, II, 632–633.
[29] #76/46.
[30] *Lenin*, II, 405–420.
[31] *Ibid.*, 420.
[32] #86/176. Refers to Lenin and another writer.

induced in him, by the absence of a "flow of ideas," a sense of "aesthetic depression."[33] Publicly, he responded to Lenin with a curt and even sharper article in which he stated that he did not know where to begin rebutting his opponent, so different were their conceptions of Marxist economics. Of Lenin's Orthodoxy he spoke scornfully: "[Lenin] apparently considers it absolutely obligatory in all cases not only to think but also to express himself à la Marx, and moreover à la Marx in Russian translation . . . I reason conditionally: 'if the labor theory of value is correct,' whereas [Lenin] must reason categorically: 'insofar as the labor theory of value says so and so.'"[34] It would be good, Struve concluded, if Lenin shook off the "spell" of Orthodoxy. It was the last time he expressed such a wish and such a hope. He had come by now to consider Lenin as impervious to arguments from logic and life as Plekhanov, and did not even bother to reply to the letters which Lenin kept on sending him.[35]

With the approach of his last summer in exile, Lenin decided to familiarize himself with the Revisionist literature, especially Neo-Kantian philosophy. To find out what it was about, he began a systematic course of self-instruction in the history of philosophy, beginning with the French materialists of the eighteenth century. His ignorance of the subject was vast ("I realize very well my lack of philosophical education," he confessed privately);[36] but so was his dislike of it, and he soon abandoned the undertaking. After some sketchy background reading, he turned to Stammler and promptly declared the book "learned nonsense and utterly useless scholasticism."[37] The Bulgakov-Struve debates of 1897 over historical causation made on him the same impression. He concluded on this thin evidence that Plekhanov was right: Neo-Kantianism was indeed a theory of the "reactionary bourgeoisie" and a "serious matter." Sharing these thoughts with Potresov on June 27, 1899, he voiced amazement at Potresov's report of an anti-Marxist reaction under way in St. Petersburg. Who was be-

---

[33] Struve to Potresov, July 26, 1899. The critics shared Struve's opinion of Lenin's book, which was neither widely nor favorably reviewed. The reviews praised Lenin's command of the factual material and his lucid presentation but complained of schematism and narrowness of conception. See *Lenin*, III, 545–555, where several of these reviews are reprinted.

[34] #84/1581, 1583.

[35] Lenin, *Pis'ma k rodnym*, 229.

[36] *Lenin*, XXVIII, 40.

[37] *Ibid.*; Lenin, *Pis'ma k rodnym*, 216.

hind it, he wanted to know. "Is it true that [Struve] and his friends have developed a tendency to unite with the liberals?" If this indeed was the case, then Struve would cease to be a "comrade" (Genosse): "This of course, will be an enormous loss to all the Genossen, because he is a man of great talent and learning — but, of course, 'friendship is friendship, and business is business,' and this will not obviate the need for war."[38]

As yet, however, he was not ready for war. Having drafted a polemical piece against Bulgakov, whom he considered the worst offender among the Revisionists, he softened the sharpest passages before dispatching the manuscript to the publisher. "I am 'Orthodox' and a decisive opponent of the 'critics' . . . *but* one must not exaggerate the differences of opinion (as Bulgakov does) in the face of common enemies," he explained to Potresov.[39]

The most severe blow to Lenin's equanimity was the receipt in late July from his sister Anne of a document called "Credo." It had been written by Catherine Kuskova, a young Marxist just returned from Western Europe, where with her husband, S. N. Prokopovich, she had investigated the labor movement. Anne had obtained the text from Kalmykova. Transcribing it for her brother, she gave it the title "Credo," a name by which it has been known ever since, although Kuskova rejected both the name and its implication of programmatic intent.[40] Like everything else that this spirited woman ever wrote, the "Credo" was inaccurate and confusing, but the portent of its thesis at least was clear: As Russian socialism matures, the party must give up trying to form an independent labor organization and join in the national struggle for constitution and civil liberties. "The party's . . . striving for a seizure of power will be transformed into a striving for a change, for a reform of existing society in a democratic direction . . ."[41]

[38] *Lenin*, XXVIII, 41.

[39] *Ibid.*, 10. Written on June 27, 1899. "One of Bulgakov's major shortcomings is precisely his failure to state where he sides with Kautsky against the Populists," he wrote in May 1899 (Lenin, *Pis'ma k rodnym*, 210) — an indication of how difficult it was for him even at this late date to give up the idea of a united front against the "Populists."

[40] The story of the "Credo" is told in *Lenin*, II, 636–639; Richard Kindersley, *The First Russian Revisionists* (Oxford, 1962); and J. L. H. Keep, *The Rise of Social Democracy in Russia* (Oxford, 1963), 65–66.

[41] *Lenin*, II, 478.

Kuskova wrote her brief essay to explain why Revisionism had come about. To her, it was an inevitable phase in the development of European socialism, a process of maturing which carried it from preoccupation with politics to concern with society and economics. But although she sympathized with Revisionism (or so it would appear, for the argument is muddled), her "Credo" in itself was not a Revisionist document, as it was subsequently made out to be in party polemics. The Revisionists wanted the working class to participate in politics: they merely excluded revolution and power seizure as political techniques. Struve, for one, during his Revisionist phase still fully expected the Russian working class to overthrow the autocracy. The roots of Kuskova's ideas lay rather in Economism. The blurring of the lines between agitation as a means to political involvement and as an end in itself had already occurred, as noted, in 1897–98.[42] In 1899–1900, Economism won the majority of the Union of Russian Social Democrats, the official organization of Russian Social Democracy abroad.[43] Kuskova, who during her stay abroad had been affiliated with the Union, merely pushed the tendencies inherent in worker agitation and Economism to their logical conclusion by urging that the second, political stage of the agitational strategy be abandoned altogether.

Plekhanov combatted these Economist tendencies in the Union, though with less vigor than he evidenced in fighting Bernstein, for he considered Economism the lesser danger of the two. Not so Lenin. As long as the "critical tendency" had confined its re-visions to theory — epistemology, philosophy of history, theories of value and profit, pauperization, even the idea of social revolu-tion — he treated it with forebearance. But when "criticism" touched the concept of an independent socialist party, his toler-ance immediately gave out.

To understand the violence of Lenin's reaction to the "Credo," one need only recall the circumstances attending his conversion to Social Democracy in 1895. At that time he gave up his essen-tially Blanquist idea of terror and power seizure because talks with Akselrod, Plekhanov, and Struve had persuaded him of the

---

[42] Economism made its appearance not only in Russia but also in the West. See P. Kampffmeyer, "Historisches und Theoretisches zur sozialdemokratischen Re-visionsbewegung," *Sozialistische Monatshefte*, No. 5 (1902), 345–354.

[43] *Lenin*, II, 641; Baron, *Plekhanov*, 153–154, 186–192.

superiority of the Social Democratic strategy: a temporary alliance
with all the opponents of autocracy in Russia, especially the
"bourgeoisie." In this alliance, according to Akselrod's formula,
the "proletariat" would exercise the role of the "hegemon": and
the "proletariat," of course, meant the Social Democratic party.
Once one gave up the idea of forming an independent Social
Democratic party to guide the political struggle against absolutism, the whole strategy became meaningless. Worse than
that, such a move would turn the Social Democrats into accomplices in the bourgeoisie's seizure of power. Dreading this prospect, he reacted urgently — one may almost say, in panic — to
a document which in fact represented only the views of its author
and her husband.[44] With an uncanny political instinct, he sensed
that it was a harbinger, the symptom of what he diagnosed as
"an impending disease" of Social Democracy.[45] He immediately
drafted a "Protest of Russian Social Democrats" against the
"Credo," which he persuaded a number of fellow exiles to sign.
In it, he reaffirmed the commitment of socialists and of labor to
political action, with copious references to Struve's manifesto of
1898.[46]

But this move did not assuage the fears that now assailed him
in earnest. In the "Protest" he denied that the Social Democratic
movement was undergoing a "crisis" — to say so, he wrote, meant
to "repeat unthinking phrases of bourgeois scribblers who try
to blow up every disagreement among socialists and transform it
into a schism of socialist parties." [47] But in his heart he knew that
the crisis had come. He worried so much over it that he lost
weight and developed insomnia.[48]

Pondering the causes of Economism, Lenin concluded that
foremost among them was the isolation of the worker groups from
each other and from the socialist intelligentsia. Thrown back on
their own resources, workers unconsciously slipped into habits of
"small deeds" and lost sight of the labor movement as a whole.
From this analysis, Lenin concluded that the most urgent task

---

[44] According to B. I. Nikolaevsky (*Potresov*, 34), even the most extreme
Economists conceded that labor had a political duty to fulfill.
[45] *Lenin*, II, 636.
[46] *Lenin*, II, 477–486.
[47] *Lenin*, II, 481.
[48] Krupskaia, *Vospominaniia*, 35.

confronting Russian Social Democrats was to infuse the Russian labor movement with a sense of class consciousness and common purpose.

This program was not entirely novel. Kautsky and Plekhanov had spoken before Lenin of the intelligentsia's duty to lead the proletariat and inject into it socialist consciousness; but no Marxist of any standing before Lenin had ever envisaged the relationship between labor and the socialist intelligentsia as other than harmonious. Because it had been generally assumed that the interests and aspirations of the two groups coincided, it was considered unnecessary to define precisely their respective functions or spheres of authority. Lenin was the first Marxist to challenge the assumption of a harmony of interest between labor and socialism. The personal experiences which he had had with the St. Petersburg labor elite in 1894–95, as well as the massive evidence of the attraction that apolitical trade unionism held for international labor, led him to the conclusion that labor was not inherently, by its nature, socialist. Left to its own devices, its instinct was to collaborate with the bourgeoisie and betray socialism. This conception, without precedent in the history of socialist thought, did not spring into Lenin's mind at once in its finished form, but germinated there in the year and a half that followed his receipt of the "Credo." He finally articulated it in December 1900 in a seminal paper called "Urgent Questions of Our Movement," wherein he stated flatly that "the labor movement separated from Social Democracy . . . inevitably turns bourgeois." [49] This contention negated the basic tenet of Marxism, that capitalism inevitably radicalized the working class and in the end left it no alternative but to struggle for socialism. It marked an even more radical departure from Marx than Revisionism and, like it, was a symptom of the malaise spreading in European Social Democracy.

To assure the flow of socialist impulses into labor, Lenin reasoned, it was imperative to organize an effective Social Democratic party. This required patient and skillful diplomacy. The movement was by now split into three factions — Orthodox, Revisionist, and Economist. Before a party organization could be constituted, the two heresies had to be neutralized. Corresponding in the second half of 1899 with Martov and Potresov, Lenin

[49] *Lenin,* IV, 56.

formed with them a joint plan of action, calling for the simultaneous pursuit of two contradictory policies: separation of the
Orthodox Marxists from the Revisionists and Economists on the
ideological level, and unification with them on the level of organization. The Orthodox Marxists were to fuse with the heretics
into a single party and, by a relentless exposure of their fallacies,
wean their following away from them.

As a first step toward this goal, the "triumvirate" (Lenin,
Potresov, Martov) decided to launch two periodicals. One, a
journal called *Zaria* (The Dawn), which Potresov suggested, was
to be devoted to theory. Its task would be to combat the Revisionist tendencies prevailing in the periodical press legally published
inside Russia. The other, proposed by Lenin, was to be a newspaper, modeled on *Der Sozialdemokrat,* the organ of the German
Social Democrats published in Switzerland during the years of
Bismarck's antisocialist law.[50] Potresov christened it *Iskra* (The
Spark).[51] Its special mission was to combat both Economism
and the government, and its editorial board was to constitute
the embryo of a central committee for the future party. Both
publications were to open their columns to Social Democrats
holding non-Orthodox views. The three friends agreed to put
this plan into execution immediately after their terms of exile had
expired.

The strategy suffered from a fatal contradiction. On the one
hand, *Iskra* and *Zaria* were to serve as organs of militant Orthodoxy for the purpose of exposing and liquidating Social Democratic heresies; on the other, they were to provide the shell for
a rudimentary party organization embracing these very heretics.
Iskra and *Zaria* were to be instruments of ideological warfare and
political amalgamation: they were at one and the same time
to separate and to unite.

To further complicate matters, the triumvirate naturally assumed that the Social Democratic organization built around their
publications would lead the national struggle against autocracy.
According to Potresov, *Iskra* was dedicated to a political ideology
"based on the idea of the hegemony of the proletariat and its Social
Democratic vanguard in the task of the political liberation of

---

[50] *Lenin,* II, 502.
[51] *Potresov,* 39.

Russia." [52] Although this was not spelled out, the implication was that the Social Democrats would exploit the liberal movement for their own purposes, while pretending to assist it. Would the bourgeoisie allow itself to be used in this manner? And what of the proletariat, which in political matters was to be asked to co-operate with the very elements which socialist propaganda depicted as its mortal class enemy?

In sum, the subtle strategy conceived by Lenin and Potresov, with Martov's rather skeptical acquiescence, rested on faith in their ability to reconcile the irreconcilable: ideological purity and political opportunism.

In January 1900, when their terms of exile simultaneously expired, Lenin and Potresov headed west; Martov, who was serving his sentence in an even remoter locality, followed them. Forbidden to settle in St. Petersburg, they chose as their legal residence Pskov, whence they could maintain contact with friends in the capital, about two hours away by train. Their base of operations was the apartment of the Radchenkos, who resided in Pskov under overt police surveillance. At their disposal was also the modest wooden house of V. A. Obolensky, who worked in Pskov as a statistician.

During February and March, Lenin and Potresov made several clandestine trips to St. Petersburg to see friends and acquaint themselves with the situation at first hand. These encounters, which took place in Kalmykova's apartment, were closely observed by the police, but for the time being no arrests were made. Lenin and Potresov were pleasantly surprised by what they found out. The situation was not as dismal as it had seemed to them in Siberia: the Economists turned out to be less antipolitical and the Revisionists less bent on fighting the Orthodox than they had thought.[53] The two also learned that emissaries whom the émigré Union of Russian Social Democrats had secretly dispatched to Russia were arranging for a second Social Democratic congress to be held in May 1900 in Smolensk. There was general expectation that this congress would at last constitute a genuine party organization. Talks with the Union's emissaries indicated that they were

---

[52] OD, I, 613.
[53] *Potresov*, 38, apparently based on information given to Nikolaevsky by Potresov.

not averse to recognizing *Iskra* as the projected party's official organ. This prospect sufficed to make Lenin and Potresov contemplate the possibility of remaining in Russia and converting *Iskra* into an underground publication.[54]

Conversations with Struve and his Revisionist friends also went well. It was very important for Lenin and Potresov to secure Struve's support for their venture. His literary connections enabled Struve to reach numerous potential contributors to *Zaria,* while contacts with prominent zemstvo people (Shakhovskoi, Rodichev, and so on) made it possible for him to obtain precise information and documentation on bureaucratic misdeeds of the kind that *Iskra* required. Furthermore, through friends in the publishing world and in public life — notably D. E. Zhukovsky, a wealthy landlord — he had access to money. Lenin and Potresov regarded Struve's literary and financial connections as essential to their cause and felt that without his help *Iskra* and *Zaria* could not be launched. They were, therefore, highly gratified to learn from Struve that notwithstanding his Revisionism he continued to consider himself a Social Democrat and was prepared to assist them in every possible way.[55] After preliminary discussion, it was agreed that as soon as Martov had arrived from Siberia, the three editors would sign a formal accord with Struve, specifying the terms on which he and his friends would participate in the projected publications. In the meantime, Lenin undertook to draft a public announcement spelling out the ideological position of *Iskra* and *Zaria.*

The task which Lenin had set himself was impossible to fulfill because it called for the condemnation of the ideology of the Revisionists and the Economists, and at the same time required justification of collaboration with them. To cope with the difficulty, Lenin divided his announcement into two distinct parts, one theoretical, the other practical.[56] In the first, he blamed the crisis convulsing the Social Democratic movement on the isolation of its constituent groups. He identified Revisionism with Economism, and called it "the parody of Marxism in Russian legal literature." [57]

---

[54] *Ibid.,* 38–39.

[55] *Ibid.;* L. Martov, *Istoriia rossiiskoi sotsial-demokratii* (Petrograd, 1918), 57; Struve, "My Contacts and Conflicts with Lenin," SR, XIII, No. 37 (1934), 75.

[56] *Lenin,* IV, 1–13.

[57] *Ibid.,* 6; this is one of the earliest instances of juxtaposition of the adjective "legal" with the noun "Marxism."

Nevertheless, once he had drawn a sharp line separating true Marxism from its aberrations, he proceeded to solicit the deviants' cooperation. Social Democracy, he explained, was prepared to assist any group fighting autocracy. He went on to state the importance of launching literary organs open to a frank discussion of the party's program.

> While we shall carry out our literary work from the viewpoint of a definite orientation, we do not, by any means, intend to put forth all particulars of our own point of view as the views of all Russian Social Democrats; we do not intend by any means to deny existing disagreements, to paper them over or to rub them out. On the contrary: we want to make our organs into organs of *deliberation* on all the problems by all Russian Social Democrats holding the most diverse views. We not only do not repudiate polemics among comrades on the pages of our organs; on the contrary, we are prepared to allot them a great deal of space . . . More than that: recognizing Russian labor and Social Democracy as the vanguard in the struggle for democracy, for political freedom, we consider it imperative to strive to make our organs *all-democratic* ones . . .[58]

It is difficult to see how Lenin and Potresov expected to secure the cooperation of the Revisionists and Economists in publications in whose editorial policy statement they were roundly abused. Upon being shown Lenin's announcement on his arrival in Pskov late in March, Martov thought the whole thing preposterous; so did Vera Zasulich, who had come surreptitiously to St. Petersburg from Geneva and was hiding out in Kalmykova's apartment. But Lenin and Potresov exuded confidence. They assured Martov that Struve would be content to "play second fiddle," especially if at the forthcoming Smolensk congress the Social Democrats succeeded in forming a party organization. In any event, they had little choice: without Struve, *Iskra* and *Zaria* would be so short of money and literary materials that they would collapse at the start. Martov had the impression that to assuage his misgivings about an alliance with Struve, whom Martov strongly disliked, Lenin intended to carry "a rock under his shirt." [59]

[58] *Ibid.*, 11–12.
[59] LS, IV (1925), 56.

Unfortunately, we are poorly informed about Struve's activities during this time. He participated in debates at the Free Economic Society[60] and worked on a book dealing with general economic theory, installments of which he published in the spring of 1900.[61] But what else he did between July 1899, when he left St. Petersburg with his family to vacation in the countryside, and April 1900, when he arrived in Pskov to negotiate with the triumvirate — of this, at present, nothing is known. Ignorance of this period in his life is particularly galling, because it is then that he first established a working relationship with liberal circles and began to gravitate toward the constitutionalist camp.

Evidence of this evolution is his collaboration on a short-lived liberal newspaper, *The Northern Courier* (*Severnyi Kur'er*). Founded by Prince V. V. Bariatinsky in November 1899 as an organ of the "intellectual conscience of Russian society," [62] it adopted as its theme Struve's slogan "The country's life is growing more complex." Following the example which he had set in his "Domestic Surveys" in the *New Word* and *The Beginning*, it attempted to illustrate from daily life the unbridgeable chasm which separated the realities of Russia's life from the anachronistic structure of its government. In an important programmatic statement published in the first issue of the paper Struve stated this theme, and predicted as explicitly as he could the inevitable disintegration of autocracy:

> In the depths of a people's historic life there always occurs something contrary to what takes place on the surface: there it is not small deeds that are accomplished to the sound of loud words, but, on the contrary, great historic facts that are created to the accompaniment of small words, or altogether without words . . . The wordless creativity of history manifests itself in one fact which under other social conditions would be self-evident but which requires conscious notice under conditions of our Russian life, which in the main fulfills its creative mission si-

[60] According to *Trudy* IVEO, he took part in the debates held on October 23 and December 4, 1899.

[61] #90.

[62] The first issue of *Severnyi Kur'er* came out on May 14/26, 1899, in a small format with these words, signed by M. Golovinsky, on the front page. At least two more issues appeared in this format, and then the paper ceased publication. It resumed in the regular large format on November 1/13, 1899, and appeared without break until December 22, 1900/January 4, 1901, when it was suppressed.

lently. The title of our article has defined this fact. It is called "The Growing Complexity of Life." It makes itself felt at every step and represents one of the manifestations of the transition of the country to new forms of economic life. This growing complexity has its quantitative and qualitative aspects. The means of communication, commercial relations, and the population movement expand; urban centers develop; village life transforms itself. And, most important, in the course of these changes among the intelligentsia and the people there emerges a new man. . . .

Life, as it grows increasingly complex, demands more complex forms of exerting influence, and, as it runs into simplified forms and means, it experiences pain each minute. It shrinks but it can neither vanish nor become simpler for the sake of exerting simplified influence. It is strong by virtue of its complexity and cannot renounce it. After all, it is life, it is the "man" for the sake of which exists the "Sabbath" — forms. Directly or circuitously, painlessly or painfully, life must adapt these forms to itself . . .

[The new] man wants and is forced by all the conditions of life to learn, but to learn not only by decree and following a set program — in the ultimate analysis, he wants to think independently and just as independently to shape his life. He wishes modern technology not to oppress and confine him, but to "straighten him out" . . . He wants scope for his material and his spiritual existence.[63]

The notion that the working class will lead the struggle for political liberty gradually yields here to a broader vision of a whole nation demanding freedom, of the seething content bursting through the rigid form. These are rumblings of the "liberational movement" of 1902–1905, which Struve was to supply with its theory.

[63] "Uslozhnenie zhizni," SK, No. 1 (November 1/13, 1899), 2. Struve first identified himself as the author of this article in a letter sent from Munich to the editors of the Brokgauz and Efron Encyclopedic Dictionary on February 10, 1901: Pushkin House, Leningrad, Fond 377. The article, which created much stir, brought the newspaper its first warning from the police: Struve, "Pamiati V. Ia. Iakovleva-Bogucharskogo," RM, June 1915, Pt. 2, 143. In the letter mentioned above, Struve also took credit for an article in *The Northern Courier* on Gradovsky (see "A. D. Gradovskii, kak publitsist," SK, No. 9 [November 9/21, 1899], 1) signed "P.I." and a third article, the title of which I was unable to decipher in the manuscript. Lenin, too, was invited to contribute to this newspaper in May 1900, possibly at Struve's suggestion, but he refused: KL, No. 1/10 (1924), 22.

At this time (February 1900), Struve seems to have entered into negotiations with an unidentified zemstvo figure (possibly D. E. Zhukovsky), who is said to have offered him money with which to move abroad and found an oppositional newspaper.[64] It was rumors of such dealings that had caused Lenin to inquire apprehensively from Siberia whether it was true that Struve had "developed a tendency to unite with the liberals."[65]

In other words, Struve was well along in cementing relations with the liberals when Lenin and Potresov invited him to collaborate on their periodicals. Believing then, as afterward, in the necessity of constituting the broadest possible coalition against the autocracy, he readily agreed, even though he thought Lenin's and Potresov's political program utopian. He did not fear collaborating with self-professed Orthodox Marxists, being convinced that Orthodoxy would soon disintegrate from contact with living reality.

In April 1900, Obolensky's dacha in Pskov was the scene of negotiations between Struve and Tugan-Baranovsky, representing the Revisionist wing in Russian Social Democracy, and Lenin and Potresov, speaking for the Orthodox editorial board of *Iskra* and *Zaria*.[66] Martov was also present but he merely observed the proceedings. The meeting opened with Lenin reading his announcement. Martov, our main witness to these events,[67] says that Tugan-Baranovsky took offense at the passages linking the "critics" with the Economists and describing their writings as a "parody" of Marxism. When Lenin finished, he angrily demanded to know why the two groups were lumped together, since the Economists renounced political action whereas the Revisionists favored it. Lenin, lawyer that he was, had come prepared, and he opened a dossier with evidence meant to prove the apolitical attitude of the Revisionists. According to Martov, it consisted of trivia, the weightiest item being Struve's refusal, on grounds of party solidarity, to associate himself with Radchenko's attack on the Economists. During the reading and the discussion which followed, Struve, like Martov, sat silent and scornful.

---

[64] *Belokonsky*, 92. Based on information supplied by an anonymous source who could have been none other than V. Ia. Iakovlev-Bogucharsky.

[65] See above, p. 244.

[66] B. N[ikolaevsky], "Iz epokhi 'Iskry' i 'Zari,' " KS, No. 35 (1927), 10; LS, III (1924), 130.

[67] LS, IV (1925), 49–61.

Martov was certain that these negotiations were a waste of time.[68] But to his surprise, once the preliminaries were over, Struve and Tugan-Baranovsky declared themselves in full sympathy with the plans of the triumvirate. The two parties reached an informal understanding but postponed the signature of a more formal agreement until the editors had consulted Plekhanov and his group. Struve and Tugan-Baranovsky promised to help *Iskra* and *Zaria* obtain funds and materials, and in return secured the right to state in these publications their own views on Marxism "as topics for discussion" ("v diskussionnom poriadke").[69] Revisionism was thus implicitly recognized by Lenin and Potresov as a legitimate variant of Social Democracy. Struve says that during these talks Lenin behaved in an opportunistic manner and Potresov in a friendly one, while Martov concealed his feelings.[70] After the offending passages in the announcement had been removed or toned down (including the one about the "parody"), the two groups parted amicably. Before leaving, Struve gave Lenin and his friends five rubles for the cause.[71]

A few days after the Pskov talks, the police seized and jailed the organizers of the Smolensk congress. The plans to form a Social Democratic party were aborted for the time being. In view of this situation, the triumvirate decided to lose no more time in moving abroad. As the seat of their editorial office they chose Germany rather than Switzerland, because they wanted to be as far as possible from Plekhanov, fearing that his intransigence would make their life difficult and prevent them from maintaining good relations with the Economists and Revisionists. Potresov was the first to leave the country. He arrived in Germany in April, and with the help of German Social Democratic friends made the technical arrangements for the printing of *Iskra* and *Zaria*. The financial resources at his disposal were meager: he had a total of 5,000 rubles for the two publications, 2,000 from Kalmykova, 1,000 from Zhukovsky, and the remainder from his own pocket.[72] How small a sum this was and why additional financial backing was essential may be judged from the fact that at this time an average Russian

[68] *Ibid.*, 57.
[69] "My Contacts and Conflicts with Lenin," 75–76.
[70] *Ibid.*, 76.
[71] LS, IV (1925), 60.
[72] *Potresov*, 39.

monthly called for an initial investment of 30,000 to 40,000 rubles. Having concluded these arrangements, Potresov proceeded to Switzerland.

Lenin was supposed to follow him there shortly, but he was delayed because he had been arrested on one of his illegal expeditions from Pskov to St. Petersburg. Although the police authorities seem to have been informed of what he and his two friends were intending abroad, they soon released him and even returned his passport. The circumstances of this curious episode are obscure; but there are indications that the Okhrana mistakenly believed that Lenin was an Economist interested in depoliticizing the labor movement who could do no harm abroad and could do some good.[73] Martov stayed in Russia for the time being to take care of transport and distribution.

While the triumvirate was making these preparations, Plekhanov was waging his own battle against Russian heretics settled in the West. In March 1900 he brought out *Vademecum,* a work directed against the Economists who were in control of the Union of Russian Social Democrats. The violence of its language shocked even his admirers, and contributed heavily to the decision of the triumvirate to stay out of his immediate reach.[74] Plekhanov's campaign failed miserably. In April 1900, at a conference of émigré Social Democrats, the supporters of the Union won a majority, whereupon Plekhanov, hurt and angry, withdrew from active politics to write a major treatise criticizing Revisionism.[75]

[73] Central State Archive of the October Revolution (TsGAOR), f. D.P. oo, 3-e d-vo, ch. 950/1899, l. 118, cited in VIKPSS, No. 1 (January 1963), 114. According to this Okhrana document, the police believed that Lenin was going abroad to take control of the Rabochee delo organization, which, of course, was dominated by Economists. Vladimir Burtsev, the unmasker of Azef, believed that Zubatov, a high Okhrana official, sponsored *Iskra* as a means of neutralizing the Socialist Revolutionaries. In his view, the police were well informed about the Pskov negotiations and the editorial arrangements which Potresov made abroad for *Iskra* and *Zaria.* He called attention to the fact the police had issued Krupskaia a passport to join Lenin in Munich, although they knew that the staff of *Iskra* was there. See: Vladimir Burtsev, "Lenin pod pokrovitel'stvom Departamenta politsii i Nemtsev," *Za svobodu* (Warsaw), No. 113 (May 19, 1927), and "Kak Departament politsii otpustil Lenina za granitsu dlia bol'shevistskoi propagandy," *Byloe* (N.S.), II (1933), 85–92. The exact Munich address of *Iskra* is indeed listed in the official annual report of the Chief of Gendarmes for 1901, together with its editorial staff, Lenin included: *Obzor,* XXV (1901), 120–121. See also *Potresov,* 36, and KL, No. 1/10 (1924), 18–26.

[74] A. N. Potresov and B. I. Nikolaevsky, *Sotsial-demokraticheskoe dvizhenie v Rossii,* I (Moscow and Leningrad, 1928), 357.

[75] Plekhanov opened his attack on Neo-Kantianism in the autumn of 1898 with a critique of Konrad Schmidt in which he called it "bourgeois opium." He fol-

Given his embattled mood, it is easy to picture his reaction to the proposal which Lenin and Potresov outlined to him on their arrival in Geneva. They proposed that he join them in sponsoring two publications on the pages of which his enemies would be allowed openly to air their views. Enraged, he accused them of incorrigible opportunism and flatly refused to give them any help. From Lenin's vivid but incoherent account, written immediately after the first meeting with Plekhanov,[76] it is known that the first subject to come up was Struve. Plekhanov reminded Lenin and Potresov that they had requested him in 1895 "not to shoot at Struve" and expressed anger at their willingness to continue "peaceful cooperation" with this man. Lenin tried to justify himself: "we must be as lenient as *possible* with Struve because *we ourselves* are not without blame for his evolution; we ourselves, and G. V. [*Plekhanov*] *among us*, did not stand up when it was necessary to do so (1895, 1897)." [77] But Plekhanov would admit to no fault on his part. He raged against "traitors" to the cause, shouting that if he had the power he would have them all shot.[78] His outbursts were so intemperate and his hatred of the heretics so ferocious that Lenin, to his surprise, found himself defending Struve.

These talks went on for several days. Lenin felt that the real issue at stake was control of *Iskra* and *Zaria*. By threats of noncooperation, Plekhanov succeeded in the end in obtaining editorial control of *Zaria* as well as a double vote on the board of *Iskra*. He hoped to use the power he had gained to assure that the two publications cleaved to the Orthodox line. But this victory was costly: Lenin who had believed him a paragon, now found him, on closer contact, to be a mere politician. In the course of these quarrels,

---

lowed it with several others. See Kh. Zhitlovsky, "Die Polemik Plechanov contra Stern und Conrad Schmidt," *Sozialistische Monatshefte*, III (1899), 277–283, and 322–330.

[76] "Kak chut' ne potukhla Iskra," *Lenin*, IV, 19–31. The editors of this edition have excised several anti-Semitic remarks by Plekhanov. They are restored in *Lenin PSS*, IV, 338–339.

[77] Lenin, IV, 19; cf. *Potresov*, 42.

[78] At about this time, Posse arrived in England. He visited Kropotkin, the venerable anarchist, who told him of his great admiration for Struve. He also said that if he, Kropotkin, returned to the Russia of Nicholas II he would be sent to Sakhalin to conduct geological investigations, whereas in a Russia ruled by Plekhanov he would be hanged: V. A. Posse, *Moi zhiznennyi put'* (Moscow and Leningrad, 1929), 240. As far as Plekhanov's intentions were concerned, Kropotkin was not far off the mark.

Lenin underwent another one of the spiritual crises which he was to experience repeatedly during this transitional period. In a note jotted down at the time he spoke of feeling "entirely reborn." [79]

The question of Struve's participation was central to these disagreements. Lenin and Potresov wanted to adhere to the verbal understanding reached at Pskov, and urged Plekhanov to agree at least to a "conditional accord" with Struve. But Plekhanov would not yield an inch: he "very coldly and drily remarked that he was in complete disagreement" and told them they had to choose between him and Struve.[80] Exhausted and dejected, Lenin and Potresov at the end of August left for Germany, without having secured from Plekhanov a promise to participate in *Iskra*. They were so discouraged that they contemplated for a while giving up everything and returning to Russia.

Iskra and *Zaria* might never have materialized were it not for the intercession of Vera Zasulich. After Lenin and Potresov had departed and Plekhanov's anger had subsided, she succeeded in making him see their point of view: that it was not reasonable to expect Struve and his backers to render *Iskra* and *Zaria* the assistance which everyone agreed was essential without giving them something in return. Plekhanov relented. In a letter sent to her in Munich, where she had gone to join Lenin and Potresov, he wrote: "After long deliberation, I admit that [Lenin's and Potresov's] tactics are correct, and I am prepared to yield to them all along the line. Let them also invite Struve and [Tugan-Baranovsky]; I agree to this as well." [81] This concession, without parallel in Plekhanov's life, enabled the negotiations to resume.

Plekhanov placed one condition on Struve's participation: that he renounce all claims to being a Social Democrat. He insisted on this point because he feared that the appearance of Revisionist articles on the pages of *Iskra* and *Zaria* would further disorient the Social Democratic rank and file and aggravate the prevailing theoretical confusion. He proposed that Struve and his party identify themselves as representatives of the "democratic opposition," and come in as friends of the Social Democrats rather than as "comrades." Lenin and Potresov accepted this stipulation. Thus, at Plekhanov's insistence, Struve was to be asked to withdraw from

[79] *Lenin*, IV, 28.
[80] Potresov and Nikolaevsky, *Sotsial-demokraticheskoe dvizhenie*, I, 74.
[81] *Ibid.*

Social Democracy as a price for being permitted to cooperate with it.

Once the disagreements with Plekhanov were resolved, Lenin rewrote the Pskov announcement. All the references which had made Plekhanov so furious — those to the need for "diversity" of opinion and to the "general democratic" nature of the new publications — were done away with, and were replaced with a laconic promise that *Iskra* would open its pages to "polemics among comrades." Whereas Lenin's Pskov draft had stressed the desirability for unity among all the currents of Social Democracy, the new version insisted on the need for separating (*razmezhevanie*) the true Marxists from the deviants. In the first draft, the allusions to Revisionism were casual and vague; in the new announcement they were brutally explicit:

> We have no intention of making our organ a mere storehouse of divergent opinions. On the contrary: we shall conduct it in the spirit of a firmly defined movement. That movement can be expressed by the word Marxism, and it is hardly necessary for us to add that we stand for the logical development of the ideas of Marx and Engels, and decidedly reject the half-hearted, diluted, and opportunistic corrections which have lately come into such fashion from the sleight of hand perpetrated by Eduard Bernstein, P. Struve, and many others.[82]

In another part of the revised announcement, "legal Marxism" was used to refer to an ideological current in the Russian Social Democracy, allegedly distinct from and antagonistic to genuine Marxism.

On October 6, 1900, Lenin and Potresov signed a formal accord with the Liberation of Labor Group. Only the first article, announcing that the signatories had reached agreement, was made public; the clauses which spelled out the terms of their collaboration remained secret. Following the conclusion of the agreement, the editors released the revised text of the announcement.

Struve presumably knew nothing of the quarrels in Geneva of which he was a central object. While Plekhanov, Lenin, and

---

[82] *Lenin,* IV, 37–41. The old and new texts are printed in parallel columns in LS, IV (1925), 62–75.

Potresov argued and shouted at each other, he was preoccupied with philosophical problems. It is at this very time (September–October 1900) that after long soul searching he decided he had no choice but to abandon strict positivism and embrace metaphysics.[83] This philosophical evolution affected deeply his whole political theory, but not his attitude toward alliance with his one-time Social Democratic friends whose immediate goal — political liberty — was the same as his.

In November 1900, Potresov arrived in St. Petersburg with the text of the revised *Iskra* announcement. This version departed so drastically from the one agreed upon at Pskov that its release without Struve's and Tugan-Baranovsky's consent constituted a clear breach of the understanding reached at Pskov. Tugan-Baranovsky interpreted it in this manner. Infuriated at the duplicity of the "Orthodox," he refused to see Potresov and would have no further dealings with *Iskra* and *Zaria* and their editors.[84] Struve, however, although probably no less angry, restrained his feelings, and avoided a break in relations. As soon as he could get away, he hurried with his wife to Munich to find out what had happened and whether anything could be salvaged of the projected partnership. There he was joined by Bogucharsky-Iakovlev.

For two months — from the end of December 1900 to the end of February 1901 — Munich was the scene of intermittent and usually stormy meetings between the enlarged board of *Iskra* and the representatives of the "democratic opposition." Ostensibly, the talks concerned the terms on which the "democratic opposition" would participate in *Iskra* and some other common publishing ventures. In fact, they involved questions far transcending editorial arrangements. At stake was nothing less than leadership of the movement for Russia's political liberation and the relationship between the two leading contenders for that post, the Social Democrats and the liberals.

This was no longer an academic issue. After nearly two decades of political quiescence, resistance to autocracy once again assumed active and sometimes violent forms. The universities were shaken by riots of an intensity unknown since the 1860's. In February

[83] #96. The subject will be discussed in Chapter 12.
[84] *Lenin*, IV, 68.

1899, students at St. Petersburg University booed their rector and fought the police sent to quell them. In the hope of stifling university unrest, the government issued in the summer of 1900 "temporary regulations" providing for the drafting of students engaged in political activity. When the universities reopened in the fall, students at Kiev demonstrated in defiance of these regulations. The public at large expressed its support of student demonstrators by means of mass rallies.

The zemstva, too, were stirring. At this time zemstvo leaders constituted an informal all-Russian caucus, which met informally behind the cover of various scientific and literary conferences. The so-called third element, the hired personnel of the zemstva, made up largely of moderate socialists, was particularly hostile to the government and its functionaries. The government took measures against the challenge from this quarter as well. In June 1900, it issued an ordinance which cut down both the taxing powers and the local authority of the zemstva, reducing considerably their already limited sphere of political activity. Zemstvo leaders known to engage in politics were ordered dismissed from their posts. The Free Economic Society, an important center of liberal opposition, was shut down.

There was trouble elsewhere too. Labor unrest showed no sign of abating after the 1896–97 strikes, and spread from St. Petersburg to other industrial centers of the empire. Among the minorities, the Finns, whose constitution had been suspended in 1899, proved particularly troublesome, protesting their loss of autonomy in a variety of ways, both active and passive.

Suddenly, the imperial government found itself confronted with the simultaneous resistance of diverse social and national groups which until then had acted individually and could be disposed of one by one. The giant wave of unrest which in 1905 was to break against the monarchy and smash its central bastion, absolutism, was visibly swelling.

As Struve's differences with the Social Democrats, both theoretical and personal, multiplied, he steadily drew nearer the constitutional groups in the zemstva. At the Munich talks he still wanted to avoid a breach with the Social Democrats, whom he continued to view as the single most effective antiautocratic force in Russia;

but he did not wish to appear overly dependent on them, either, for fear of losing standing with his new friends in liberal circles. "I saw quite clearly," he wrote afterward, "that my influence among the Liberals and Democrats would dwindle, or even be reduced to nothing and become a negative quantity, should I submit to the 'Orthodoxalists.' This is why I was resolute and firm." [85] When requested by the editors of *Iskra* to renounce his Social Democratic allegiance, he readily consented, despite the fact that he still thought of himself as a socialist. But once he agreed to represent something called the "democratic opposition," he insisted on doing so as a partner, not as a client.

And this insistence clashed head on with the vision the Social Democrats had of the "liberal bourgeoisie" and its role in the movement for political liberation. The idea of hegemony meant to them that they led and the others followed. Lenin in particular had a very narrow notion of hegemony. To him it meant not winning the nonproletarian classes as allies but utilizing them to serve Social Democratic purposes.[86] In a revealing letter to Potresov written in 1899, he assailed Akselrod's notion of "support of and union with" the liberal bourgeoisie: the bourgeois opposition, he wrote, should form the "tail" of the movement, and follow it, sometimes even gritting its teeth.[87] In effect, to him hegemony meant monopoly: the Social Democrats were to be the only organized party of the opposition; there were to be no others.

Disagreements broke out at the first meeting between the *Iskra* board and Struve, held in Munich on December 29, 1900. Struve declared at the outset that the revised announcement of *Iskra* precluded the kind of cooperation agreed upon at Pskov. He saw no point in arranging for the flow of money and literary materials to a publication which abused him as an "opportunist" and "bourgeois apologist." But, he continued, he still saw the possibility of cooperation on a more modest scale in the form of joint publication of a third periodical, issued as a regular supplement to *Zaria*, of which he would be sole editor. This publication he proposed to call *Contemporary Review* (*Sovremennoe obozrenie*). It was to steer clear of disputes in the socialist camp, and make it its job to rally public opinion against the autocratic regime.

[85] "My Contacts and Conflicts with Lenin," 78–79.
[86] F. I. Dan, *Proiskhozhdenie bol'shevizma* (New York, 1946), 329.
[87] *Lenin*, XXVIII, 25.

Lenin immediately interpreted Struve's motive in terms of his own political conduct, that is, as a power ploy. Struve was no longer prepared to play the part he had assigned to him, that of second fiddle in the Social Democratic orchestra — he now aspired to become concertmaster of a more prestigious ensemble, an independent liberal party. Given this situation, Lenin had no interest in further collaboration with him or the liberals. Indeed, such collaboration now struck him as distinctly dangerous. With their vast financial resources, with their numerous adherents in zemstva and municipal governments, the liberals could overwhelm their Social Democratic allies and press them into service for their own interests. The Social Democrats would be reduced to liberal handmaidens. As he watched Struve negotiating with Potresov and Vera Zasulich the details of his proposal, Lenin's feelings toward Struve turned into cold hatred. He suddenly began to see him in an entirely different light: no longer as an errant comrade, but as a renegade, a Judas, who had all the time pretended to be a Social Democrat in order to betray his colleagues and make a career as a liberal politician. By inspiring the amorphous nonsocialist democratic opposition to organize and come forth on their own, he was destroying carefully laid strategic plans on which he, Lenin, had pinned all his hopes since 1895.

At two in the morning of December 30, 1900, Lenin sat down to record his feelings about the first day of these negotiations.

I should like to record my impressions of today's talk with Struve. It was a notable and "historic" meeting of sorts (Potresov, Vera Zasulich, Struve and his wife, and myself) — at any rate, it was historic in my life, a summing-up of a whole epoch, or at any rate, of a way of life; one that will determine for a long time to come my conduct and life path.

From Potresov's initial account I understood that Struve was moving toward us and wanted to make concessions. It turned out to be just the opposite. This strange error probably came about because Potresov was too anxious to have that with which Struve "lured" us, namely political materials, correspondence, etc., and "what you want, you believe." Potresov believed in the possibility of that with which Struve lured, he wanted to believe in his sincerity, and the possibility of a decent *modus vivendi* with him.

And it was precisely this meeting that finally and irreversibly refuted this faith. Struve showed himself from an entirely new side, he showed himself a "politician" of the first water, a politician in the worst sense of the word, a "politico," an artful dodger, a huckster, and an impudent boor. He arrived *completely convinced of our impotence;* this is how Potresov himself formulated the results of the discussions, and his formulation was entirely correct. Struve came convinced of our impotence, he came to offer us terms of our *surrender,* and he did so in an exquisitely artful manner, without uttering a single sharp word, but revealing nonetheless what a coarse, hucksterish, run-of-the-mill liberal nature lies concealed beneath that refined, civilized cover of the most up-to-date "critic."

To my questions (which opened the business part of the meeting) why he does not want to join us simply as a collaborator, Struve replied quite firmly that it was psychologically impossible for him to work for a journal in which he was "torn to shreds" (literally his expression); that we must not think we can abuse him and he will "write political articles" for us (literally!); that collaboration was possible only on terms of full equality (that is, apparently, of the critics and the orthodox); that after the Announcement his comrade and friend [Tugan-Baranovsky] did not even want to come to see Potresov; that he, Struve, proceeded not so much from the [text of the] Announcement, and not even from the Announcement at all, but from the fact that earlier he had wanted to confine himself to "benevolent assistance"; that now he had no intention of confining himself to this but wanted also to be an editor (he virtually said so!!). All this Struve did not blurt out at once. Discussions of his collaboration went on rather long (too long, in the opinion of Potresov and Vera Zasulich), but to me they showed quite clearly that one will get nowhere with this gentleman.

He then began to press his proposition: why not found a third political organ on equal footing? This will be convenient for him as well as for us (he will provide materials for the paper, we shall "earn" something from the resources given to it). He proposed that the cover should carry no mention of the Social Democrats, nothing referring to our firm, and that we must

— morally, not formally — undertake to furnish this organ also with all of our general political material.

The matter became clear, and I said that the founding of a third organ is out of the question, that the issue reduces itself to the following: *whether Social Democracy should conduct the political struggle, or whether the liberals should do so independently* and *self-sufficiently*. (I expressed myself more clearly and concretely, more precisely.) Struve understood, became angry, and declared that after I had expressed my views with "anerkennentwerter Klarheit" [commendable clarity] (literal words!), this subject was finished, and one ought to talk only about commissions: commissions of symposia. This is the same kind of a third journal (I began to say). All right, then a commission for only one pamphlet which *is at hand*, declared Struve. Which one? I asked. Why must you know? Nina Struve impudently replied. If you approve in principle, then we shall decide; if not, then there is no need for you to know. I asked about the conditions of printing: such and such a publisher, and nothing else, nothing need be said about your firm; except for the publisher, there must be no connection with your firm, Struve declared. I began to argue against this as well, demanding that our firm be indicated. But Potresov began to contradict me and the conversation stopped.

Finally, having agreed to defer a decision, Potresov and Zasulich continued to press Struve, demanded from him explanations, argued. I remained silent, laughed (so that Struve could clearly see), and the discussion promptly drew to a close.[88]

For Lenin this particular evening indeed marked a milestone, the end of an "epoch." It was then that he decided further collaboration with the "bourgeoisie" was futile, because the "bourgeoisie" was about to "conduct the political struggle . . . independently and self-sufficiently." Henceforth he would go his own way.[89]

---

[88] *Lenin*, IV (1925), 67–68. The translation above reproduces the complete text of the document, with the code names deciphered. The italics on the page above from the words "whether Social Democracy" to "self-sufficiently" are mine. During the Munich negotiations, formal minutes were kept (LS, III, 129), but these have not been published so far.

[89] More information on Lenin's break with the "liberal bourgeoisie" at this time

As soon as he had reached this conclusion, Lenin wanted to break off all further negotiations with Struve. But now Plekhanov restrained him. Having compelled Struve to withdraw from Social Democracy, he saw no reason to deprive *Iskra* and *Zaria* of the help he and his liberal friends had to offer the Orthodox in combatting the Economists. The others agreed, and Lenin, a minority of one, had to acquiesce.

A formal agreement was finally reached on January 30, 1901. (On the insistence of Plekhanov, who had briefly come to Munich to participate in the negotiations, it was put in writing.)[90] Its text has not been made public to this day,[91] but the main clauses can be reconstructed from a draft prepared by Lenin (first published in 1959) and from partial summaries found elswhere.[92]

The contracting parties were identified as the "Social Democratic Group *Zaria* and *Iskra*" and the "Group of Democratic Opposition Svoboda [Freedom]." The latter, a fictitious firm, was to stand for those groups in Russia which undertook by all *legal* means to resist the autocratic regime. The agreement stipulated that Struve and other designated members of his party would collaborate in the two Social Democratic publications in the name of this opposition, but that they were not to interfere in any discussions involving questions of Social Democratic theory or practice. The two groups agreed to bring out jointly a periodical supplement to *Zaria* called *Contemporary Review,* under Struve's editorship. The Social Democratic Group apparently retained some kind of veto over its contents, but this is not certain. The *Survey* was to devote most of its space to materials incriminating the imperial government. These were to be supplied by both groups, and the Social Democrats reserved to themselves the right to print them also in *Iskra* and *Zaria.* The Social Democratic Group assumed responsibility for the printing, transport, and dis-

---

can be found in my "The Origins of Bolshevism: The Intellectual Evolution of Young Lenin," in Richard Pipes, ed., *Revolutionary Russia* (Cambridge, Mass., 1968), 63–66.

[90] *Perepiska G. V. Plekhanova i P. B. Aksel'roda,* II (Moscow, 1925), 139.

[91] The text of the agreement (unavailable to me) is preserved at the Dom Plekhanova in Leningrad, Arkhivnyi Fond 1, Edinitsa khraneniia 29, List 2.

[92] "K proektu soglasheniia so Struve," *Lenin PSS,* IV, 389–390. That this draft is not identical with the final version is evident from a reference to an Article 7 in Lenin's letter to Plekhanov of January 30, 1901 (LS, III, 1924, 128). Lenin's draft has only six articles.

tribution of the *Review*. In return, the Group of Democratic Opposition undertook to cover the expenses connected with the publication and distribution of *Iskra* and *Zaria*.

The agreement of January 30, 1900, represented something much more significant than a mere publishing contract. It was an act of political coalition between Social Democracy and the as yet unformed liberal-democratic movement, entailing a division of spheres of activity, the one to pursue revolutionary methods, the other legal ones.[93] In return for services rendered, the liberals were to finance the Social Democratic organization centered on *Iskra* and *Zaria*. The delicate nature of this arrangement, so embarrassing to both parties subsequently, after their paths had diverged, explains why it has been so assiduously concealed or obfuscated in the historical literature.

Lenin was dismayed by the terms of the accord and appealed to Plekhanov (who had returned to Geneva before the agreement was concluded) to "raise the banner of rebellion." If this agreement went through, he wrote, Struve "would be boss, because he has the money and 99 percent of the materials." Social Democratic "hegemony" would turn into "cant." Struve would make a great liberal career, destroying, in the process, *Iskra* and *Zaria*.[94] But Plekhanov disagreed: "The circumstances are such that a break *now* would destroy us; and *later on* we shall see." [95] In the end, Lenin seems to have signed the agreement.[96]

For the public at large, the two groups prepared separate declarations announcing their agreement to cooperate. The declarations never actually came out, and they are known only in fragmentary versions.[97] The Social Democratic declaration, written by Plekhanov, stated that the overthrow of the autocracy required all

[93] In a letter to Akselrod dated March 20, 1901, Lenin demanded that the announcement of the "coalition" with Struve not be released, which indicates that the January agreement was just that: *Lenin PSS*, XLVI, 90.

[94] *Lenin*, XXVIII, 213.

[95] LS, III (1924), 133.

[96] The editors of *Perepiska Plekhanova i Akselroda* (II, 143) say that Lenin refused to sign the agreement with Struve. This is highly doubtful, for if it had been the case Lenin would not have been so anxious to nullify the agreement afterward (see note 93 above); nor would Lenin's refusal to sign have gone unrecorded by the author of a recent Soviet article, L. V. Shirikov, who makes a desperate effort to justify the Munich agreement by the most questionable interpretation of the evidence: VIKPSS, No. 4 (1961), 139–144.

[97] A. N. Potresov in OD, I, 615–616; reprinted in LS, III (1924), 130–132.

progressive elements to join forces. While for various reasons it was undesirable for these elements to merge into a single party, it was advantageous for them to coordinate efforts against a common enemy. The legal oppositional activity envisaged by the Group of Democratic Opposition Freedom would supplement and bolster the revolutionary activity of the Social Democrats. The *Contemporary Review,* which the two groups were to bring out jointly, would welcome all strains of opinion except those inimical to the cause of political liberty.[98]

The other declaration was written by Struve. Its known portion reads as follows (all the ellipsis dots are in the original):

> In our desire to diffuse among broad public circles the idea of freedom, we are not concerned with elaborating any kind of a party program that would predetermine in detail some particular constitutional arrangement for our multinational and multilingual country. . . . We shall give equal attention to the "illegal," or so-called revolutionary, struggle and to all efforts actually made and possible to fight the existing political system on its own ground. We declare beforehand that one of the main tasks of our literary undertaking will be to deliberate politically the legal struggle against the . . . superbly organized absolutism of the bureaucracy . . . In our opinion one of the most important achievements of political awereness of recent times is the conviction that there exists an indissoluble historical link between so-called legal and cultural activity and that which aims directly and openly to change the existing political order — a conviction which becomes ever more rooted among both the Russian opposition . . . and . . . the government. . . . We do not reject the necessity of certain compromises in legal public activity, but we shall recognize only those compromises that are dictated by the steadfast striving to win for Russians more quickly and more securely the conditions of respectable political life. Beyond these limits, political realism transforms itself into lack of principle, as contemptible morally as it is dangerous politically . . . Finally, we believe it necessary to stress that — like the Social Democratic group that joins us in the common task — we assign a prime political importance and mission to

[98] OD, I, 615–616; LS, III (1924), 131–132.

the Russian labor movement. In this movement, the political thought of the Russian intelligentsia has found a powerful ally, with whose growth henceforth the fate of political liberty in Russia will be indissolubly linked. We count on the *Contemporary Review*'s meeting with sympathy and support from all the oppositional elements. Its task is to unite all those elements in a single literary undertaking, in the closest union with Social Democracy, the only organized force among the Russian opposition.[99]

Struve's editorial policy statement contained in embryo the principles which he later enunciated in the program of *Osvobozhdenie* (Liberation), the émigré journal which he launched in June 1902. Its essential feature was the idea of a broad antiautocratic front (rather than that of the hegemony of any one group), alliance with the revolutionary movement, and, coupled with it, willingness to refrain for the time being from formulating any detailed program that would alienate potential supporters.

The two statements were to have been issued in February by Dietz, the publisher of the German Social Democrats. But Dietz decided against publishing them because the references to "revolutionary activity" could get him into trouble with the German police.

After the agreement had been signed, Struve produced the pamphlet which had so intrigued Lenin. It was the manuscript of a secret memorandum, prepared by Witte, to which Struve gave the title "Autocracy and Zemstvo," and which he had probably received from some high government official sympathetic to the liberal cause. During the protracted Munich negotiations, he had written for it a long and important introduction. It was agreed that the *Iskra-Zaria* group would publish as a book Witte's memorandum with this introduction. One can form an idea of how advantageous financially the arrangements with Struve were for the Social Democrats from the fact that for the publication of the Witte book Struve paid them 6,000 rubles. Of this, 1,800 was to cover printing costs, and the remaining 4,200 — a sum almost

[99] OD, I, 616. The full text, with Plekhanov's marginalia, is at the Dom Plekhanova in Leningrad, Arkh. Fond 1, Ed. khr. R. 29, 1g. The unpublished portions apparently contained the important political passages defining the coalition of Social Democrats and the "democratic opposition": VIKPSS, No. 1 (1963), 143.

equal to their entire initial capital — was to subsidize *Iskra* and *Zaria*.[100]

At the beginning of March 1901, Struve left Munich for St. Petersburg to make financial and editorial arrangements for the *Contemporary Review* and close down his household. He expected to be back in Germany shortly.

[100] *Obzor*, XXV (1901), 121. The police learned the amount of money given for the publication of Witte's memorandum but not its source; they never discovered how *Iskra* got hold of the manuscript.

11.   THE SOCIAL DEMOCRATS BREAK
WITH THE LIBERALS

When Struve returned to St. Petersburg, a fresh wave of antigovernmental disturbances had just broken out. On January 11/24, 1901, the 183 students previously arrested for demonstrating at the University of Kiev were ordered inducted into the army. Three days later, in retaliation against this ruling, a terrorist attacked and fatally wounded the Minister of Education, N. P. Bogolepov. Protest meetings and demonstrations demanding the immediate revocation of the "temporary regulations" and amnesty for the Kievan students occurred throughout the country. The grandest of these demonstrations was scheduled by the student organizations of St. Petersburg for March 4/17 in front of the Kazan Cathedral. The prestigious Union of Writers of St. Petersburg voted to join the students on this occasion.[1]

March 4/17 fell on a Sunday. Life in the center of the capital city came to a standstill as groups of students and intellectuals converged on the cathedral. By noon the crowd had grown to an estimated three thousand people, standing shoulder to shoulder in the square fronting the cathedral. At half past twelve someone in the crowd read aloud a proclamation, copies of which were distributed. A red flag was unfurled; there were shouts of "hurrah." At this point, a detachment of Cossacks trotted out from a side street. The Kazan Cathedral is a miniature replica of St. Peter's and has a similar colonnade. The Cossacks formed a line between the wings of that colonnade, pinning the demonstrators against the façade of the church and cutting them off from sympathizers and onlookers gathered opposite, on Nevsky Boulevard. Caught in the trap, some of the demonstrators threw snowballs

[1] Struve attended the dramatic meeting of the Union on the evening of March 3/16, at which it was decided to take part in the demonstration: *Osv*, No. 14 (January 2/15, 1903), 218.

and rubber boots at the Cossacks. One of these flying objects (according to official accounts, a rock or an iron mallet) struck an officer in the face, drawing blood. The Cossacks were given the command to charge. Drawing their vicious leather *nagaiki*, they rode straight into the massed crowd, indiscriminately meting out blows left and right. The crowd pressed against the walls of the church and spilled inside, where services were in progress. The violence lasted ten minutes, during which some demonstrators, including several women, had their heads bloodied.[2]

Struve was in this crowd, and he was among those struck. Ariadna Tyrkova, a school friend of Nina who had come to the square accompanied by Tugan-Baranovsky, spotted him after the Cossacks had retreated:

> He was in an utter frenzy. Having noticed Tugan-Baranovsky, he lunged forward and, waving his arms, in a choking voice shouted: "What the devil is this? How dare they! How dare they strike me on the legs with a nagaika! You understand? — me! — " He pounded his hands on the overcoat, on which the nagaika had left its dirty marks. We were all excited and indignant at what was taking place around us. But life likes to mix the tragic with the comic. Looking at the ruffled red hair and red beard of Struve, at his face distorted with indignation, hearing his senseless, incoherent shout, repeated several times — "me! me!" — I nearly burst into laughter.[3]

By one o'clock the action was over. After the Cossacks had withdrawn and reformed their lines, the police moved in to arrest the demonstrators. These proceedings occupied the entire afternoon. By five o'clock nearly one thousand people, among them Struve, were taken to jail. Some were promptly released, but many remained in prison for several days, after which they were ordered to leave St. Petersburg and take up residence in a provincial town of their choice for periods ranging up to three years. During this time, they were to be subject to police surveillance.

[2] Documents on the student disturbances of this period are printed in KA, No. 2/75 (1936), 83–112, and No. 4–5/89–90 (1938), 258–308.

[3] A. Tyrkova-Villiams, *Na putiakh k svobode* (New York, 1952), 70–71. The official police report is in KA, No. 2/75 (1936), 103–105; a newspaper account, hostile to the demonstrators, is in StPV, March 7/20, 1901.

Struve drew a one-year sentence. He chose to settle in Tver, a leading center of the zemstvo constitutionalist movement. Kalmykova, who had helped organize the Kazan square demonstration and had also taken part in it, drew a three-year term. She shut down her business and left for Germany.

Judging by the letters which they exchanged in the spring of 1901, the editors of *Iskra* and *Zaria* were anything but crushed by reports of Struve's arrest. Except for Potresov and Vera Zasulich, who still sympathized with him and were nicknamed "die Struvefreundliche Partei," the Social Democratic leaders so mistrusted Struve that they were almost relieved not to have to live up to the terms of their agreement. To Plekhanov, the "very existence of [Struve] in this world was an injustice." [4]

Behind this unconcern, however, lay not so much personal feelings, which would have been held under control had the interests of the cause demanded it, as the fact that the need for an alliance with Struve and his supporters rapidly diminished. *Iskra* fared far better than had been anticipated. It was well received by socialist intellectuals tired of the moderation of the Revisionists and Economists, and it obtained so much literary material that after a few issues it changed from a monthly to a biweekly. Finances also improved. In March 1901 the situation had still been so desperate that the editors of *Iskra* demanded from Struve as a condition of further collaboration on the *Contemporary Review* a firm pledge of sufficient money to cover all their current expenses. [5] But shortly afterward money seems to have become available from other sources, and *Iskra* acquired a greater degree of independence than its founders had had reason to hope.

Thus, partly because of Struve's inability to return to Germany, and partly because of *Iskra's* lessened dependence on him and his friends, the agreement of January 30, 1901, was stillborn. The *Contemporary Review* failed to materialize; and so, with a couple of minor exceptions, did the other projected joint ventures. The only concrete results of the agreement were the appearance of a

[4] LS, III (1924), 205.
[5] The draft of a letter to this effect, undated and unsigned, is in the Potresov Archive, International Institute of Social History, Amsterdam. Cf. Lenin's letter to Akselrod, March 20, 1901, in *Lenin PSS*, XLVI, 90, which refers to this document.

two-part article by Struve in *Iskra*, called "Autocracy and Zemstvo";[6] the publication, in book form, of Witte's memorandum under the same name, with Struve's lengthy introduction;[7] and the appearance of an article by Iakovlev-Bogucharsky in *Zaria*.[8]

In the *Iskra* article Struve called attention to the contribution made by the zemstva in the struggle against the autocratic regime, and pleaded with labor and Social Democracy to come to their assistance. The implication of his argument was that labor and zemstva acting in concert would bring autocracy down.

Witte wrote his memorandum to discredit his adversary, the Minister of the Interior, I. L. Goremykin. In it, he argued against Goremykin's proposal that zemstva be introduced into the western provinces of the empire (where there were none), on the grounds that zemstva were in the long run a deadly danger to absolutism. No new ones should be created, and those in existence should be abolished.

In the Introduction to this work, Struve agreed with Witte's premise but not with his conclusion. In some ways, zemstva indeed endangered the monarchy, he wrote, but they also protected it from a greater danger, namely, revolution; it was in the government's long-term interest to preserve them and expand their sphere of activity. The autocratic principle was beyond salvation: it had simply become impossible to rule a country of Russia's complexity and dynamism by bureaucratic means. The country had to have political freedom; the only realistic question was whether such freedom would be gained by legal or by violent means.

> If the government takes the road indicated by Witte and abolishes zemstva, it will — without being compelled to do so by any immediate necessity — deprive society of the main forum for the gradual and legal improvement of the social and constitutional order in Russia, and force the center of gravity of public initiative [*obshchestvennaia samodeiatel'nost'*] to shift

[6] #99.

[7] S. Iu. Vitte, *Samoderzhavie i zemstvo* (Stuttgart, 1901). There was a second edition, brought out by Struve in Stuttgart in 1903 (#190). Witte also published it in 1914 under the title *Po povodu neprelozhnosti zakonov gosudarstvennoi zhizni*. Petrunkevich says that Witte was not the document's true author: ARR, XXI (1934), 328.

[8] "Byvalyi," "O starom i novom," *Zaria*, No. 1 (April 1901), 137–142. Bogucharsky-Iakovlev is identified as author in I. F. Masanov, *Slovar' psevdonimov*, I (Moscow, 1956), 175.

toward the realm of the illegal . . . The abolition of zemstva will hand revolutionary propaganda a superb trump card. We say this quite objectively, being neither in any way repelled by what is usually called revolutionary activity, nor enthusiastic or carried away by this particular form of struggle for political and social progress.[9]

Such a shift was bound to occur, Struve continued, because the moderate elements of Russian society, hitherto content with non-political forms of expression, would if deprived of zemstva have no choice but to turn to politics. This spelled revolution, insofar as in autocratic Russia all politics was by definition revolutionary. A development in this direction would imperil the monarchy much more than did peaceful zemstvo activity:

Of itself, an illegal liberal party, as an organization composed of the most moderate and least volatile oppositional elements, can develop neither a particularly broad nor a particularly intense activity. But, given the presence of such broad and intense activity on the part of other parties, notably the Social Democratic or Labor party, the Liberal party — even without entering with the Social Democrats into a direct accord — could become a very serious factor.[10]

Once the monarchy found itself challenged by a revolutionary minority, it would sorely miss the moderating influence of the zemstva.

In short, to prevent a disastrous revolution, the monarchy should do the opposite of what Witte recommended and strengthen the moderate elements and their organizations. These elements were less dangerous to it acting legally in the zemstva than illegally in a liberal party. The Introduction ended with an appeal for "rights and a sovereign [vlastnoe] all-Russian zemstvo" — Aesopian language for constitution.[11]

Struve's Introduction to Witte contained some remarkable prophesies, but as a political program it was singularly inept. The

[9] S. Iu. Vitte, Samoderzhavie i zemstvo, 2nd ed. (Stuttgart, 1903), xxxiv.

[10] Ibid., xli–xlii.

[11] Ibid., xlvii. See Struve's note in the second edition of the Witte memorandum (Ibid., xiin) in which he charges Lenin with deliberately misinterpreting this appeal and pretending not to understand that it was a veiled appeal for constitution.

probability of its persuading Nicholas II to curry favor with the
liberals was low, whereas the likelihood of its offending the Social
Democrats was great and real. It is difficult to understand how
Struve expected the Social Democrats to acquiesce in a policy
statement in which they — formal allies of his group — were
treated as an expendable item, used as a threat to secure from
the government a constitution. It was *Realpolitik* at its worst.

For Lenin, this was the last straw. His strong suspicion, first
aroused by Struve's insistence on editorial independence in running the *Contemporary Review*, that the liberals had entered into
an alliance with the Social Democrats in order to subvert and
destroy them, now turned into certainty. He replied to Struve
with an essay called "Oppressors of Zemstva and Hannibals of
Liberalism." [12] Zemstva, he wrote, were not at all centers of
political opposition; they were mere tools of autocracy, institutions by means of which it solidified its hold on the country. The
liberals would become useful allies of the Social Democrats only
if they were prepared to form an underground party. If they persisted in waging the struggle legally, through the zemstva, they
would become, in fact, agents of the counterrevolution. Lenin's
essay was the most outspoken attack on Russian liberals to come
from the pen of an authoritative Social Democratic spokesman.

Plekhanov and Akselrod had grave misgivings about Lenin's
tactic. "Soften it, my friend," Plekhanov urged after reading
Lenin's essay, *"Liberalism must not be rubbed against the grain
right now. This is a great mistake!"* [13] And Akselrod wondered
whether it was not too early to inform the liberals by such a frank
statement how the Social Democrats intended to use them.[14]

Lenin agreed to Plekhanov's and Akselrod's editorial suggestions, but he was adamant on matters of policy:

> In general, I am not all that stubborn about softening individual
> passages, but in principle I cannot renounce the idea that we
> have the right (and the duty) to tear [Struve] to bits for his
> political juggling. He is precisely a political juggler — of this

---

[12] *Lenin*, IV, 119–157. "Hannibals of Liberalism" refers to a passage in Struve's
Introduction to Witte (2nd ed., p. ix) calling on the nation to swear a "Hannibal's
oath" to win freedom for Russia similar to the one it had sworn fifty years earlier
to give freedom to the serfs.
[13] Plekhanov to Lenin, July 14, 1901, in LS, III (1924), 204.
[14] *Lenin*, IV, 576.

I have become finally convinced while reading and rereading the Introduction. And into my criticism I poured everything brought about by the past few months (that is, negotiations with the "calf" [Struve], the attempt at an agreement, and so forth.) Squaring my accounts with this fellow, I unburdened my heart, so to say. To me, the center of gravity of the whole article lay in settling the question of the constitutionality of the zemstvo. "Zemstvo" liberalism represents in terms of its effect on society an equivalent of what "Economism" represents in terms of its effect on labor. We must persecute both of these minimizations.[15]

Struve's long association with Social Democracy now drew to an end; and so did his personal relationship with its leaders. Once the ideological bonds had snapped, there was no opportunity for friendship among people who recognized no line separating personal relations from service to the cause.

For Lenin, Struve developed a hatred that was unique in that it showed no effort at objectivity, so pronounced in his treatment of everyone and everything else that came under his scrutiny.

Lenin reciprocated with a vengeance. Once Struve had ceased to be useful, he became fair game for him to hunt with any weapon, including character assassination. In this hunt Martov joyfully seconded him, lending the enterprise both his superior imagination and greater journalistic skill. The two missed no opportunity to "expose" Struve as an enemy of Russia's working class, as a Judas who pretended to fight autocracy while in fact working on its behalf.[16] In these polemics, Lenin sometimes did not hesitate to hint that Revisionism was a product of police sponsorship.[17]

---

[15] LS, III (1924), 219–220.

[16] Among Lenin's attacks on Struve are a reference to him as one who had torn off his mask and revealed himself for what he really was — a leader or lackey [both!] of the liberal landlords — and a statement that the liberal camp harbored traitors who should be exposed: Lenin, V, 145, 198. The following is a fair sample of Martov's polemical style: "The constitutionalists seek to organize the liberal bourgeoisie not so much in order to struggle for the overthrow of the autocracy as *to prepare it for the struggle aimed at winning the exclusive right to lord it in Russia after the victory of the people over the autocracy:* [Iu. O. Martov], "Programma russkikh liberalov," Iskra, No. 23 (August 1, 1902). See also his "Vsegda v men'shinstve," Zaria, No. 2/3 (1901), 191–193, 201. Such abusive language in political controversies shocks today much less than it did before World War I when different manners were observed.

[17] E.g., Lenin, IV, 375.

The viciousness with which Lenin hounded Struve after 1900 was motivated not only by fear of the liberal movement as a potent rival in the struggle for political power, but also by the need to obliterate the man who was the living reminder of his own past mistakes.

The methods which Lenin and Martov employed to destroy Struve's reputation had a significance transcending that which it held for the relationship of the three men: it was symptomatic of a definitive breach between Russian Social Democracy and liberalism. The emergence of a liberal movement with its own identity nullified the idea of hegemony, and with it the whole strategy which had hitherto guided the Russian Social Democratic movement. No longer able to count on leading the national movement for political liberation, the Social Democrats had to reexamine fundamentally their policies.[18] Some among them — the future Mensheviks — decided henceforth to concentrate on organizing labor, others — led by Lenin — to form a tight clandestine party of professionals capable at a suitable moment of seizing power. The roots of the historic Menshevik-Bolshevik split which occurred at the 1903 London Congress thus lay in the collapse two years earlier of the idea of hegemony, of which the rift with Struve was the outstanding manifestation. But the rift between the Social Democrats and the liberals had even more momentous historic consequences. Having given up hope of leading the "bourgeoisie," the Social Democrats now veered to the left and most of them became antiliberal, anticonstitutional, and antiparliamentarian. Henceforth, liberalism and socialism in Russia would fight not only the government but each other, with results that in 1917 were to prove calamitous to nearly all concerned.

The personal campaign against Struve waged by Lenin and Martov with Plekhanov's acquiescence shocked many readers of Iskra, even though they were accustomed to the polemical device of translating every intellectual disagreement into personal abuse. Its tone was indeed sharper than anything hitherto known. Among those who objected to it was N. K. Takhtarev, one of the proponents of Economism. On one occasion he told Lenin in his face that he thought it wrong to call Struve "a traitor, a renegade, and a new Tikhomirov." Such accusations needlessly inflamed Iskra's readers, and could have unforeseen consequences. For ex-

[18] F. I. Dan, *Proiskhozhdenie bol'shevizma* (New York, 1946), 320–321.

ample, what would happen, he asked, "if a worker really dedicated to the cause, under the influence of the badgering of Struve
on the pages of *Iskra,* were suddenly to get the idea he should
take care of Struve, and perhaps even kill him?" To which Lenin
replied, unperturbed: "Ego i nado ubit'" — "He ought to be
killed." [19]

Fanaticism, in the words of Santayana, consists in redoubling
one's efforts after one has forgotten one's aims.

[19] N. K. Takhtarev, "V. I. Lenin i sotsial-demokraticheskoe dvizhenie," *Byloe,* No. 24 (1924), 22.

PART THREE

LIBERATION

The idea of freedom is the only secular idea able to set hearts on fire.

*— Struve in Paris,
January 22, 1932*

12. THE PHILOSOPHY AND POLITICS OF LIBERALISM

Struve once asked himself why it was that Pushkin, whom the Russians revered as their greatest writer, received relatively little recognition abroad. He answered the question by saying that Westerners were attracted to Russian culture by its exotic quality, and that for them Pushkin was too "Western," too much like their own writers. *Mutatis mutandis,* the same explanation can be given for Western indifference to Russian liberalism. During the fifty years preceding the downfall of the old regime, liberalism was the dominant political philosophy of Russia's educated classes; and from the Great Reforms of the 1860's to the constitutional charter of 1906, it was the force behind all the major constructive changes carried out by the imperial government. And yet, how few are concerned with the history of Russian liberalism, and how little is known about it! [1] But then, there was nothing exotic about Russian liberals, as there was about the anarchists or the Slavophiles: the liberals had in their ranks no Bakunins, Nechaevs, or Dostoevskys, who intrigue the Westerner and enable him to regard Russia as a country so strange and foreign that its fate can be of no immediate concern to him.

In fact, Russia's tradition of liberalism — defined as a theory holding that political authority must be restrained by law and representative institutions — is as ancient as the autocratic tradition. From the moment the Russian monarchy staked its claim to absolute and undivided authority, it had to contend with individuals and social groups who insisted that it had a right to neither. Beginning with the early sixteenth century, every major political crisis in Russia involved a conflict between the forces and ideolo-

---

[1] The best history of the Russian liberal movement until the founding of the Constitutional Democratic party is George Fischer's *Russian Liberalism: From Gentry to Intelligentsia* (Cambridge, Mass., 1958). The basic work on the Union of Liberation is *Shakhovskoi.*

gies of absolutism and those of liberalism. This was true of the
dispute over monastic landholdings in the sixteenth century, of
the wars in the "Time of Troubles" in the seventeenth, and of the
succession crises in the eighteenth. From the reign of Catherine
II onward, the desire for some formal limitation on the monarchy
became so much a part of Russian political life that the monarchy
had no choice but to pay obeisance to it and acknowledge the
principle of legality and occasionally even that of constitutionalism.[2]

It is true, of course, that liberalism in Russia did not attain its
ultimate aim. The constitutional experiment inaugurated in
1905–1906 lasted too short a time to accomplish what the liberals
wanted, and except for one decade — 1906–1917 — Russians
never really enjoyed much semblance of civil liberty or representative government. In that sense, Russian liberalism may indeed be
said to have "failed." But the question of the ultimate efficacy of
an idea or movement must be kept distinct from that of its actual
historical significance. We can determine with some degree of
precision and objectivity what influence a historic force exerts on
its own time because the study of contemporary documents enables us to relate intention to accomplishment. But on what criteria
are we to judge whether or not any historic phenomenon has
"succeeded"? Obviously such judgment depends entirely on one's
vantage point. If one waits long enough, in the end everything
turns to dust, everything "fails." Napoleon "failed," and so did the
conservative monarchies that defeated him, so did the liberals
who dislodged the conservatives, and so, finally, did the socialists
who replaced the liberals. On closer investigation, all claims to
historic "success" appear to rest on the judge's arbitrarily choos-
ing a position in time most favorable to his argument, and all
judgments of "failure" turn out to be veiled acknowledgments
of the mortality of man and his works.

But the historian's job is not to give awards: it is not to sum up
but to count.

In tracing the story of Russian liberalism during the second
half of the nineteenth century, it is difficult to identify behind
it motives of social or economic self-interest. Its proponents were

[2] The subject is traced in B. B. Glinsky, *Bor'ba za konstitutsiiu, 1612–1861 gg.*
(St. Petersburg, 1908).

not industrialists and merchants eager to lift restraints on their business, such as those who had provided the backbone of English liberalism. Quite the contrary: operating in an underdeveloped and precarious economic environment, Russian businessmen looked to the government to protect them from the demands of the working class and the competition of foreign countries. Politically, they inclined toward conservatism, whose ideal, modeled on the German *Rechtsstaat*, was legality rather than freedom. As Max Weber pointed out in 1905–1906, Russian liberalism was a movement not of socioeconomic interest but of ideas.[3] Its principal social support came from the educated gentry, a class which stood nothing to gain and much to lose from the principles of political democracy and social (especially agrarian) reform which the liberal party espoused.

The inspiration of post-Reform Russian liberalism was not economic interest but thwarted individualism and frustrated patriotism. The spread of liberal sentiments among the educated class was an understandable reaction to the government's persistent refusal to accompany its programs of enlightenment and nationalism with suitable means of expression and action for the educated, patriotic citizenry. First by compelling the gentry to learn and then by encouraging them to do so, the monarchy inculcated in them a sense of judgment and of taste, which entailed an awareness of alternatives, of choices, of identity as individuals. As the history of the West indicates, this awareness can be a source of immense creativity and therefore of national power, but only if given scope; thwarted, it turns into a source of destructiveness. This scope the imperial government was unwilling to concede. It granted its subjects almost undisturbed access to knowledge, it promoted learning and the arts, it permitted travel abroad, it fostered a sense of national pride, but it would not allow the Russian who learned, traveled, and developed feelings of patriotism those personal safeguards and those outlets for political self-expression which he had come to consider indispensable. Even the most loyal and respectable Russian citizen was subject to indignities at the hands of the police. He had no say in how the country was to be governed, how its money was to be spent,

[3] Max Weber, "Zur Lage der bürgerlichen Demokratie in Russland," ASS, XXII (1906), 243–244, 247. Weber's views are discussed in my article "Max Weber and Russia," *World Politics*, VII, No. 3 (April 1955), 371–401. This point was sometimes made also in Russian literature: see, e.g., RR, No. 9 (July 1902), 4.

how its resources were to be used, how and where its armed forces were to be employed. One often speaks of Russians of the old regime as being "oppressed," but this word does not accurately convey their predicament. Russians, as individuals, were not really oppressed because as long as they steered clear of political action no one bothered them. They were, rather, humiliated and frustrated by being treated like a nation of mischievous children long after they had proven they were a great and creative people. This is what educated Russians found so intolerable and why so many of them lived in a state of permanent inner opposition to the imperial government.

By and large, however, this sense of personal and national frustration did not lead to political activism, and this for two reasons. First, because of the code of gentlemanly behavior inculcated in them, the educated elite found it distasteful to engage in illegal activity. Second, many among them feared the peasant masses, whom they suspected of harboring deep destructive passions; this fear inhibited them from doing anything the peasants could construe as a weakening of authority. Most post-1861 Russian liberals were therefore liberal conservatives rather than liberal democrats. Instead of engaging in politics, they concentrated on practical cultural and social work, hoping by such activity gradually to lift the country's intellectual and material standards to the point where in the remote future it could support a free society. They joined zemstvo boards, participated in municipal self-government, served as justices of the peace, and helped found rural cooperatives. This program of "small deeds" deliberately avoided ideology and politics.

Until the turn of the century, Russian liberals only twice ventured outside these confines into the forbidden territory of politics, and on both occasions without much success.

The first outburst of constitutional activity occurred immediately after the Emancipation, in 1862, when several Assemblies of the Nobility put forth demands that exceeded considerably the moderate program of reforms contemplated by the government. Some adopted the proposal made in January 1862 by Ivan Aksakov for the abolition of gentry privileges and the introduction of legal equality. The nobility of Tver went further yet and by a nearly unanimous vote urged the tsar to convoke a representative and democratically elected assembly of the entire nation. The authorities made short shrift of these challenges by arresting and exiling the leading figures of the liberal party. Unable to elicit support from the country at large, the movement faltered. It collapsed completely in 1863, when Polish rebellion enabled the government to rally nationalist sentiment to its side and turn it against the internal opposition.[4]

Constitutionalism remained dormant during the fifteen years that followed. Its second chance came toward the end of the reign of Alexander II. Confronted for the first time with a determined revolutionary movement, the government ventured in 1878 to solicit support from society. It now appealed to the citizenry for help in the fight against sedition, hinting that in return it would initiate political reform. The bureaucratic apparatus interpreted the new course as a command to show forbearance toward the political self-expression of "respectable" social circles. It did not, therefore, interfere, when in 1878 several zemstva revived demands for political liberalization. In March 1879, the chairmen of four provincial zemstva (Poltava, Tver, Chernigov, and Samara) were permitted to meet in Moscow, and there to form a Zemstvo Union (Zemskii Soiuz), pronouncedly constitutionalist in its orientation. The leading figures in this organization were F. I. Rodichev of Tver and I. I. Petrunkevich of Chernigov. With the financial backing of the Union, the Ukrainian publicist Michael Dragomanov founded in Geneva a liberal-constitutionalist organ, the journal *Free Word* (Vol'noe slovo), which advocated political decentralization with broad autonomy for the national minorities, a constitution, a two-chamber parliament, and civil liberties. In the same year, Petrunkevich initiated negotiations with the People's Will, hoping to persuade its leaders to suspend the terror and join the zemstva in the struggle for political liberty. The liberal-radical coalition was well under way when, on March 1, 1881, an assassin's bomb killed the tsar and thereby cut the ground from under the forces in the administration which, with his support, had worked for conciliation with society.[5]

[4] On the constitutional movement of 1862, see D. I. Shakhovskoi, "Politicheskie techeniia v russkom zemstve," *Iubileinyi zemskii sbornik, 1864–1914* (St. Petersburg, 1914), 441–447; and N. I. Iordansky, *Konstitutsionnoe dvizhenie 60-kh godov* (St. Petersburg, 1906).

[5] The constitutional movement of 1878–1881 is treated in Shakhovskoi, "Politicheskie techeniia," 453–462; *Belokonsky*, 17–34; V. Ia. Bogucharsky [Iakovlev],

Later that year, after momentary hesitation, the government decided to deal with further challenges to its authority not by concessions but by repression. The Ministry of the Interior was now placed in charge of an expanded and centralized police force, and transformed into a powerful agency of political control. The era of "counterreform" began. The promises made in 1879–1881 were forgotten.

In the face of this reaction, the constitutional movement speedily collapsed. Appalled by the murder of the tsar, the bolder *zemtsy* lost the appetite for political involvement which they had barely managed to acquire; others had never been prepared to engage in politics unless formally invited to do so by the monarchy. After 1881, Russian liberals once again ceased to call for a constitution and reverted to the practice of "small deeds." Their appeals now were for legality rather than for freedom, by which they meant scrupulous observance on the part of the bureaucracy of the law of the land given by the autocrat. The daily *Russian News* (*Russkie vedomosti*) and the monthly *Messenger of Europe* were the leading publications advocating this kind of pragmatic, legalistic, apolitical liberalism. Such was the climate of opinion in 1885 when Struve became a liberal, and it accounted for his decision to join Social Democracy. It was the pronounced apoliticism of the Russian liberals in the 1880's and early 1890's that allowed the Social Democrats to claim leadership in the political struggle against the autocracy and to aspire seriously to hegemony over the national movement for political liberation.

The majority of the zemtsy might have been perfectly content to practice "small deeds" for the rest of their lives had the monarchy allowed them to do so. But the government of the last two tsars, not content to deny society political self-expression, was determined to deprive it even of that modest sphere of nonpolitical public activity which it had been allotted by the reforms of Alexander II. The assault on local self-government began in earnest in the fall of 1886 when the Minister of the Interior, Dmitry Tolstoy, confidentially proposed the formal abrogation of the Zemstvo Statute of 1864. His argument was that this statute had created in Russia a schizophrenic system of local administration, partly bureaucratic, partly elective, which made effective

---

"Zemskii soiuz kontsa 70-kh i nachala 80-kh gg. XIX veka," *Iubileinyi zemskii sbornik*, 233–259.

government impossible. Tolstoy did not ask that zemstva be abolished outright, but he wanted them subordinated to the regular bureaucratic apparatus.[6] His proposal was rejected as too "radical," but subsequently measures were taken to curtail the effectiveness of the institutions of local self-government. A decree of July 12, 1889, abolished the post of justice of the peace, which had been very popular with the liberal gentry, and transferred his functions to the land commandant, an appointed official chosen from the landed gentry but responsible to the bureaucracy. A decree of June 12, 1890, subjected zemstva to stricter administrative controls, and increased further the preponderance in them of gentry landowners. Governors were now authorized to withhold confirmation of the office of persons elected to their offices by the zemstva.[7]

Although these measures caused no panic in zemstvo circles, they did have the effect of shaking some of the more conservative liberal elements out of their political lethargy. In the early 1890's zemstvo leaders from various parts of the empire revived the custom of holding informal consultations, first begun in 1878. The zemstvo personnel most angered by the government's repressive measures were the hired specialists, later called the Third Element. These salaried agronomists, statisticians, teachers, doctors, and other experts depended for their livelihood on the zemstva and keenly cared for their survival. Politically to the left of the elected zemstvo deputies, they also began to convene at this time. The 1897 census revealed that there were 47,000 people in this social group.[8]

The death of Alexander III in 1894 aroused momentary hopes that the new government might abandon its repressive course and revert to the liberal policies of the 1860's. These hopes, as has been noted, were dashed in 1895 by the "senseless dreams" speech of Nicholas II. As Struve had correctly predicted at the time in his open letter to Nicholas II, the policy of permanent bureaucratic-police rule proclaimed in this speech had the effect

---

[6] The government drive against the zemstva has been recently described on the basis of archival materials by L. G. Zakharova, *Zemskaia kontrreforma 1890 g.* (Moscow, 1968).

[7] Fischer, *Russian Liberalism*, 12–13; Hugh Seton-Watson, *The Russian Empire, 1801–1917* (Oxford, 1967), 469.

[8] L. K. Erman, *Intelligentsiia v pervoi russkoi revoliutsii* (Moscow, 1966), 13. On the organizational activities of the Third Element, see *Belokonsky*, 36–46.

of forcing moderate elements in the zemstva leftward, toward political action. In 1895, zemstvo leaders founded in Moscow a semilegal center which organized regular informal meetings for the purpose of discussing problems of local self-government. The principal figure in this center was the head of the Moscow zemstvo council, D. N. Shipov, a man of pronouncedly conservative views and a foe of parliamentarism and constitutionalism. That a man of his opinions should have been moved to engage in activity of this kind is an indication of the disgust which the government had by this time aroused among some of its most loyal subjects.[9]

In 1899, Shipov and several outstanding zemtsy with constitutional sympathies (among them, the twins Peter and Paul Dolgorukov, D. I. Shakhovskoi and P. S. Sheremetev) founded a society called Symposium (Beseda) to provide a forum for the discussion of problems confronting zemstvo boards. Its membership was confined to elected zemstvo deputies, the so-called *zemskie glasnye*. (The society's permanent secretary, the lawyer V. Maklakov, was the one exception.) The Symposium had a floating membership of some forty or fifty people, all aristocrats by origin and men of wealth, who met in Moscow several times a year, apparently with the tacit approval of the police. After the June 1900 ordinance curtailing the zemstva's power to tax, the Symposium directed its discussions toward political topics, for this measure suggested that the government was indeed determined to destroy local self-rule in Russia and that it had become unrealistic to ignore broader political issues. Witte's confidential memorandum, *Autocracy and Zemstvo,* brought out by the Social Democrats under Struve's editorship early in 1901, which urged the tsar to abolish zemstva as incompatible with absolutism, made a strong impression on zemstvo circles, helping to push some hesitating moderates leftward.[10]

[9] According to Maklakov, the Minister of the Interior, Goremykin, knew of these meetings and gave them grudging approval: V. A. Maklakov, "Iz proshlogo," SZ, No. 48 (1932), 358. The historian E. D. Chermensky says they were illegal: "Zemsko-liberal'noe dvizhenie," IsSSSR, No. 5 (1965), 44.

[10] The archive of Beseda is preserved at the Manuscript Division of the Moscow State Historical Museum, Fond 31. For accounts of its activities, see Maklakov, "Iz proshlogo," 354–359, where, however, he mistakenly traces its origin to the early 1890's; Chermensky, "Zemsko-liberal'noe dvizhenie," 44–46; E. P. Mikheeva, "Neskol'ko dopolnenii k istorii 'Besedy,'" IsSSSR, No. 2 (1966), 241–243; and Peter D. Dolgorukov in Kn. Pavel Dm. Dolgorukov, *Velikaia razrukha* (Madrid,

The Symposium had difficulty, however, translating its growing political concerns into action because its membership, like that of the zemstva at large, was at this time split into two factions, liberal-conservative and liberal-constitutionalist.

The first of these factions was headed by Shipov, a man widely respected for his judgment and personal qualities even by those who rejected his political program.[11] To him and his friends the enemy was not the autocracy but the bureaucracy. Shipov's conception of the political system suitable for Russia was not unlike that which Karamzin had formulated nearly a century earlier in his *Memoir on Ancient and Modern Russia*: by virtue of its historic traditions, Russia required strong monarchical authority, but that authority had to function in a strictly legal manner and refrain from interfering with the "legitimate" concerns of society. The bureaucracy, by wedging itself between the tsar and the people, prevented the monarch from maintaining his traditional rapport with the people; it was mainly responsible for the lawlessness prevailing in Russia. Shipov's remedy was not to weaken the autocracy by subjecting it to constitutional and parliamentary restraints, but to strengthen it and transform it into a "true" monarchy. This was to be achieved by buttressing the existing institutions of self-rule against bureaucratic encroachments and by utilizing all legal means of persuasion to influence the tsar.[12]

The constitutionalist zemtsy, led by Petrunkevich, Peter Dolgorukov, and Shakhovskoi, considered Shipov's program utopian. To them, the bureaucracy was merely a tool of the monarchy. They saw no point in attacking the symptom of Russia's political malaise and ignoring the cause. The real culprit was absolutism. Hence, they revived the constitutional slogans of 1862 and 1878–1882.[13]

Because there was no way of reconciling these contrary points of view, the constitutionalists in the Symposium (where they

1964), 332–335. On the effect in zemstvo circles of Struve's introduction to Witte, see D. N. Shipov, *Vospominaniia i dumy o perezhitom* (Moscow, 1918), 177.

[11] Chermensky, "Zemsko-liberal'noe dvizhenie," 44.

[12] Shipov, *Vospominaniia*, 269–271; Leonard Schapiro, *Rationalism and Nationalism in Russian Nineteenth-Century Political Thought* (New Haven and London, 1967), 143–167.

[13] Chermensky ("Zemsko-liberal'noe dvizhenie," 44) lists in the constitutional faction Peter and Paul Dolgorukov, F. F. Kokoshkin, G. E. Lvov, V. A. Maklakov, Iu. A. Novosiltsev, I. I. Petrunkevich, A. A. Svechin, E. N. and S. N. Trubetskoi, M. V. Chelnokov, and D. I. Shakhovskoi.

were in a minority) agreed for the time being to keep in abeyance
their demand for a constitution, and to collaborate with their
conservative colleagues on a program of common minimum demands: strengthening local self-government and restraining the
bureaucracy. The Symposium undertook an ambitious publishing
program in Russia and abroad, bringing out a series of books
whose purpose it was to educate the Russian public in questions
of politics and economics.[14] The constitutionalist faction, however, did not confine its activities to the Symposium. It established
contact with groupings to the left, including the Social Democrats and the Third Element. Plekhanov and Akselrod, even if
they did not maintain regular relations with the zemstvo constitutionalists, were well disposed to them. Struve says that from
private conversations with the two leaders of the Liberation of
Labor Group (Akselrod especially) he discovered that they "had
always been attracted, both spiritually and emotionally" to democratic Liberalism.[15]

Thus, around 1900, the Russian "liberational movement"
(*osvoboditel'noe dvizhenie*) began to take concrete shape. It embraced a wide spectrum of opinion, from liberal-conservative to
democratic-revolutionary, but its spokesmen, for all their differences as to ultimate aims, agreed that the bureaucratic-police
regime had outlived its usefulness. In the center of this loose
coalition stood zemstvo constitutionalists, who sought to provide
the link connecting the conservatives with the radicals.

For Struve, open identification with the constitutional cause
required no profound inner conversion. He had been a liberal
and a constitutionalist since the age of fifteen, and if he had originally cast his lot with the Social Democrats it was only because
between 1885 and 1900 Russia had had no effective liberal movement. But by 1900 the situation had changed. From then on, the
zemstvo movement was unmistakably moving away from its traditional apoliticism, and its constitutionalist faction, although nu-
merically still in the minority, was more active than the conservative and was steadily gaining adherents at its expense as a result
of the government's relentless pressures on the zemstva. Struve

---

[14] A partial list of Beseda's publications can be found in *Belokonsky*, 80, and
Dolgorukov, *Velikaia razrukha*, 336–338. See also Maklakov, "Iz proshlogo," 354–
355, 357.
[15] Struve, "My Contacts with Rodichev" SR, XII, No. 35 (January 1934), 363.

had maintained friendly personal relations with the zemstvo constitutionalists for some time. When in 1900–1901 he was ejected from Social Democratic ranks, he found a natural home in their midst.

But before formally associating himself with the zemstvo constitutionalists, he had to resolve to his own satisfaction the philosophical questions implicit in liberal politics. Liberalism in Russia, as elsewhere, assumed the existence of absolute and eternal ethical norms, the most important being the supreme value of the individual. Struve instinctively believed in the existence of such norms but he had difficulty reconciling them with his philosophy of critical positivism. (Intellectual consistency was to him always a matter of utmost concern.) As a positivist he could not acknowledge "absolute and eternal ethical norms," because there was no way in which these could be derived from empirical evidence, the positivist's criterion of reality. Furthermore, as a critical positivist and a follower of Riehl he could not grant that values were in any sense "necessary," that is, obligatory, because, according to Kant, the realm of values was one of freedom, not of necessity. The question of how to reconcile positivism with ethics had long troubled him. He became acutely conscious of it as a result of his quarrel with Plekhanov and Lenin, which had raised in a very personal manner the whole issue of proper conduct in conflicts pitting personal integrity against political expediency.

In *Critical Remarks* he had still made light of the matter. Citing Riehl and Simmel, he wrote there that consciousness was determined by being (meaning that moral values were subsumed under and derived from existence), and defined freedom as the recognition of necessity.[16] But as he confessed afterward, he had never been satisfied with this facile solution. In a pseudonymous essay, published in 1903, in which he traced his intellectual evolution, he wrote: "Only a very attentive and sensitive reader [of *Critical Remarks*] could even then have detected behind Struve's peremptory judgments hidden inner doubts about the correctness of the accepted solution. These doubts tormented the author, but he denied and suppressed them." [17] That this was indeed the case emerged during his debate with Bulgakov in 1896–97, in

[16] #15/40, 42.
[17] #191/89.

the course of which he made some surprising concessions to idealism, saying that while freedom viewed from the point of view of science was indeed an illusion, it had an indubitable reality viewed from the point of human psychology, and that social ideals were formed independently of social reality.

Ostensibly, however, until 1900 he remained a critical positivist. For metaphysics he retained the profoundest kind of contempt. In the spring of 1897, reviewing a recent article by Vladimir Soloviev, he heaped abuse on metaphysics and metaphysicians. Metaphysics was at best a branch of aesthetics: "Without poetry and outside poetry, metaphysics . . . is dull and futile." The "moral imperative," which Soloviev preached, was gibberish from the logical point of view:

> Until now, we had believed, together with the antiquated philosopher Kant, that in the world of phenomena there exists only one necessity, expressed in the law of causality, and that the realm of the ethical, as that which *ought to be,* is dominated by the concept of freedom, which is not applicable to the realm of phenomena, and for that reason is also unsuitable for the empirical scientific explanation of human actions. But Mr. Soloviev, while "not denying the inevitability of human actions," at the same time speaks calmly of "moral necessity." Would it not have been better simply to write *free necessity,* and thus openly to declare one's full independence from all the constraining fetters of science and logic?[18]

Yet for all the arrogance with which he dismissed Soloviev's idealism, the ethical problem continued to trouble him: how could one justify the existence of values which were "necessary," in the sense of being morally binding? The choice, as Struve saw it, reduced itself to two options: "A positivist, if he reasons critically and consistently, must be in ethics, defined as a doctrine of the morally imperative, either an absolute skeptic (or, what is the same, a cynic, in the vulgar sense of the word), or, at any rate, an extreme subjectivist." [19]

[18] #41. Struve reprinted this article (originally published in the *Messenger of Samara*) in a volume of his selected papers (*Na raznye temy,* St. Petersburg, 1902, 187–197); but when he edited this volume he had ceased being a positivist, and embarrassed by his attacks on metaphysics, removed the offending passages from the essay.
[19] #96/liii.

He investigated the possibility of adopting "absolute skepticism" in morality and carefully read Nietzsche. But having done so, he rejected Nietzsche's solution. Nietzsche, he concluded, sought to eliminate the moral problem by suppressing the idea of moral duty.[20] Yet this sense of duty indubitably existed, as he well knew from personal experience. In a statement which bears a strong autobiographical imprint, Struve wrote:

> All moral activity should clear the soul: it should cut down much and uproot. In short, it involves a struggle, the stage of which is the soul — a struggle of the individual not against external forces but within himself, within the individual who has undergone a bifurcation, who divides within himself. No matter how free it is, if it is conscious creative activity, moral endeavor always brings a great deal of suffering, bitterness, and sorrow, such as is indissolubly bound up with conflict. But once this conflict is over, the victor not only gains an upper hand but also a free hand — or more precisely, a free soul. He has not only subordinated his opponents — he has swept them aside: they no longer reside in the soul, they are destroyed or driven underground.[21]

The "subjective method," the other alternative open to the positivist, Struve was not able to adopt either, because he remained loyal to the Kantian dualism which strictly separated the necessary from the free. There could be no formal bridges between the two:

> Existence contains no freedom and creativity. These concepts are alien to existence. The present has been completely determined by the past; the future is determined by the present (its own past). Thus everything is determined or predetermined. The whole realm of the existent is necessary. It could not and cannot be other than it was, is, and shall be, in accordance with the unalterable law of its existence.[22]

In 1900, Nicholas Berdiaev, a young Marxist in political exile, sent him the manuscript of a book, his first, in which he analyzed

[20] #107/190.
[21] #107/194.
[22] #191/78.

critically Mikhailovsky's theory of sociology.[23] Struve arranged
for its publication and took advantage of the opportunity to
expound in a twenty thousand word introductory essay his own
views on the matter. He still found the "subjective method" as
unacceptable as ever. In the first place, it confused the phenomenal with the normative, "psychological subjectivism with epistemological [subjectivism]."[24] Second, it provided no reliable
guide for determining values. Ultimately, positivist ethics reduced
itself always to eudemonism (hedonism). But to identify the
good with the pleasing was to commit a tautology: " 'Happiness
is the criterion of morality.' But it is necessary to provide an
evaluation or a definition of that 'happiness for which it is obligatory to strive.' An evaluation — from the point of view of
happiness? But in that case we are turning in a vicious circle."[25]
Struve cites at length and with evident relish Nietzsche's dev-
astating critique of eudemonistic morality. He returns time and
again in his writings to Mikhailovsky's ethics, which he describes in one place as an attempt to satisfy a metaphysical
need within the framework of positivism.[26] He now acknowledges
Mikhailovsky's achievement in having realized the moral difficulty implicit in positivism, but he rejects his solution as resting
on an unacceptable derivation of the normative from the ex-
istent.[27]

In the end, there was no way out: positivism had to be abandoned, at any rate in its strict sense as a doctrine claiming universal validity. Because moral imperatives could be neither denied
nor empirically deduced, it inescapably followed that moral values
belonged to a different realm, a transcendental one, existing independently of phenomena:

The compulsive presence in every normal human consciousness of the moral problem is beyond doubt, and so is the

[23] Nicholas Berdiaev, *Sub"ektivizm i individualizm* (St. Petersburg, 1901). Frank,
24. This book, which launched Berdiaev on his literary career, was reviewed by
Mikhailovsky in RB, No. 1 (1901), Pt. 2, 77–97.
[24] #96/xviii.
[25] #96/lx. The words in quotation marks are from Mikhailovsky's "What Is Happiness?"
[26] #191/87.
[27] #191/85. On November 14/27, 1900, on the occasion of the fortieth anniversary of Mikhailovsky's literary activity, Struve spoke at a dinner given in his
honor: Kalmykova to Potresov, undated letter, probably from November 1900.

impossibility of resolving this problem empirically. Once we admit the impossibility of resolving the moral problem objectively (that is, empirically), we acknowledge at the same time the *objective nature of ethics as a problem, and, accordingly, arrive at a metaphysical postulate of the moral world order, independent of subjective consciousness.*[28]

Philosophically, this passage, written in the autumn of 1900, marks Struve's Rubicon. Were we concerned with his intellectual evolution exclusively, we would here draw the line between his early and late biography. In these words, at last, he gives up positivism as an all-embracing system, and accepts a dualistic philosophy with two parallel realms, one empirical, the other transcendental, or metaphysical. Each is objectively real. Each has its own laws: that something exists does not signify that its existence is justified, anymore than the desirability of something's coming to pass assures that it will do so.[29]

In his search for a metaphysic, Struve was led to Fichte. The road was not direct, but circuitous. First he read Bernstein's writings on Lassalle; then he intensively read Lassalle; and from Lassalle, who had been Fichte's philosophical disciple and an authority on his thought, he was led back to the source itself.[30] The Fichte whom Lassalle, Bernstein, and Struve admired was, of course, not the familiar chauvinist of the *Speeches to the German Nation* and the *Closed Commercial State*, but the largely forgotten young Fichte, the humanist author of the *Destiny of Man.*[31] In Struve's immediate post-1900 philosophical and political writings the influence of this early Fichte is always near at hand.

Like Fichte, Struve conceives the human being in terms of the "ego" — the conscious and eternally striving individual who real-

---

[28] #96/liv.

[29] Struve's rejection of strict positivism did not lead him to accept the subjective method. Unlike Mikhailovsky and the other "subjectivists," after 1900 he came to regard moral values as objectively valid, that is, as absolute and eternal.

[30] Ferdinand Lassalle, "Fichte's politisches Vermächtniss und die neueste Gegenwart" and "Die philosophie Fichte's," in Eduard Bernstein, ed., *Ferdinand Lassalle's Reden und Schriften*, I (Berlin, 1892), 365–395, 425–461. Struve's most important statement on Lassalle is #95, where he concludes with an appeal to socialists to return to Lassalle and Fichte (#95/299).

[31] C. Trautwein, *Ueber F. Lassalle und sein Verhältnis zur Fichteschen Sozialphilosophie* (Jena, 1913), and G. Leibholz, *Fichte und der demokratische Gedanke* (Freiburg, 1921). According to Leibholz, the democratic side of Fichte's thought became generally known in Germany only after the conclusion of World War I. With Kant, he became the spiritual founder of the Weimar Republic.

izes himself in constant interaction with the external world of
"non-egos." He departs from Fichte, however, in defining the
ego in religious terms. The human soul is a God-given, "eternal
and self-determining substance." [32] As a substance, it is, by definition, capable of acting without external interference, that is, it
is free. All metaphysics must rest on the religious concept of man:
a metaphysical system, like dialectical materialism, which fails
to do so is, therefore, unacceptable.[33] Life is a never-ending quest
for self-fulfillment or self-realization of the ego, in the course of
which it becomes conscious of itself. All morality derives from
the fact of the absolute worth of the individual and posits his
absolute right to self-fulfillment. "Absolute good consists in . . .
every man freely containing in himself and creating absolute
truth and absolute beauty." [34]

Although moral values are absolute and eternal, Struve main-
tains, moral conduct is never automatic. Though "necessary,"
morality does not manifest itself with the same ironclad sequence
that prevails in the empirical realm:

> If the moral or the morally imperative is universally binding,
> it is so in a different sense from the existential. The univer-
> sality of the morally binding presupposes always not only the
> possibility, but even the reality of its rejection. "You ought
> to" always presupposes: "You can also refuse the obligation."
> "You see, you understand" always means: "You cannot not see,
> you cannot not understand." [35]

It is the peculiarity of ethics that although its tenets have an
imperative quality, their acceptance involves spiritual conflict.
Moral duty is recognized only after an intense dialogue within
the bifurcated human soul. All morality presupposes free, conscious choice;[36] its secret is the peculiar fusion of duty and choice,
obligation and freedom.[37] This whole conception of ethics is
very close to Fichte's. Struve calls freedom indispensable to
ethical behavior, because unless one can choose between alterna-

[32] #107/196.
[33] #93/13 and #96/l–lviii.
[34] #96/lxiii.
[35] #96/xxxix.
[36] #96/lxix.
[37] #107/191.

tive courses of action, unless one can experience the inner conflict, one cannot be said to act morally:

> [The formal aspect of morality] consists in the recognition of individuality, freedom, and equality as indispensable conditions of the realization in man of absolute good or highest welfare. Without these formal conditions, the supreme value of life — the embodiment in man of absolute truth and absolute beauty — is not only unattainable but can turn into its very opposite, into profound immorality . . .[38]

Why "equality" as well as individuality and freedom?

> I am deeply convinced that the idea that all men have equal worth . . . rests on the idea of the substantial being of the spirit, and that, in this sense, the term "Christian-democratic morality" is absolutely correct.[39]

While no formal link connects the existential and transcendental realms, the two may be said to be joined by a psychological bridge in the sense that the conviction that things are on our side strengthens our ideals:

> There are phenomena whose essence, real meaning, and aesthetic charm reside in the unique and mysterious symbiosis of contrary principles. Thus the ideal toward which we strive cannot be for us entirely necessary. Should it be entirely colored in the hues of necessity, our exertions would be no more required for its realization than they are for the movements of celestial bodies and the sedimentation of seashores. But, on the other hand, we should feel terribly weak if on the side of our ideal stood only one force — our desire to bring it about. We always consciously seek or unconsciously attach to this force a powerful ally: the force of things. The more the load is taken up by the unconscious, spontaneous force of things, the more convinced we are that our ideals must be realized. Our *free activity* can never fully disappear from the conception of the ideal — otherwise the ideal disintegrates as

[38] #96/lxiii–lxiv.
[39] #96/lxviii.

such and becomes transformed from a form of human creativity into part of the natural flow of things. But the more the latter cooperates with us and works for us, the more confidently will we look forward to the future. The ideal, as such, requires for its existence our free activity. But to be powerful and feasible, this ideal, as an objective fact, requires the greatest possible participation of the force of things in its realization. And insofar as everything human consists, without remainder, of these two quantities [the force of things and free human activity], then obviously the growth of one means the diminution of the other. But in this case, the diminution displays a uniquely peculiar characteristic: it constitutes neither a reduction of the strength nor a reduction of the moral value of free activity. While free activity decreases in relation to the objective factor, free activity objectively grows stronger from this reduction and, at the same time, in no way yields its inner worth. Free activity loses sense where the whole territory is seized by the force of things; but psychologically it can occupy a great deal of space and have a great deal of meaning, even if in the realistically founded image of the future, objectively it has to recede completely before the force of things.[40]

Anyone inclined to view ideas as mere "functions" or "sublimations" of psychic drives would do well to take seriously these reflections. In acknowledging an independent realm of moral values, Struve found not only a solution to a problem which had troubled him for many years, but also an inexhaustible source of spiritual strength. Henceforth, facing the many disappointments which life held in store for him, he never felt the need to accommodate himself to "reality." He thought in terms of two realities, the invisible one of moral imperatives being no less "real" than the other, the visible world of happenings. The morally proper for him was henceforth insulated from the batterings of experience. This philosophical conviction allowed him to absorb the shocks of defeat with supreme fortitude.

On the basis of his new philosophy, Struve constructed a theory of liberalism, outlined most fully in a marvelous essay called

[40] #107/191.

"What Is True Nationalism?" [41] Steeped in the thought of Fichte, Lassalle, and Ivan Aksakov, his ideas were not quite original, and yet his theory has considerable importance as the most ambitious attempt in the history of Russian political thought to formulate a consistent doctrine of democratic and national liberalism. (The only other systematic liberal theory in Russia, that of Boris Chicherin, was of a nondemocratic, conservative variety.)

The starting point of Struve's liberal theory is the human individual endowed with a God-given soul who, in order to become himself, needs to think and act in freedom. The point of view is strictly nominalist. The individual is the only proper subject of politics, and under no circumstances must one hypostatize such concepts as state or nation:

> Uncritical or unconscious realism or universalism in sociology and politics in practice often leads to coarse errors, pregnant with harmful consequences. Thus, when one fashions in one's mind a fantastic creature under the name "state," one readily sacrifices to it the real interests (in the broadest sense) of the human beings united in the political community. But insofar as the *being* called by this name is fantastic, insofar as it does not exist in reality, its place, of course, is at once taken by a more or less numerous group of living people for whom it is very convenient to ascribe to their interests, sometimes of a base nature, an elevated state sanction. This occurs almost invariably when the fluid, sociolegal relationship between men, called the state, is transmuted into an independent being or substance conceivable apart from living people and their relations. [42]

Although this statement was meant to apply to the conservative nationalism of the imperial regime and its theoreticians, in writing it Struve undoubtedly also had in mind Marxists like Plekhanov and Lenin and their notion of the revolutionary "cause."

The individual requires rights, both civil and political, for only when he enjoys them can he fulfill his destiny as a human being.

---

[41] #106. A few years later Struve wrote that this essay was his farewell to Russia as he was about to depart for his voluntary exile in the West: *Rech'*, No. 47 (February 24/March 8, 1908).

[42] #106/501.

Such rights are not historic phenomena, connected with the "bourgeois" phase of history. They are religious in origin. Drawing on the writings of Georg Jellinek, Struve contends that the notion of freedom of conscience and of speech originated in the Protestant dissent of the seventeenth and eighteenth centuries in Britain and the American colonies. Like all moral values, liberties are not relative but eternal and absolute:

> Natural law is not only ideal or desired law, brought in or moving in to take the place of effective or positive law. It is *absolute* law, whose roots repose in the ethical concept of the individual and his self-realization, and which furnishes the measure of all positive law . . . The idea of absolute law . . . constitutes the essential and eternal content of liberalism. The problem of liberalism . . . is not in the least exhausted by the question of *organization of government*. Thus it is broader and deeper than the problem of democracy. Democracy is in many respects only a method or a means of realizing liberalism . . . Liberalism is cosmopolitan and ideal in its origin. It arose in response to questions of religious conscience, and received flesh and blood in truly democratic communities, constituted not by a mythical but by an actual "social contract" on the virgin lands of America. The first word of liberalism was freedom of conscience. And this fact is something that ought to be well realized and firmly kept in mind in every country where liberalism has not yet uttered a single word. I use the term "liberalism" intentionally. Contrary to the prevailing view of liberalism as something soft-bodied, half-hearted, and shapeless, I understand this term to mean a severe, precise, and uncompromising viewpoint which draws a sharp line separating law from lawlessness.[43]

Because of the strength of the Russian conservative tradition, whose supporters believed that in Russia law had as its purpose not to guarantee individual rights (as in the West) but to pre-

[43] #106/507-509. Cf. Georg Jellinek, *Die Erklärung der Menschen- und Bürgerrechte* (Leipzig, 1895). Max Weber, who was familiar with Struve's writings from the *Liberation* period (he had learned Russian at that time to follow news of the Russian Revolution), commented that in the twentieth century mass movements had rendered obsolete the ideal of individual rights and liberties. He viewed Struve's liberalism with great sympathy but even greater skepticism: Max Weber, "Zur Lage," 280.

serve order, Struve went to great lengths to show that formal legality was not enough. Law had to have a specific content, namely guarantees of individual rights. In the essay "Pravo i prava" ("Law and Rights"), he argued persuasively against a formalistic approach to legality:

> What [Russian citizens] need is not abstract law, not "due process" divorced from all content, but concrete rights. "Due process" and "legality" are valuable and they are valued by people not because of an alleged worth inhering *within* these principles, but because in the actual legal life of the people they combine with concrete content, with "rights" which are of value to the individual and whole social groups . . . The legal order is valuable not only because it assures the rule of objective and dispassionate law, but also because the rule of objective and dispassionate law assures the most important interests of the individual, embodied in the form of rights . . . For the citizen-peasant to have reason to "cross himself" before the law, it is necessary that "law" comfort him not only with its form, but also with its content, that it extend the peasant's freedom, that is, elevate his personality, give him "rights." [44]

It had always been important to guarantee individual rights, but under modern conditions it was more so than ever, because technology had vastly enhanced the scope of state power. Struve did not regard this phenomenon as necessarily deleterious, but he did feel that it had to be counterbalanced by a corresponding growth in the individual sphere:

> At no time, during no period in history, has the absence of individual rights founded in law posed so great a cultural threat as in the age of gigantic states with their superb networks of railroads, telegraphs, and telephones, and with their accurately functioning, "enlightened" bureaucratic "apparatus." Modern technology, of course, performs great services for the individual and his bold search for new outlets and contents of

[44] #100/89–90. Cf. the favorable comment in VE, No. 2 (February 1901), 888–889. Struve made the same point in 1897, while in his most "orthodox" Marxist phase: #42/230. The leading exponent of formal legalism in Russia was probably N. M. Korkunov: see his *Russkoe gosudarstvennoe pravo*, I (St. Petersburg, 1893), 215–222.

life. But not for nothing is it based on the principles of concentration and centralization of power, whose device reads: he who has little shall lose little, he who has much shall gain much. Where the centralized state mechanism directs everything, prescribes to everything its limits and measure, penetrates everywhere, detects everything, manages the present and attempts to preordain the future — there contemporary technology (in the broadest sense of the word) benefits the centralized apparatus incomparably more than it does the independently active individual.

If "Christianity required neither freedom of the press nor freedom of assembly to conquer the world" (Renan), that was only because it enjoyed, in effect, virtually unlimited freedom of expression and communication. At a time when the technical means of the state and the government were highly imperfect and arbitrariness was not as yet systematized, its rule was far less all-embracing and hence less detrimental to cultural and especially spiritual activity than it is in our own day. There were then no books, no journals, and no newspapers, but there were also no censorship and no police, and there could have been none, because these institutions, too, require for their development and perfection certain technical means. It is well known that in the classical country of freedom of the press, censorship fell not only or not so much because of the clear realization of its illegality as such, but by virtue of the technical imperfectibility of the police apparatus . . . English liberty in general is historically connected with the clumsiness of the government, or, in other words, of the administrative apparatus of England.

From this it clearly follows that where subjective rights are not fixed in law, technical progress (in the broad sense of the word), which is seized upon and adapted best and most fully by the centralized state apparatus, in certain respects, and very essential ones, has worsened and continues to worsen the position of the individual as the creator of new culture, as the seeker of new paths.

Here lies the immense cultural evil, the source which amply feeds the crudest materialism in society and threatens national culture with the impoverishment of life-giving spiritual strength, passions, and interests. Indeed, the sphere of cultural creativity is arbitrarily cut in two. That part which represents the immediate arena for the human spirit, where religious, political, and social culture is being created, is in every conceivable way fenced off from the penetration of the free act of the individual and of free associations. Here rules the principle recently cast with slave-like cynicism into the formula "no doubts about the soundness of the given command." In return, the individual and the free associations are compensated [for this deprivation] by being fairly "liberally" allowed to dispose of the low country of material interests. Here a certain degree of freedom is allowed and here flows the main stream of paternalistic cares, coarsely, in an oriental manner, reproducing the celebrated *enrichissez vous*. The search for new paths for the spirit and for life is replaced with pursuit of material comforts and pleasures. Thus national culture is suffused and infected with the poison of practical materialism. This is particularly and even exclusively pernicious for the higher classes of the population, for whom participation in the benefits of enrichment is much easier and more tangible than for the mass of people, who until now invariably have been and still continue to be excluded from the banquets of this world. And it is from these classes that the major part of the intelligentsia is recruited for the bureaucracy, which wields such a commanding influence over the entire life of the people.[45]

The material might of the contemporary state is thus an entirely new and specific factor, characteristic of our age. Obviously, its cultural import varies greatly, depending on whether the government, armed with all the up-to-date acquisitions of industrial, administrative, and other techniques, confronts an individual armed with rights or not. In other words, what means the growth of the material might of the state, fostered and assured by all kinds of technical progress, where the rights of the individual have not been embodied in law, where the rule or recognition of objective law is not accompanied by unqualified recognition of subjective rights? This problem is of enormous interest to the philosophy of culture, and, accordingly, to that of law. At the same time, it is our firmest conviction that it is the fundamental problem of con-

[45] #106/524–527.

temporary Russian culture, before which all the others recede.[46]

Genuine nationalism — Struve's ultimate concern — must rest on liberal foundations. Copiously quoting from Aksakov, Struve attacks the whole ideology of official nationalism, which identifies the national spirit with some specific ethos set for all eternity. The national spirit is never fixed, it never "freezes," it forever flows and changes. This is an additional argument in favor of individual rights and freedoms.

> Liberalism in its pure form, that is, the sense of the recognition of the inalienable rights of the individual standing above the encroachments of every collective, supraindividual entity, no matter how organized and how designated — such liberalism is the only species of true nationalism, of genuine respect for and self-respect of the national spirit. It entails the recognition of the right of its living carriers and creators to free creativity and seeking, to the erection and rejection of goals and "forms" of life.[47]

In a lovely metaphor, he envisions man in relation to his country as both child and parent: child in that he inherits, parent in that he bequeathes.

Struve was convinced that Russia stood on the threshold of an unprecedented surge (*pod"em*) of national culture, unmistakable evidence of which he saw in the religious debates of the end of the nineteenth century.[48]

> It is possible to have a society which lives merely spontaneously, which feels no necessity and has no strength to promote culture, that is, *consciously* to pose and autonomously (*samochinno*) to solve its tasks — a society where everything can move forward only at the government's beck, by its power, by its decree; a society which regards culture as a duty owed the state and for which culture is represented by the police (not in the figurative but in the scientific sense of the word). Such, on the whole, has been Russian society throughout the

[46] #106/523.
[47] #106/512.
[48] #106/523–524.

eighteenth century. But contemporary Russian society is different. From the summits of the intelligentsia (in the person of the national hero of thinking Russia, Leo Tolstoy) to the depths of national life, Russia consciously and autonomously creates culture, working on the solution of its higher tasks — religious tasks, which it raises, as did Christianity during the first centuries and during the modern Reformation — alongside and in connection with moral and social problems. We attach immense importance to this peculiarity of our times: the stubborn travail of national consciousness over the religious problem — a travail which is not simply an agonizing *perplexity*, such as the Schism was. In it we perceive the distinct sign of the cultural maturity of the Russian people as a whole and the welcome portent of a broad surge of national culture. No matter how oppressive the conditions under which the process of the formation of national culture is taking place, we are ready to echo with a joyful heart the classic words of Hutten: "Die Geister sind erwacht: es ist Lust zu Leben!" —— "The spirits are awake — what joy it is to be alive!"

13. THE ORIGINS OF THE UNION OF LIBERATION

If one were to treat each episode in Struve's life in proportion to its biographical and historical importance, at least as much space would have to be allotted his liberal as his Social Democratic phase. In disposing of such issues, however, we are not entirely free to follow our judgment, because of our dependence on the sources of information. These, in the case of Russian liberalism, are far from adequate. The archive of the Union of Liberation — the main collection of source material on the formative years of the Constitutional Democratic party, when Struve made his principal contribution to liberalism — has vanished, and may well have been destroyed before any historian had a look at it.[1] Nor is the situation much better with materials whose whereabouts are known. Most of these repose in Soviet archives controlled by the Central Archive Administration of the Ministry of the Interior, that is, the police. This guardian has been understandably reluctant to release documents bearing on the history of Russian liberalism,

---

[1] According to Professor Gleb Struve, Peter Struve's son, the archive of the Union of Liberation was in his father's apartment when the Revolution of 1917 broke out. At the end of 1917, when Peter Struve went south to join the Whites (still according to his son), he entrusted it to the care of S. F. Oldenburg, the President of the Russian Academy of Sciences. There is independent evidence that the archives of the Constitutional Democratic party, in which the Union of Liberation dissolved, was indeed concealed after the Bolshevik power seizure in the Manuscript Division of the Academy, for here it was discovered in 1930 by the Commission for the Purge of the Academy. After their discovery, these materials were transferred to the Central Historical Archive (KA, No. 46, 1931, 38, 42), and from there to the Central State Historical Archive in Moscow (TsGIAM), where they presently repose. However, according to the descriptive catalogue of this archive (Tsentral'nyi Gosudarstvennyi Istoricheskii Arkhiv v Moskve, *Putovoditel'* [Moscow, 1946], 104), Fond 523, which holds the papers of the Constitutional Democratic Party, has no documents antedating 1905. This information suggests that it has no materials from the *Liberation* period. Because there are no references to archival materials on the Union of Liberation in any Soviet study which I have examined, I conclude that this archive has either perished or remains hidden somewhere in the USSR.

because they could be used to refute the official version of history, which depicts the Bolshevik party as the only resolute and uncompromising foe of the imperial government. The historian here confronts a piquant situation in which the Communist police protects from his eyes dossiers on the opposition to tsarism compiled by the tsarist police. Among these materials are the papers of the Constitutional Democratic party and of the Russian Historical Archive in Prague, the latter of which the Soviet government acquired in 1945.[2] In view of the paucity of available materials, it is simply not possible to trace Struve's liberal period in the desirable detail.

We have left Struve in March 1901 as he was about to depart from St. Petersburg for Tver as an administrative exile. He arrived there in the early days of April and at once plunged into research on the agrarian history of the region. The findings, admirably supporting his general thesis on Russia's pre-Emancipation economy, were later incorporated into the revised version of his papers on the subject, brought out in 1913 in book form.[3] In Tver he also wrote several of the seminal essays on liberal philosophy and politics discussed in the preceding chapter, and collected for publication his miscellaneous articles for a book called *On Various Themes*, which appeared in the spring of 1902.[4]

But clearly, at a time when the country was seething with discontent and various oppositional groupings were organizing themselves into parties, a man of Struve's political passions could not confine himself to historical and editorial work. He chafed in his exile, and dreamt of going abroad. Petrunkevich, who was also living under police surveillance in the Tver province, recalls

[2] Some materials on the Union of Liberation gathered by the foreign agencies of the police are at the Okhrana Archive in the Hoover Institution, Stanford, California, and will be cited below. Among the manuscripts lost to Western scholars when the Prague Archive was sent to Moscow is an unpublished history of the Union of Liberation by V. Vodovozov: George Fischer, *Russian Liberalism* (Cambridge, Mass., 1958), 142n–143n.

[3] *Krepostnoe khoziaistvo* (St. Petersburg and Moscow, 1913).

[4] It is known that Struve completed the editorial work on this book (#132) while in Tver from his undated letter sent to S. A. Vengerov from there (Pushkin House, Leningrad, Fond 377, No. 10476). The Preface, which bears the date March 1902, must have been written in Germany. Struve was surprised that the censors had approved this book for publication, for ever since his arrest in March 1901 he had had to publish his articles anonymously: Struve to Hans Delbrück, July 9, 1902, enclosing a copy of *On Various Themes*.

Struve's telling him he was determined to leave Russia, even illegally, if necessary.[5]

His desire was to publish the *Contemporary Review* or some other publication that would articulate the country's stifled voice of conscience, as Herzen's *Bell* and Dragomanov's *Free Word* had done in their time. Later, when this desire was fulfilled, he explicitly compared his literary undertaking with those of his two forerunners: "To continue [the work of] Herzen and Dragomanov does not mean simply to repeat their ideas. It means feeding and spreading that broad spirit of struggle for complete freedom of the individual and of society, unfettered by any doctrine and yet steadfast, which both of these fighters for the free Russian word have always held high like an unquenchable flame."[6]

While Struve was laying these plans, the constitutionalist members of the Symposium made their own decision to publish an organ of their party abroad.[7] The two obvious candidates for the post of editor of such an organ were Miliukov and Struve, and both were given close scrutiny. Of the two, Miliukov appeared preferable: he was older (forty-two, compared to Struve's thirty-one), he had a record of political opposition untainted by radical associations, and while he was superbly informed on a wide variety of subjects he did not display the intellectual eccentricities of Struve. (It has been said of him that he could compose single-handed an entire newspaper, from the political news on the front page to the chess section on the last.) But Miliukov had only recently returned from voluntary exile in Bulgaria, where he had spent several years after losing his post at the University of Moscow. It seemed cruel to ask him to migrate once again, this time perhaps forever. Furthermore, a man of Miliukov's political abilities could prove more useful in Russia than outside it. In the end, Miliukov and the constitutionalists agreed that he should remain where he was (that is, in Finland), and there await further political developments.[8]

---

[5] I. I. Petrunkevich, "Iz zapisok obshchestvennogo deiatelia," ARR, XXI (1934), 336. Petrunkevich dates the meeting as having taken place in 1902, which is wrong.

[6] #254/15. Struve frequently drew analogies between the situation in Russia in Herzen's day and his own: e.g., #98/xiii–xiv; #111/2; #124/105.

[7] The decision seems to have been taken toward the end of June 1901 at a secret meeting of the zemtsy: E. D. Chermensky, "Zemsko-liberal'noe dvizhenie," IsSSSR, No. 5 (1965), 50.

[8] Petrunkevich, "Iz zapisok," 337.

There were no such hesitations about Struve, who was politically expendable; but in his case there were inhibitions of a different kind. Struve had made a favorable impression on the constitutionalists with his forceful liberal essays, especially the introduction to Witte's *Autocracy and Zemstvo* and "Law and Rights." [9] But although his commitment to liberal values seemed genuine, no one could really be certain of his politics. He was known for his unpredictable intellectual leaps and his insistence on the freedom to make them at any time the urge came over him. His recent and well publicized friendship with the Social Democrats also did not help, because it could alienate from the constitutional cause *zemtsy* holding conservative views. For these two reasons, the constitutionalists did not approach Struve immediately after Miliukov's candidacy had been dropped.[10] Petrunkevich, who was in frequent contact with him in Tver and kept him abreast of developments in the constitutionalist camp, hints in his memoirs that he did not even inform Struve of the group's decision to launch an émigré paper.[11]

The actual circumstances which finally led Struve to move abroad and assume the editorship of *Liberation* are obscure. Miliukov says that, having turned down the offer, he suggested Struve in his stead.[12] Struve has left no detailed account of this episode; he merely states that sometime in 1901 D. E. Zhukovsky suddenly appeared in Tver and placed before him 30,000 rubles in gold, saying that it was for an émigré newspaper "devoted exclusively to the propaganda of the idea of constitutional government in Russia." [13] Zhukovsky, previously mentioned as one of the

[9] Shakhovskoi, 85; OD, I, 386–387; D. N. Shipov, *Vospominaniia i dumy o perezhitom* (Moscow, 1918), 177, 186.

[10] Belokonsky, 92–93; Petrunkevich, "Iz zapisok," 336–337.

[11] Petrunkevich, "Iz zapisok," 337.

[12] In his memoirs, Miliukov takes credit for recommending Struve (*Vospominaniia*, I [New York, 1955], 197), but his account of the *Liberation* period, written from memory in wartime France, is full of errors.

[13] Struve, "My Contacts and Conflicts with Lenin," SR, XII, No. 36 (April 1934), 81. Struve does not mention Zhukovsky by name because when these recollections appeared, Zhukovsky was still living in the Soviet Union, and could have suffered unpleasant consequences from such publicity. His last known post was that of a lowly assistant in the Faculty of Botany at the Crimean Pedagogical Institute in Simferopol: Akademiia Nauk SSSR, *Nauchnye rabotniki SSSR bez Moskvy i Leningrada* (Leningrad, 1928), 131. He was arrested sometime in the 1930's and seems to have perished during the purges: A. Tyrkova-Viliams, *Na putiakh k svobode* (New York, 1952), 172–173. That he presented Struve with 30,000 rubles in gold is known from Struve's casual remark in a letter to N. A. Tsurikov, dated March 31, 1938, in the possession of Prof. Gleb Struve.

supporters of *Iskra* and the stillborn *Contemporary Review,* was a
friend and follower of Struve. It was the lure of his money that in
large measure accounted for the eagerness with which Lenin and
Potresov sought to involve Struve in their publishing ventures. He
had enough money to produce the 30,000 rubles from his own
pocket. Perhaps he did so; or perhaps he collected the sum from
other admirers of Struve. In any event, the money does not seem
to have come from the fund of the zemstvo constitutionalists, who
had collected 100,000 rubles for their own organ, because this
money was offered to Struve only the following year. Struve, however, did not much trouble about the source of this money; he only
wanted to know whether as editor he would enjoy full independence. Zhukovsky replied affirmatively; the one condition he posed
was that the projected publication not depend in any way on the
socialists.[14]

With Zhukovsky's money in hand, Struve decided to delay his
departure no longer and applied for a passport for himself and his
family. The application ran into administrative snags. Late in the
year, the authorities finally issued the passport to Nina, who was
in the seventh month of pregnancy. She arrived in Montreux with
the children in mid-November (NS). At that time she was still
uncertain when her husband would come.[15] He joined her at the
end of December, having left Russia by an unknown route (probably by way of Finland) and without a valid passport.[16] He took
this step fully aware of its gravity. He believed that he was condemning himself to at least twenty years of émigré life, and that
perhaps, like Herzen, he might never again see Russia[17] — so great
was his and his generation's awe of the imperial regime.

The instant he found himself on Swiss soil, Struve sent out letters in all directions to solicit support. He counted on receiving
help from every émigré political group — socialist, liberal, nonpartisan, ethnic minority — for a literary enterprise whose only
program was to be the abolition of autocracy.

[14] "My Contacts and Conflicts with Lenin," 81. The *Contemporary Review,* which
Zhukovsky was also to have financed, was, of course, intended to come out under
Social Democratic auspices.

[15] Nina Struve to Potresov from Montreux, November 3/16, 1901.

[16] Struve to Akselrod from Montreux, December 30, 1901.

[17] Struve, "O chem vedetsia tiazhba?" *Vestnik Partii Narodnoi Svobody,* No. 2
(January 11, 1907), 77; *Frank,* 32.

Among the first whom he contacted were his one-time Social Democratic friends. On December 30, 1901, he wrote to Akselrod: "Although I have parted in my views from you and your closest collaborators, I nevertheless retain toward you the friendliest feelings." Whether or not this letter elicited an answer is not known. At the beginning of the new year he went to Munich to talk with the editors of *Iskra*. Lenin flatly refused to see him. Krupskaia, who showed up at Vera Zasulich's to see Nina, her friend since school days, says the encounter "reeked with heavy Dostoevskyism," as Struve complained of being insulted by *Iskra* and tried to amuse the company at his own expense. She concluded that Lenin was right: Struve had become a total stranger to the party. The following day Nina sent her a jar of marmalade, and there the attempt of creating a basis for cooperation with the *Iskra* group ended.[18] Clearly, no assistance could be expected from this quarter. Plekhanov and Lenin, by now undisputed leaders of the movement, would no longer collaborate with the "liberal bourgeoisie." This decision dealt a serious blow to Struve's hopes for a national antiautocratic coalition, in which the Social Democrats, given their strong commitment to political liberty, could have been the strongest allies of the liberals. He resolved, however, to bide his time. He was so utterly convinced that Russian Social Democracy, like the German movement, would evolve to the right, toward liberal reformism, that he held extended the spurned hand of friendship, and made it a matter of firm editorial policy to ignore *Iskra*'s taunts.[19]

He had an easier time establishing a working relationship with the Socialist Revolutionaries. The SR's were not competing with the liberals, and proved willing to join them in the war against the autocracy. "For us it will be more advantageous to deal with a liberal regime than an autocratic one," *Revolutionary Russia*, the SR organ wrote. "We realize not only our ability to perform great

[18] LS, III (1924), 43–44.
[19] Kuskova states categorically that in 1902 Struve and Lenin agreed to collaborate: *Novoe Russkoe Slovo*, October 21, 1945. This assertion contradicts everything known of Struve's and Lenin's relations after 1900, as well as Struve's explicit denial of any relations with Lenin during the *Liberation* period ("My Contacts and Conflicts with Lenin," 82). Kuskova may have confused the January 1901 agreement concerning *Contemporary Review* with *Liberation* and the events of 1902. On October 11, 1902, Struve wrote Akselrod a letter in which he spoke more in sorrow than in anger about *Iskra*'s polemics against all political rivals, and added: "To raise the issue of 'hegemony' in the revolutionary struggle evokes nothing but moral astonishment and pity."

services for the liberals — of course, provided the liberals know how to utilize our work — but also that of the liberals (if they so desire) to perform no mean services for us, for our common task of the political liberation of Russia." [20] The socially diversified and politically amorphous following of the constitutionalists seemed to the SR's a happy hunting ground for recruits. Individual Socialist Revolutionaries took an active part in all the undertakings sponsored by the constitutionalists, and contributed materially to their success. Especially active was the faction which later split off from the SR's and formed the Party of Popular Socialists (Partiia Narodnykh Sotsialistov).

Among the minorities, Struve established a close working relationship with the Finnish opposition and also, apparently, with the Jewish Bund.[21]

He had originally intended to call his paper *Liberty* (*Svoboda*), the name of the fictitious organization on whose behalf he had concluded the January 1901 agreement with *Iskra*. But during his stay in Tver, this name had been appropriated by a splinter Socialist Revolutionary group with its own publication series. He therefore abandoned it and took the name *Liberation* (*Osvobozhdenie*). The printing and distribution were contracted for with the Stuttgart firm of J. H. W. Dietz, the principal publisher of the German Social Democratic party. Dietz also brought out *Iskra* and *Zaria* and had on his staff three Russian typesetters.

In March 1902, Struve moved to Stuttgart. Rather than settle in the city proper, he rented quarters in the suburban village of Gaisburg. The choice was probably dictated by considerations of security. Gaisburg was a village of a few hundred inhabitants, mostly Social Democrats, who knew each other well, and consequently it was a place where outside police agents would have difficulty protecting their anonymity. The choice proved a wise one, and the German branch of the Okhrana ran into great trouble trying to

[20] RR, No. 9 (July 1902), 5.
[21] In July 1902 Martov, having heard from Plekhanov of Struve's dealings with the Bund, wrote to Plekhanov volunteering to write an attack on the Bundists titled "Is It True?": "Is it true that a certain socialist organization has decided for money to render substantial services to a bourgeois party gathered around *Liberation?*" (Martov to Plekhanov, from Paris, July 12, 1902, Dom Plekhanova, Leningrad, V.281.9). He seems to have forgotten that, barely a year and a half before, his own colleagues, Plekhanov among them, were perfectly willing to render similar services for money to the same "bourgeois" party.

shadow Struve and his contacts. In Gaisburg, Struve leased six rooms in a large house on Schlosstrasse 84, called The Castle. These quarters were to serve both as the residence for his family (four children, Nina's widowed mother, and two Russian domestics) and the editorial office of the paper. The house was shared by a retired German gymnasium teacher and the widow of a German architect, with both of whom the Struves established friendly relations. R. Streltsov, a young Russian radical whom Struve engaged as editorial secretary, rented rooms nearby.[22]

While Struve was completing the publishing arrangements in Germany, Iakovlev-Bogucharsky, whom he had chosen as his principal editorial collaborator, was busy rounding up literary contributors in Russia. A one-time Narodovolets who had taken the well trodden road leading from terrorism by way of Social Democracy to social liberalism, he had assumed responsibility for laying the organizational groundwork for *Liberation*. (He had been intended by Struve to perform a similar function for the *Contemporary Review*.) In the course of a trip in February 1902, Bogucharsky visited Tula, Kursk, Kharkov, and the Crimea, meeting everywhere with a favorable response.[23] Among the writers who promised to contribute to *Liberation* were Gorky (then a great admirer of Struve)[24] and Chekhov. Posse, however, whom Bogucharsky approached with an invitation to join the staff, refused, saying he had decided to move to London to resume publication of his suppressed monthly *Life* (*Zhizn'*).[25]

Up to this point, Struve and Bogucharsky were acting entirely on their own behalf. Struve had no formal ties with the zemstvo constitutionalists, although some of them had promised him personal support.[26] One year after they had resolved to bring out an émigré organ, the constitutionalists still had no editor and no paper. In February 1902, having learned that Struve was abroad and about to launch an independent liberal publication, they dispatched D. I. Shakhovskoi and N. N. Lvov to Stuttgart to see

---

[22] Okhrana Archives, Hoover Institution, Index XIIIb(1), Folder 1C.

[23] *Belokonsky*, 92–93. The identity of the unnamed person whose account Belokonsky cites can be established from *Frank*, 31, and *M. Gorkii i A. Chekhov* (Moscow, 1937), 87.

[24] V. A. Posse, *Moi zhiznennyi put'* (Moscow and Leningrad, 1929), 242.

[25] *Belokonsky*, 93; Posse, *Zhiznennyi put'*, 292.

[26] *Shakhovskoi*, 85.

whether it would be possible to join forces.[27] The two emissaries
arrived in Stuttgart in March, carrying a programmatic statement
drafted by Miliukov and endorsed by a meeting of constitutionalists held in Moscow.[28] Miliukov's program anticipated strikingly
the provisions of the October Manifesto: guarantees of civil liberty and of legal equality, and the establishment of a democratically elected parliament with control over the administration and
the regular budget.[29]

Personally, Struve was in complete sympathy with Miliukov's
program, and he said so when introducing it in the first issue of
Liberation.[30] Nevertheless, he firmly refused the request of Shakhovskoi and Lvov to adopt this program as the platform of his
paper. In 1902 Struve regarded support of the zemstva, the only
centers of oppositional activity allowed to function legally in Russia, as essential to the success of the constitutional movement. The
majority of the zemtsy were known to be anticonstitutional. To
identify *Liberation* with the constitutional cause, therefore, was
tantamount to rejecting the support of the zemstvo movement.
Struve was as confident that in time the Slavophile zemtsy would
move to the left as he was that the Social Democrats would move
to the right: life would see to that. But such evolution had to occur
gradually and naturally, in response to intensified autocratic oppression, not to the pressures of the constitutionalists. Altogether,
he felt at this time, the less said about the regime that would replace autocracy, the better. The rallying cry of *Liberation*, as he
envisaged it, should be simply: "Down with autocracy!" On this
basis it would be possible to construct a nationwide united front.
As he put it in the editorial that launched *Liberation* and that,
printed as a broadsheet, was widely circulated in Russia:

[*Liberation*] will develop a positive program of broad political
and social reforms. This does not mean, however, that the edi-

[27] Petrunkevich, "Iz zapisok, 337. Shakhovskoi says that he visited Struve in the
company of two zemtsy whom Struve had not previously met (*Shakhovskoi*, 86–
87); all the other sources refer to two visitors only (e.g., *Belokonsky*, 93).
[28] *Belokonsky*, 93.
[29] "Ot russkikh konstitutsionalistov," *Osv*, No. 1 (June 18/July 1, 1902), 7–12.
In his memoirs, Miliukov depicts himself in 1902 as a conciliator who sought to
keep the movement from adopting Struve's leftward orientation: *Vospominaniia*,
I, 236, 238.
[30] *Osv*, No. 1 (June 18/July 1, 1902), 7.

torial board will present its readers on its behalf with a ready-made program containing, point by point, the solution of all the basic problems which the fundamental transformation required by the country raises. Such a program must still be worked out by the public figures of our country and, first and foremost, by those working in the organs of self-government. The editorial board of *Liberation* counts not on providing them with a program, but on receiving one from them.[31]

Liberation was to be the midwife of Russian liberty. This negative policy agreed with the one he had formulated the year before for the *Contemporary Review.*

Struve spent two days with his visitors, hotly debating the basic questions of strategy, the resolution of which in no small measure determined the future of the liberal movement in Russia.[32] At issue were two different political strategies. Miliukov wanted to create a political party as a counterweight to the existing parties of the socialists (the SD's and SR's), and for this reason needed a specific program. Struve thought in broader, national terms. He wanted to arouse all the political factions, all the social classes, all the ethnic groups. He envisaged what in more recent political language would be called a popular front. A specific program would preclude the formation of such a front, because it would immediately bring to the surface all kinds of disagreements.[33] From this conflict, which inaugurated a political rivalry between the two men that flared up intermittently until their death forty years later, it was Struve who emerged victorious. Under his influence, the constitutionalists agreed to postpone formulating a specific program and to advance the antiautocratic slogan in its bare, negative form. Thus, instead of a liberal party there emerged the "liberational movement" (osvoboditel'noe dvizhenie) which Struve had been advocating since 1899. In this sense, it may be said that Struve was the author of the grand strategy adopted by the liberal

[31] #111/5. The editorial also made a stir abroad. Delbrück translated it for *Preussische Jahrbücher* (August 1902, 364–368) and called the readers' attention to the combination in it of "European ideas with Russian national patriotism."

[32] *Shakhovskoi*, 86–87.

[33] Other disagreements concerned Miliukov's demand for a constituent assembly connected with the existing institutions of self-government. Struve feared that this demand would alienate potential radical supporters: Struve to Delbrück, July 24, 1902.

movement during the years 1902–1904 which decided the fate of autocracy.

He also had his way in editorial matters. Shakhovskoi and Lvov turned over to him the 100,000 rubles which their colleagues had collected for a constitutionalist organ. From now on, the constitutionalists bore the main financial burden of supporting *Liberation* and its subsidiary publications. This they agreed to do even though Struve insisted on retaining the editorial independence which he had secured from Zhukovsky. The arrangement he made with his principal backers was of a most peculiar kind, without precedent in the history of Russian émigré journalism in that (as he put it in a private letter) *Liberation* "was neither the organ of any revolutionary group nor the personal enterprise of the editor" but the common outlet for all those who desired "a fundamental peaceful transformation of the wholly untenable bureaucratic order." [34] Although generally considered the official organ of the zemstvo constitutionalists and, after its formation in 1903–1904, of the Union of Liberation, *Liberation* was never that in reality. It was a publication independent of the editor, who managed it, and the constitutionalists, who financed it.[35] The best way to describe it would be with the words "national forum of opinion."

Miliukov's program appeared in the first issue of *Liberation*, personally endorsed by the editor as an expression of the views of a group of "Russian constitutionalists." Alongside, Struve printed another, more conservative statement of policy emanating from the zemtsy. The constitutionalist program committed neither the journal, nor its contributors, nor its supporters.

The first issue of *Liberation* carried the dateline June 18/July 1, 1902. Its appearance was preceded by a flurry of excitement among the Russian Social Democrats, because Dietz had erroneously advertised it as an organ of their party. Lenin was beside himself with rage, but a few days later *Vorwärts*, the German Social Democratic paper, carried Struve's correction, and the storm abated.[36]

[34] Struve to Delbrück, July 9, 1902.
[35] "*Liberation* is not an organ authorized in any sense to speak on behalf of the 'Union of Liberation.' In accord with the common wish of our friends and ourselves, *Liberation* fully retains its literary independence" (#247/185). Written November 30/December 13, 1904.
[36] LS, IV (1925), 122–123, 129–131, 134.

In fact, nothing was further from Struve's mind than linking his paper with any party. In its statement of policy he wrote: "Its calling is to serve as the organ . . . of the broad national mission and of all those who champion a new, free Russia. It wishes to be their echo, their word, their tocsin." It was dedicated to the task of achieving a revolutionary aim by legal means:

> We shall preach not accommodation to the existing political regime, which saps the best energies of our nation, but, on the contrary, the struggle against it. We shall not skirt diplomatically all the conclusions which follow from the demand for political freedom . . . Our task is not to divide but to unite. The cultural and political liberation of Russia can be neither the monopoly nor the main burden of a single class, a single party, a single doctrine. It must become a national cause, a cause embracing all the people, one that will evoke a response from every heart capable of distinguishing between what is moral and what is amoral in politics, a heart which, for that reason, is unwilling to come to terms with the violence and arbitrariness of a band of bureaucrats who administer a great people without being subjected to any controls and without owing any responsibility.[37]

He promised on the pages of *Liberation* to expose bureaucratic misrule and lies and to give the fullest publicity to all oppositional movements, particularly those involving industrial workers and the revolutionary intelligentsia. One of its main functions was to serve as a "supplement" to the official *Government News* (*Pravitel'-stvennyi Vestnik*).[38]

In the issues which followed, Struve laid down a steady and accurate barrage against the imperial administration. With the help of friends in Russia, some of them evidently in high places, he exposed innumerable instances of repression and corruption, citing names, dates, and places, and sometimes reprinting in their entirety top secret government circulars. This information filled much space in *Liberation*, and contributed greatly to its popularity

[37] #111/2.
[38] #194.

in Russia. The exposures were frequently accompanied by Struve's commentaries.

Struve's critique of the imperial regime rested on premises familiar from his political writings of the 1890's. Their intellectual roots were those ideas of Ivan Aksakov which Struve had assimilated and recast while in secondary school. Political democracy was not only necessary for Russia's well-being; it had been made inevitable by the whole progress of Russian culture. The autocratic government was done for; Nicholas II had completed the destruction which his father began: "'Autocracy' in the Russia of today is impossible, and it no longer exists." [39] What passes for autocratic monarchy is in reality a police state administered by means "of a ubiquitous surveillance, secretly carried out on the basis of secret instructions and circulars." The instant the powers of the police were curbed, the sham would be exposed and "autocracy" would collapse. [40] The question was no longer whether Russia would win political liberty but how soon and under what circumstances, peaceful or violent, evolutionary or revolutionary. The choice lay in the hands of the emperor and his ministers. If they promptly introduced basic reforms, they could spare the country a bloody revolution; if they failed to do so, revolution would become unavoidable. In either event, the demise of autocracy was certain.

In the second half of 1902, Struve believed that reform was the more likely of the two alternatives, because the government was too strong and the opposition too weak for a successful revolution to take place in Russia. As he envisaged it, change would take the form of gradual concessions by the regime as it found itself increasingly less able to administer the country by means of the bureaucracy:

> We have no doubt whatever that, if the government fails to undertake fundamental political and economic reforms, sooner or later Russia will undergo revolution, and the nation, in the literal sense of the word, will itself undertake the necessary reforms. We are frightened not only and not even mainly by the victim which might accompany this "revolutionary explosion."

[39] #118/64.
[40] #150/357–358.

We cannot contemplate without indignation and chagrin those immense sacrifices and losses of all kinds which the country must suffer for each day of conservative politics. Yes indeed, immeasurable and terrible are they, those victims not only of the day of revolutionary reckoning, but of the gray working days of the existing order. And if we believed that revolution was imminent, we would call upon it with one blow to put an end to this disgraceful political torment of a great people. But we are certain that the day of the inevitable revolution — inevitable should the government persist in its stubbornness — is not yet near at hand. At the present time, the Russian opposition lacks material means sufficient to liquidate the bureaucratic regime by itself, but it has behind it immense moral strength. The Russian autocratic government, on the other hand, with immense material means at its disposal, suffers from total moral impotence. It is incapable of moving life forward, it is devoid of all creative power. Russia is ready for a fundamental political transformation and awaits it, but the revolutionary elements in our country, fortunately or not, have not yet matured. The revolution will come when the sum total of the victims of the present order grows terribly large, when the cup overflows. The country will not be compensated for these victims by the soundness of those reforms which will come in the wake of the revolution. Such, in brief, is our view of the situation in Russia. That is why we appeal for peaceful reforms, that is why we desire concessions from the government. Drawing before it the inevitable specter of revolution, we only express our scientific conviction. Calling on the government to prevent revolution by timely and fundamental reforms, we obey the voice of our moral political conscience, which is outraged by the reigning falsehood.[41]

It is because he considered reforms both preferable to revolution in principle and more realistic under the existing conditions that he gave such weight to the alliance of all oppositional groups, and refused at first to commit *Liberation* to any positive program. There was no one "highroad" to freedom, he wrote in his early editorials, and "Slavophiles" should join hands with revolutionaries.[42]

[41] #122/102.
[42] #124/104.

But by and large, however, from the beginning he favored the left over the right. This was partly because he considered the left more militant and less likely to sell out, but also because the principal audience of *Liberation* was the inchoate "democratic" element of the Empire. The official organ of the Socialist Revolutionary party thus described this constituency:

> Represented here above all is the so-called Third Element. Here one can find that segment of the revolutionary intelligentsia which is either unable to choose between the Social Democrats and the Socialist Revolutionaries or which, because of its character or status, cannot muster enough "guts" for the life of penal servitude of the illegal revolutionary. Here are not a few skeptics, disillusioned Marxists, "half-baked" (as well as "over-baked") socialists; "fathers" irritated by the punishment meted out to their "sons" — revolutionaries — and propagandized by them; professional people, zemstvo ideologists, and the petty intelligentsia in private or public service. Here one can also encounter the commoner [*raznochinets*], the declassé, the lower civil servant, the salesman, and even the worker, peasant, petty bourgeois, and small artisan. In short, here, in this broad, unformed stream, emerges the democratic "street," many elements of which can furnish cadres for the revolutionary socialist army, do so already, and will even more in the future. Now, however, they are "neither fish nor fowl." They have broken with the "old world," but they have not yet joined the new. They are, most of them, "sympathizers." [43]

Struve was prepared to go far to wean this group from the socialists and attract them to the constitutionalist cause. Even in 1902 he went out of his way to express sympathy for the revolutionaries, especially the SR's, with whom he and his friends were on good terms. He supported SR terror as "a historically inevitable and morally justifiable" response to the terror inflicted by the bureaucracy on the country,[44] and pleaded with the liberals to show understanding for revolutionaries.[45] The incessant appeal to the left gave *Liberation* a pronouncedly radical-liberal character. It explains

[43] RR, No. 56 (December 5, 1904), 5.
[44] #113/14; #114/19; #120/82.
[45] #124.

why the Symposium in the summer of 1902 refused to associate itself with it.[46]

This "listing to portside," as Kuskova called it, became even
more pronounced in the winter of 1902–1903, when Struve decided
that further courting of the conservative zemtsy was useless.

His shift was a reaction to a successful counteroffensive launched
against the constitutionalists by Plehve, the new Minister of the Interior. Certain that the conservative majority of the zemtsy felt
uncomfortable in their role as a semilegal faction whose left wing
was in collusion with terrorists, he coldly proceeded to detach
them. The event occurred in the summer of 1902.

In March of that year, the government had announced the composition of a special conference on the needs of rural industries, to
which it invited no elected zemstvo deputies. The fact that the authorities turned to bureaucratic organs rather than to the zemstva
and that they did not think it necessary to involve elected deputies
incensed many zemtsy who felt that the procedure adopted jeop-
ardized the very survival of local self-government in Russia. To
formulate a common zemstvo response to this latest challenge,
Shipov convened toward the end of May in his Moscow apartment
another one of those semilegal zemstvo meetings held there peri-
odically over the past several years.[47] The mood of the assembled,
more than half of them members of the Symposium, was militant.
The constitutionalists, led by Petrunkevich, demanded that the
zemtsy declare a total boycott of the conference and refuse in any
manner to cooperate with it. Shipov succeeded in neutralizing this
group, but the meeting adopted a strong resolution, one article of
which (Article IV) fairly insisted that the government assure adequate representation of the zemstvo deputies in the special conference.[48] The sense of the resolution was that the government
could not properly resolve questions affecting rural industry, or,
for that matter, any others, without consulting the elected members of the organs of local government. At this time, too, a per-

[46] Chermensky, "Zemsko-liberal'noe dvizhenie," 45. Shakhovskoi, however, says
that under the influence of *Liberation*, the Symposium turned to political subjects
and even contemplated sending programmatic articles to *Liberation: Shakhovskoi*,
104.
[47] Shipov, *Vospominaniia*, 156–161.
[48] *Ibid.*, 161–168; first published in *Osv*, No. 5 (August 19/September 1, 1902),
65–66. The text of the minutes of this meeting can be found in S. Iu. Vitte,
Samoderzhavie i zemstvo, 2nd ed. (Stuttgart, 1903), lviii–lxviii.

manent bureau of zemstvo congresses was created under the chairmanship of Shipov.

Plehve, who promptly learned of these defiant proceedings, might not have attached particular significance to them were it not that they were soon followed by the first issue of *Liberation*. Apparently, its appearance was a great and disagreeable surprise to him.[49] The prospect painted by Struve of the zemstva's coordinating their activities with radical circles forced Plehve to take steps. On June 28/July 11, ten days after the publication of the first issue of *Liberation*, he invited Shipov and M. A. Stakhovich, spokesmen for the nonconstitutionalist majority of the *zemtsy*, to visit him in St. Petersburg. In his conversation with Shipov, a record of which may be found in the latter's memoirs,[50] Plehve mingled threats with assurances of friendliness and promises of cooperation. He told Shipov that he had every intention of involving him and his colleagues in administrative functions, but on condition that they abstain from any further involvement in politics; in other words, that they agree to a break with the constitutionalists. Witte, whom Shipov saw next, made essentially the same point.

As Plehve had anticipated, Shipov eagerly seized the proffered hand. In August, he convened another zemstvo meeting, which he persuaded to repeal Article IV of the May resolutions, the one that had particularly displeased Plehve. Stakhovich did not lag behind in demonstrating his loyalty. His opportunity came in November 1902, when the government barred Peter Dolgorukov from serving on the Kursk zemstvo because of his recruiting on behalf of the constitutionalist party. Some members of the Kursk zemstvo wished to lodge a formal protest against this decision, but Stakhovich dissuaded them. In an address delivered to this zemstvo at the time, Nicholas II restated Plehve's offer to Shipov: abstention from national politics as a condition for being allowed to participate in local government.[51]

Struve witnessed the capitulation of the zemstvo conservatives with astonishment and dismay. He thought that in their quarrel with the bureaucracy the zemtsy held all the trump cards: what would the government do, he asked, how would it administer the

---

[49] *Belokonsky*, 96–97, 102, Maklakov says that for the government *Liberation* was an "act of war": V. A. Maklakov, *Vlast' i obshchestvennost' na zakate staroi Rossii* (Paris, 1936), 142.

[50] Shipov, *Vospominaniia*, 171–184.

[51] *Osv*, No. 13 (December 19, 1902/January 1, 1903), 203–205; OD, I, 389.

country, should they decide all at once, in a body, to tender their resignation? [52] Confident that Plehve's transparent maneuver would fail, he urged them to fight back and openly demand the convocation of a *zemskii sobor*.[53] By December 1902, however, his editorials grew angry at the "Slavophiles": Shipov's actions in Moscow in August and Stakhovich's in Kursk in November, he wrote, were grievous blunders, which could only benefit the bureaucracy.[54]

The fruit of these disappointed expectations was an influential editorial which Struve wrote for the twelfth issue of *Liberation* (December 2/15, 1902). Here he came out for the first time publicly in favor of a formal liberal organization (but not, as yet, a party) and hinted that such an organization should adopt a constitutional platform. "Events are unfolding with a relentless logic," he said in the key passage, "the situation grows increasingly complex and at the same time increasingly acute. It demands, first and foremost, that *the liberal elements of Russian society organize themselves into some kind of solidary and purposefully acting entity (edinstvo).*"[55] Only such an entity would prevent the bureaucracy from pursuing the divisive tactics so successful against an inchoate body of individuals. Furthermore, as the example of Boris Chicherin showed, Struve continued, referring to Chicherin's recent book, even liberals of a conservative bent like him were compelled by events to recognize that there was no way of restraining the bureaucracy except by constitutional means.[56] Struve still left the door open for the Shipovs and Stakhovichs to join the organization he had in mind; but his bow in the conservative direction now was perfunctory, and his true enthusiasm was reserved for the revolutionaries. Speaking of the "objective need" for Russia's liberation, he said that it was met

by the enormous creative energy of the revolutionaries, bursting with protest and the desire for action. This energy constitutes the inner strength of Russian revolutionary parties, which no

[52] #119/67.
[53] #120/81–82; #128/149–150; and #129/176. The idea of a *zemskii sobor* (land assembly), meaning a consultative rather than a legislative body of representatives, was popular among the more conservative zemtsy.
[54] #125/115; #128/149–150; #131/203.
[55] #130/186.
[56] #130/188. The reference is to a book Chicherin published anonymously in Berlin in 1900, *Rossiia nakanune dvadtsatogo stoletiia*.

police can eliminate. The revolutionary parties unite the best, the most active, and the most self-sacrificing elements of the young generation of the incessantly growing intelligentsia. This intellectual and moral flower of the nation . . .[57]

And so on, issue after issue. How he would come to rue these words! The day was not far off when these "best elements," this "intellectual and moral flower of the nation," would turn for him into maggots. But now and for the next two years, his loathing of the autocracy blinded him to everything. He was so utterly confident of the constructive energy pent up in the Russian people and, at the same time, so impressed by the sheer physical might of the imperial regime that he dreaded no violence from below. Privately he had few good words for revolutionary methods. According to S. Frank, at this very time he spoke of the assassination of Alexander II as Russia's "greatest tragedy."[58] But publicly, in the role of a political strategist, he spared no praise for the revolutionaries and did all he could to persuade the liberals to suppress their distaste for them. He viewed each act of revolutionary violence as another turn of the screw applied to the body of the imperial regime as it lay stretched on the torture rack of history. When enough of these turns were made and the pain became unbearable, the government would yield. The glorified revolutionary methods on the pages of *Liberation,* apparently quite unmindful that, once unleashed, Bakunin's "evil passions" might not subside, even after the country had been given its freedom. He shared at this time a delusion common to many intellectuals, that violence enlisted in a "good" cause somehow differs from other kinds of violence and can be contained.

Miliukov promptly responded to Struve's editorial, and was pleased to have his rival give up the idea of a common front with

[57] #130/186. See also #131/202, where Struve describes the propaganda by "revolutionaries" as "fulfilling a great cultural mission by transforming the spontaneous and biological movements of the masses into a conscious struggle, permeated with human dignity and inspired by the idea of law." In July 1902 Struve sent Delbrück two indignant letters protesting a statement in *Preussische Jahrbücher* that the intelligentsia "barbarized Russia." He characterized this view as typical of "Baltic aristocrats" and said that the intelligentsia should not be blamed for the sins of modern Russian absolutism: Struve to Delbrück, July 15, 1902. See also his letter of July 9.

[58] *Frank,* 34.

the conservatives. He agreed that the time had come to organize, but before organizing, he cautioned, one had to have some idea with whom one joined and to what end. *Liberation* had tried to serve too broad a circle of readers, he warned. It had sought to unite instead of separating: now it had become necessary to separate before uniting.[59]

Struve concurred with an alacrity suggesting that he had independently reached a similar conclusion. He volunteered to spell out the principles called for by Miliukov on the basis of which the liberals could separate themselves into an organization, and in so doing went beyond Miliukov's program of the previous spring. He listed two principles: constitutionalism and democracy.[60] In this laconic formula Struve identified the twin pillars on which Russian liberalism as an organized movement was henceforth to rest, and, incidentally, coined the name which the liberal party was to adopt when it formed in October 1905.

Through their brief exchange on the pages of *Liberation*, Miliukov and Struve perceptibly diverted the course of Russian liberal politics. Until the winter of 1902–1903, the Russian liberals had cooperated closely with the conservatives. I have noted to what lengths the zemstvo constitutionalists went as late as 1900–1901 to maintain unity with their conservative partners in the Symposium. Now the constitutionalist-conservative coalition broke apart: the constitutionalists severed ties with their conservative friends and turned left, toward radical programs and allies. Miliukov and Struve — the leading theorists of the liberal movement — agreed that in the projected liberal organization there would be no room for Shipov and Stakhovich: they and their followers could remain friends but could no longer be members.[61] From this point onward, Russian liberalism ceased to be a movement predominantly identified with the landed gentry and transformed itself into one catering to the "democratic" intelligentsia.[62] This meant, in matters of doctrine, a readiness to accept the universal franchise and a fairly

[59] *Osv*, No. 17 (February 16/March 1, 1903), 289–291. Cf. Miliukov, *Vospominaniia*, I, 239ff.

[60] #140/291.

[61] Struve, #140/291; Miliukov ("ss"), *Osv*, No. 17 (February 16/March 1, 1903), 289–291.

[62] The leftward reorientation of the constitutional movement is stressed by Kuskova (e.g., SZ, No. 44, 1930, 366–395) and Fischer (*Russian Liberalism*, 117–155). See also OD, I, 390–391.

radical program of economic and social reform; and in political practice, an all-out effort to draw into liberal ranks the Third Element, the salaried personnel of private enterprises, journalists, and so forth.

The reorientation was to some extent a tactical maneuver consciously executed to counter Plehve's successful tactic in splitting the zemstvo movement. But for Struve, at any rate, it represented more than that. He was convinced that in modern times a liberalism that was unwilling to link itself with political and social democracy had no hope of success. Commenting on the German Reichstag elections of 1903, he pointed to the miserable showing made by the German liberals and blamed their steady decline on their short-sighted support of Bismarck's antisocialist legislation of 1878:

> The ruin of German liberalism followed quite inevitably from the fact that in the most critical moments of its existence it broke living contact with the social and political tasks of democracy . . . Liberalism which comes forth against Social Democracy denies its own principles; it assumes the point of view of class defense of political and social privilege, and thereby rejects itself.[63]

During his entire liberal period, Struve consistently advocated a program of political and social democracy, similar to the platform on which the English Liberal party was to campaign in the parliamentary elections of 1906.

V. Maklakov and, following him, other conservative historians have treated this leftward evolution of Russian liberalism as a calamity for the liberal cause as well as for the country. Maklakov blamed *Liberation* for splitting what had hitherto been a united movement and "deforming" liberalism by affiliating it with revolution.[64] It is his contention that if the liberals had remained loyal to their tradition of working for progress within the framework of law they would have succeeded in reaching an accommodation

---

[63] #150/4.

[64] Maklakov, *Vlast' i obshchestvennost'*, I, 242–245, and "Iz proshlogo," SZ, No. 48 (1932), 355. More recently, the point has been made eloquently in V. Leontovitsch's *Geschichte des Liberalismus in Russland* (Frankfurt, 1957), 285 and *passim*.

with the imperial government from which Russia would have acquired genuinely liberal institutions. But the idea of a "loyal opposition" in imperial Russia looked more feasible contemplated from the Paris of the 1930's, where Maklakov reminisced, than from the Russia of the early years of this century. A loyal opposition presupposes a loyal administration: it calls for a modicum of good will on the part of the government and some readiness to share power with society. Neither were in evidence in pre-1905 Russia. Shipov, the Russian statesman who came closest to Maklakov's ideal, learned from personal experience how impossible it was in Russia to act the role. He had tried to cooperate with Plehve: a more devoted and forthright supporter of the monarchy would have been difficult to find outside government circles. And yet as his reward he was to be barred two years later from running for the post he had so long and honorably held, that of chairman of the Moscow zemstvo board. Then even he had to admit that Plehve had deceived him.[65] As will be seen below, disenchanted, he agreed in November 1904 to participate in the zemstvo conference which, in effect, launched the 1905 Revolution. All of which suggests that the liberal-conservative program which Maklakov in retrospect wished that his friends had pursued was not feasible.

The following are excerpts from the reports on the surveillance of Struve sent by the chief of the Okhrana's Berlin agency, Arkady Mikhailovich Harting (alias Heckelman-Landesen), to the head of the Paris Okhrana Bureau, Leonid Aleksandrovich Rataev:[66]

[November 1902]

As I have had the honor to report to your Excellency in the telegram from 12/25 inst., the editorial office of the oppositional organ *Liberation* is located in Russia. Peter Struve merely prints and publishes this journal, maintaining relations with like-minded Russians. Struve carefully conceals his place of residence, paying frequent visits to Switzerland and Stuttgart

[65] Shipov, *Vospominaniia*, 197.
[66] Okhrana Archives, Hoover Institution. File numbers, in order of citation: Index XIIb, Folder 2; Index XVIIr-1, No. 92; Index XIIIa, Folder 5A, No. 101; Index XIIIa, Folder 5A, No. 144; Index XIIIa, Folder 5A, No. 174; Index XIIIa, Folder 5A, No. 186; Index XIIIc(3), Folder 14.

. . . Notwithstanding the evident hostility of revolutionary organizations active abroad, the émigrés attach major importance to this liberal group, because, as they maintain, the constitutional movement in Russia is steadily gaining ground, and gradually acquiring influence over all of educated society. The most competent [émigré] elements, viewing the newspaper *Liberation* as an undertaking that merits political attention and respect, maintain that the liberal movement in Russia has allegedly solidified and organized itself to the point at which, in time, and this in the not too distant future, it will become an inevitable factor in the downfall of autocracy.

[January 27/February 9, 1903]

In view of the extreme difficulties which our secret agents, already ten days in Stuttgart, have experienced in establishing the identity of Peter Struve, I have the honor respectfully to beg Your Excellency for at least an approximate description of his distinctive features . . . I communicate briefly the report of the secret agents: Struve lives not in Stuttgart but in the suburban village of Gaisburg, which has a population of two to three hundred inhabitants. When the agents walk the streets of the above-mentioned village, they are stared at as if they were wild animals. One of them has managed to find quarters in a side street, but observation from there is extremely difficult. The other, so far, has not yet found a place to live nearby. However, on the day of their arrival here the agents ran into Ruvim (Rubin) Streltsov, born in 1875 in Taganrog, who had left Berlin on October 10 of the previous year. Streltsov was seen here in the fall in the company of a young woman with whom he is presently living in Gaisburg. The agents have observed him several times in the course of the ten days leaving his home (he resides two steps from Struve) carrying whole packs of letters, which he dropped into the Gaisburg mail box, and packets of pamphlets, which he took to a certain house, the occupant of which has not yet been identified.

[April 13/26, 1904]

Struve spends entire days in his house in the village and rarely goes to Stuttgart to the printing press. Thus, the agents see him sporadically. Sometimes they see nothing of him for stretches of six to eight days . . . The conditions for surveillance in Stuttgart are in the highest degree unfavorable, because the persons who are of interest to us live in isolated localities [and] in houses whose windows face the street, which greatly hinders observation. The Stuttgart police is not a national but a metropolitan one, and the city administration is almost entirely in the hands of Social Democrats. It is only with the utmost difficulty that I can secure from there the least bit of information, and in view of the fairly insignificant results obtained so far by the surveillance, I request that the agents be recalled from Stuttgart. To begin with, all these people work more or less tolerably under steady supervision but without it display, unfortunately, very little presence of mind. Second, I am experiencing here a shortage of agents, because under prevailing conditions it is necessary to watch railway stations and not residences, and this I am unable to arrange without having at my disposal all the men.

[May 13/26, 1903]

On May 13/26 an unidentified person arrived in Stuttgart. He put up at the Hotel Marquardt, where he signed the register as Doljoff (probably Dolgov or Dolzhov) from Moscow.[67] He stayed at Struve's apartment until 11:00 P.M. and the next day, May 14/27, left Stuttgart at 12:48 P.M. for Frankfurt-am-Main. The agents write that he will proceed from there to Moscow, but they give no basis for this surmise. He had apparently given Struve a sizable sum of money, because after his departure Struve and his wife did a great deal of shopping in various stores, whereas previously they had been without a penny.

[June 1903]

On about June 8 (NS) Struve had a visit from an Englishman, who spent entire days with him and his wife, and in whose company he visited the printing firm which prints *Liberation* (for example, on 2/15 inst.) . . . The Englishman put up at the Stuttgart Hotel Marquardt under the name D. D. Braham from London. One of our agents succeeded in overhearing a few

[67] Peter Dolgorukov, who used "Dolgov" as his pseudonym: Petrunkevich, "Iz zapisok," 348.

phrases from Struve's conversation with this Englishman. To Struve's question: "What language did you speak with . . . ?" (the agent could not make out the name), he replied, "French." Struve: "I am surprised, for an Englishman you also speak good German." Braham: "Yes, I speak German very well, but my Russian is still poor." I presume that D. D. Braham is the well-known *Times* correspondent recently expelled from Russia.

[June 1903]

On June 8/21, at night, the writer Victor Berdiaev from Kiev arrived in Stuttgart.[68] Before his arrival he spent several days in Berlin. Berdiaev spent all day June 22 in the company of Peter Struve, slept at his house in Gaisburg, and on the 23rd dispatched his sizable baggage to Heidelberg, all the time accompanied by Struve. On the 24th he took a daytime train to Heidelberg. Struve escorted him to the railway car. They parted very amicably, exchanging numerous embraces . . . After long efforts and a certain expenditure of money it has been possible to learn that in recent times Struve has sent registered letters to the following persons or institutions [there follows a list of some forty names, many of them garbled, in Russia and Western Europe].

[Telegram from Rataev in Paris to Harting in Berlin, dated August 17, 1903]

Director orders stop special surveillance Struve. Léonide.

The Director, that is, the head of the Okhrana in St. Petersburg, ordered the suspension of surveillance because the two clods who shadowed Struve — a Russian by the name of Prodousov and a German named Shlivert (Schliewert?) — picked up bits of small talk but failed to detect preparations made under their very noses for the first national conference of constitutionalists. After the Miliukov-Struve exchange in the pages of *Liberation*, the "Russian friends," as the supporters of the journal inside Russia were known to one another, decided to convene in Western Europe in order to talk with Struve and work out the base for the liberal organization which he had proposed. The exact time and

[68] Nicholas Berdiaev, of course.

place of the meeting were left for Struve to decide. He, in turn, entrusted the arrangements to Zhukovsky, the ubiquitous éminence grise of the constitutionalist movement.[69]

Because all the invited participants, with the exception of Struve, lived in Russia and would probably incur most disagreeable consequences should the Okhrana learn of their presence at such a meeting, Zhukovsky went to great lengths to disguise the conference as an innocent tourist outing. For his base of operations he chose the Swiss frontier city of Schaffhausen, on Lake Constance, a short trip by steamer from Germany. There he booked for the participants rooms in several inconspicuous hotels ("democratic inns," as Petrunkevich calls them). They were to leave each morning in small groups for a village in the vicinity of Schaffhausen and gather for business at a designated restaurant.[70] The first day of the three-day meeting, August 1, 1903 (NS), coincided with the Swiss national holiday. The planning was so meticulous that the Okhrana apparently learned nothing of the conference at the time. Its Stuttgart agents thought that Struve had left for Russia and alerted the frontier guards.

The delegates who assembled in Schaffhausen belonged to two principal groups. Eight of them — approximately half of the delegation (its exact number cannot be established) — were zemstvo constitutionalists: V. Vernadsky, Peter Dolgorukov, D. E. Zhukovsky, S. A. Kotliarevsky, N. N. Lvov, I. I. Petrunkevich, F. I. Rodichev, and D. I. Shakhovskoi.[71] The other group consisted of professional writers and publicists. The latter were drawn mostly from the ranks of former Social Democrats, either those who had broken with Marxism on theoretical grounds (Struve, Berdiaev, Bulgakov, and Frank) or those who still thought of themselves as socialists but could find no place in a Social Democratic party dominated by Plekhanov and Lenin (Kuskova, Prokopovich, and Iakovlev-Bogucharsky). Among those present was B. Kistiakovsky.[72] The first of the two groups of onetime Social Democrats formed something like an ideological party, following Struve's

---

[69] Petrunkevich, "Iz zapisok," 337–338; *Shakhovskoi,* 102–103.

[70] Petrunkevich, "Iz zapisok," 338–339.

[71] *Ibid.,* 338; Chermensky, "Zemsko-liberal'noe dvizhenie," 51.

[72] Chermensky, "Zemsko-liberal'noe dvizhenie," 51. Petrunkevich gives a somewhat different list, omitting Bogucharsky, but adding P. Novgorodtsev, I. Grevs, and V. Vodovozov: "Iz zapisok," 338.

lead and abandoning positivism in favor of philosophic idealism. In the winter of 1902–1903 members of this group published an important symposium, *Problems of Idealism,* in which they attempted to provide a generalized metaphysical and religious foundation for liberal politics.[73] The twenty-odd participants at the Schaffhausen conference came from different political backgrounds, but it would be wrong to try to fit them into fine social rubrics.[74] All were gentry by origin and intellectuals by choice, and none spoke on behalf of any identifiable social and economic interest group. Indeed, the persistent unwillingness of such vested interest groups to involve themselves in the Russian liberal movement remained a source of its weakness.

According to Shakhovskoi, to whom we owe the fullest available history of the constitutionalist movement, the Schaffhausen conference followed a systematic agenda.[75] Of the questions raised, the most urgent was the organizational one raised by Miliukov and Struve. The issue boiled itself down to the alternative: a political party or a national front? The majority of the delegates opted for the second alternative, thereby endorsing Struve's "broad" rather than Miliukov's "narrow" platform. (Miliukov, then on a speaking tour in the United States, was absent.) The conference voted to form immediately, in every major Russian city, "Unions of Liberation," which every person who wished to end the autocratic regime would be eligible to join. These Unions were to perform two tasks: (1) mobilize all the strata of public opinion against the autocratic regime by means of demonstrations and petitions; and (2) furnish *Liberation* with data discrediting the bureaucracy.[76] It was assumed that some day the Unions of Liberation would merge into a liberal party. Until then, they were to enjoy full freedom of opinion on all issues save the cardinal one of political liberation.[77]

The conference also endorsed Struve's tactic of an alliance with the radicals. Claiming that the liberals "had no enemy on

[73] *Problemy idealizma* (St. Petersburg, 1903). I shall return to this book in the second volume of the biography.

[74] As is done, for example, by Fischer in *Russian Liberalism*, 141–142.

[75] *Shakhovskoi*, 106.

[76] V. Vodovozov, "Soiuz Osvobozhdeniia," B&E, Supplementary Vol. III, 354; Weber, "Zur Lage," 253–254.

[77] Chermensky, "Zemsko-liberal'noe dvizhenie," 51–52.

the left," Petrunkevich backed Struve when, in debating with Rodichev, he urged liberals to ignore attacks on them in the radical (presumably Social Democratic) press.[78]

In addition, other matters were taken up, including the crisis in Russo-Japanese relations, the agrarian question, and the nature of the franchise in the postautocratic, constitutional Russian state. On all domestic questions, the participants inclined toward a fairly radical line and on the agrarian issue they even spoke, although guardedly, of forcible alienation of private land.[79] But since their opinions on these matters had no binding force, they are not of great significance, and serve only to indicate the strong leftist tendency of the constitutionalist group.

In the autumn of 1903, back in Russia, the participants in the Schaffhausen meetings went to work to implement its principal resolution. Conferences of the friends of *Liberation* were held in the principal cities, as a result of which by the end of the year numerous branches of the Union were set up. On January 3–5/16–18, 1904, fifty persons, representing some twenty of these branches[80] at a gathering in St. Petersburg, organized the Union of Liberation. Some of the participants objected to naming the organization after an independent paper over whose opinions they had no control, but these objections were overruled. The conference adopted the following resolution concerning the purpose of the Union of Liberation:

The Union of Liberation assumes as its first and principal task the political liberation of Russia. The Union regards political freedom even in its most minimal dimensions as utterly incompatible with the absolutist character of the Russian monarchy, and for that reason it will struggle above all for the liquidation of autocracy and the establishment in Russia of a constitutional regime. In defining the concrete forms which the constitutional regime can assume in Russia, the Union of Liberation will exert all its efforts to see to it that the political problem is solved in the spirit of broad democracy. It recognizes

---

[78] Fischer, *Russian Liberalism,* 142, referring to Vodovozov's unpublished history.
[79] Vodovozov, "Soiuz Osvobozhdeniia," 354; *Shakhovskoi,* 106; *Belokonsky,* 172–183.
[80] They are listed in *Shakhovskoi,* 110.

above all that in essence it is indispensable to place at the foundation of political reform the principle of a universal, equal, secret, and direct vote.

While placing prime emphasis on political demands, the Union of Liberation acknowledges the necessity of defining the principles underlying its attitude toward the socioeconomic problems which life itself brings to the fore. In the realm of socioeconomic policy, the Union will be guided by the same basic principle of democratism, assigning its activity the direct aim of defending the interests of the working class.

As pertains to the national question, the Union recognizes the right to self-determination of the various nationalities living in the Russian state. In regard to Finland, the Union identifies itself with the demand for the restitution of the constitutional order prevailing there until illegally violated during the present reign.[81]

The principal practical achievement of the first founding congress of the Union was the formation of a ten-member council (Sovet) whose functions were to coordinate the activities of the local branches, to maintain contact with Struve, and to enter into agreements with other political organizations. Its composition, as nearly as it can be established (the results of the secret ballot were not announced to the participants), was as follows: I. I. Petrunkevich (chairman), Peter D. Dolgorukov, N. N. Kovalevsky, N. N. Lvov, D. I. Shakhovskoi, V. Ia. Iakovlev-Bogucharsky, E. D. Kuskova, S. N. Prokopovich, A. V. Peshekhonov, and V. M. Khizhniakov — the familiar half-and-half distribution between zemtsy and intellectuals from the professions.[82] As far as can be established, the police did not learn either of this congress or of the council which it had elected.

Thus an organization was created which had as its express purpose to lay siege to the autocracy by means of a massive and overt public campaign. A coalition of liberals and radicals, it was

[81] *Listok Osvobozhdeniia*, No. 17 (November 19/December 2, 1904), 2. Cf. *Shakhovskoi*, 109–114, on the course of the discussions.

[82] E. P. Mikheeva, "Neskol'ko dopolnenii k istorii 'Besedy,'" IsSSSR, No. 2 (1966), 243. Other sources give slightly different lists: BSE, LII (1947), 342; Chermensky, "Zemsko-liberal'noe dvizhenie," 53.

the only successful revolutionary organization in the history of imperial Russia. Before two years passed, it succeeded where all the others had failed: it forced the autocratic regime to give up its monopoly on political power.

14. LIBERALS AT THE HELM

Less than one month after the founding congress of the Union of Liberation, in February 1904, the Japanese launched a surprise attack on the Russian forces in the Far East, and Russia was at war. No episode in Struve's early life reveals better the consistent strain of nationalism in his psyche than his tortured reaction to this event. Like all the opponents of the autocratic regime, he was happy that it had stumbled into a war which it could not possibly win (of that he was certain) and which would leave it weaker and less prestigious. But unlike some other intellectuals in the camp of the opposition, he could not bring himself to profit from the government's embarrassment by inciting the population to sabotage the war effort. He worried about the long-term consequences for the country of Witte's Far Eastern policy, from which he expected nothing but disaster regardless of whether or not it attained its immediate objectives. This worry in large measure vitiated his satisfaction in the government's plight. The position he took on the war was, as a result, so ambivalent that his readers had great difficulty deciding where he stood.

Struve had all along watched Russia's penetration into the Far East with misgivings. He was convinced that even under the most favorable circumstances Russia could not establish over China and its dependencies the kind of political and economic hegemony which Witte desired. Any commercial markets that Russia succeeded in opening up in the Far East would benefit not its own underdeveloped and overpriced industries, he felt, but the advanced economies of England, Japan, and the United States. The potential benefits to Russia of Witte's *Drang nach Osten*, therefore, were nil, its only possible beneficiary being Russia's competitors, whereas its potential dangers were great and real, for in its eastward expansion Russia encroached on the sphere of influence of the other great powers. Half a year before the Japanese attack on Port Arthur, he wrote:

The East Asian policy of the St. Petersburg government represents a squandering of national resources on a monstrous scale. It does not promise and cannot promise in the foreseeable future any advantages, moral or material. This entire policy is sufficiently characterized by the fact that Russia's political conquests are the result not of its economic strength but of its economic weakness in the Far East. This weakness will prevent Russia from effectively exploiting its conquests. Siberia has been placed under the sovereignty of the Russian nation as a result of spontaneous incursions and the steady pressure of colonization. Manchuria has been seized by generals and diplomats, with the aid of vast subsidies from the state treasury, subsidies which will soon attain the sum of one billion rubles. While hundreds of millions of rubles have been squandered on Manchuria, the peasant in the heartland of Russia has been sinking into poverty, and the government has been left without money for reforms other than the introduction of the state sale of alcoholic beverages, the strengthening of the police, and the extension of aid to the gentry. Is this not the case, gentlemen patriots with sonorous-sounding voices and light-weight thoughts? Why is Russia protecting Turkey, a country incapable of political development, and convulsively holding on to Manchuria, which is good for nothing? Why does it conduct an inglorious and senseless foreign policy that weakens the bonds of friendship with France and risks conflict with Japan, England, and America? [1]

· Struve's steadfast opposition to expansion in East Asia was inspired not so much by hostility to imperialism as such as by his conviction that the legitimate objects of Russian imperial ambition lay in the Near East. In his early economic writings, in the course of debates with the opponents of Russia's industrialization, he had already hinted that the markets for the products of this industry would be found in this region. In 1904, while condemning

[1] #161/34; also #179/222–223 and #194/3. The leadership of the Union of the Liberation shared Struve's opposition to Russia's expansion in East Asia: *Shakhovskoi*, 114.

Russian military activity in the Far East, he wrote in *Liberation* of the expulsion of the Turks from Europe as a "great cultural task." [2]

After the war with Japan broke out, he noted in an excited editorial called "War Jubilee and the Jubilee War," that it occurred exactly fifty years, almost to the day, after the outbreak of the Crimean War. The coincidence of dates carried a deep meaning for him, because he believed that Russia found itself at this time in a situation closely resembling the one in which it had been in the middle of the nineteenth century. The "Jubilee War," he predicted, would end like the Crimean: with the government's capitulation, first to the enemy on the field of battle, and then, at home, to Russian society. [3]

As principal spokesman for the liberal cause, Struve immediately confronted the problem of formulating a policy on the war. Proceeding on the assumption that Russia's defeat was unavoidable, he thought that the liberals would be wise to draw a clear line separating the government which had provoked the war from the military which had to fight it. Once the army had suffered defeat, he believed, it should prove possible to direct the brunt of its frustration against the imperial government and in this manner to gain the support of the military for the cause of political liberty. His policy was publicly to support the army while inwardly anticipating and welcoming its defeat. In his earliest pronouncement on the war, Struve referred to the soldiers leaving for the front as "heroes." [4] He spoke even more explicitly in favor of the army in the first issue of *Flysheet of Liberation* (*Listok Osvobozhdeniia*), a supplement to *Liberation* which he founded in response to the war, whose function it was to print accurate reports on the progress of military operations and on foreign opinion. In a famous "Letter to Students" published there, he advised young Russians to flock to patriotic meetings sponsored by the authorities and to join in the shouts "Long live the army!" but in the same breath to cry out: "Long live Russia!" "Long live freedom!" "Long live free Russia!" and "Down with Plehve!" [5] In editorials sub-

---

[2] #200/301. Compare his statement of June 1905: "In both economic and cultural respects, Russia confronts the Black Sea and Asia Minor" (#281/354).

[3] #200; also #198.

[4] #198.

[5] #202/2–3; cf. #283, where he appeals directly to the army.

sequently published in *Liberation* and its supplements, he asserted time and again the necessity of linking the patriotic movement which the war had engendered with the struggle for national liberty. As he saw it, the war had given the liberals a precious opportunity to penetrate groups of society — the armed forces and the ordinary, nationalistically inclined citizenry — which so far had eluded them. The task was to convince these groups of the unpatriotic and unnational character of the bureaucratic-police state. To benefit from this opportunity the liberals could not simply assume a defeatist stance and cheer every debacle of Russian arms.

Struve adopted this position as the editorial policy of his paper without consulting his colleagues in the Union of Liberation; and he persisted in it even after it had become apparent that most of them did not approve of it. By virtue of the arrangement which he had with the Union, he was certainly entitled to have his way on the editorial page. But his haste in defining policy on a matter of such importance without prior consultation angered the liberals at home and lowered his standing among them.[6]

The political strategy which Struve had worked out in response to the war promptly elicited attacks from both the nationalists of the right and the liberals of the left. The war had split Russian opinion. Conservatives, including a large proportion of conservatively inclined liberals, backed the government, although with varying degrees of conviction. The zemtsy decided for the duration of the war to observe a cease fire in their skirmishing with the bureaucracy. A resolution to this effect was adopted by the Symposium on February 14/26, 1904.[7] Some prominent veterans of the liberal movement, among them K. K. Arseniev, the idol of Struve's youth, even joined one of the delegations which called on Nicholas II to express its patriotic sentiments.[8] Struve found such behavior disgusting. He was appalled at how easily people allowed themselves to be hoodwinked by the bureaucracy. Those who declared a truce against the government for the duration of the war were, in his opinion, exceedingly short-sighted: objectively, he wrote, Plehve presented a greater danger to Russia than did the Japanese.[9] The government should not be granted reprieve from the

[6] *Shakhovskoi,* 118.
[7] E. D. Chermensky, "Zemsko-liberal'noe dvizhenie," IsSSSR, No. 5 (1965), 54.
[8] #203.
[9] *Ibid.*

mounting pressure for political liberty just because it had goaded Japan into launching an attack. Sentiments of this kind, expressed with Struve's customary incisiveness, caused publicists of the extreme right to accuse him of unpatriotic behavior and even to hint at treason.[10]

The Union of Liberation, especially its powerful left wing, was not pleased with his position either, on the grounds that it was *too* nationalistic. Copies of the first issue of the *Flysheet of Liberation,* with Struve's appeal to students, caused an uproar when they reached Russia. One of the members of the St. Petersburg Union — Struve believed it was Kuskova — even put out a mimeographed leaflet to protest his stand on the war and to disassociate the St. Petersburg Union from it.[11] In some localities shipments of the *Flysheet* were destroyed in bulk by infuriated Union members.[12] Miliukov, who was steadily gaining status as the spokesman of the liberal "regulars" and liked to miss no opportunity to embarrass his chief rival, took Struve to task in a letter to the editor of *Liberation.* The masses of the population in Russia, he wrote, were indifferent to the war; it was simply not possible for the students to join in patriotic demonstrations. "As long as the Russian army remains a brutal symbol of Russian boorishness . . . we shall not shout 'Long live the Russian army!' " Patriotic feelings, Miliukov counseled, should be held in reserve to be lavished on the free Russia of the future.[13]

But Struve refused to yield. To those of the right who accused him of lacking in patriotism, he replied that in this particular instance Russia's patriotic interests required the country's defeat:

> The point of view of true national interest and statesmanship does not permit one to treat war as some sort of condition which allegedly cannot be terminated save by a victory. War is a political act, and, as such, it must be appraised from the point of view of the wisdom and expediency of that policy of which it is one of the links. One must not say: the war has

[10] Struve cites some of these right-wing attacks on him in #210.

[11] *Rossiia,* No. 18 (December 24, 1907).

[12] *Frank,* 41–42.

[13] *Osv,* No. 19/43 (March 7/20, 1904), 330. In his memoirs, however, Miliukov concedes that the war with Japan did provoke a surge of nationalism in Russia: P. N. Miliukov, *Vospominaniia, 1859–1917,* I (New York, 1955), 239.

to be waged to its end regardless of whether it makes any sense to wage it at all. Such an attitude is especially inappropriate in this case, when it is more than unclear to what end — victory or utter exhaustion — the war will have to be waged . . . Every lucid, sober, and dispassionate mind realizes with striking clarity what may be called the *paradox of the Russo-Japanese War*. This paradox lies in the complete objective coincidence between the immediate political aims of hostile Japan and the national-political interests of the Russian people in the Far East. *Japan endeavors to eject Russia from Manchuria; the Russian people have an interest in leaving that region with the smallest possible losses.*" [14]

It was not true that Russia would suffer fatally from the loss of Far Eastern possessions. There is much historical evidence, Struve contended, to indicate that teritorial losses of the greatest magnitude could be a prelude to a national surge: as examples he cited France's loss of Canada and Britain's loss of the North American colonies.[15]

To those of the left who accused him of being too nationalistic, he retorted that they misread the mood of the country. Reports of correspondents scattered throughout Russia indicated that the population did care about the war and that some groups were seized by a patriotic frenzy.[16] The country's reaction to the war came as a surprise to him, because before the outbreak of hostilities he had expected it not to support the government.[17] But once he realized he had been wrong, he concluded that the liberals had no choice but to identify themselves with the nationalist sentiment and use it for their own ends.[18]

To the historian, his position appears perhaps not very realistic but certainly not inconsistent. Nonetheless, among Struve's contemporaries it caused a confusion which persisted long after the events. Some were convinced that in 1904–1905 Struve had supported the war;[19] others were equally certain that he had hoped

[14] #231/65.
[15] #209/385.
[16] #204/319.
[17] #179/223.
[18] #207/331–332.
[19] V. A. Maklakov, *Vlast' i obshchestvennost' na zakate staroi Rossii*, I (Paris, 1936), 238; *Shakhovskoi*, 118.

for defeat.[20] Struve himself, after the 1917 Revolution, sided with those who depicted him as a supporter of the war,[21] but his writings of the time contradict him. In 1904–1905 he had repeatedly blamed Russia for the war, had prophesied its defeat, and argued that, for all the hardships that defeat would bring, in the long run it would benefit Russia. His appeal for support of the armed forces, which had earned him the reputation of a hawk in some circles, was a tactical move designed to gain mass support for the liberals. And yet it must be conceded that Struve's defeatism had an ambivalence about it that gave it a very different quality from that of the radicals. He never lost sight of the interests of the Russian nation and the Russian state, even while plotting the downfall of the Russian government. His defeatism was qualified, tactical, cerebral, and therefore not entirely convincing.

One month after the outbreak of the war, the Okhrana ordered a resumption of the regular surveillance of Struve.[22] This time the watch proved somewhat more rewarding because Harting's Stuttgart agents had succeeded sometime before in gaining access to Struve's incoming correspondence. With the connivance of German postal authorities, the agents perlustrated all letters addressed to him, copied or summarized them, and forwarded the information to St. Petersburg.[23] However, Struve and his correspondents wrote so guardedly that little was learned from the intercepted mail. The Okhrana had no more success in planting an agent provocateur among the leadership of the Union of Liberation, which consisted of prominent public figures of the utmost probity. The impractical scholar and his aristocratic and literary friends actually succeeded better than fulltime professional revolutionaries in concealing from the imperial police their seditious activities.

The outbreak of the Russo-Japanese War disrupted the ambitious plans for a national campaign of agitation which the

---

[20] For example, A. F. Kerensky, cited by Struve in *Rossiia*, No. 18 (December 24, 1927); *Frank*, 37.

[21] *Rossiia*, No. 18 (December 24, 1927).

[22] Okhrana Archives, Hoover Institution, Stanford, California, Index XIIIa, Folder 7, Document 93, dated March 1904.

[23] The Okhrana's German branch began the perlustration of Struve's incoming mail in Stuttgart in August 1903: Okhrana Archives, Index XIIIa, Folder B, document dated August 26/September 8, 1903.

Union of Liberation had laid at its founding congress a month before. With Russian soldiers and sailors dying on the Far Eastern front, it had become quite impossible to incite the population against the government, especially because the majority of the zemtsy wished to undertake nothing that might jeopardize the war effort. Police repression, intensified during the war, caused further difficulties. Several members of the Union's national council were arrested and exiled, although not for their connections with the council, of whose existence the Okhrana was apparently still unaware. The council replaced its lost members by coopting new ones, and continued to meet once a month, alternating between Moscow and St. Petersburg.[24]

At this time, the central apparatus of the Union, its nerve center and its brain, was in Moscow. Here, in the city and in the neighboring countryside, lived the country's most prestigious constitutionalists, including four of the five zemtsy elected to the original council. The Moscow Union had many branches, which convened as autonomous caucuses to discuss political programs and to plan political action. Each such branch was designated by a letter of the alphabet. Eventually, there were so many branches that the Union ran out of letters to assign — a fact which gives some idea of the scope of its organization. The most prestigious was the oldest branch, Group A, which disposed of a sizable budget and engaged the services of a fulltime, paid secretary. Group A occupied itself with questions of broad political strategy, and among its many contributions to the liberal cause was drafting the major part of the constitutional project which the Union adopted in 1905.[25] It also formed and directed several sections with more specialized functions. Of these, the key one was the Technical Section, which assumed responsibility for receiving and distributing *Liberation* literature, maintaining links with other branches of the Union, and organizing political banquets. Other sections occupied themselves with agitation among women and peasants. There was also a Historians' Section, whose membership included M. Pokrovsky, subsequently the marshal of Soviet historical scholarship.[26]

[24] *Shakhovskoi*, 122.
[25] *Ibid.*
[26] My information on Group A derives largely from G. I. Shreider, a Socialist Revolutionary whom N. N. Lvov and D. I. Shakhovskoi engaged in the autumn of 1903 as secretary of the Moscow Union of Liberation. The late Boris I. Nikolaevsky

If the Moscow organizations of the Union of Liberation were dominated by zemtsy and people with a straightforward liberal-constitutionalist orientation, the St. Petersburg organizations were in the hands of politicians who were radicals first and liberals second. Among them, many were defectors from Social Democracy and some were active Socialist Revolutionaries. Leadership of this group was exercised by the four *intelligenty* on the Union's council, among whom the indefatigable Kuskova was the outstanding figure.[27] The St. Petersburg *osvobozhdentsy*, by political background and general predilection alike, preferred to concentrate their propaganda and agitation on the industrial proletariat. They established good relations with organized labor in the city, which later on were to pay handsome dividends.

In the provincial towns, the condition of the Union seems to have been less brilliant. Kuskova, who made a tour of Kursk, Orel, Saratov, and Kharkov on behalf of the Union in the spring of 1904, found its branches torn by feuds and in a general state of disarray. The cause of the trouble, in her opinion, lay not so much in ideological disagreements as in the basic social differences dividing the membership of the Union. The provincial Unions of Liberation, she noted, tended everywhere to structure themselves on the pattern of a two-tiered arrangement, with an "upper house" composed of zemtsy and people with professional status and a "lower house" consisting of hired zemstvo personnel and other representatives of the "democratic intelligentsia." Whatever the political link binding them, socially the two groups had very little in common. Their innate mistrust of each other expressed itself in constant bickering, which precluded effective political action. In some localities members of the Union from the Third Element crashed banquets organized by the zemtsy for themselves and their kind, bringing along with them gangs of manual workers.[28] A member of the Saratov Union independently confirmed Ku-

---

interviewed Shreider in Brussels in 1928, and kindly lent me his notes of the interview.

[27] Shreider lists eight members of the St. Petersburg Union: N. F. Annensky, A. V. Peshekhonov, Ia. Ia. Gurevich, S. N. Prokopovich, E. D. Kuskova, V. V. Khizhniakov, V. Ia. Iakovlev-Bogucharsky, and N. P. Asheshev. Miliukov (*Vospominaniia*, I, 266) speaks of a "Large St. Petersburg Group" of twelve to fourteen members, of whom he names Iakovlev-Bogucharsky, Khizhniakov, Kuskova, N. D. Sokolov, Miklashevsky, and Kuprianova.

[28] E. D. Kuskova, "Kren nalevo: Iz proshlogo," SZ, No. 44 (1939), 389–390.

skova's depressing account.[29] By and large, the Union appears to have succeeded only in those provinces which had zemstva; elsewhere, it had difficulty gaining a foothold.[30]

All the sources agree that the Union did not give its members enough to do and that, during the initial six months of its existence (the first half of 1904), the activity of its rank and file confined itself largely to the distribution of the literature which Struve published in Stuttgart. Correct as this estimate undoubtedly is, it does not convey adequately the political potential of the Union. The Union had not been intended as a political party, and hence winning followers, creating an internal party structure, and engaging in overt political action were nowhere as important for it as they were for the Social Democrats or the Socialist Revolutionaries. The Union was a political pressure group; its purpose was by incitement to exert on the government unbearable pressure for a constitution. To fulfill this task, it needed little formal organization or overt activity. Indeed, the very looseness of its organization and the lack of a specific program proved a great boon by making the Union fairly impervious to police harassment. As soon as the political climate for constitutional agitation became more favorable, that is, after Plehve was assassinated (July 1904), the Union amply demonstrated its vitality and effectiveness.

The main business of the Union, as stated, was to incite minds against the autocracy. The principal vehicle of this incitement was *Liberation* and the other literary productions which Struve wrote and edited.

Liberation appeared fortnightly in two editions. One, printed on ordinary paper, was for distribution outside the Russian Empire through subscriptions and bookstore sales. The other, on India paper, was for smuggling into Russia. To protect recipients from police harassment, the India paper edition carried in the left upper corner the printed statement: "We found your address in a directory, and take the liberty of sending you our publication." Our only information on the number of copies printed comes from

[29] D. Protopopov, "Iz nedavnego proshlogo," RM, No. 11 (1907), Pt. 2, 16–38. See also OD, I, 391–392.
[30] *Belokonsky*, 192.

Max Weber, who in turn obtained it from Bohdan Kistiakovsky. Weber speaks of a total printing of 12,000 copies, of which 4,000 were on ordinary paper and 8,000 on India paper; but after the latter figure he places a question mark.[31] This figure is only slightly below that of the known printing of *Iskra* (13,000–15,000).[32] In addition to *Liberation*, Struve brought out several related publications. Mention has been made of the *Flysheet of Liberation*, twenty-six numbers of which came out. As a vehicle for longer theoretical writings, Struve published an annual, also called *Liberation*, which appeared twice (1903 and 1904).[33] Major collections of documentary materials on such subjects as labor legislation in Russia, anti-Jewish pogroms, important zemstvo congresses, and constitutional projects were published in a series of occasional pamphlets.[34] Finally, Struve sponsored several monographs relating to the history of the struggle against the autocracy, including a collection of the political writings of Dragomanov, a history of public opinion under Alexander II by A. A. Kornilov, and the first complete edition of the memoirs of the revolutionary V. Debogory-Mokrievich.[35] As can be seen, Struve ran not just a fortnightly periodical, but a major publishing enterprise, modeled on and comparable to Herzen's Free Russian Press.

The principal audience for this voluminous literary output was in Russia, behind a tight cordon of frontier customs. To get it past the regiments of frontier guards, postal inspectors, and police agents assigned the job of ferreting out seditious literature, Struve had to devise an elaborate smuggling machinery. Its management was in the hands of Nina. (Krupskaia performed a similar service for Lenin.)

According to Shakhovskoi, the bulk of the materials published by Struve was caried into Russia by individual citizens unconnected with *Liberation*, on their person or in their luggage upon their return to Russia from foreign countries.[36] Since in a typical

[31] Max Weber, "Zur Lage der bürgerlichen Demokratie in Russland," ASS, XXII (1906), 237.

[32] OD, I, 403.

[33] *Osvobozhdenie: Kniga Pervaia* (Stuttgart, 1903), see #186; and *Osvobozhdenie: Knika Vtoraia* (Paris, 1904), see #254.

[34] A list of these pamphlets is given in Fischer, *Russian Liberalism*, 218–219.

[35] M. P. Dragomanov, *Sobranie politicheskikh sochinenii i statei*, 2 vols. (Paris, 1905–1906); [A. A. Kornilov], *Obshchestvennoe dvizhenie pri Aleksandre II (1855–1881)* (Paris, 1905); *Vospominaniia Vl. Debogory-Mokrievicha* (Stuttgart, 1903). Struve reviewed the last in #189.

[36] *Shakhovskoi,* 123.

turn of the century year some 200,000 Russian citizens traveled abroad for an average stay of eighty days,[37] it is not surprising that so much literature could come in by this means. From Struve's point of view, this particular method of distribution was the most convenient because it paid for itself and presented no danger to the organization. But it was not a dependable way, permitting a systematic saturation of the Russian reading public, and for that reason other means had to be devised as well.

One of them was the regular mail. To escape detection by Russian postal authorities, copies of *Liberation* sent by post were elaborately disguised. Nina engaged the services of numerous friends, supporters, and even hired help to stuff copies of the paper into envelopes bearing false letterheads, address them to individuals in Russia in various handwriting styles, and drop them one by one or in small batches into mail boxes. Much of the material sent by post was disguised as business catalogues. Because it would have been an easy matter for the Russian postal authorities to intercept this mail if all of it bore the Stuttgart postmark, Nina sent batches of *Liberation* for posting to accomplices scattered throughout European countries, including Germany, Italy, Switzerland, Austria, and England. The archive of Arvid Neovius, *Liberation*'s Finnish correspondent residing in Stockholm (he wrote under the initial "F"), has a number of letters from Nina instructing him to forward or arrange for the forwarding from Sweden to Russia of the enclosed materials.[38]

Finally, much material, often mixed with Social Democratic literature, was transported by a complicated contraband operation in which Memel in East Prussia and the Helsinki-Viborg railroad line in Finland were the focal points.

The existence of a center for smuggling socialist and liberal materials from East Prussia into Russia was discovered by the Prussian authorities in the fall of 1903 through a tip from the Russian police. Several German Social Democrats were arrested, including one Treptow, among whose effects was found a letter from Nina Struve. The police in Königsberg passed this information on to the government of Würtenberg, on whose territory Stuttgart lay, and requested a search of the Struve household.

[37] B. Ischchanian, *Die ausländischen Elemente in der russichen Volkswirtschaft* (Berlin, 1913), 5n.
[38] Archive of A. Neovius, Finnish State Archive, Helsinki.

This was carried out on December 9, 1903, in a surprise raid, which yielded a vast quantity of printed material in Russian, envelopes and postage stamps of various European countries, and lists of addresses in Russia and abroad.[39] The raid on the Struves caused a minor public scandal in Germany. German liberals and Social Democrats had for some time voiced disapproval of the connivance of the German and Russian police and of the liberties which their government allowed the Okhrana on German territory. The East Prussian arrests of German citizens and the related search of Struve was grist for their mills and was used to embarrass the government. Hans Delbrück referred to it in an article on Russian police activities in Germany in the influential monthly *Prussian Yearbooks*,[40] and August Bebel threatened to speak on the matter in the Reichstag. (Struve was on friendly terms with both men.) The Foreign Office in Berlin reprimanded the Würtenberg authorities for having carried out such a sensitive mission without prior consultation. Würtenberg replied that it understood Struve was a dangerous anarchist; it promised, however, not to molest him further after being assured that he was no anarchist but a "thoroughly respectable man" (*ein durchaus achtbarer Mann*).[41] The Stuttgart police apparently caused all this trouble and political embarrassment to no purpose. According to Nina's letter to Neovius, written shortly after the raid, the whole affair ended "satisfactorily," which can only mean that the police found no incriminating evidence.[42]

The Finnish route seems to have been the single most important means of bulk smuggling to Russia.[43] After February 1899, when

[39] Staatsarchiv Ludwigsburg, Germany: Bestand E 150, Bund 1608, document dated December 15, 1903, signed "Nickel." The trial of the German Social Democrats arrested in East Prussia in 1903 is reported in *Osv*, No. 54 (August 19/September 1, 1904), 70–78.

[40] "Politische Korrespondenz: Russische Polizei in Deutschland," *Preussische Jahrbücher*, No. 2 (February 1904), 394.

[41] Staatsarchiv Ludwigsburg, documents from Berlin dated January 5, 1904, signed "Varnbüler"; February 2, 1904, signed "v. Soden"; and February 3, 1904, signed "Nickel."

[42] Nina Struve to Neovius, December 18, 1903; Neovius Archive, Finnish State Archive, Helsinki. This is confirmed by Okhrana records: Harting to Lopukhin, coded telegram, December 8/21, 1903; Okhrana Archives, Hoover Institution, Index XIIIa, Folder B.

[43] I owe my knowledge of the Finnish route of literary contraband mostly to the generosity of Mr. William Copeland of Kuopio, Finland, who specializes in the history of relations between Russian liberals and Finnish nationalists during this

the Russian government unilaterally curtailed the power of the Finnish parliament, the Finnish nationalists organized a contraband operation to bring into the country anti-Russian literature printed abroad. Both *Iskra* and *Revolutionary Russia* utilized this apparatus, paying the Finnish nationalists on the average between one and one and a half Finnish marks for each kilogram of materials delivered to Finland. Struve made a similar arrangement with the Finns, probably in August 1902 when he met with Neovius in Stuttgart.[44]

The kingpin of the Finnish contraband operation was Koni Zilliacus, the most energetic and least scrupulous of the Finnish nationalist politicians, then residing in Stockholm. The Struves sent shipments of their literature to various cover addresses in Sweden. Zilliacus retrieved these materials, had them repacked, and forwarded them to Finland either disguised as commercial freight or concealed in false-bottomed trunks. Crossing the Swedish-Finnish frontier was a relatively easy matter because the customs there were in the hands of Finns, many of them sympathetic to the nationalist cause. The couriers deposited the consignments at designated points in Helsinki or along the Helsinki–St. Petersburg railroad. Here Struve's and Zilliacus's responsibility came to an end: the transport of the materials across the Finnish-Russian frontier was the job of the Union of Liberation. The scope of the smuggling operation engaged in by the Finns may be gauged by the fact that in a single year (1902) they are estimated to have illegally transported into Finland ten tons of seditious literature of all kinds. For publications which were very topical and required rapid delivery, the Finns provided also an express service employing professional smugglers. This service cost up to five times the fee charged for the regular transport. Presumably, the *Flysheet of Liberation* was shipped in this manner.

Because Russians crossing into Finland required no international passports, there was a great deal of movement across the frontier at all times, especially during the summer season when

---

period. On the Social Democratic use of the Finnish apparatus, see V. M. Smirnov [A. Paulson], "Revoliutsionnaia rabota v Finlandii, 1900–1907 gg.," PR, No. 1/48 (1926), 119–157.

[44] Struve to Neovius, August 23 [1902], Neovius Archive.

vacationers went to their dachas on the Finnish lakes. It was, therefore, a relatively easy matter for the Union to arrange for the smuggling of literature by this route. How this was accomplished can be learned from the facts uncovered when the police succeeded in intercepting couriers. The most famous case of this kind occurred in November 1903: the arrest on the Finno-Russian frontier of Ariadna Borman (Tyrkova) and E. V. Anichkov. From evidence introduced at the trial and from Tyrkova's memoirs we learn how their mission had been organized. Tyrkova was approached by Kuskova and asked to go to Finland to bring across the frontier a shipment of *Liberation*. Although she was not connected with the Union and had only a vague idea of its existence, Tyrkova consented without a moment's hesitation — such was the spirit of the times. For company, she took along a friend, a young philologist named Anichkov. Following Kuskova's instructions, the two rented separate rooms in Helsinki's best hotel. There they were visited by unknown Finns carrying long bags stuffed with *Liberation* and other publications of Struve's, which they were instructed to sew inside their clothing. They did as they were told, but Anichkov for good measure stuffed a few copies of *Liberation* into the pocket of his overcoat. During the crossing of the frontier, a Russian customs official ran his hands along this overcoat, which Anichkov had suspended from a rack, and discovered the newspapers. This was bad enough; but Anichkov made matters worse yet by calling out to Tyrkova, who was innocently sitting in the adjoining compartment: "Ils ont trouvé!" The two were arrested and searched. The inspection uncovered on Anichkov 106 copies of *Liberation*, and on Tyrkova no fewer than 227, as well as several pamphlets. Their trial took place behind closed doors, but its record became available to Struve and was published in *Liberation*. Had smuggling of *Liberation* been their only offence, the two smugglers would have gotten away with light sentences. But following their arrest, the police searched their apartments, which yielded a great deal of seditious literature, including a handwritten manifesto praising Struve. Tyrkova and Anichkov received sentences of two and a half years in prison, subsequently lowered by the tsar to one year. Tyrkova requested and was granted bail on medical grounds, and was subsequently spirited out of the country by the Union of Liberation to join Struve's staff.[45] Poor Anichkov, however, had to serve out his full term. Among others arrested for smuggling *Liberation* from Finland was D. E. Zhukovsky. He was released after three days' detention.[46] Despite such occasional failures, the literary contraband traffic across the Finnish frontier flowed steadily and without serious interruptions.

By these elaborate, devious, and costly means, the Union succeeded in bringing into Russia a large quantity of illegal literature. The usual lapse between publication in Stuttgart and distribution in Russia was three to four weeks.[47] As far as the extent of distribution is concerned, the absence of detailed studies does not permit precise estimates, but it must have been considerable. The correspondence columns in *Liberation* indicate that the paper penetrated the most remote provinces, that it was avidly read and earnestly discussed, and that its opinions were taken seriously. Vodovozov says that *Liberation* "belonged to the most widely distributed and most influential illegal Russian periodical publications, competing, in this regard, with Herzen's *Bell*";[48] and because he was both a prominent member of the Union and its historian, his opinion on this matter carries weight.

With time, *Liberation* also became a prime source of information on events and conditions in Russia for the foreign press. When in early 1903 the Russian government expelled the correspondent of the *Times*, D. D. Braham, for his honest reporting on the Kishinev pogrom, the *Times* did not bother to replace him. Instead, it assigned a special Russian correspondent, Harold Williams, to Struve in Stuttgart. Williams's reporting clearly bore the stamp of Struve's information and opinions.[49] Max Weber's

[45] Tyrkova's and Anichkov's arrest and trial are described in A. Tyrkova-Viliams, *Na putiakh k svobode* (New York, 1952), 131–169, and *Osv*, No. 24/48 (May 21/June 3, 1904), 426–431. See also *Belokonsky*, 171n–172n, and *Shakhovskoi*, 125–127.

[46] *Belokonsky*, 172n; Tyrkova-Viliams, *Na putiakh*, 172; *Shakhovskoi*, 124.

[47] *Shakhovskoi*, 125.

[48] V. Vodovozov, "Osvobozhdenie," B&E, Supplementary Vol. III, 353. Cf. *Shakhovskoi*, 102–103. Tyrkova-Viliams, *Na putiakh*, 199, also draws a comparison with Herzen's *Bell*.

[49] Tyrkova-Viliams, *Na putiakh*, 185. She wrote a biography of Williams, whom she married, titled *The Cheerful Giver* (London, 1935). Struve says that after Braham's expulsion from Russia he, Struve, was offered his job as *Times* correspondent there. He could not accept the offer for obvious reasons, and proposed instead to supply the *Times* with information. In response to this offer, the *Times* assigned Williams to him as a special correspondent. RiS, No. 1 (December 1, 1928).

two well-known essays on Russia also reveal the influence of the
Union of Liberation and its publications.[50]

Just as Struve had always annoyed his socialist friends by
insisting on personal and intellectual liberty, so he now annoyed
his new liberal friends with his stress on national priorities. One
example of such behavior was his attitude toward the Russo-
Japanese War. Another was his reaction to the Kishinev pogrom,
which alienated not a few Jewish intellectuals.

Like any civilized person, Struve did not judge people by their
national or religious allegiance, and had a natural immunity to
any kind of prejudice. None of his writings reveal the slightest
trace of anti-Semitism. But in dealing with the so-called Jewish
problem ("so-called" because insofar as it is a problem at all
it is not one for Jews but for the others), he was always first and
foremost a Russian nationalist. His great mission in life was to
assure the political emancipation and cultural flowering of the
Russian people. For the strivings of the individual national minorities inhabiting the Empire he never evinced the slightest understanding. He was willing to concede autonomy and possibly even
independence to Finland and Poland. But for the Ukrainians,
Muslims, Georgians, and the many other national minorities inhabiting the Russian Empire who, through their intelligentsia,
claimed their national rights, he had no patience. To him, they
were Russians all and, as such, certain to attain satisfaction of all
their needs the instant Russia became a free country. In that
free country, Russians would be the dominant nationality. The
Jews too were Russians. Their duty was to help liberate Russia
from the yoke of absolutism; anything that distracted them from
this overriding task was despicable.

Struve was sickened by the Kishinev pogrom, seeing in it yet
another futile effort by Plehve to divert the country's political
and social discontent into channels less dangerous for the regime.
Liberation and its publications reported fully on the massacre; it
is from this source that the Russian public first learned what had
happened behind the closed doors of the court where the trial

---

[50] Weber, "Zur Lage," and "Russlands Uebergang zum Scheinkonstitutionalis-
mus," ASS, XXIII (1906).

of those implicated was held.[51] For Jews as a people he had warm
sympathy:

> [The autocratic system] has produced a cruel and senseless
> body of legislation on Jews which transforms them into some-
> thing resembling animals, herded into a confined space and
> there hunted down. Whoever you may be — friends or enemies
> of Jews — put your hand on your heart and say: can one con-
> sider as human beings rather than as animals people who can-
> not move freely even within the limits of their designated "pale
> settlement," people among whom father and mother cannot
> follow son or daughter, and so on, if they have differing
> "residence rights"? . . . Jews are in a worse position than
> animals.[52]

For Jews as Russian citizens he had less admiration. He took advantage of the opportunity provided by the Kishinev pogrom to
preach them a little sermon:

> One can only marvel at the humility with which the Jewish
> inhabitants of Russia still suffer their lawless situation and the
> destitution that ensues from it! Jews, whatever their profession
> or class status, should first of all renounce this slave-like humility
> and initiate an energetic struggle for law. From this point of
> view, the Zionist movement represents a dual, innerly self-
> contradictory phenomenon. On the one hand, it signifies the
> gathering, development, and strengthening of the cultural forces
> of Judaism, and as such deserves full sympathy. On the other,
> by nurturing the idea of a Jewish nationality and even of state-
> hood, and thereby thoughtlessly extending a hand to vile anti-
> Semitism, Zionism in every possible way sidesteps the political
> struggle, the struggle for Jewish emancipation. And yet, the
> solution of the Jewish problem can only be found in full
> emancipation. Jewish nationalism, as embodied in Zionism, re-

---

[51] The materials on the Kishinev pogrom were published seriatim in *Liberation*,
beginning with No. 12/36 (November 24/December 7, 1903). Additional materials
were made public in the pamphlet *Kishinevskii pogrom* (Stuttgart, 1903), released
by *Liberation*. See Struve's Introduction to this pamphlet: #193. Also, *Shakhovskoi*,
100.
[52] #151/377.

fuses to pose in a straightforward manner this plain task, the solution of which will cut the ground from under both crude Judophobia and Jewish nationalism. Herein lies Zionism's great sin before Jewry and before Russian society . . . [The term] Judaism applies to a race: the Jews constitute a separate religious community, but the idea of a Jewish nationality is a fantastic and sick product of the abnormal legal conditions of the multi-million *Jewish population of Russia*. Let the Jews, if they wish and are able to, establish a separate Jewish state in Palestine: we shall neither hinder them nor help. But within the confines of the Russian state they should — in the common interest of Jewry itself and the cultural progress of the entire Russian people — become equal Russian citizens. In the person of its wealthy representatives, Russian and international Jewry disposes of vast economic power. Its failure to employ this power for the emancipation of Russian Jewry is the great sin of the class of wealthy Jews and of that Zionism which inspires it.[53]

For some reason, this editorial was interpreted by many Russian Jews as anti-Semitic. *Liberation* received numerous letters complaining that it had slurred Jews by singling them out for subservience to the imperial regime and denying them the status of a nationality. Struve, of course, did not relent. The controversy was a precursor of the much more bitter dispute over the existence of Ukrainian nationality and culture in which he was to become embroiled in 1911–12.

Liberation got under Plehve's skin. On June 24, 1904 (NS), he approached the German envoy in St. Petersburg to inquire whether German laws provided grounds for the suppression of the paper or, at least, for the expulsion of its editor. Reporting on this conversation to his Foreign Office, the ambassador wrote that Plehve told him he felt no need to explain how "extraordinarily inconvenient" *Liberation* had become for the Russian government and how greatly it would appreciate German assistance in its liquidation.[54] Because under the constitution of the German Em-

---

[53] #151/378.
[54] Excerpt from a secret communication of the German Legation in St. Petersburg, No. 527, June 24, 1904, signed "Romberg," Staatsarchiv Ludwigsburg.

pire this matter came within the competence of the government of
Würtenberg, Berlin passed on Plehve's request to Stuttgart. Someone — probably a Social Democratic friend in the Würtenberg
administration — must have immediately forewarned Struve, because on June 28 (NS) he and his wife were observed by the
Okhrana in Paris looking for a place to live.[55] In the early days
of July they rented a two-story villa in Passy (Rue Bellini 14) and
returned to Stuttgart. Later that month Struve appeared before
the authorities at Gaisburg to declare his intention of moving to
Paris,[56] thereby sparing the government of Würtenberg any further embarrassment which his residence might cause. In September, after having taken holidays with his family in the Black
Forest, he transferred the household and the editorial office of
Liberation to Paris.

With the exception, later, of Lenin, Struve hated no figure of
prerevolutionary Russia as much as Plehve. To Struve he was the
"evil spirit" of the regime, the official champion of "Asiatic culture," the "protector and, at the same time, the gravedigger of
autocracy." [57] When in July 1904 the assassin's bomb killed Plehve,
he wrote:

The corpses of Bogolepov, Sipiagin, Bogdanovich, Bobrikov,
Andreev, and von Plehve are not melodramatic whims or romantic accidents of Russian history. These corpses mark the
logical development of a dying autocracy. Russian autocracy,
in the person of its last two emperors and their ministers, has
stubbornly cut off and continues to cut off the country from
all avenues to legal and gradual political development, and, at
last, has come face to face with the terrible reality of unavoidable political murders, one after the other. The terrible
thing for the government is not the physical liquidation of the
Sipiagins and von Plehves, but the public atmosphere of resentment and indignation which these bearers of authority create
and which breeds in the ranks of Russian society one avenger
after another. Political conspiracy and terrorist organizations

[55] Okhrana Archives, Hoover Institution, Index XVIIIr(1), Report No. 170,
dated June 25/July 8, 1904, signed by Rataev.
[56] Staatsarchiv Ludwigsburg, communication of July 25, 1904, No. 10216.
[57] #141/306; #150/344; #192; #203/1.

can be ferreted out and suppressed. A tense political atmosphere which breeds assassins cannot be rarefied and rendered harmless by any police. Exactly two years ago von Plehve boasted that by skilled police measures he would suppress Russian disorders. And what has happened? Employing the immense resources of the Department of Police he has shown himself unable, even in the technical sense, in regard to his own person, to solve the tasks of external security. At the time of his appointment, von Plehve was welcomed as a wise man. But, in fact, how great was the narrow-minded police mentality of that almighty minister! He thought that by tormenting the national minorities for the amusement of an inane nationalism, by demolishing constitutional Finland, by choking the Russian press, by systematically undermining the zemstva, and by reopening to the police the doors to universities and secondary schools he would stamp out the detested "trouble." He thought that by substituting for a genuine program of basic reforms the carefully thought out reactionary designs and seductive unclarities of the celebrated manifesto of February 26, 1903, he, as the great reformer of Russian autocracy, would inaugurate a new era in its history and launch its triumphal, irresistible advance. He thought that an autocracy which introduced the police into everything was conceivable — an autocracy which transformed legislation, administration, scholarship, church, school, and family into police operations — that such an autocracy would be able to dictate to a great nation the laws of its historical development. And the police of von Plehve were not able even to avert a bomb. What a pitiful fool! [58]

[58] #225. Struve commented on the manifesto of February 26, 1903, in #141. His joy at the assassination of Plehve is described by Tyrkova-Viliams, *Na putiakh*, 176.

15. FULFILLMENT — 1905

Monarchical absolutism in Russia expired after an agony of a year's duration which began with the so-called Paris conference of "oppositional and revolutionary" parties in October 1904 and concluded with the Manifesto of October 17, 1905. In the Manifesto, the monarchy capitulated unconditionally to the ultimatum given it by the Union of Liberation. For Struve personally, the Manifesto was the realization of everything he had striven for since 1885. No Russian writer of his generation had fought more consistently and more persuasively for the cause of political liberty which now triumphed. Had death struck him on October 17, 1905, he would have died a happy man.

But he was destined to live nearly four decades longer, in the course of which — brief interludes excepted — the scope of personal liberty in Russia was to be steadily restricted until there was nothing left. The tragic disappointments attending these events form the substance of the second half of this biography and will be related in due course. It must be noted now, however, that even as the hour of triumph approached Struve had premonitions of what lay ahead. His genius as a political thinker and his misfortune as a politician were always to be a step ahead of his time: to encourage others when their spirits lagged and to caution them when they were jubilant. In his writings of 1905 one can discern, breaking through the dominant sounds of optimism, unmistakable notes of fear that the successful revolution could turn into a counterrevolution. By the time the October Manifesto was proclaimed, he was already experiencing pangs of the "patriotic alarm" that from then on was never to leave him.

As soon as it had become apparent that the autocracy was breathing its last — that is, after the "Bloody Sunday" of January 9/22, 1905 — the coalition of oppositional groups and parties, of which Struve had been the foremost theorist and champion, began to dissolve. The "liberational movement" had done its job. Its largely negative mission lost relevance in the new political atmosphere in which the political parties, having written off the autocratic regime, were beginning to compete for the mass electorate of tomorrow. Struve was afraid neither of this competition nor of the effect it could have on the largely illiterate masses, because he had a strong faith in the peasants' and workers' sense of rational self-interest. What he did fear was the consequences that would ensue if the liberals failed to press for and achieve a constitutional system based on genuine political and social democracy. If tsarist absolutism was replaced by a "landlord constitution" (*barskaia konstitutsiia*), Russia's peasants and workers would remain permanently frustrated, and in this condition fall prey to the antiliberal extremists of both the right and the left. Under these conditions the government could exploit mass discontent to reestablish the bureaucratic-police regime, or the radicals could keep the country in a state of chronic revolutionary paralysis. In either event, political liberty in Russia would perish at birth.

These considerations caused Struve to plead with the liberals to assume on political and social issues the most radical position compatible with their principles. It was essential that peasants and workers acquire an opportunity to defend their interests in a legal manner, and that in their minds there form an indissoluble association between their economic well-being and the principle of political liberty. Only when this happened would extremists be prevented from seizing leadership of the masses. Struve was never as desperately radical as in 1905. In his scattered recollections, this period of his life remains virtually unrecorded, for he preferred later to expunge from memory the ideas he had then advocated.

After Plehve's assassination, the government delayed for a whole month naming his successor. Its difficulty was not so much finding a high civil servant willing to take over the Ministry of the Interior, for, the personal risks notwithstanding, there was no shortage of candidates. The problem was deciding what kind of man to choose: whether to entrust the post to someone committed to Plehve's policy of repression, or to depart from the practice of a quarter of a century and select an official committed to conciliation. The decision — as it turned out, a fatal one for the autocracy — was to opt for the second alternative. Prince Sviatopolk-Mirsky whose appointment was announced in mid-August 1904, had the reputation of a man who felt strongly about the necessity of bridging the chasm that had grown between government and society. On taking office, he proclaimed a "New Course," intended to restore national unity and mutual trust. To lend credibility to his words, he promptly instituted a number of reforms, including abolition of corporal punishment in the village and the army, partial amnesty for political prisoners, and easing of censorship. There were hints of more reforms to come.

Mirsky's appointment to the most important administrative post in the Empire, the tenor of his speeches and the substance of his reforms, aroused in the country greater enthusiasm than the government had anticipated and probably desired. Expectations rose very quickly, creating a situation fraught with danger.

The constitutionalists welcomed Mirsky's gestures of conciliation, but were unwilling either to place faith in the government's promises or to accept its implied offer of a truce. They interpreted Mirsky's appointment as a holding operation, designed to soothe popular discontent until the government could conclude the war with Japan and bring back the armies needed to suppress it. The imperial government now had to pay a heavy price for its failure to make good on the promises it had made to society in 1879–1881. Its credit with educated Russians was exhausted. Those to whom it now turned for confidence and support would accept nothing but hard cash: written guarantees assuring that henceforth the legislative and administrative activities of the Russian government would be subject to controls and accounting. In other words, a constitution.

Struve agreed with the position taken by his friends in Russia. Upon learning of Mirsky's appointment, he immediately warned readers of *Liberation* not to be misled: personally, the new minister could indeed be an honest liberal, but this mattered little because he was a captive of the system. He would be used by it, intrigued against, and discarded as soon as his usefulness was over. His policies conveyed the "smell" of reforms, not the reality. He was dangerous because he could be used by the monarchy to split the forces presently combined against it.[1] Russia needed only one reform — constitution. If Mirsky meant what he said, he should allow the constitutional question to be raised openly in Russia. Nothing less than that would do.[2]

This policy of "unconditional surrender" was frequently voiced in the constitutionalist press during Mirsky's ministry. In two articles in *Liberation,* called "The New Course" and "The Fiasco of the New Course," Miliukov, like Struve, rejected out of hand any suggestions of a cease fire in the conflict against the government. It was all or nothing: constitution or war. There could be no "intermediate positions" between autocracy and constitutional government.[3] The juridical weekly *Law* (*Pravo*), which the constitutionalists had captured, took a similar stand. An unsigned editorial in the issue of October 3/16, 1904, reminded its readers that Plehve, too, on his appointment two years earlier, had made the country promises of reform only to give it the reality of police repression.[4] In subsequent editorials, *Law* expressed with growing fearlessness the political position which Struve had been advocating for the past several years. The response of the constitutionalists in Russia to Mirsky's New Course was: "We need not reforms, but reform."[5] They were not going to allow the government to use palliative measures either to divide the liberal movement or to gain itself a respite.

The military mentality behind this political conduct was very much in evidence and sometimes explicitly stated. Struve alluded to it in a metaphor that was to crop up frequently in liberal debates during the first two Dumas: "The autocratic government has fully evacuated numerous positions. But it has not yet abandoned the central one — autocracy. And insofar as the conflict is precisely over that position, one's estimate of the

---

[1] #234.

[2] #242.

[3] *Osv,* No. 57 (October 2/15, 1904), 113–114, and No. 60 (November 10/23, 1904), 161–162. In his memoirs Miliukov says that his own attitude to Mirsky was decisively influenced by Witte's statement to Petrunkevich that the tsar was dead set against granting a constitution: P. N. Miliukov, *Vospominaniia, 1859–1917,* I (New York, 1955), 241.

[4] *Pravo,* No. 40 (October 3/16, 1904), 1911–1916.

[5] *Shakhovskoi,* 129. The reactions of the press to Mirsky are reflected in editorials reprinted in A. N. Achkasov, ed., *Poveialo vesnoiu . . . ,* 2nd. ed. (Moscow, 1905).

situation and society's conduct must be determined by the prospects of its seizure." [6]

For Struve, any concessions or promises of concessions made by the autocratic government were danger signals. He interpreted them as attempts to split the opposition and, as such, as moves demanding organizational countermeasures. So it had been in 1902, and so it was now, in 1904. In response to Mirsky's New Course, he joined preparations for a clandestine conference to be held in Paris for the purpose of coordinating the activities of all the antiautocratic parties of the Russian Empire.

The origin of this so-called Paris conference is difficult to establish. The proposal is said to have originated with the Polish Socialist party (PPS) at the Amsterdam Congress of the Socialist International.[7] But there is also evidence that the initiative come from N. V. Chaikovsky and F. V. Volkhovsky, two veterans of the socialist-revolutionary movement of the 1860's living in London who had long espoused the idea of a united front.[8] Whatever the source of the idea, there is no disagreement that its most energetic promoters were Finnish nationalists led by Koni Zilliacus. An "activist" friendly to the Socialist Revolutionaries and a strong advocate of armed uprising, Zilliacus received subsidies from the Japanese government,[9] but this fact was not generally known at the time. Struve certainly had no inkling of any Japanese involvement. Had he known or even suspected it, he would undoubtedly have refused to have anything to do with the proposed conference. The Japanese, pleased by the stand *Liberation* took on the war, at one point approached him through a Russian SR with

[6] #251/201.
[7] "Doklad Rataeva ot 9/22 Oktiabria 1904 g., za No. 282," *Russkii politischeskii sysk za granitsei* (Paris, 1914), 182–183; KS, No. 3/32 (1927), 60–61.
[8] L. Mechelin Archive, Finnish State Archive, Helsinki, No. 1617 6/2, unsigned letter to Struve, probably from L. Mechelin and probably from May 1904. The idea of a national front against autocracy, popularized by *Liberation,* was first formulated in the 1890's by these London émigrés, most of them veterans of the social-revolutionary movement of the 1860's and 1870's, among whom the leading figure was S. M. Stepniak-Kravchinsky. The subject is discussed in a doctoral dissertation in progress at Harvard University by Mr. Donald Senese.
[9] Koni Zilliacus, *Revolution und Gegenrevolution* (Munich, 1912), 88–89; Michael Futrell, "Colonel Akashi and Japanese Contacts with Russian Revolutionaries in 1904–5," St. Antony's Papers, No. 20, *Far Eastern Affairs,* No. 4, ed. G. F. Hudson (1967), 7–22. It seems that the Japanese distributed copies of *Liberation* to their Russian prisoners of war.

an offer of money. As soon as he heard the proposition, he booted his visitor out of the house.[10]

Struve was informed in May 1904 of the proposal to hold the Paris conference by a letter from the Finnish nationalist Leo Mechelin. The main purpose of the meeting, he was told, was to agree on "practical action" against the government.[11] Exactly what was meant by this expression the letter did not say, but it clearly referred to an armed insurrection. Mechelin requested Struve to find out whether his friends were interested. From the correspondence preserved in Mechelin's archive in Helsinki it appears that the Union of Liberation did not want to become implicated in any preparations for an insurrection, and refused.[12] But later, probably in the aftermath of Plehve's assassination, the Union changed its mind and agreed to come, on the understanding that the meeting would adopt a "minimum program" acceptable to all the participating parties — a formulation that excluded from the agenda the question of an armed uprising.

The Finnish organizers issued invitations to eighteen parties, Russian and national minority; eight accepted. The Union of Liberation was represented by Struve and three emissaries sent from Russia — Miliukov, Iakovlev-Bogucharsky, and Peter Dolgorukov. The Socialist Revolutionaries, who with their allies among the national minorities dominated the proceedings, had on their delegation the agent provocateur Azef. It was he who told the police what happened at the closed sessions. (Struve's and Miliukov's presence at this meeting became publicly known only in February 1909, when Stolypin revealed it to the Duma during a debate of the Azef affair.)[13] The other six participating parties came from the borderlands.[14]

The Russian Social Democrats were conspicuous by their absence. They had intended to come, and unanimously voted a resolution to this effect at a caucus held in early June.[15] But on

---

[10] A. Tyrkova-Viliams, *Na putiakh k svobode*, (New York, 1952), 194–195.

[11] Mechelin Archive, Finnish State Archive, Helsinki, two letters from May 1904, marked 1617 6/2.

[12] Two letters from the summer of 1904, Mechelin Archive.

[13] *Slovo*, February 12/25 and 14/27, 1909.

[14] They were the Polish Socialist party (PPS), the Polish National League, the Latvian Social Democratic Labor party, the Georgian Party of Socialist Federalist Revolutionaries, the Finnish Party of Active Resistance, and (toward the end of the meeting) the Belorussian Gromada.

[15] KS, No. 3/32 (1927), 57–72. Lenin was present at this meeting.

the eve of the conference they reversed themselves, partly because they had gotten wind of Japanese backing and partly because they feared being outnumbered by a coalition of Socialist Revolutionaries and liberals.[16]

The conference opened in Paris on September 17/30, 1904, at the Hôtel d'Orléans in the Rue Jacob, and met for nine days. Little is known of its proceedings, for they were shrouded in secrecy; what is known comes mainly from Azef's confidential account to the police and Miliukov's memoirs.[17] The liberals justified their opposition to the idea of an armed uprising and outlined their own designs for a massive national campaign of banquets, demonstrations, and petitions demanding a constitution, which seem to have been drawn up by the council of the Union of Liberation in August. Much time was taken up by discussion of the national question, which loomed large because of the heavy representation of minority parties. Miliukov says he was astonished at how far Struve was prepared to go to accommodate the minorities. In fact, it is known from statements which Struve made publicly in 1904 and 1905 that he favored not only the full restitution of the constitutional rights of Finland — a proposal which in all probability most liberals would have readily accepted — but also the restitution to Poland of the constitutional charter which Alexander I had granted it in 1815 and Nicholas I had abrogated after the uprising of 1830.[18] Miliukov rejected these proposals and held up the proceedings for a day and a half until all specific recommendations on the nationality question were struck from the program.[19]

The resolutions of the Paris Conference reaffirmed the principle of democracy and demanded that the autocratic system be replaced by a constitutional and democratic one. As for the nationalities, the resolution spoke of granting the "right to national self-determination" — a formula which could be interpreted to mean anything one wanted. Legal disabilities suffered by the minorities and the policy of Russification, however, were explicitly condemned.[20] The conference also agreed on concrete measures of

[16] PR, No. 12/35 (1924), 119–22.
[17] "Doklad Rataeva," and Miliukov, *Vospominaniia*, I, 241–244.
[18] #267/279.
[19] Miliukov, *Vospominaniia*, I, 243.
[20] *Listok Osvobozhdeniia*, No. 17 (November 19/December 2, 1904), 1–2. The

cooperation in combatting the imperial regime, but these were not made public and remain unknown to this day. There is reason to believe that they included the promise of active assistance to the Union of Liberation in its forthcoming constitutional campaign.

The conference, in the words of the SR organ, *Revolutionary Russia,* did not aim at a political union but a "provisional coalition for the purpose of synchronizing pressures" on the government.[21] Each of the participating parties retained full independence in questions of theory and action.

At the request of the representatives of the Union of Liberation, it was agreed not to release any news of the conference before December in order to give the Union the opportunity to make a public declaration of its existence.[22] This was done in mid-November (OS), at which time the eight parties simultaneously published in their organs the protocols and resolutions of the Paris Conference. The effect of this announcement was considerable, because never before in the history of the Russian oppositional movement had its diverse parties been able to set aside their differences long enough to agree on a common program.

The Paris Conference was formally called "Conference of Oppositional and Revolutionary Organizations of the Russian State," the distinction between the two types of organizations being drawn in order to distinguish those which renounced methods of armed violence from those which approved of them. Once the joint sessions were over, the four "revolutionary" parties held a secret private conference of their own at which they formed a bloc to coordinate insurrectionary strategy and tactics. This fact, too, was announced in December.[23]

The equivalent in the Russian Revolution of the French National Assembly of 1789 was the great zemstvo congress held in St. Petersburg between November 6/19 and 9/22, 1904. It was at this meeting that a majority of the country's only elected offi-

documents are translated in George Fischer, *Russian Liberalism* (Cambridge, Mass., 1958), 169–170.

[21] RR, No. 56 (December 5, 1904), 2.

[22] *Shakhovskoi,* 137.

[23] RR, No. 56 (December 5, 1904), 1–2. Miliukov says that at the time he did not know of this conference: *Vospominaniia,* I, 244.

cials, after due deliberation, solemnly and in full awareness of their action, voted to demand a representative legislative body. Once the constitutional movement received this high sanction, the wave of revolution began to roll unchecked.

The initiator of this act of defiance, as of so much else that happened in Russia during the crucial six months that followed Plehve's death, was the council of the Union of Liberation. Sometime in August, as has been said, the council began to think of activating plans for the national constitutional campaign that it had been charged to organize at its formation in January, but had had to shelve when the war broke out. In order to exert the maximum pressure on the government, it was thought desirable to have as many provincial zemstvo assemblies as possible adopt resolutions favoring constitutional government. Late in August (OS) two members of the council, who also happened to serve on the Moscow bureau of zemstvo congresses, approached Shipov, the bureau's chairman, with the suggestion that it convene a national conference of zemstvo deputies to formulate a common policy in this matter.[24] Because the bureau had been inactive since its altercation with Plehve two years earlier, the council placed little faith in its suggestion, and concentrated on organizing banquets, demonstrations, and petitions.[25]

To the Union's great surprise, the idea of a national zemstvo congress immediately caught on. Many of the conservative zemtsy had by now been driven to desperation by the bureaucratic regime, whose incompetence Russia's miserable showing against Japan had demonstrated even to the most obtuse. Normally, strong dynastic loyalties would have inhibited them from expressing their dissatisfaction in public. But some of Mirsky's pronouncements had led them to believe that the monarchy desired them to speak their minds. In this mistaken belief they joined the constitutionalists and gave their consent to a national zemstvo congress. On September 8/21, the bureau of zemstvo congresses decided to hold this congress in Moscow at the beginning of November (OS). The agenda was to include, in addition to the usual apolitical zemstvo questions, a debate on the country's political future. Mirsky, who had accidentally learned of these plans (though not

[24] *Shakhovskoi,* 129–130.
[25] *Ibid.,* 130.

the full agenda), not only gave them approval but volunteered
to ask the tsar for his blessing.[26] With such august backing, it is
not surprising that the zemstvo congress generated tremendous
excitement in the country. There was a widespread feeling that
the congress was intended by the government as the first of a
series of public consultations for the purpose of creating a consensus concerning the country's political future, on the model of the
consultations that had preceded the decree abolishing serfdom.
From them, it was thought, there certainly would issue some kind
of a constitutional charter. Mirsky, by legitimizing discussion of
the constitutional question, inadvertently pushed within the orbit
of the Union of Liberation conservative, nationalist elements
which until then had resisted its blandishments. This was the
critical factor assuring the success of the Union's endeavors.

On the eve of the zemstvo meeting, the Union of Liberation
held its second congress. Here several tactical resolutions were
adopted that were to exert considerable influence on the course
of events in the months that followed. The delegates voted to
emerge from the shadow world of conspiracy into the open light
of public activity by formally proclaiming the Union's existence.
This was publicized in no. 17 of the *Flysheet of Liberation,* dated
November 19/December 2, 1904. Furthermore, the congress resolved: to take active part in the forthcoming zemstvo congress
and there to do everything possible to have it adopt a formal
resolution favoring a constitution; to induce the provincial zemstvo
assemblies to pass resolutions demanding a constitution of a democratic kind; to initiate throughout the country, on the occasion of
the fortieth anniversary of the court reform (November 20/
December 3), a campaign of public banquets that would also
center on demands for a democratic constitution; and, finally, to
form a Union of Unions (Soiuz Soiuzov) embracing the various
professional associations of the empire.[27] Thus, through the
zemstvo assemblies, convened separately and nationally, through
gatherings of notables and professionals, Russian society, with
one voice, was to cry out for constitution. Shortly before its adjournment, the congress received from Paris the draft of a political program prepared by Struve with the assistance of several
members of the Union (probably the three delegates to the Paris

[26] *Belokonsky,* 213.
[27] *Shakhovskoi,* 131–132.

Conference). Because time was short, the draft was not dealt with but was forwarded for discussion to the branches of the Union.[28]

The zemstvo congress assembled on November 6/19 in a festive mood. At the last minute, its fate appeared to hang in the balance, for Mirsky had been pressured to rescind the permission he had granted its organizers. But once he realized that the congress would take place with or without his permission, he gave authorization on condition that it transfer its seat to St. Petersburg and assume the form of a "private consultation" (*chastnoe soveshchanie*). The proceedings of this congress — the most important public assembly held in imperial Russia up to that time — need not detain us, since Struve was not present.[29] What concerns us are its consequences, which completely altered the political climate of Russia and deeply affected both his life and his thought. The delegates voted in favor of granting all Russian citizens inalienable civil rights, including equality before the law, and creating an elected representative body with authority to participate in legislation, to control the budget, and to supervise the administration. The word "constitution" was not mentioned in order to placate the Slavophiles; but it was implicit in everything the congress voted. Shipov and his followers — approximately a fourth of the one hundred delegates present — signed the resolutions, although with a dissenting minority clause concerning Article 10, which defined the powers of the proposed parliament.[30]

The November congress was no ordinary meeting of zemtsy, such as had been convening unobtrusively at Shipov's residence from time to time since the mid-1890's. This was a revolutionary assembly which publicly stated the need to abolish autocracy in Russia. The country's population instinctively sensed its historic significance. Delegates departing for the congress were accompanied to railway stations by crowds of well-wishers. On their arrival in St. Petersburg they found that even though the meet-

[28] *Ibid.*, 135. Revised, this program came out as *Osnovnoi gosudarstvennyi zakon Rossiiskoi imperii: Proekt russkoi konstitutsii vyrabotannyi gruppoi chlenov "Soiuza Osvobozhdeniia"* (Paris, 1905).

[29] The records of this conference were published under the title *Chastnoe soveshchanie zemskikh deiatelei proiskhodivshee 6, 7, 8, i 9 noiabria 1904 g. v S.-Peterburge* (Moscow, 1905). It is described in Fischer, *Russian Liberalism*, 177–191.

[30] *K mneniiu men'shinstva chastnogo soveshchaniia zemskikh deiatelei* (Moscow, 1905).

ings were held in private residences that had not been publicly advertised and shifted their locale from day to day, the cab drivers unerringly knew where to take them; and if they did not, friendly policemen in uniform or plain clothes offered them directions. Each day, a flood of congratulatory telegrams poured in. Addressed simply "Zemstvo Congress, St. Petersburg," they were delivered by the postal authorities to the correct destination. These telegrams exhorted the delegates to speak on behalf of the entire nation, not just the zemstva, and openly to advocate a constitution. One of the delegates, who affixed his signature to the congress's resolutions at a ceremony in the house of Vladimir Nabokov (the father of the writer) on Bolshaia Morskaia 47, exclaimed that future generations would commemorate their deed with a marble plaque.[31]

Struve commented on the congress as follows:

We are hardly likely to be proven wrong when we say that the congress of November 6 will mark an epoch in the history of Russia's political development. The congress demonstrated that the turn of our internal policy does not depend on the will of any one person. For the first time, public opinion, the country's true sovereign, has spoken up, clearly, firmly, and openly. After this event, any attempts on the part of the government to avoid a straightforward statement of the constitutional question will represent a pitiful dodge, doomed to utter failure. The repressive measures dreamt of by the various General-Adjutants Sergeis, Kleingels, and Kutaisovs would at present be acts of madness. Despite the weakness of the tsar and of Prince Sviatopolk [-Mirsky], owing to the decisiveness and courage of the zemtsy, the door to a peaceful constitutional transformation remains still unshut for the government. To take this road, firmly and decisively, will constitute an act of elementary political wisdom. Will such wisdom be available? History has given perhaps its final warning. Will it be heeded?[32]

The Union's constitutional banquet campaign was inaugurated on November 20/December 3 with a huge dinner in St. Peters-

[31] R. Budberg, "S"ezd zemskikh deiatelei 6–9 noiabria 1904 goda v Peterburge (Po lichnym vospominaniiam)," Byloe, No. 3/15 (March 1907), 70–88; D. N. Shipov, Vospominaniia i dumy o perezhitom (Moscow, 1918), 258–259.
[32] #245.

burg, chaired by the writer V. G. Korolenko and attended by 650
well-known authors, scholars, and professional people. All those
present affixed their signatures to the resolutions of the Union of
Liberation calling for a democratic constitution. Similar banquets
were held in other cities of the Empire, some of which adopted
resolutions that even went beyond those proposed by the Union
and demanded not only the granting of a democratic constitution
but also the convocation of a constituent assembly that would
determine the future of Russia's system of government and would
presumably have the option of abolishing the monarchy altogether.[33] At their regular winter sessions, many zemstvo assemblies also passed constitutional resolutions.[34] Although the leadership of this unprecedented campaign lay in the hands of the
liberals, the Socialist Revolutionaries and even Social Democrats
lent a willing hand.[35] Thus the atmosphere of a crisis was built
up that soon carried along the undecided, the faint-hearted, and
the opportunistic. The spectacle of the country's intellectual and
professional elite openly defying the authorities proved irresistible
to such fence sitters. The success of this, as of any other revolution, became assured once it required more civic courage to defend the status quo than to assail it.

An unforeseen by-product of the Union of Liberation's campaign was the so-called Bloody Sunday. The workers who took
part in the procession to the tsar on that Sunday, January 9/22,
1905, belonged to a police-sponsored union headed by an agent
provocateur, the priest Gapon. These police unions had been set
up because some high Okhrana officials concluded (as, with different results, did the Economists and Lenin) that Russian labor
was interested not in political revolution but in economic and
social self-improvement. From this fact they deduced that under
proper guidance the nascent Russian labor movement could well
be steered into safe, loyal channels. Zubatovshchina, as police-
sponsored trade unionism in imperial Russia was known, was a
forerunner of the much vaster and more effective system of social

[33] *Belokonsky*, 238–239.
[34] *Ibid.*, 240–257.
[35] The *Iskra* group, at this juncture dominated by Akselrod and Potresov, seems
to have worked out some kind of an arrangement with the constitutionalists
enabling them to take part in the banquet campaign: RR No. 61 (March 15,
1905), 5. Plekhanov and especially Lenin opposed this policy, which made the
Social Democrats into a "tail" of the liberals: see Lenin's intraparty memorandum
Zemskaia kampaniia i plan 'Iskry' (Geneva, 1904), reprinted in *Lenin*, VII, 1–20.

controls introduced by the Bolsheviks after 1917. In imperial Russia, the experiment was not very successful. Like many of the priests whom the Catholic Church in France and Italy sent into the factories after World War II, Gapon soon identified himself with those whom he was supposed to pacify, and before long emerged as a bona fide labor leader, the first in Russia with a national reputation.

In October 1904, Gapon took the initiative in getting in touch with the St. Petersburg branch of the Union of Liberation. From then on, the Union's three most active figures — Kuskova, Prokopovich, and Iakovlev-Bogucharsky — regularly attended the meetings of the "staff" which directed Gapon's labor organizations and made every effort to politicize it. Their aim was to link the economic demands made by the workers of St. Petersburg in late 1904 with the national campaign for civil liberty and constitution inaugurated by the Union of Liberation.[36] To popularize the political idea among the rank and file of labor, the Union of Liberation launched in November 1904 two newspapers, *Our Life* (*Nasha zhizn'*) and *Our Days* (*Nashi dni*). These dailies, subsidized by the wealthy industrialist Savva Morozov, were in large measure edited by Socialist Revolutionaries affiliated with the Union. Both were avidly read by industrial workers.[37] Toward the end of 1904, Gapon was in Paris and paid Struve a visit, during which the two had what Struve described as "long and agreeable talks." [38]

Gapon hesitated to follow the advice pressed on him by the Union of Liberation to endorse its constitutional demand, for his outlook was fundamentally Christian-reformist and apolitical. Finally, in late November (OS), he yielded and agreed to inject into his unions systematic political propaganda based on the resolutions of the recently concluded zemstvo congress.[39] Throughout December, when a major industrial strike was in progress in

[36] L. Ia. Gurevich, "Narodnoe dvizhenie v Peterburge 9-go ianvaria 1905 g.," *Byloe*, No. 1 (January 1906), 195–223; V. Nevsky, *Rabochee dvizhenie v ianvarskie dni 1905 goda* (Moscow, 1930), 134; *Belokonsky*, 211; Fischer, *Russian Liberalism*, 196; BSE, XX, 799. Shakhovskoi says that although the Union of Liberation held many meetings with Gapon prior to the January events, no joint plan of action was worked out: *Shakhovskoi*, 145.

[37] Gurevich, "Narodnoe dvizhenie," 197; *Belokonsky*, 211.

[38] #276/332 and "Pis'ma iz Peterburga; pis'mo pervoe," RV, No. 314 (November 28, 1905).

[39] Gurevich, "Narodnoe dvizhenie," 197–198.

St. Petersburg, Gapon's organization set up branches in all quarters of the capital and in a number of provincial cities. By means of this apparatus, the osvobozhdentsy gained access to large numbers of industrial workers, whom they persuaded to adopt political slogans alongside economic ones. They also seem to have played a large part in planning the January 9/22, 1905, procession to the tsar, which accorded with their program of public demonstrations and petitions.

The petition which Gapon's workers carried to the Winter Palace on that fateful Sunday was written in the language of humble peasants imploring the master to save them from imminent death. Most of it dealt with economic grievances. But inserted in it was a political section which bore the unmistakable imprint of the Union of Liberation and which had probably been written or at least formulated by one of its St. Petersburg representatives:

Russia is too vast, its needs too varied and too numerous, for it to be administered only by officials. The people must help themselves: after all, they alone know what their true needs are. Do not reject their help, accept it: Order at once, right now, [the convocation of] an assembly of representatives of the Russian land, of all the classes, of all the estates. Let in this assembly sit capitalist and worker, official, priest, physician, and teacher. Let all, no matter who they be, elect their representatives. Let all have equal and free voting rights and to that end command that the elections to the constituent assembly take place under conditions assuring universal, secret, and equal voting: this is our most important request; everything depends on it; it is the best, the only ointment for our painful wounds, without which they will never cease bleeding and soon bring us to death.

For all its folksy language, this pronouncement merely echoed the political platform of the Union of Liberation — a fact equally evident in the accompanying specific demands for civil liberty, a responsible cabinet, and guarantees assuring that the administration would function in accord with the law.[40]

---

[40] *Osv*, No. 65 (January 27/February 9, 1905), 241–242. F. I. Dan says that Gapon and his people, "under the influence of the Social Democrats," included political demands in their petition; but he gives no evidence for this assertion,

The demonstration, which Gapon had organized and led, was everywhere interpreted as another "manifestation" of the Union of Liberation. The police, having gotten wind of it, on the eve of Bloody Sunday arrested the entire council of the Union, which had to be replaced by a hastily assembled ad hoc body.[41]

The ability of the Union to persuade the only legally functioning labor organization in the country to place political liberty at the head of its demands and to express willingness to join all the other classes in the construction of a constitutional government was its greatest single victory. Struve's fondest wish had come true: the entire nation — from the Slavophile aristocrat to the manual worker — now rallied under the banner of political liberty. It was his program and his strategy that triumphed: liberty was acknowledged as a sine qua non of every class and almost every party. It had ceased to be an ideal of "bourgeois" landlords and had become a national task.

The Union had hoped that the various manifestations of solidarity which followed in the wake of the zemstvo congress would force the government to concede a constitution peacefully. But the hope of political reform from above was shattered by the bullets that greeted Gapon's workers. The "last warning" of which Struve spoke in his comments on the zemstvo congress had not been heeded. The copy of *Liberation* released immediately after Bloody Sunday carried in bold type the headline "Revolution in Russia" and underneath it Struve's emotional editorial, "The People's Executioner":

> The people went to him, the people waited for him. The tsar met *his* people. To words of sorrow and trust he replied with whips, sabers, and bullets. The streets of Petersburg run with blood and the bond between the people and this tsar has been broken forever. No matter who he is — a haughty despot, unwilling to descend to the people, or a contemptible coward, fearful of confronting that elemental force from which he had drawn strength — after the events of January 9/22, 1905, Tsar Nicholas II has openly become an enemy and an executioner

---

which seems highly dubious both because the SD's regarded Gapon with utmost suspicion and stayed away from his labor unions and because the political demands made in the petition run contrary to the Social Democratic platform: F. I. Dan, *Proiskhozhdenie bol'shevizma* (New York, 1946), 337.

[41] *Shakhovskoi*, 145.

of the people. We shall say no more of him — after this, we shall not speak to him. He has destroyed himself in our eyes and there can be no return to the past. None of us can forgive this blood. It chokes us with spasms, it overwhelms us, it leads us on and will bring us where we must proceed and get to.

Yesterday there were still controversies and parties. Today the Russian liberational movement must have one body and one spirit, one twin (*edinaia dvuedinaia*) thought: revenge and freedom, come what may. This oath sears the soul and, with its insistent call, steels the mind.

Against the terrible crimes perpetrated by the tsar's orders on the streets of Petersburg must rise all who possess an ordinary human conscience. There can be no argument that the crime must be punished and that its root must be extirpated. We cannot live that way any longer. The chronicle of autocratic oppression, outrage, and crimes must be brought to an end.

We must neither think nor write about anything except revenge and freedom.

Revenge will free us, freedom will avenge us.[42]

At this point, when the influence of Struve's ideas had reached its zenith, the influence of his publications waned. His fate was not that of Herzen, who after 1863 lost his following because he had identified himself with an unpopular cause, the Polish insurrection. Struve did not fall out of step with Russian public opinion. On the contrary: according to Shakhovskoi, his editorials and programmatic essays in *Liberation* accurately reflected and sometimes uncannily anticipated developments in the Union of Liberation.[43] What happened was that, with the relaxation of censorship by Mirsky, control of the press in Russia rapidly broke down and there was less need for a journal published abroad and smuggled in with considerable delay and expense. From November 1904 onward, it was possible to purchase for a few pennies on any newstand papers and journals that in an increasingly open manner espoused the *Liberation* platform. In *Our Life* and *Our Time*, and their variously titled successors, the Union of Liberation had two house organs. In May 1905, the St. Petersburg Union even put out its own *Flysheet* (*Listok Soiuza Osvobozh-*

[42] #259.
[43] *Shakhovskoi*, 150.

deniia).[44] Furthermore, several old, established publications, edited either by members of the Union or by its sympathizers, began now to advocate the Union's constitutional and democratic program. This held true of *Law, Rus', Russian News* (*Russkie vedomosti*), and a number of others.

As the need for *Liberation* declined, Struve abandoned the regular fortnightly publication schedule. After February 1905, *Liberation* appeared irregularly, usually once a month. Between February and October a total of twelve numbers was issued.

After January 1905, Struve's attention shifted to programmatic problems. The constitutional question as such seemed settled: the question now was no longer whether Russia would have a constitutional government but what kind it would be.

There were three possible answers, identified with the three factions into which the liberal movement had split by 1905. On the right wing stood the Slavophiles, headed by Shipov, who endorsed the constitutional principle, but with reservations, for they were unable to reconcile themselves to the idea of a legislative parliament. They no longer carried much weight, however, the spectrum of opinion having shifted during the past three years to the left. The middle was occupied by a large body of liberals who accepted representative government of some kind, but feared the masses acting alone or in collusion with reactionaries or revolutionaries, and therefore sought an arrangement that would keep this hydra down. To this wing belonged probably the majority of the zemtsy. On the left stood adherents of the Union of Liberation, who espoused a radical type of liberalism dedicated to the democratic franchise and comprehensive agrarian and social reform. The right wing of the liberal movement desired a constitution but an impotent parliament; the center, an effective parliament but one that would assure the preponderance of the prosperous and the educated; the left, a parliament that was not only effective but also genuinely representative and active in social legislation. As one proceeded from right to left, one found increasing faith in the political maturity of the Russian masses.

Struve, who was with the left, contributed in no small measure to the Union of Liberation's early and lasting commitment to political and social democracy. He did so, in the first place, on philo-

[44] *Ibid.*, 157.

sophical grounds: as noted already, he considered all genuine liberalism to rest on the ideal of human equality. But in his writings of 1904–1905, addressed largely to the right and the center of the liberal movement, he justified democracy more by pragmatic than by philosophic arguments. It was his contention that the best way to make the Russian *muzhik* that savage beast whom the antidemocratic liberals so dreaded was to deprive him permanently of his democratic rights. Russian peasants and workers had healthy social instincts: they knew what they needed and even what they could realistically hope to get. Under a political system that enabled them to advance their interests lawfully they would behave responsibly; under any other, they would turn violent and destructive. In late 1904 and throughout 1905, Struve exerted great efforts to convert to these views liberals who did not acknowledge the Union's platform. I shall let him speak for himself. I only wish to call attention to the underlying sense of the precariousness of Russian freedom breaking through these appeals, especially after March 1905, when with the first thaws of spring came rumblings of jacquerie.

Today, when the class lines and differences in the style of life separating the intelligentsia from the people have been wiped out, when the intelligentsia strives in every way possible to meet with the people and the people produces its own intelligentsia — today, the conscience of the Russian intelligentsia will never acquiesce in political privilege. This means that unless the political structure of constitutional Russia is grounded on a democratic foundation, Russia will of necessity have to be administered against the intelligentsia, in a constant struggle with it, that is, at the cost of an immense waste of national energies. At the same time, any constitution, no matter how undemocratic, will of itself create conditions permitting *radical* elements to engage in a struggle — conditions under which it will become increasingly necessary to treat radical elements as *direct representatives of the masses.*

In a constitutional Russia, Social Democracy will cease to be what it is today — an organization of the intelligentsia which expresses the interests and formulates the needs of the proletariat — and it will become a *genuine* proletarian or *labor* party. In constitutional Russia, the peasantry, too, will speak up on its own behalf. Both these events will occur very quickly. And one can state with full confidence that only a democratic reform will at once bring both the working class and the peasantry into the normal channel where the struggle for their interests is carried out by *peaceful means of a lawful struggle for law.*

Under the autocratic system, Russia exists in a condition of chronic revolution, a revolution concealed, or, to be more precise, exiled into the interior of the national organism but steadily expanding in depth and breadth. If major reform is not carried out, this revolution will undoubtedly assume an acuter form. A *small constitution* can, or more exactly, must immediately breed further political action, which, in the event of the obduracy of the upper classes, *will inevitably produce a large revolution.*[45]

I am profoundly persuaded of the justice of an electoral system based on the universal franchise, and firmly convinced that it accords with the principles of true and broad liberalism. But here I intend to defend its appropriateness in contemporary Russia not as a liberal and not as a democrat, not from the point of view of my ideals of political justice, but from the point of view of the social pacification (*umirotvorenie*) of the country and the rooting in it of a stable political order. If the striving for these blessings be called conservative, then I am prepared to argue that for Russia the universal vote is dictated by sane and far-sighted conservatism. Before demonstrating this thesis, I must refute the objection made by liberal opponents of the universal vote, who assume that this electoral system will subject Russia to the domination of an ignorant mob manipulated by reactionaries.

This objection represents, in fact, a hypothesis conjectural in the highest degree and resting on shaky historical analogies. It has not the slightest basis in the concrete conditions of Russian reality. In Russia, as everywhere else, the masses will follow those political currents and those leaders who can promise them and achieve the true satisfaction of their pressing needs. And in Russia the satisfaction of the most pressing needs of the masses can be achieved only by way of broad economic reforms carried out in the spirit of democracy — reforms of a kind with

[45] #237/129.

which none of the reactionary forces actually existing or conceivable in Russia can sympathize. Furthermore, democratic economic reforms in contemporary Russia are so complex as to be entirely beyond the capacity of a government apparatus controlled by reactionaries. The circumstances surrounding the democratic Caesarism of Napoleon III, which to this day hypnotize many politicians hostile to universal franchise, are in no serious way analogous to contemporary Russian reality. Under the Second Empire, France had no peasant problem and there could be no question of peasant reform. The French peasant was politically conservative because his economic interests required no reforms that would bring him in contact with authority and inspire him with the idea that political self-expression had for him genuine meaning . . .

But, we are told, the crux of the matter is that under universal franchise the politically reactionary Russian government, at the cost of satisfying all the economic needs of the Russian peasantry, will enter with it into an alliance and stamp out every free movement in the country. Those who foresee such results from universal franchise forget that the government of a country is not an abstract category that can be arbitrarily inserted for specific purposes into any desired combination of social and political forces. The reactionary Russian government is a political phenomenon — alive, historically determined and grown out of given social bases. It cannot be shifted onto an entirely new and socially alien foundation. Land commandants, governors, ministers, bureaucrats, grand dukes with their administrative appanages, the autocratic tsar — all these are not abstractions, but living phenomena. They — or, in other words, the reactionary Russian government — cannot suddenly, for the sake of its self-preservation, turn into a servant of the peasantry and begin to lean on it. This would be a social miracle which there is no need to fear. A radical political reform such as universal franchise can be introduced in a lasting form only as a result of such a radical shift of the social forces in our country, which would cut the ground from under any reaction and utterly preclude its triumph for any significant period of time.

Finally, to those who fear that the peasant, by virtue of his ignorance and helplessness, will become an easy prey of electoral deception, we shall say that the Russian peasant will be in large measure protected from such large-scale deception at the very outset of free political activity by the true sociopolitical instinct inherent in the masses that our reactionaries have dreaded and continue to dread with such good cause. Once the country has been swept by the vivifying breath of political freedom, once political banners and slogans have been everywhere freely hoisted, the peasants will learn quickly to distinguish their friends from their enemies, and find the true peasant banner.

Those who fear the perverting pressure of reactionary factors on peasant elections do not make allowance for the enormous cleansing that will be carried out at once by the very fact of the liquidation of the autocratic-bureaucratic regime and that will enlighten to an enormous degree the sociopolitical consciousness of the masses. One must keep in mind that Russia is in the throes of a whole revolution, that is, of an enormous social upheaval in the course of which the alignment of political forces must undergo radical change.

But if this be the case, then what is the meaning of the belief, expressed above, that for Russia the universal vote is dictated by healthy conservatism? Do these two assertions not stand in irreconcilable contradiction? It is our deep conviction that they are not only not self-contradictory, but that one flows from the other with inexorable logic.

The enormous social "displacement" presently occurring in Russia requires, for its peaceful resolution, the broadest possible political reform. The process of social change experienced by Russia represents one of those combinations in which a radical solution of the political question alone can bring peace and assure true order.

Political reform comes to Russia not too early but too late for any kind of a transitional solution. Those "opportunists" who triumphantly pointed out that the Russian people are indifferent to constitutional reform and from this fact deduced that such reform was unnecessary ignored the fact that political apathy and passivity of the masses are a *conditio sine qua non* of the kind of moderate political reform in which it is possible to ignore the masses as a political factor. Waiting for the autocracy itself to grant political reform, the "opportunists" have come too late with their solution of the political problem. Too late in two senses: they will not be permitted to realize their transitional solution, and such a solution, even if realized, will not pacify the country.

Russia confronts not only a political transformation. More precisely, in its political transformation converge, as in a focus, all its urgent needs, all the great and complex social problems which autocracy has proven itself utterly impotent to deal with. The masses have awakened and are stirred. Their motion indicates that they have emerged from inertia, that they sense their strength. The life of the masses has posed all kinds of difficult questions and tasks. The Russian intelligentsia, in its various currents, has long experienced and borne the pain of these questions; it has accumulated various solutions, some more thought out, some less. It is necessary to provide an open outlet for all [these] forces, to allow all the solutions an opportunity to engage in competition on the wide stage of free political life.

Only the universal vote will give all the elements of society an equal opportunity to test their real strength. It alone will give us an idea of the true measure of all things in the country. We are being frightened by radical programs and by the fascination which the masses will evince for them under universal franchise. But the existence of radical programs and the political awakening of the masses are facts which must be taken into account now. Even more will they have to be taken into account the day after political reform has been put into effect, no matter how remote it may be from universal franchise. And it may be boldly asserted that the less commandingly and responsibly the masses participate in the shaping of political life, the more powerful and, at the same time, the more futile will be the influence of radical programs on these masses.

As long as the masses do not participate on equal terms with the propertied classes in legislation, they will always remain in the throes of an anxiety and discontent that will steadily feed all kinds of troubles (*smuty*). Does the strike movement still in progress not demonstrate that the working masses, when deprived of an opportunity to satisfy their needs by means of political self-determination, take the path of economic struggle, which is simply disastrous for themselves and ruinous to the other classes of the population? Do we not see that in this struggle the workers frequently pose demands which, viewed

objectively, cannot be met — demands which, under conditions of political freedom and equality, neither they nor their
friends could support for an instant? If the peasants had normal
avenues by which to exert influence on legislation, would
agrarian disorders spread through a vast territory like a forest
fire? Would then those same political influences which now
manifest themselves in all worker and peasant turbulence not
seek and find in a democratic order more direct and efficacious
avenues for the achievement of their goals?

The only way to direct the enormous social movement presently stirring Russia's urban and rural working population into
the channel of lawful (*zakonomernyi*) struggle for their interest is to invite the entire population, on equal rights, to share
in the political life — that is, to institute universal franchise.
Give political freedom and political equality, and life itself will
freely sweep away all that which is premature and unrealizable
in radical programs. But let everything in these programs that
is viable, necessary, and valuable for the masses find in the political system of renewed Russia an opportunity for full realization, because only under these conditions will there come to
Russia the normal development of political and social life. To
those who anxiously or enthusiastically expect universal franchise to produce either the horrors of cultural barbarism or the
miracles of social revolution — to them we will say: it will bring
no horrors and no miracles; the masses, called on to participate
in political and social construction, will astonish us neither with
their obscurantism nor with their radicalism. The universal vote
will indicate to everyone his proper place and provide every
social force with an unmistakable yardstick.

Under the universal franchise the masses, having become responsible managers of their own destiny, will learn and understand what is possible and what is not. Until the masses are
given a chance to declare and realize their will by means of
legislation, disposal of state revenues, and control over government, the road to the pacification of society will always remain
barred by the fact that the people are excluded from exercising
proper influence over government activities and that their interests, therefore, remain ignored and unsatisfied. This means
that the masses, unable to feel like sovereigns of the state, will
turn against it. Given the existence of a strong revolutionary

tradition among the Russian intelligentsia, given the existence of well-organized socialist parties, given the ancient and profound cultural estrangement of the masses from educated society — any solution of popular representation other than the universal vote will represent a fateful political error which will be followed by heavy reckoning.[46]

A more eloquent expression of the faith in the omnipotence of democracy prevalent among the old Russian intelligentsia would be difficult to find.

Struve was so carried away that in some of his writings of 1904–1905 he no longer spoke of a liberal or constitutional party but of a "democratic" one, as if expecting the Union of Liberation to break away from the constitutional movement at large.[47] He also supported the notion of a popularly-elected constituent assembly that would draft the country's fundamental laws.[48]

So much for *political* democracy. Struve insisted with equal vigor on *social* democracy, that is, agrarian reform and social legislation. In its early phase, the Union of Liberation had not spelled out precisely what it thought on this subject (although its sentiments were made clear at the Schaffhausen meeting), for it preferred to concentrate its propaganda on constitutional demands. But in the winter of 1904–1905, as social tension in Russia rose, it became necessary to take an unequivocal stand on the matter. Struve again led the discussion, and placed himself on record as an advocate of a liberal democratic party strongly committed to social justice. The following passage was written in March–April 1905:

The merger of the diverse elements of the intelligentsia into a solid democratic party has now become an absolute necessity. The time is critical. Precisely because of its spontaneous character — one might say, because of the suddenness of its onslaught — the liberational movement demands the presence of a highly activist democratic party. The real masses are making their appearance on the stage. At such a time, the democratic party

[46] #300/vii–x; cf. #286a.
[47] E.g., #267; #269/281; #277/337.
[48] #267/278.

has no right passively to observe the mass movement. Passivity is especially impossible in view of the mounting movement of the peasantry.

The peasant movement, of course, is spontaneous and unorganized. But if the intelligentsia (the zemtsy included) were to confront it passively, the intelligentsia would find itself politically squeezed between a rebellious peasantry and a government bent on saving autocracy. The government is not averse . . . to sicking the peasantry on the educated classes, the liberal landlords included. And yet it itself fears, and with good reason, the peasant movement, because it cannot make serious concessions to the peasantry. As long as the Black Hundreds, mustered by the police and swollen by some deluded volunteers from the people, beat up the intelligentsia on city streets, the autocratic government can contentedly rub its hands. But a peasant agrarian revolution it must fear even more than do the landlords. Should the government support the peasants, it would arouse against itself the landlords; should it support the landlords and gun down the peasants, it would carry out with its own hands a Gapon-like experiment on the peasantry, that is, lay down a perfectly solid, immovable foundation for a Russian political revolution. Such is the logic of events. The Russian opposition — not only the democratic one but also the moderate constitutional one — should proceed at the present critical moment on the assumption that *the agrarian revolution in the country has begun.* If this is the case, then from all points of view the only sensible tactic is to master the revolution from the very outset and, acknowledging its essential legitimacy, direct it into channels of rational (*zakonomernaia*) social reform carried out in connection with the complete political transformation of the country, using the means furnished by the democratic constitution.

This is the reason that in [our] program of the democratic party we have inserted a solution of the agrarian question in the most unambiguous form. Personally, I regard such a sharp formulation of the agrarian question in the program as the only sensible move, obligatory not only for democrats but for constitutionalists in general. In exactly the same manner, in the present phase of the Russian troubles (*smuta*), I regard an *active, revolutionary* tactic to be the only sensible one for

Russian constitutionalists to adopt. If they should miss now the opportunity to engage in an active tactic, then the "law of action" will be dictated to Russian constitutionalists, or, more precisely, imposed on them, on the one hand by the Russian autocracy and on the other by the spontaneous movement of the masses and the conduct of the socialist parties. In this instance I intentionally speak not only of democrats but of all Russian constitutionalists, and I even particularly have in mind the constitutionalists from the landowning class.

They must understand that in present-day Russia political reform has become closely linked with social problems, and that furthermore the agrarian revolution in Russia has begun under conditions unique in both its own and world history. The country has socialist parties and a labor movement. And the socialist parties and even more the labor movement over which the socialists exercise influence impart and will continue to impart revolutionary energy to the peasant mass.

The destitution of the peasantry, linked with socialist agitation and socialist reeducation of the working class, will produce a movement of a kind which it would be senseless to fight. Wise men, men endowed with a true political sense, in general do not fight revolutions. Or, to put it into different words: the only way to fight a revolution is to accept its premises and goals, and strive only to change its methods . . .

A revolution, we repeat, cannot be defeated: it can only be mastered.[49]

He made the same point in an exchange with Jean Jaurés on the pages of *Humanité*: "Russia needs a strong government which will not fear revolution because it will place itself at its head . . . *The Revolution in Russia must become government.*"[50]

The anxiety concealed behind these radical sentiments did not escape some perceptive observers from the socialist camp. Karl Kautsky, in a commentary on the Russian situation in July 1905, noted with condescension that Russian liberals like Struve were growing apprehensive of mass anarchy and beginning to pine for authority. He thought their fears quite unfounded: as French his-

[49] #269/281–282.
[50] Struve, "La Révolution russe et la Paix: Lettre ouverte au citoyen Jean Jaurés," *Humanité*, No. 417 (June 8, 1905); Russian translation: #281. Cf. #282.

tory had demonstrated, the working class matured best under revolutionary conditions. "Permanent revolution (*die Revolution in Permanenz*), therefore, is what the Russian proletariat needs," Kautsky concluded, adding that it was also what it would most likely get.[51] According to Struve, this passage, addressed to him, first gave currency to the concept of "permanent revolution."[52]

Struve spelled out in March 1905 the specific social reforms he had in mind. In the forefront of his concerns stood the peasantry. The high tariffs on foreign industrial goods which he had endorsed in his Social Democratic days he now rejected: tariffs had to be substantially lowered because they enriched a small group of industrialists at the expense of the rural population. Agrarian reform was essential. Peasant communities short of land should be given additional land allotments. "This augmentation, insofar as it involves land belonging to private landowners, should be accomplished by means of compulsory purchase at government cost." The industrial workers should be allowed to organize trade unions and to strike, and should be given social protection, including state insurance. Court reform and school reform that would assure all Russians of elementary education and liberate the educational establishment from church and police tutelage were also among his recommendations.[53]

In advocating political and social reform Struve meant to forestall the radicalization of the Russian masses. In the spring and summer of 1905 he did not yet think this danger imminent. In reply to a writer from Russia who asked on the pages of *Liberation* how the liberals could compete with the radicals for influence over the masses and yet remain true to themselves, Struve drew a distinction between "revolution" and "revolutionism." Revolution was a spontaneous and fundamentally legitimate movement of the population which became dangerous only when thwarted. Revolutionism was a state of mind, most prevalent among a part of the intelligentsia, whose distinguishing quality was lack of contact with the realities of life. It meant "the tendency to subordinate living political activity to an abstract radical program and a doctrinaire re-

[51] NZ, XXIII, No. 41 (July 5, 1905), 462.
[52] RVed, No. 19 (January 25, 1907).
[53] #267/279. Cf. *Shakhovskoi*, 150.

jection of all compromise." Russian radical parties were addicted to revolutionism because they were composed of intellectuals who lacked mass following. Once they had gained such a following — as was inevitable under a democratic system — they would either deradicalize or disappear from the scene. In other words, under conditions of political and social democracy revolutionism presented no serious threat to Russia.[54]

In the autumn of 1905 he began to revise his overly optimistic estimate. News from Russia indicated that the radicals, especially the Social Democrats, had succeeded much better than he had believed possible in winning adherents among students and industrial workers and in turning them away from the struggle for political liberty and the satisfaction of just grievances, toward "revolutionism." In some universities, Social Democratic students managed to bring instruction to a standstill and even to enforce a boycott of professors suspected of "reactionary" attitudes. Elsewhere, they prevailed on the workers to advance demands that obviously could not be met. To Struve, these were alarming developments:

> The tactics of Social Democracy, of course, are determined by its character as a narrow body of intellectuals which aspires to represent the working class. But this is only one source of its tactics. The other lies in the very world outlook of Social Democracy, which lacks any *idea of law*. Social Democracy wishes to overcome the reactionary violence of autocracy with the revolutionary power of the people. It has in common with its enemy the cult of power: it merely desires a different carrier of power and assigns it different tasks. In its world outlook, law is not the idea of the just but the command of the *strong*.[55]

Having learned that two Russian university professors accused by students of reactionary opinions had submitted their case to a court of honor, Struve exploded:

[54] #277. This was a reply to "Kak ne poteriat' sebia?" by "U-v" in *Osv*, Nos. 69–70 (May 7/20, 1905), 333–334.
[55] #294/497. Dated October 12, 1905 (NS). In "My Contacts and Conflicts with Lenin," SR, XIII, No. 37 (July 1934), 83, Struve says that in writing this passage he had Lenin in mind.

I would not only refuse to be judged myself were I accused of being a "reactionary"; I would never judge anyone else for this offense. And I would not only refuse to judge, but I would loudly protest against being invited to such proceedings. I acknowledge the right to be "unreliable" in principle, philosophically, as an inalienable right, no matter who determines the criteria of "reliability." In this matter, I want to subordinate myself to no authority, to no police station, regardless of how it is decorated: with the double-headed eagle or the Phrygian cap, whether its "mirror of justice" descends from Peter the Great or from Karl Marx.[56]

In August, Struve and the family left Paris for Brittany. They rented a villa at Point St. Cast and there spent several quiet weeks away from political turbulence and worries, in the company of Tyrkova and a young friend recently arrived from Russia, Simeon Frank.[57]

But when they returned to Paris in September there was no more escape from politics. Every day the newspapers brought from Russia a stream of reports of riots and strikes indicating a progressive breakdown of authority. Struve now made up his mind to return home even at the risk of being arrested at the frontier, for he desperately wanted to be near the eye of the storm. But he could not leave right away because Nina was again pregnant and expecting any day. Tyrkova, who was with him at the time as a member of the editorial staff of *Liberation*, recalls that during these last days of autocracy he completely lost his head:

He ran ten times a day to the newspaper kiosk at the metro station, grabbing all editions: morning, evening, early, late, noontime, and afternoon, regular and extra. These were put out by all the newspapers. Whole pages were full of Russia, and each brought new details confirming the vehemence of the movement. Struve walked the streets of Passy, the paper open in front of him like a shield, risking falls under carriages, bump-

[56] *Ibid.* See also Struve's Introduction to M. P. Dragomanov's *Sobranie politicheskikh sochinenii*, I (Paris, 1905), v–vii, and "Betrachtungen über die russische Revolution," in Josef Melnik, ed., *Russen über Russland* (Frankfurt-am-Main, 1906), 1–15.
[57] Tyrkova-Viliams, *Na putiakh*, 206–207; *Frank*, 44.

ing into passers-by, impervious to their deserved abuse. At home, he looked senselessly into all the rooms, muttered incomprehensible words, stared at us with unseeing eyes . . .

Suddenly, on the evening of October 17, extra editions came out bearing in enormous letters the memorable words: "The Tsar Gives In — Concedes Constitution."

Just that day Nina was in labor with her fifth child. She did not go to a hospital but stayed home to carry on her usual work. As befitted the wife of the editor of a constitutional journal, she chose for her delivery the memorable day of October 17, the day of the constitution . . .

A disheveled Struve, shaking a pile of newspapers, shoving everyone aside, burst into the bedroom where his wife was straining in the last pangs of childbirth.

"Nina! Constitution!"

The midwife took him by the arm and pushed him out of the bedroom. Half an hour later, the fifth Struve was born.[58]

Friends later joked that Struve's political evolution was faithfully reflected in the birthdates of his children: the first born on May 1, the last on October 17.

Now he was free to leave.[59] A friend, the writer Maximilian Voloshin, offered him his passport, and with it in his pocket Struve departed on October 19/November 1 for Berlin. He arrived there the following day and tried to proceed to St. Petersburg, but he found that no trains were leaving for Russia because of the general strike there. Berlin was full of Russians converging from all directions and, like him, desperate to return home. To accommodate them, the German government arranged for a special train to the port city of Stettin, where steamships departed regularly for the Russian capital. As he arrived at the terminal to board the boat train, he was met by Iollos, the head of the Berlin office of the St. Petersburg Telegraphic Agency, who had come to see him off.

---

[58] Tyrkova-Viliams, *Na putiakh,* 209–210. A pedantic correction, however: Struve learned of the October Manifesto not from French newspapers, but from a telegram sent him by Iollos from Berlin: RiS, No. 196 (August 27, 1932).

[59] The following account of Struve's return journey to Russia is based on his reminiscences in *Rossiia,* No. 24 (February 4, 1928), and RiS, No. 196 (August 27, 1932); see also V. A. Posse, *Moi zhiznennyi put'* (Moscow and Leningrad, 1929), 402–403, and RVed, October 27, 1905.

Iollos brought him the news he had just received over the wire: the tsar, at Witte's request, had granted him pardon.

After a brief sea voyage, on Tuesday, October 25/November 7, 1905, Struve landed in St. Petersburg, and beheld his native country which he had expected never to see again.

BIBLIOGRAPHY
INDEX

BIBLIOGRAPHY

The bibliography which follows lists primary and secondary works utilized in the writing of this volume. Nearly all of these works either date from or deal with the first thirty-five years of Struve's life. The monographic literature on the historical background is not listed, except for a small number of frequently cited fundamental studies. The abbreviations used are explained on pp. xi–xiii.

Archival Materials

Unpublished Writings of Struve

International Institute for Social History, Amsterdam

Fifty-seven letters to A. N. Potresov, 1891–1904 (includes some letters of his wife, Nina, as well).
Seven letters to P. B. Akselrod, 1896–1902.
Two letters to Karl Kautsky, 1896, 1897.
One letter to E. Bernstein, 1899.

Dom Plekhanova, Leningrad

Seven letters to G. V. Plekhanov, 1895–1899 (not available to me).

Central State Historical Archive, Moscow (TSGIAM)

Struve Archive (Fond Struve, 604), thirty-nine units (not available to me).

Institute of Literature (Pushkin House), Leningrad

Five letters to Z. A. Vengerova, 1897–1899.
Two letters to K. K. Arseniev, 1894, 1907.
Three letters to S. A. Vengerov, 1901.

Deutsches Bundarchiv, East Berlin

Three letters to Hans Delbrück, 1902.

Finnish State Archives, Helsinki

Ten letters to A. Neovius, 1902–1906.

Other Unpublished Materials Relating to Struve

International Institute for Social History, Amsterdam

One hundred ninety-two letters from A. M. Kalmykova to A. N. Potresov, 1894–1905.
Four letters from A. N. Potresov to P. B. Struve, undated.
Two letters from P. N. Skvortsov to P. B. Struve, 1895.
One letter from Karl Kautsky to P. B. Struve, 1895.

Hoover Institution, Stanford, California

Okhrana Archives: scattered reports on the surveillance of Struve, 1902–1904.

Staatsarchiv Ludwigsburg, Ludwigsburg, Germany

Papers relating to *Osvobozhdenie,* 1903–1904: Bestand E 150, Bund 1608.

Private possession, Professor Gleb Struve,
Berkeley, California

A. Meiendorf, "P. B. Struve," manuscript of 46 pages, written in 1944–45.

B. I. Nikolaevsky, Archive, Hoover Institution,
Stanford, California

Recollections of P. B. Struve by V. A. Obolensky, written in 1944.

Works by P. B. Struve, 1892–1905, Exclusive of Newspaper Articles, in Order of Publication

#1. "Novaia kniga Gumplovicha," RB, XI, No. 6 (June 1892), Pt. 2, 25–30.
#2. "Zur Auswanderungsfrage in Russland," SC, I, No. 28, (July 11, 1892), 343 346.
#3. "Die Wirtschaftliche Entwickelung Russlands und die Erhaltung des Bauernstandes," SC, I, No. 34, (August 22, 1892), 415–417.
#4. "Die Bauernpacht in Russland," SC, II, No. 1, (October 3, 1892), 2–4.
#5. Review of *Itogi ekonomicheskogo issledovaniia Rossii po dannym zemskoi statistiki* (Moscow and Dorpat, 1892); ASGS, V (1892), 498–517, and VI (1893), 172–176.
#6. "Zur Landarbeiterfrage in Russland," SC, II, No. 23 (March 6, 1893), 269–271.
#7. "Die Sozialstatistik der Missernten in Russland," SC, II, No. 27 (April 3, 1893), 320–321.

#8. "Avstriiskoe krest'ianstvo i ego bytopisatel'," VE, XXVIII, No. 6 (June 1893), 569–585; reprinted in *Nrt*, 317–334.

#9. "Zur Beurtheilung der kapitalistichen Entwickelung Russlands," SC, III, No. 1 (October 2, 1893), 1–3.

#10. Review of I. A. Hourwich, *The Economics of the Russian Village* (New York, 1892); ASGS, VI (1893), 630–633.

#11. "Der Arbeitslohn und die Lebenshaltung der Fabrikarbeiter in Gouvernement Moskau," SC, III, No. 20 (February 12, 1894), 234–235.

#12. "Nemtsy v Avstrii i krest'ianstvo," VE, XXIX, No. 2 (February 1894), 796–828; reprinted in *Nrt*, 335–368.

#13. Review of Nikolai -on [N. F. Danielson], *Ocherki nashego poreformennogo obshchestvennogo khoziaistva* (St. Petersburg, 1893): ASGS, VII (1894), 350–358.

#14. "Die neure russische Gesetzgebung über den Gemeindbesitz," ASGS, VII (1894), 626–652; signed "P.S."

#15. *Kriticheskie zametki k voprosu ob ekonomicheskom razvitii Rossii,* Vypusk I (St. Petersburg, 1894).

#16. "Der Lodzer Projekt einer gesetzlichen Regelung der Arbeitszeit in den Fabrik- und Handwerksunternehmungen Russlands," SC, IV, No. 4 (October 22, 1894), 45–46.

#17. "Zarabotnaia plata," B&E, XII (1894), 284–295.

#17a. "Zemledel'cheskoe gosudarstvo," B&E, XII (1894), 424–425.

#18. "Izbytok rabochikh ruk (Bezrabotitsa)," B&E, XII (1894), 820–822.

#18a. "Imperskie finansy," B&E, XIII (1894), 18.

#19. "Imushchestvennyi nalog," B&E, XIII (1894), 25–28.

#20. "Otkrytoe pis'mo k Nikolaiu II." Mimeographed on January 19/31, 1895. Reprinted in V. Burtsev, ed., *Za sto let, 1800–1896* (London, 1897), Pt. 1, 264–267.

#21. "Moim kritikam," *Materialy k kharakteristike nashego khoziaistvennogo razvitiia* [St. Petersburg, 1895]. Book impounded and destroyed by censorship. First published in *Nrt*, 1–59.

#22. Review of I. I. Ianzhul, *Promyslovye sindikaty* (St. Petersburg, 1895); ASGS, VIII (1895), 514–519.

#23. "Karteli," B&E, XIV (1895), 610–616.

#23a. "Katedersotsializm, k.-sotsialisty," B&E, XIV (1895), 723–724.

#24. "Kautskii," B&E, XIV (1895), 772–773.

#25. "Neskol'ko slov po povodu stat'i g. Obolenskogo, 'Novyi raskol v nashei intelligentsii' (Pis'mo v redaktsiiu)," RM, XVII (February 1896), No. 2, Pt. 2, 100–114; reprinted in *Nrt*, 233–251.

#26. Critique of report by N. V. Levitsky on agricultural artels in the Kherson province, delivered on January 13/25, 1896; *Trudy* IVEO, No. 2 (March–April 1896), 190–193, 214–216, 222.

#27. Critique of report by V. I. Kasperov on the economic consequences of monetary reform, delivered on April 2/14, 1896: *Trudy* IVEO, No. 3 (May–June 1896), 208–214. Reprinted in *Reforma denezhnego obrashcheniia v Rossii* (St. Petersburg, 1896), 208–214.

#28. "Zwei bisher unbekannte Aufsätze von Karl Marx aus den vierziger Jahren," NZ, XIV, Pt. 2 (1895–96), No. 27 (March 25, 1896), 4–11, and No. 28 (April 1, 1896), 48–55.

#29. "Marx und der 'wahre' Sozialismus," NZ, XIV, Pt. 2 (1895–96), No. 33 (May 6, 1896), 219–220.

#30. Review of G. P. Rosenberg, *Zur Arbeiterschutzgesetzgebung in Russland* (Leipzig, 1895), ASGS, IX (1896), 297–304.

#31. "Agrarnyi vopros i sotsial'naia demokratiia v Rossii," in *Doklad, predstavlennyi delegatsieiu russkikh sotsial-demokratov mezhdunarodnomu rabochemu sotsialisticheskomu kongressu v Londone v 1896 godu* (Geneva, 1896), 22–32. Anonymous, identified as Struve's in *Perepiska G. V. Plekhanova i P. B. Aksel'roda,* I (Moscow, 1925),

145. Reprinted in German translation in NZ, XIV, Pt. 2 (1895–96), No. 44 (July 22, 1896), 560–566.

#32. "Lange, F. A.," B&E, XVII (1896), 312–314.

#32a. "Lassal', F.," B&E, XVII (1896), 363–366.

#33. "Makler slug," B&E, XVIII (1896), 426–427.

#33a. "Mandevil', B.," B&E, XVIII (1896), 530–531.

#34. "Manufaktura," B&E, XVIII (1896), 563–564.

#34a. "Manchesterskaia shkola," B&E, XVIII (1896), 568.

#35. "Marks, K.," B&E, XVIII (1896), 662–667.

#36. "Monopoliia," B&E, XIX (1896), 782–784.

#37. "Die Arbeiterbewegung in Russland," SP, VI, No. 2 (October 8, 1896), 25–30. Anonymous, Struve identified as author in LS, IV, 18, note 31.

#38. "Studien und Bemerkungen zur Entwicklungsgeschichte des wissenschaftlichen Sozialismus," NZ, XV, Pt. 1 (1896–97), No. 3 (October 7, 1896), 66–81; XV, Pt. 2, No. 34 (May 12, 1897), 228–235, and No. 35 (May 19, 1897), 269–275.

#39. "Die Deutsche Brüsseler Zeitung' vom Jahre 1847," NZ, XV, Pt. 1 (1896–97), No. 12 (December 9, 1896), 380–381.

#40. "Osnovnye poniatiia i voprosy politicheskoi ekonomii," MB, V, No. 12 (December 1896), 105–115.

#41. "Filosofiia ideal'nogo dobra ili apologiia real'nogo zla?," SoV, No. 5 1897); reprinted with major revisions in Nrt, 187–197.

#42. "Novaia kniga po russkoi istorii i literature," SoV, No. 20 (1897); reprinted, with minor changes, in Nrt, 221–232.

#43. "Svoboda i istoricheskaia neobkhodimost'," VFP, VIII, No. 1/36 (January–February 1897), 120–139; reprinted in Nrt, 487–507.

#44. "Nashi utopisty," NS, No. 6 (March 1897), Pt. 2, 1–20; reprinted in Nrt, 60–83.

#45. "Tekushchie voprosy vnutrennei zhizni," NS, No. 6 (March 1897), Pt. 2, 157–172; signed "P.B."

#46. "G. Chicherin i ego obrashchenie k proshlomu," NS, No. 7 (April 1897), Pt. 2, 34–62; reprinted in Nrt, 84–120. Signed in NS "Novus."

#47. "Tekushchie voprosy vnutrennei zhizni," NS, No. 7 (April 1897), Pt. 2, 229–243; signed "P.B."

#48. "Ocherki iz istorii obshchestvennykh idei i otnoshenii v Germanii v XIX veke," NS, No. 7 (April 1897), Pt. 1, 83–96, and No. 8 (May 1897), Pt. 1, 154–167; NO, V, No. 4 (April 1898), 785–795. The NS articles are signed "S.T.R."

#49. "Eshche o svobode i neobkhodimosti," NS, No. 8 (May 1897), Pt. 2, 200–208.

#50. "Na raznye temy: 'Muzhiki' g. Chekhova," NS, No. 8 (May 1897), Pt. 2, 42–51; signed "Novus." Reprinted in Nrt, 121–132.

#51. Review of J. Beloch's Istoriia Gretsii, I (Moscow, 1897); NS, No. 8 (May 1897), Pt. 2, 57–60. Unsigned.

#52. "Tekushchie voprosy vnutrennei zhizni," NS, No. 8 (May 1897), Pt. 2, 207–229; signed "P.B."

#53. "Tekushchie voprosy vnutrennei zhizni," NS, No. 9 (June 1897), Pt. 2, 190–214; signed "P.B."

#54. "K voprosu o bezrabotitse," NS, No. 10 (July 1897), Pt. 1, 92–106. Reprinted in Dzh. Gobson (J. Hobson), Problemy bednosti i bezrabotitsy (St. Petersburg, 1900), 040–000.

#55. "'Ekonomicheskie etiudy' N. V. Vodovozova," NS, No. 10 (July 1897), Pt. 2, 56–62; reprinted in Nrt, 419–426.

#56. "Tekushchie voprosy vnutrennei zhizni," NS, No. 10 (July 1897), Pt. 2, 216–243; signed "P.B."

#57. Review of P. Novgorodtsev, Istoricheskaia shkola iuristov (Moscow,

1896); NS, No. 10 (July 1897), Pt. 2, 75–78. Unsigned; identified in *Nrt*, 79n.

#58. Remarks on a book edited by A. I. Chuprov and A. S. Posnikov on bread prices, delivered on March 1/13 and 2/14, 1897: *Trudy* IVEO, No. 4 (July–August 1897), 19–21, 78–83.

#59. "Mezhdunarodnyi kongress po voprosam zakonodatel'noi okhrany rabochikh," NS, No. 12 (September 1897), Pt. 2, 145–181. Reprinted in *Nrt*, 369–418.

#60. "Po povodu s.-peterburgskoi stachki," *Rabotnik* (Geneva), No. 3–4 (1897), iii–xvi; signed "Peterburzhets." Identified as Struve's in OD, II, Pt. 2, 314–315.

#61. Remarks on G. V. Butmi-de-Katsman's report on currency reform, delivered on April 7/19 and April 30/May 11, 1897; Trudy IVEO, No. 5 (September–October 1897), 111–115.

#62. "Na raznye temy," NS, No. 13 (October 1897), Pt. 2, 55–84; signed "Novus." Reprinted in *Nrt*, 113–146.

#63. Review of Paul Miliukov, *Ocherki po istorii russkoi kul'tury*, 2nd ed., Vols. I and II (St. Petersburg, 1897); NS, No. 13 (October 1897), Pt. 2, 89–94.

#64. "Tekushchie voprosy vnutrennei zhizni," NS, No. 13 (October 1897), Pt. 2, 246–266; signed "P.B."

#65. "Miscellanea," *Nrt*, 170–186. Original publication place unknown: probably an installment of "Na raznye temy" in the December 1897 NS issue destroyed by the censors.

#66. "Napriazhennost' ili intensivnost' truda," B&E, XX (1897), 557–559.

#67. "Narodnoe khoziaistvo," B&E, XX (1897), 590–591.

#68. Introduction to translation of Maks Schippel' (Max Schippel), *Denezhnoe obrashchenie i ego obshchestvennoe znachenie* (St. Petersburg, 1897), i–xiii.

#69. Introduction to G. Shultse-Gevernits (G. von Schulze-Gäwernitz), *Krupnoe proizvodstvo* (St. Petersburg, 1897), i–xx.

#70. *Manifest rossiiskoi sotsial-demokraticheskoi rabochei partii.* Unsigned. First distributed in April 1898 as a leaflet: cf. LR, No. 2 (1928), 180.

#71. "Marks o Göte (k kharakteristike dvukh umov)," MB, VII, No. 2 (February 1898), Pt. 1, 177–182; reprinted in *Nrt*, 252–258.

#72. "Istoricheskoe i sistematicheskoe mesto russkoi kustarnoi promyshlennosti (Otvet P. N. Miliukovu)," MB, XII, No. 4 (April 1898), Pt. 1, 188–200; reprinted in *Nrt*, 427–447.

#73. "Die neue Fabrikgesetzgebung Russlands," ASGS, XII (1898), 475–515. Unsigned. Authorship identified in LS, IV, 10.

#74. "Nauchnaia istoriia russkoi krupnoi promyshlennosti," *Nrt*, 448–464. Original place and date of publication unknown.

#75. Introduction to Pol' de Ruz'e (Paul de Rousiers), *Professional'nye rabochie soiuzy v Anglii* (St. Petersburg, 1898), i–iii.

#76. "K voprosu o rynkakh pri kapitalisticheskom proizvodstve (Po povodu knigi Bulgakova i stat'i Il'ina)," NO, VI, No. 1 (January 1899), 46–64.

#77. "Popytki artel'noi organizatsii krepostnykh krest'ian. Iz etiudov o krepostnom khoziaistve," N, No. 1–2 (January–February 1899), Pt. 1, 296–318. Reprinted in *KrKh*, 171–212.

#78. "Vnutrennee obozrenie," N, No. 1–2 (January–February 1899), Pt. 2, 292–316.

#79. "Romantika protiv kazenshchiny," N, No. 3 (March 1899), Pt. 2, 177–191. Reprinted in *Nrt*, 203–220.

#80. "Vnutrennee obozrenie," N, No. 3 (March 1899), Pt. 2, 224–258.

#81. Review of B. Kistiakovsky, *Gesellschaft und Einzelwesen* (Berlin, 1899); ASGS, XIV (1899), 222–226.

#82. "Die Marxsche Theorie der sozialen Entwicklung. Ein kritischer

Versuch," ASGS, XIV (1899), 658–704. French translation in *Etudes de Marxologie* (Paris), No. 6 (1962), 105–156.

#83. Review of Eduard Bernstein, *Die Voraussetzungen des Sozialismus* (Stuttgart, 1899), and Karl Kautsky, *Bernstein und das sozialdemokratische Programm* (Stuttgart, 1899); ASGS, XIV (1899), 723–739.

#84. "Otvet Il'inu," NO, No. 8 (August 1899), 1580–1584.

#85. Introduction to Russian translation of Karl Marks (Karl Marx), *Kapital*, Vol. I, Bk, I (St. Petersburg, 1899), xxvii–xxxiv.

#86. "Protiv Ortodoksii," Zh, III, No. 10 (October 1899), 175–179.

#87. "Osnovnye momenty v razvitii krepostnogo khoziaistva v Rossii v XIX v. (Istoricheskii etiud)," MB, VIII, No. 10 (October 1899), Pt. 1, 180–194; No. 11 (November 1899), Pt. 1, 271–289; No. 12 (December 1899), Pt. 1, 254–283. Reprinted, with changes, in *KrKh*, 1–170.

#88. "Rabochii klass," B&E, XXVI (1899), 25–28.

#89. "Osnovnaia antinomiia teorii trudovoi tsennosti," Zh, IV, No. 2 (February 1900), 297–306.

#90. "K kritike nekotorykh osnovnykh problem i polozhenii politicheskoi ekonomii," Zh, IV, No. 3 (March 1900), 361–392, and No. 6 (June 1900), 249–272.

#91. "Pervaia popytka vozbuzhdeniia krest'ianskogo voprosa v tsarstvovanie Aleksandra II," Zh, IV, No. 4 (April 1900), 455–466. Reprinted in *KrKh*, 288–308.

#92. "Iz letnikh nabliudenii," MB, IX, No. 9 (September 1900), Pt. 1, 193–210. Reprinted in *Nrt*, 465–486.

#93. "Vladimir Solov'ev," MB, IX, No. 9 (September 1900), Pt. 2, 13–15. Reprinted in *Nrt*, 198–202, as "Pamiati Vladimira Solov'eva."

#94. "Novoe izdanie *Promyshlennykh krizisov* M. I. Tugan-Baranovskogo (Kriticheskaia zametka)," MB, IX, No. 10 (October 1900), Pt. 1, 259–279.

#95. "F. Lassal' (Po povodu 75-letiia so dnia ego rozhdeniia)," MB, IX, No. 11 (November 1900), Pt. 1, 294–299. Reprinted in *Nrt*, 259–266.

#96. Introduction to Nicholas Berdiaev, *Sub"ektivizm i individualizm* (St. Petersburg, 1901), i–lxxxiv.

#97. "Na raznye temy," MB, X, No. 1 (January 1901), Pt. 2, 13–19. Reprinted in *Nrt*, 279–290, as "Zametki o Gauptmane i Nitsshe."

#98. Introduction to S. Iu. Vitte (Witte), *Samoderzhavie i zemstvo* (Stuttgart, 1901), iv–xliv. Cf. #190.

#99. "Samoderzhavie i zemstvo," *Iskra*, No. 2 (February 1901), 2, and No. 4 (May 1901), 2–3. Unsigned. Identified as Struve's in LS, I, 34.

#100. "Pravo i prava," *Pravo* (St. Petersburg), No. 2 (January 7, 1901), 88–91. Unsigned. Reprinted in *Nrt*, 522–525.

#101. "Na raznye temy," MB, X, No. 3 (March 1901), Pt. 2, 108–113. Reprinted in *Nrt*, 267–278, as "Eshche o Lassale."

#102. "Na raznye temy," MB, X, No. 6 (June 1901), Pt. 2, 12–27. Reprinted in *Nrt*, 291–316, as "Protiv ortodoksal'noi neterpimosti — Pro domo sua," and "Pamiati N. V. Shelgunova."

#103. "Liubopytnyi obyvatel'skii protest protiv shkol'nogo klassitsizma XVIII veka," MB, X, No. 7 (July 1901), Pt. 1, 186–202.

#104. Review of Simeon Frank, *Teoriia tsennosti* (St. Petersburg, 1900); MB, X, No. 8 (August 1901), Pt. 2, 113–117.

#105. "Krepostnaia statistika (Iz etiudov o krepostnom khoziaistve)," NO, VIII, No. 9–10 (September 1901), 22–45. Reprinted in *KrKh*, 213–250.

#106. "V chem zhe istinnyi natsionalizm? (Posviashchaetsia pamiati Vladimira Seergevicha Solov'eva)," VFP, XII, No. 59 (September–October 1901), 493–528. Reprinted in *Nrt*, 526–555. Originally signed "P. Borisov."

#107. "K voprosu o morali," MB, X, No. 10 (October 1901), Pt. 1, 186–197. Signed "P.I." Reprinted in Nrt, 508–521.
#108. "Novyi trud po agrarnoi ekonomii Rossii," NO, VIII, No. 11 (November 1901), 16–24. Reprinted in KrKh, 317–335, as "O knige V. G. Bazhaeva."
#109. "K literaturno-obshchestvennoi istorii krest'ianskogo voprosa," in Pomoshch Evreiam postradaiushchim ot neurozhaia — Literaturno-khudozhestvennyi sbornik (St. Petersburg, 1901), 139–153. Reprinted, with changes, in KrKh, 251–287, as "Iz istorii idei krest'ianskogo zemleustroistva."
#110. Introduction to G. Shultse-Gevernits (G. von Schulze-Gäwernitz), Ocherki obshchestvennogo khoziaistva i ekonomicheskoi politiki Rossii (St. Peterburg, 1901), vii–xvi.
#111. "Ot redaktora," Osv, I, No. 1 (June 18/July 1, 1902), 1–7.
#112. Introduction to "Pis'ma v redaktsiiu," Osv, I, No. 1, (June 18/July 1, 1902), 12–13.
#113. Introduction to "Materialy i svedeniia po delu ob ubiistve Sipiagina," Osv, I, No. 1 (June 18/July 1, 1902), 14.
#114. Editorial, Osv, I, No. 2 (July 2/15, 1902), 17–21.
#115. Editorial, Osv, I, No. 3 (July 19/August 1, 1902), 33–35.
#116. Remarks on "Gosudarstvennyi podlog," Osv, I, No. 3 (July 19/August 1, 1902), 38.
#117. Editorial, Osv, I, No. 4 (August 2/15, 1902), 49–50.
#118. Review of A. P., Samoderzhavie, biurokratizm i zemstvo (Berlin, 1902); Osv, I, No. 4 (August 2/15, 1902), 64.
#119. Editorial, Osv, I, No. 5 (August 19/September 1, 1902), 65–68.
#120. "Ot redaktsii," Osv, I, No. 6 (September 2/15, 1902), 81–85.
#121. Editorial, Osv, I, No. 7 (September 18/October 1, 1902), 97–100.
#122. "Po povodu odnogo upreka," Osv, I, No. 7 (September 18/October 1, 1902), 102.
#123. "Kodifikatsiia' tsenzurnykh zapretov," Osv, I, No. 7 (September 18/October 1, 1902), 102–104.
#124. "Liberalizm i t.n. 'revoliutsionnye' napravleniia," Osv, I, No. 7 (September 18/October 1, 1902), 104–105.
#125. Editorial, Osv, No. 8 (October 2/15, 1902), 113–116.
#126. "Po povodu predlozhenii M-va Finansov ob otmene nakazanii na stachki," Osv, I, No. 8 (October 2/15, 1902), 119–120. Identical with #133.
#127. Editorial, Osv, I, No. 9 (October 19/November 1, 1902), 129–132.
#128. Editorial, Osv, I, No. 10 (November 2/15, 1902), 145–150.
#129. "K sobytiiam," Osv, I, No. 11 (November 18/December 1, 1902), 175–176.
#130. Editorial, Osv, I, No. 12 (December 2/15, 1902), 185–190.
#131. Editorial, Osv, I, No. 13 (December 19/January 1, 1902), 201–203.
#132. Na raznye temy (1893–1901 gg.) — Sbornik statei (St. Petersburg, 1902).
#133. Introduction to Russkii zakon i rabochii (Materialy po rabochemu voprosu, Vyp. I) (Stuttgart, 1902), iii–vi. Cf. #126.
#134. Introduction to Kratkii ocherk pravitel'stvennykh mer i prednachertanii protiv studencheskikh besporiadkov (Materialy po universitetskomu voprosu, Vyp. I) Stuttgart, 1902), iii–iv.
#135. Editorial, Osv, I, No. 14 (January 2/15, 1903), 217–218.
#136. "Razboinitskaia moda," Osv, I, No. 14 (January 2/15, 1903), 232–233.
#137. "'Ob"edinenie' v oblasti narodnogo obrazovaniia," Osv, I. No. 14 (January 2/15, 1903), 243.
#138. Editorial, Osv, I, No. 15 (January 19/February 1, 1903), 249–251.
#139. Editorial, Osv, I, No. 16 (February 2/15, 1903), 265–267.

#140. "K ocherednym voprosam," *Osv*, I, No. 17 (February 16/March 1, 1903), 291–292. (Pt. 1 of this article, signed "ss" was written by Paul Miliukov).

#141. "Tri avtora," *Osv*, I, No. 18 (March 2/15, 1903), 305–307.

#142. "Na zloby dnia," *Osv*, I, No. 18 (March 2/15, 1903), 307.

#143. "Finansovo-ekonomicheskoe polozhenie Rossii i politika g. Vitte"; Pt. 1: *Osv*, I, No. 18 (March 2/15, 1903), 307–309; Pt. 2: *Osv*, II, No. 2/26 (July 2/15, 1903), 22–24.

#144. "O chem dumaet odna kniga?" *Osv*, I, No. 18 (March 2/15, 1903), 311–312.

#145. "Nashi reformatory," *Osv*, I, No. 19 (March 19/April 1, 1903), 326.

#146. "K politiko-ekonomicheskoi biografii kn. V. P. Meshcherskogo," *Osv*, I, No. 19 (March 19/April 1, 1903), 332–333.

#147. "Voisko i natsiia," *Osv*, I, No. 19 (March 19/April 1, 1903), 339–340.

#148. Editorial, *Osv*, I, No. 20–21 (April 18/May 1, 1903), 345–348.

#149. "Zubatov v Peterburge ili prerekaniia polits. vedomstv po rabochemu voprosu," *Osv*, No. 20–21 (April 18/May 1, 1903), 352–353.

#150. "Rossiia pod nadzorom politsii"; Pt. 1: *Osv*, I, No. 20–21 (April 18/May 1, 1903), 357–358; Pt. 2: *Osv*, II, No. 5/29 (August 19/September 1, 1903), 86–87; Pt. 3: *Osv*, II, No. 6/30 (September 2/15, 1903), 110–111; Pt. 4: *Osv*, II, No. 9/33 (October 19/November 1, 1903), 165; Pts. 5 and 6: *Osv*, II, No. 11 (November 12/25, 1903), 185–187; Pt. 7: *Osv*, II, No. 19/43 (March 7/20, 1904), 342–344.

#151. Editorial, *Osv*, I, No. 22 (May 8/21, 1903), 377–379.

#152. "Kto pritupliaet obshchestvennoe soznanie?" *Osv*, I, No. 23 (May 19/June 1, 1903), 409–411.

#153. "Neobkhodimoe ob"iasnenie," *Osv*, I, No. 23 (May 19/June 1, 1903), 411–412.

#154. "Geroi dnia," *Osv*, I, No. 23 (May 19/June 1, 1903), 412.

#155. Editorial, *Osv*, I, No. 24 (June 2/15, 1903), 425–429.

#156. "Konets malen'kogo samoderzhaviia," *Osv*, I, No. 24 (June 2/15, 1903), 429.

#157. Editorial, *Osv*, II, No. 1/25 (June 18/July 1, 1903), 1–3.

#158. "Germanskie vybory," *Osv*, II, No. 1/25 (June 18/July 1, 1903), 3–5.

#159. Comment on "Usilenie gubernatorskoi vlasti," *Osv*, II, No. 1/25 (June 18/July 1, 1903), 11–12.

#160. Editorial, *Osv*, II, No. 2/26 (July 2/15, 1903), 17–21.

#161. Editorial, *Osv*, II, No. 3/27 (July 19/August 1, 1903), 33–35.

#162. Editorial, *Osv*, II, No. 4 (August 2/15, 1903), 49–53.

#163. Editorial, *Osv*, II, No. 5/29 (August 19/September 1, 1903), 73–74.

#164. Editorial, *Osv*, II, No. 6/30 (September 2/15, 1903), 89–92.

#165. "Zemskoe delo," *Osv*, II, No. 6/30 (September 2/15, 1903), 96–97.

#166. "Vnutrennii politseiskii nadzor za ofitserami rossiiskoi armii," *Osv*, II, No. 7/31 (September 18/October 1, 1903), 113.

#167. "Pleve, Gertsl' i evrei," *Osv*, II, No. 7/31 (September 18/October 1, 1903), 125.

#168. Editorial, *Osv*, II, No. 8/32 (October 2/15, 1903), 129–131.

#169. "K prebyvaniiu tsaria zagranitsei," *Osv*, II, No. 8/32 (October 2/15, 1903), 131–133.

#170. Introduction to "Chudesa politsii v Sarove," *Osv*, II, No. 8/32 (October 2/15, 1903), 132.

#171. "Figliar, pouchaiushchii liubvi k otechestvu," *Osv*, II, No. 9/33 (October 19/November 1, 1903), 158–160.

#172. "K Kishinevskomu protsessu," *Osv*, *II*, No. 9/33 (October 19/November 1, 1903), 166.

#173. "Lozung vremeni," *Osv*, II, No. 10/34 (November 2/15, 1903), 169/173.

#174. Comments on "Studencheskoe obshchestvo v Moskve," *Osv*, II, No. 10/34 (November 2/15, 1903), 180/182.
#175. "Torg i peretorzhka," *Osv*, II, No. 11/35 (November 12/25, 1903), 190–192.
#176. "Poprishchin, kak redaktor 'S.-Peterburgsk[ikh] Vedomostei," *Osv*, II, No. 12/36 (November 24/December 7, 1903), 201.
#177. "K arestu V. L. Burtseva," *Osv*, II, No. 12/36 (November 24/December 7, 1903), 213–214.
#178. "Naglyi obman, ili tsinicheskoe izdevatel'stvo?" *Osv*, II, No. 13/37, (December 2/15, 1903), 221.
#179. "Zametki," *Osv*, II, No. 13/37 (December 2/15, 1903), 222–224.
#180. "Davlenie na senat," *Osv*, II, No. 13/37 (December 2/15, 1903), 224–225.
#181. "Eshche g. Stolypin," *Osv*, II, No. 13/37 (December 2/15, 1903), 239.
#182. "Russkoe samoderzhavie pered sudom ego byvshego storonnika," *Osv*, II, No. 14/38 (December 25, 1903/January 7, 1904), 241–242.
#183. "Samoderzhavie i zemstvo," *Osv*, II, No. 14/38 (December 25, 1903/January 7, 1904), 252–253.
#184. "Vsepronikaiushchii sysk samoderzhaviia," *Osv*, II, No. 14/38 (December 25, 1903/January 7, 1904), 253–254.
#185. Introduction to "Mery pravitel'stva v bor'be s dvizheniem sredi zheleznodorozhnykh rabochikh," *Osv*, II No. 14/38 (December 25, 1903/January 7, 1904), 254.
#186. Introduction to *Osvobozhdenie: Kniga Pervaia* (Stuttgart, 1903), iii.
#187. Afterword to "Materialy po noveishei istorii russkoin tsenzury," in *Osvobozhdenie: Kniga Pervaia* (Stuttgart, 1903), 204.
#188. "Ne v ochered'," in *Osvobozhdenie: Kniga Pervaia* (Stuttgart, 1903), 225–239.
#189. Review of Vladimir Debogory-Mokrievich, *Vospominaniia*, in *Osvobozhdenie: Kniga Pervaia* (Stuttgart, 1903), 243–253.
#190. Introduction to second edition of S. Iu. Vitte (Witte), *Samoderzhavie i zemstvo* (Stuttgart, 1903), xlviii–lxxii.
#191. "K kharakteristike nashego filosofskogo razvitiia," in P. I. Novgorodtsev, ed., *Problemy idealizma* (Moscow, 1903), 72–90. Signed "P.G."
#192. Introduction to *Doklad voronezhskogo uezdnogo komiteta o nuzhdakh sel'sko-khoziaistvennoi promyshlennosti* (Stuttgart, 1903), 3.
#193. Introduction to *Kishinevskii pogrom* (Stuttgart, 1903), vii–viii.
#194. Introduction to *Ministr Finansov i gosudarstvennyi sovet o finansovom polozhenii Rossii* (Stuttgart, 1903), 3–4.
#195. Introduction to *Zakonodatel'nye materialy k zakonu o starostakh v promyshlennykh predpriiatiiakh* (*Materialy po rabochemu voprosu*, Vyp. II, Stuttgart, 1903), v–xx.
#196. "Usilenie gubernatorskoi vlasti," *Osv*, II, No. 15–16/39–40 (January 19/February 1, 1904), 275–279.
#197. "Zemstvo, dvorianstvo i samoderzhavie," *Osv*, II, No. 15–16/39–40 (January 19/February 1, 1904), 289–291.
#198. "Voina," *Osv*, II, No. 17/41 (February 5/18, 1904), 297.
#199. "N. K. Mikhailovskii — Nekrolog," *Osv*, II, No. 17/41 (February 5/18, 1904), 297.
#200. "Voennyi iubilei i iubileinaia voina," *Osv*, II, No. 17/41 (February 5/18, 1904), 297–301.
#201. "Polozhenie del na teatre voiny," *Osv*, II, No. 17/41 (February 5/18, 1904), 312.
#202. "Pis'mo k studentam," *LisOsv*, No. 1 (February 11/24, 1904), 1–3.
#203. "Nel'zia molchat'," *LisOsv*, No. 2 (February 18/March 2, 1904), 1–2.
#204. "Voina i patriotizm," *Osv*, II, No. 18/42 (February 19/March 3, 1904), 319.

#205. "Voina, finansy i valiuta," *Osv*, II, No. 18/42 (February 19/March 3, 1904), 321–323.
#206. "B. N. Chicherin — Nekrolog," *Osv*, II, No. 18/42 (February 19/March 3, 1904), 323.
#207. "Voina i russkaia oppozitsiia," *Osv*, II, No. 19/43 (March 7/20, 1904), 330–332, and No. 21/45 (April 2/15, 1904), 379. The sections signed "ss" are by P. N. Miliukov.
#208. "Neskol'ko slov o patrioticheskikh adresakh," *LisOsv*, No. 6 (April 15/28, 1904), 1–2.
#209. Editorial, *Osv*, II, No. 22/46 (April 18/May 1, 1904), 385–386.
#210. "Set' lzhi," *Osv*, II, No. 22/46 (April 18/May 1, 1904), 386–390.
#211. "12 protiv 50," *Osv*, II, No. 22/46 (April 18/May 1, 1904), 390–391.
#212. "Po povodu porazheniia na Ialu," *LisOsv*, No. 7 (April 26/May 9, 1904), 1–2.
#213. Editorial, *Osv*, II, No. 23/47 (May 2/15, 1904), 409–410.
#214. "Samoderzhavie protiv ranenykh i zemstva," *Osv*, II, No. 24/48 (May 21/June 3, 1904), 425–426.
#215. Remarks on "Delo Anichkova i Borman," *Osv*, II, No. 2/48 (May 21/June 3, 1904), 430–431.
#216. "Nikakogo politseiskogo znacheniia'," *Osv*, II, No. 24/48 (May 21/June 3, 1904), 436.
#217. "S teatra voiny," *LisOsv*, No. 10 (May 27/June 9, 1904), 1.
#218. "Politika vnutrenniaia i politika vneshniaia," *Osv*, II, No. 25/49 June 2/15, 1904), 441–442.
#219. Introduction to "Voina," *Osv*, II, No. 56 (June 2/15, 1904), 446.
#220. "Pravda li, chto russkoe pravitel'stvo somnevaetsia v blagodati Sv. Kreshcheniia?" *Osv*, II, No. 25/49 (June 2/15, 1904), 454.
#221. Remarks on "Eshche odin podvig g. f.-Pleve," *Osv*, II, No. 25/49 June 2/15, 1904), 455–456.
#222. "Experimentum in anima populi," *LisOsv*, No. 11 (June 9/22, 1904), 1.
#223. "Gubernatorskii gipnoz," *Osv*, III, No. 50 (June 25/July 8, 1904), 1–2.
#224. "Lev Tolstoi o voine," *Osv*, III, No. 51 (July 2/15, 1904), 17–22.
#225. "Konets f.-Pleve," *Osv*, III, No. 52 (July 19/August 1, 1904), 33.
#226. "Znal ili ne znal tsar'?" *Osv*, III, No. 52 (July 19/August 1, 1904), 35–36.
#227. "Iz russkoi zhizni," *Osv*, III, No. 52 (July 19/August 1, 1904), 44–46.
#228. "Oblichenie gnili," *Osv*, III, No. 53 (August 2/15, 1904), 49–50.
#229. "Tsar' v narode," *Osv*, III, No. 53 (August 2/15, 1904), 50.
#230. "Iz russkoi zhizni," *Osv*, III, No. 53 (August 2/15, 1904), 61–62.
#231. "Gosudarstvennaia vozmozhnost' nemedlennogo prekrashcheniia voiny," *Osv*, III, No. 54 (August 19/September 1, 1904), 65–67.
#232. "Milosti mladentsa Alekseia," *Osv*, III, No. 55 (September 2/15, 1904), 81–82.
#233. "Nashi neprimirimye terroristy i ikh glavnyi shtab," *Osv*, III, No. 55 (September 2/15, 1904), 83–84.
#234. "Novyi Ministr Vnutrennikh Del," *Osv*, III, No. 55 (September 2/15, 1904), 84–85.
#235. "Znachenie Liaoianskogo boia," *Osv*, III, No. 55 (September 2/15, 1904), 90.
#236. "Chto zhe teper'?" *Osv*, III, No. 56 (September 7/20, 1904), 98–99.
#237. "Organizatsiia i platforma demokraticheskoi partii," *Osv*, III, No. 58 (October 14/27, 1904), 129–130.
#238. "Otstuplenie kn. Sviatopolka?" *Osv*, III, No. 58 (October 14/27, 1904), 135.

\#239. "Otkrytoe pis'mo k prof. kn. E. N. Trubetskomu," *Osv*, III, No. 58 (October 14/28, 1904), 136–137.

\#240. Introduction to "Dva pis'ma k ministru vnutrennikh del," *Osv*, III, No. 58 (October 14/27, 1904), 137.

\#241. "Prizrak voiny s Angliei," *Osv*, III, No. 59 (October 28/November 10, 1904), 145–147.

\#242. "Kn. Sviatopolk-Mirskii i vopros o konstitutsii," *Osv*, III, No. 59 (October 28/November 10, 1904), 158–159.

\#243. "Intrigi protiv kn. Sviatopolka-Mirskogo," *Osv*, III, No. 59 (October 28/November 10, 1904), 159–160.

\#244. "Glasnost' kniazia Sviatopolka-Mirskogo," *Osv*, III, No. 60 (November 10/23, 1904), 178.

\#245. "Zemskii s"ezd," *Osv*, III, No. 60 (November 10/23, 1904), 183.

\#246. Introduction to "Delo ob ubiistve f.-Pleve," *LisOsv*, No. 19 (November 27/December 10, 1904), 1.

\#247. Editorial, *Osv*, III, No. 61 (November 30/December 13, 1904), 185.

\#248. "Zhores o soglasovannykh deistviiakh russkoi oppozitsii," *Osv*, III, No. 61 (November 30/December 13, 1904), 185–186.

\#249. "K sobytiiam," *Osv*, III, No. 61 (November 30/December 13, 1904), 197–198.

\#250. "*Vorwärts* o deklaratsii oppozitsionnykh i revoliutsionnykh partii," *Osv*, III, No. 61 (November 30/December 13, 1904), 200.

\#251. "Novye obeshchaniia i novye ugrozy," *Osv*, III, No. 62 (December 18/31, 1904), 201–203.

\#252. "Po povodu nekotorykh noveishikh politicheskikh raskopok," *Pravo*, No. 51 (December 19, 1904), 3518–3522. Signed "S." Identified in RM, No. 11 (November 1911), Pt. 2, 131n.

\#253. Po povodu noveishikh izbienii," *LisOsv*, No. 22–23 (December 30, 1904/January 12, 1905), 5.

\#254. "Otkuda i kuda?" in *Osvobozhdenie: Kniga Vtoraia* (Paris, 1904), 15–29.

\#255. Introduction to *Usilenie gubernatorskoi vlasti: Proekt fon Pleve* (Paris, 1904), vii–xiv.

\#256. "Komitet Ministrov i Komitet Reform," *Osv*, III, No. 63 (January 7/20, 1905), 217–219.

\#257. "Nasushchaia zadacha vremeni," *Osv*, III, No. 63 (January 7/20, 1905), 221–222.

\#258. "Inostrannaia pechat' o russkikh delakh," *Osv*, III, No. 63 (January 7/20, 1905), 229–230.

\#259. "Palach naroda," *Osv*, III, No. 64 (January 12/25, 1905), 233.

\#260. "On proshchaet ikh," *Osv*, III, No. 65 (January 27/February 9, 1905), 241.

\#261. "Smirenno-sviateishie lguny," *Osv*, III, No. 65 (January 27/February 9, 1905), 254–255.

\#262. "Maksim Gor'kii i Akademiia Nauk," *Osv*, III, No. 65 (January 27/February 9, 1905), 256.

\#263. "Otkrytoe pis'mo k ofitseram russkoi armii," *Osv*, III, No. 66 (February 12/25, 1905), 257–258.

\#264. "Anarkhiia samoderzhaviia," *Osv*, III, No. 66 (February 12/25, 1905), 259–260.

\#265. "Neizbezhnoe," *Osv*, III, No. 66 (February 12/25, 1905), 260.

\#266. "Chernaia sotnia i belyi flag," *Osv*, III, No. 67 (March 5/18, 1905), 273.

\#267. "Demokraticheskaia partiia i ee programma," *Osv*, III, No. 67 (March 5/18, 1905), 278–279.

\#268. "Mukden," *Osv*, III, No. 67 (March 5/18, 1905), 280.

\#269. "Voprosy taktiki," *Osv*, III, No. 67 (March 5/18, 1905), 280–282, and No. 68 (April 2/15, 1905), 294–295.

#270. "V chem iskhod?" *Osv*, III, No. 68 (April 2/15, 1905), 289–290.
#271. Chto zhe budut na samon dele otstaivat' gg. dvoriane?" *Osv*, III, No. 68 (April 2/15, 1905), 297–298.
#272. "K programme Soiuza Osvobozhdeniia," *Osv*, III, No. 69–70 (May 7/20, 1905), 307–308.
#273. "Vserossiiskii s"ezd advokatov," *Osv*, III, No. 69–70 (May 7/20, 1905), 309–311.
#274. Introduction to "Dve agrarnye programmy," *Osv*, III, No. 69–70 (May 7/20, 1905), 327.
#275. "Zemstvo i demokratiia," *Osv*, III, No. 69–70 (May 7/20, 1905), 330–331.
#276. "Iz russkoi zagranichnoi pechati," *Osv*, III, No. 69–70 (May 7/20, 1905), 331–333.
#277. "Kak naiti sebia?" *Osv*, III, No. 71 (May 18/31, 1905), 337–343.
#278. "Kazn'," *Osv*, III, No. 71 (May 18/31, 1905), 351.
#279. "Sobstvennaia Ego Velichestva voina," *Osv*, III, No. 71 (May 18/31, 1905), 351–352.
#280. "V posledniuiu minutu," *Osv*, III, No. 71 (May 18/31, 1905), 352.
#281. "La Révolution russe et la Paix: Lettre ouverte au citoyen Jean Jaurés," *Humanité*, No. 417 (June 8, 1905). Translated into Russian in *Osv*, III, No. 72 (June 8/21, 1905), 353–355. Reprinted in RM, No. 3–4 (March–April 1917), Pt. 2, 95–101.
#282. "Po povodu otveta Zhoresa," *Osv*, III, No. 72 (June 8/21, 1905), 355–356.
#283. "S natsiei ili s pravitel'stvom — pis'mo k ofitseram," *Osv*, III, No. 72 (June 8/21, 1905), 360–361.
#284. "Torzhestvo zdravogo smysla," *Osv*, III, No. 72 (June 8/21, 1905), 362–363.
#285. "Pamiati Mikhaila Petrovicha Dragomanova," *Osv*, III, No. 72 (June 8/21, 1905), 364.
#286. "Eshche o Kuropatkine," *Osv*, III, No. 72 (June 8/21, 1905), 366.
#286a. "O vseobshchem izbiratel'nom prave v russkikh usloviiakh," *Pravo*, No. 25 (June 26, 1905), 2028–2034. Signed "P.S." and identified on the basis of internal evidence.
#287. "Nezhnaia uvertiura k groznomu konfliktu," *Osv*, III, No. 73 (July 6/19, 1905), 369–370.
#288. "'Kniaz' Potemkin' i chto zhe dal'she?," *Osv*, III, No. 73 (July 6/19, 1905), 371–372.
#289. "Priamoi otvet na krivye rechi g. Suvorina," *Osv*, III, No. 73 (July 6/19, 1905), 373–374.
#290. "Rozhdaetsia natsiia," *Osv*, III, No. 74 (July 13/26, 1905), 416.
#291. "Voina i mir," *Osv*, III, No. 75 (August 6/19, 1905), 437–439.
#292. "Iz ruk tsaria — iz ruk Mikado i Anglii," *Osv*, III, No. 76 (September 2/15, 1905), 442–444.
#293. "Le bourreau est le premier ministre d'un bon prince," *Osv*, III, No. 77 (September 13/26, 1905), 479–480.
#294. "Zametki o sovremennykh delakh," *Osv*, III, No. 78–79 (October 5/18, 1905), 495–498.
#295. "K obrazovaniiu konstitutsionno-demokraticheskoi partii," *Osv*, III, No. 78–79 (October 5/18, 1905), 503–504.
#296. "Kniaz' S. N. Trubetskoi," *Osv*, III, No. 78–79 (October 5/18, 1905), 504.
#297. Announcement of the discontinuation of *Osvobozhdenie*. Loose sheet, sent to subscribers, dated "Moscow, November 26, 1905."
#298. Introduction to *Zemskii s"ezd 6-go i sl. noiabria 1904 g., kratkii otchet* (Paris, 1905).
#299. Introduction to *Zemstvo i politicheskaia svoboda* (Paris, 1905), v.
#300. Introduction to *Osnovnoi gosudarstvennyi zakon Rossiiskoi Imperii*

(*Materialy po vyrabotke Russkoi konstitutsii,* Vyp. I) (Paris, 1905), vii–xv.

#301. Introduction to *Proekt osnovnogo zakona Rossiiskoi Imperii* (*Materialy po vyrabotke russkoi konstitutsii,* Vyp. 3) (Paris, 1905), iii–iv.

Principal Reminiscences and Secondary Works Dealing with the Young Struve

Frank, Simeon, *Biografiia P. B. Struve.* New York, 1956. Recollections of Struve by a friend. Cited as *Frank.*

Nikolaevsky, B. I. "P. B. Struve," NZh, No. 10 (1945), 306–328.

Valentinov, N. "Iz proshlogo: P. B. Struve o Lenine," SoV, No. 8–9 (673–674) (1954), 169–172.

Vodov, S. "Petr Berngardovich Struve," *Studencheskie gody* (Prague), No. 1/18 (1925), 33–35.

In addition, much biographical material can be found in the works listed below, especially those by Ariadna Tyrkova-Viliams and A. M. Voden.

Frequently Cited Collections, Memoirs, and Monographs

Angarsky, N. *Legal'nyi marksizm: populiarnyi ocherk,* Vol. I. Moscow, 1925.

Belokonsky, I. P. *Zemskoe dvizhenie.* Moscow, 1914. Cited as *Belokonsky.*

Chermensky, E. D. "Zemsko-liberal'noe dvizhenie nakanune revoliutsii 1905–1907 gg.," IsSSSR, No. 5 (1965), 41–60.

Fischer, George. *Russian Liberalism: From Gentry to Intelligentsia.* Cambridge, Mass., 1958.

Kindersley, Richard. *The First Russian Revisionists.* Oxford, 1962.

Lenin, V. I. *Pis'ma k rodnym, 1894–1919.* Leningrad, 1934.

Lenin, V. I. *Sochineniia,* 3rd ed., 30 vols. Moscow, 1926–1937. Cited as *Lenin.*

Maklakov, V. A. *Vlast' i obshchestvennost' na zakate staroi Rossii,* Vol. I. Paris, 1936.

Martov, L. *Zapiski sotsial-demokrata.* Berlin, 1922.

Marx, Karl and Friedrich Engels. *K. Marks, F. Engel's i revoliutsionnaia Rossiia.* Moscow, 1967. Cited as MERR.

Mendel, Arthur. *Dilemmas of Progress in Tsarist Russia.* Cambridge, Mass., 1961.

Miliukov, P. N. *Vospominaniia, 1859–1917,* Vol. I. New York, 1955.

Nikolaevsky, B. I. Introduction to *A. N. Potresov: Posmertnyi sbornik proizvedenii* (Paris, 1937), 9–90. Cited as *Potresov.*

Petrunkevich, I. I. "Iz zapisok obshchestvennogo deiatelia," in *Arkhiv russkoi revoliutsii,* XXI (1934).

Pipes, Richard, ed. *Revolutionary Russia.* Cambridge, Mass., 1968.

Pipes, Richard. *Social Democracy and the St. Petersburg Labor Movement, 1885–1897.* Cambridge, Mass., 1963.

Posse, V. A. *Moi zhiznennyi put'.* Moscow and Leningrad, 1929.

Shakhovskoi, D. I. "Soiuz Osvobozhdeniia," *Zarnitsy* (1909), Pt. 2, 81–171. Cited as *Shakhovskoi.*

Shipov, D. N. *Vospominaniia i dumy o perezhitom.* Moscow, 1918.

Tyrkova-Villiams, A. *Na putiakh k svobode.* New York, 1952.

Voden, A. "Na zare 'legal'nogo marksizma," LM, No. 3 (1927), 67–82, and No. 4 (1927), 87–96. Cited as *Voden.*

Index

Abramkin, V. M., 215n, 216n, 219n
Achkasov, A. N., 362n
Adler, Victor (1852–1918), 57n
Agriculture, Russian: and capitalism, 37–39; Danielson's views on, 80–83; Struve's views on, 86–89, 112–113, 148–151, 167; Struve's research on agrarian history, 196–207
Aksakov, Ivan (1823–1886), 13, 16, 17–19, 20, 21–23, 55, 286, 301, 306, 320
Akselrod, P. B. (1850–1928), 50, 59, 141, 212n, 218, 236, 245, 246, 262, 273n, 276, 292, 312n, 313, 371n
Alexander I (1777–1825), 365
Alexander II (1818–1881), 16–17, 50, 287, 288, 326
Alexander III (1845–1894), 18, 153, 289
Amfiteatrov, A. V., 151–152
Andreev, 357
Andreevsky, S. A., 24n
Angarsky, N. S. (1873–1943), 95n, 123n, 125n, 137n, 152n, 176n, 189n
Angel, Pierre, 56n, 57n, 211n
Anichkov, E. V. (1866–1937), 13n, 352–353
Arseniev, K. K. (1837–1919), 23–24, 74–75, 126, 153, 181, 341
Ascher, Abraham, 237n
Asheshev, N. P., 346n
Aveling, Eleanor Marx (1856–1898), and Edward B. (1851–1898), 96n
Azef, E. F. (1870–1918), 256n, 364, 365

Bagration, Prince P. I. (1765–1812), 6
Bakunin, M. A. (1814–1876), 88, 283, 327
Bariatinsky, V. V. (1874–?), 252
Baron, Samuel, 213n, 235n, 245n
Bartenev, V. V., 126
Bauer, Bruno (1809–1882), 158, 159
Bauer, K. K. (d. 1906), 70, 71n, 147n
Bebel, August (1840–1913), 350

Beginning, The (Nachalo), Struve's journal, 215–220, 236, 239, 241, 252
Belinsky, V. G. (1811–1848), 94
Bell, The (Kolokol), Herzen's newspaper, 310, 353
Belokonsky, I. P., 254n, 292n, 311n, 315n, 316n, 324n, 347n, 353n, 368n, 371n, 372n
Berdiaev, Nicholas (1874–1948), 295–296, 332, 333
Bernstein, Eduard (1850–1932): Revisionism, 56n, 59, 159, 169, 208–209, 211–212, 226, 236, 297; Struve on, 213–214, 219–222; Lenin on, 240–241; Plekhanov on, 218, 245
Beseda, see Symposium
Billington, James, 33n
Bismarck, Otto von (1815–1898), 66, 67, 161, 248, 328
Blanquism, 51, 99, 224, 245
Bloody Sunday (Jan. 9/22, 1905), 359, 371–375
Blum, Jerome, 204n
Bobrikov, N. I. (1839–1904), 357
Boehm-Bawerk, Eugen von (1851–1914), 227–228, 231
Bogdanovich, N. M. (1856–1903), 357
Bogolepov, N. P. (1846–1901), 271, 357
Bolshevik-Menshevik split (1903), 278
Braham, D. D., 331–332, 353
Braun, Heinrich (1854–1926), 86, 89
Brentano, Lujo (1844–1931), 77, 87n, 88, 110–111
Brokgauz and Efron Encyclopedic Dictionary, 157, 231n, 253n
Bücher, Karl (1847–1930), 205–206, 239
Budberg, R., 370n
Bulgakov, Sergei (1871–1944): debate with Struve on freedom and necessity (1896–1897), 184–189, 243, 293; as Revisionist, 214, 217, 228, 239, 241, 242, 244, 333
Bund (Jewish), 190, 191, 314
Burtsev, Vladimir (1862–1942), 256n

Russian Research Center Studies

1. *Public Opinion in Soviet Russia: A Study in Mass Persuasion,* by Alex Inkeles
2. *Soviet Politics — The Dilemma of Power: The Role of Ideas in Social Change,* by Barrington Moore, Jr.*
3. *Justice in the U.S.S.R.: An Interpretation of Soviet Law,* by Harold J. Berman. Revised edition, enlarged
4. *Chinese Communism and the Rise of Mao,* by Benjamin I. Schwartz
5. *Titoism and the Cominform,* by Adam B. Ulam*
6. *A Documentary History of Chinese Communism,* by Conrad Brandt, Benjamin Schwartz, and John K. Fairbank*
7. *The New Man in Soviet Psychology,* by Raymond A. Bauer
8. *Soviet Opposition to Stalin: A Case Study in World War II,* by George Fischer*
9. *Minerals: A Key to Soviet Power,* by Demitri B. Shimkin*
10. *Soviet Law in Action: The Recollected Cases of a Soviet Lawyer,* by Boris A. Konstantinovsky; edited by Harold J. Berman*
11. *How Russia Is Ruled,* by Merle Fainsod. Revised edition
12. *Terror and Progress USSR: Some Sources of Change and Stability in the Soviet Dictatorship,* by Barrington Moore, Jr.
13. *The Formation of the Soviet Union: Communism and Nationalism, 1917–1923,* by Richard Pipes. Revised edition
14. *Marxism: The Unity of Theory and Practice*—A Critical Essay, by Alfred G. Meyer
15. *Soviet Industrial Production, 1928–1951,* by Donald R. Hodgman
16. *Soviet Taxation: The Fiscal and Monetary Problems of a Planned Economy,* by Franklin D. Holzman
17. *Soviet Military Law and Administration,* by Harold J. Berman and Miroslav Kerner*
18. *Documents on Soviet Military Law and Administration,* edited and translated by Harold J. Berman and Miroslav Kerner
19. *The Russian Marxists and the Origins of Bolshevism,* by Leopold H. Haimson
20. *The Permanent Purge: Politics in Soviet Totalitarianism,* by Zbigniew K. Brzezinski*
21. *Belorussia: The Making of a Nation*—A Case Study, by Nicholas P. Vakar
22. *A Bibliographical Guide to Belorussia,* by Nicholas P. Vakar*
23. *The Balkans in Our Time,* by Robert Lee Wolff (also American Foreign Policy Library)
24. *How the Soviet System Works: Cultural, Psychological, and Social Themes,* by Raymond A. Bauer, Alex Inkeles, and Clyde Kluckhohn†
25. *The Economics of Soviet Steel,* by M. Gardner Clark*
26. *Leninism,* by Alfred G. Meyer*
27. *Factory and Manager in the USSR,* by Joseph S. Berliner†
28. *Soviet Transportation Policy,* by Holland Hunter
29. *Doctor and Patient in Soviet Russia,* by Mark G. Field †
30. *Russian Liberalism: From Gentry to Intelligentsia,* by George Fischer
31. *Stalin's Failure in China, 1924–1927,* by Conrad Brandt
32. *The Communist Party of Poland: An Outline of History,* by M. K. Dziewanowski
33. *Karamzin's Memoir on Ancient and Modern Russia: A Translation and Analysis,* by Richard Pipes
34. *A Memoir on Ancient and Modern Russia,* by N. M. Karamzin, the Russian text edited by Richard Pipes*

* Out of print.
† Publications of the Harvard Project on the Soviet Social System.
‡ Published jointly with the Center for International Affairs, Harvard University.